Dedication

I dedicate this book to the memory of Barbara Olson, who lost her life on September 11, but who lives on through her 2 books *Hell to Pay and The Final Days*. *It is my sincere hope that her work will have helped to lead to the inevitable incarceration of the Clintons..*

Acknowledgments

There are many people I want to thank, and if your name is not mentioned here, please don't be offended. First, I must thank Andrew Culver, my research assistant, proofreader, and editor. Thanks to my good friend Kimberly Haas, who is the greatest friend anyone could hope for. Like my late mother Augusta Greenblatt, Kim has been a tremendous influence on me, since I first met her almost 10 years ago. Thanks to my fellow writers, Larry "Ratso" Sloman and Michael Simmons, who have given me lots of helpful ideas. Thanks to Chris Ruddy and Carl Limbacher, from Newsmax.com. I am proud to be associated with Newsmax. Chris Ruddy- you are my hero. Thanks to the folks at Bookman Marketing & Publishing. Special thanks to Larry Nichols, Larry Patterson, and my many friends on the LAPD, who provided me valuable information over the course of the writing of this book. Shalom to all my friends at the Chabad of Hancock Park, especially Levi Raichik and his wife Miriam, who invited me to their home for *shabbos* throughout the time I was writing this book. Thanks to Michael Goldberger for all the encouragement. If it wasn't for you, I never would have met Chris Ruddy. Thanks to Doug Goodstein and everyone at E! Entertainment. Thanks to my pal Ali Sadri, who is a great American!

Feiner, thanks for the best *chullent* I have ever had. Jim Florentine and Artie Lang, you rock! And of course, thanks to Howard Stern and his staff for all the airtime over the years. Thanks to Cousin Richie and Cousin Julie of Fort Lauderdale, and thanks to my cat, who was always there for me by my side as I wrote this book. My kitty is a short-haired Bombay named Robin Quivers, who has shown me unconditional love for the past 5 years. All of you readers who are dog or cat owners know that our pets really give us unrequited love. My kitty knows nothing about the Clintons, nothing about footnotes, or deadlines, but she is always there for me. Thanks to my beloved parents, the late Augusta and I.J. Greenblatt, who taught me never to give up, to dig deeply for the truth, and to never be afraid of speaking the truth.

And last, thanks to all the fans of Melrose Larry Green and the readers. If by some chance the Clintons have me killed, I hope you enjoy this book.

Melrose Larry Green
Los Angeles, CA
May, 2004

Why I Wrote This Book

This book is not a scholarly study. It is not a legal treatise. It is not a political statement of any sort.

Rather, it is simply a factual account of how Bill and Hillary Clinton have led their lives. I will talk about a lot of things in this book. I will try to share with you the reader many facts about Bill and Hillary Clinton that you do not know. Do not expect to find "50 Reasons why the Clintons Belong in Prison".

The fact that the Clintons are not in prison makes a compelling case for a complete overhaul of the criminal justice system in this country. For you, the reader to understand why I think the Clintons belong in prison, you must see where I am coming from. Before I go any further, let me tell you the reader a little about myself and my concept of *family*.

I am a 53 year-old man who was brought up in the Five Towns of Long Island, New York. My parents, I.J. and Augusta Greenblatt, bought a $12,500 house in 1950 in Woodmere, New York, on a Government GI loan. Unlike the Clintons, who both come from dysfunctional families, my parents were always there for me. Neither my mother nor my father abused me. Neither of them were alcoholics. Neither of my parents had extramarital affairs.

My politics and religion can be covered in 2 words- (1) Democratic (2) Jewish. The Five Towns is a predominantly Jewish neighborhood. Now, it is largely Orthodox Jews, but when I lived in Woodmere, there were all types of Jews, if you will. The Greenblatts were Democrats. As a child, I remember Horace Kramer, who was the Democratic Party activist who lived on Peninsula Blvd. Horace Kramer was a good friend of my parents, and he taught me a lot about government and civic responsibility.

When I grew up, there was no doubt that I was a Democrat. Why? Because everyone else in town was a Democrat too. I distinctly remember my parents pointing out to me where a certain family lived who voted *Republican.* I think they were named the Goldfeders. Every time we drove past the Goldfeder house, I was warned to keep a distance from them- they were *Republicans.* All my friends were aghast- in our own sick world, we thought of them as "traitors".

Throughout my teenage years, I was a solid Democrat. I can vividly remember attending a rally at the Woodmere Fire House in 1964, when Bobby Kennedy was running for the Senate in N.Y. It was a thrill to catch a peek at Bobby Kennedy, right there at the firehouse. I supported JFK, LBJ, Hubert Humphrey- all of them.

Things started to change when I went away to college. I attended Brandeis University, in Waltham, Massachusetts. Coincidentally, Brandeis is just a few miles down the road from Wellesley, which is where Hillary Rodham-Clinton studied. One of my many jobs at Brandeis was delivering pizzas. Unlike Hillary Clinton, I have a great memory. I remember delivering pizzas to her dorm at Wellesley. One thing I never forgot about Hillary. She never gave me a tip! (By the way, I delivered pizzas for Senor Pizza, although most Wellesley students preferred the Wellesley House of Pizza!)

At Brandeis, I got a four-year course in phony liberals. This was the tumultuous late 60's and early 70's. Vietnam, police brutality, anti-American imperialism- these were the buzzwords on campus.

Most of my fellow Brandeis students were very intelligent, very wealthy Jewish kids whose parents gave them everything. But the underlying theme was a contempt for the American system. Everyone on campus hated Richard Nixon. It reminded me of the irrational hatred today's liberals have for George Bush. At Brandeis, there were lots of student demonstrations. But around 1970, I started to change. Student protesters had been killed at Kent State. In 1971, 2 girls from Brandeis- Kathy Power and Sue Saxe- were involved in a robbery/murder on a Boston bank. I distinctly remember the FBI coming to my dorm to question us about those two wackos. I knew Catherine Power- she once lent me a bread pan! Suddenly, Brandeis was on the network news at night. (Saxe and Power were wanted by the FBI for years. Power, like many other "revolutionaries", changed her name, got married and raised a family. She was defended by none other than Rikki Klieman, wife of LAPD Chief Bill Bratton. Both Bratton and Klieman are big-time supporters of the Clintons; both have slept in the Lincoln bedroom).

Little did I realize it then, but many of my Brandeis fellow alumni would go on to important jobs in the Administration of Bill Clinton, some 20 years later!

After graduating Brandeis in 1972, I was admitted to Cornell University, Ithaca, NY, where I earned my MBA in 1974. I worked in hospital administration for two years, before moving to Houston in 1976. In Houston, I published and edited a fitness newspaper, with the assistance of Dr. Donald Baxter. During my years in Houston (1976-1980), I actually met George Bush Sr. We were running together at Memorial Park. I recall him as being quite a nice guy. Don Baxter pointed out George H.W. Bush to me. At that time, Jimmy Carter was President. Little did I know that I had met a future President!

I moved to Los Angeles in June, 1980. It was my goal to get into show business. I have been living in Los Angeles for the past 24 years. I make a living as an income tax preparer. The apartment I live in now I have rented for 14 years. Although I am now a middle-aged man, I remember Woodmere, Brandeis, Cornell, and Houston, as if it were yesterday. In the summer of 1992, I remember hearing a guy speak at a political rally in West Hollywood, CA. To me, it was reminiscent of the rally with Bobby Kennedy, 28 years earlier at the Woodmere Fire House. I knew little about this man, *but he sure sounded great! And the ladies loved him!* He had all sorts of great ideas to improve the country. That night I decided I was going to vote for him. Who was that guy? His name was Bill Clinton.

My thinking has changed tremendously since that summer night in 1992. I must thank my friend Chris Ruddy of *Newsmax.com* for changing my life. Actually, it was my friend Michael Goldberger, who worked at a lingerie company in Lower Manhattan (where I used to store copies of my first book), who first gave me an article written by Chris Ruddy about the Strange Death of Ron Brown. Chris wrote a book called *The Strange Death of Vince Foster*. After I read that book, I read Ruddy's brilliant research into the strange death of Ron Brown. Then I started hearing about other people associated with the Clintons dropping dead- old girlfriends, a former security aide, 2 boys on a railroad track in Arkansas who might have been murdered...a White House intern who worked at Starbuck's who was killed in the summer of 1997...

Soon I started to really get scared. This guy Clinton was *not* a good person! Then I started doing some research on his wife, Hillary. And I started reading books. And did I ever read books!

Thanks to Chris Ruddy, I got to meet State Trooper Larry Patterson, who has told me many things about his experiences with Bill Clinton. I have spoken with Larry Nichols, who has known and worked with the Clintons for years. I have become an expert on the Clintons, and I want to share with you the results of my research.

Since 1992, I have been a recurring guest on the *Howard Stern Radio Show*. I am proud of my association with Howard Stern. He is a very intelligent guy. Howard says it like it is, and that's why he has so many listeners, all over the country. Although I don't do the show now as much as I used to, I am forever grateful to Howard for all his help over the years. When I did his show in late January, 2004, he allowed me to plug this book.

In 1993 and 2001, I ran for Mayor of Los Angeles. Although I didn't win the election, I learned a lot about the political process. Back in 1996, I wrote my first book *Melrose Larry Green, Everybody!* From March through November 2000, I hosted a nightly talk radio show in Los

Angeles, from midnight to 2 a.m. Larry Nichols was a frequent caller.

My most recent election was for the City Council of Los Angeles. It was a special election, to fill the seat of John Ferraro, who had passed away after many years of devoted service to the City of Los Angeles. During that campaign, a young man named Andrew Culver worked me. At the time, Andrew was a student at USC. Amazingly, the date of that election was a day that America will never forget- September 11, 2001.

Sometime around May, 2003, I heard from Andrew Culver again. He was graduating USC, and he was looking for work. So Andrew Culver became my research assistant and editor for this book. I could never have written this book without Andrew's help, and he knows how much I value his contributions to the project. Every writer needs an Andrew!

Finally, I must thank my best friend West of New York and Washington D.C., Kimberly Haas. Kim, you are a special person, who has been my buddy through good times and bad. My only regret is that my mother and father never had a chance to meet you.

Melrose Larry Green
Los Angeles, CA
May, 2004

Contents

Chapter 9- the Clinton Body Count- the death of Jerry.... 347
Parks- Bill Clinton and the Cocaine connection- The
unexplained deaths of Ron Brown and Vince Foster-
The murder of a White House intern who knew too
much- Other deaths- More lies told by the Clintons-

Appendices

CHAPTER ONE

Number Ten Reason the Clintons Belong in Prison

Filegate- Somehow, 900 FBI files containing "sensitive personal information" about Republicans were ordered by the Clinton White House from the FBI. To this day, no one knows why those files ended up in the White House. Coincidentally, the year when Filegate took place- 1996- was the *same year Bill Clinton was up for re-election.* Dick Morris and Linda Tripp both thought that Hillary Clinton was the one behind Filegate.. During the Nixon era, Charles Coulson went to prison for illegally obtaining FBI files. Bill and Hillary should have been brought up on similar charges. Imagine- 900 FBI files on Republicans in the *White House illegally and Bill and Hillary know nothing about it!*

The Washington Post of June 28, 1996 wrote this in on its editorial page: "The question of why hundreds of unjustifiably collected FBI reports on Republicans ended up in the Clinton White House remains unanswered. But another mystery looms even larger. How did Craig Livingstone end up on the White House payroll? No one professes to know...At this stage, nobody at the White House will claim credit for Craig Livingstone. It gets you wondering...Are there no papers in the payroll part of the operation that indicate Mr. Livingstone was actually hired or okayed by someone?[1]

---

(1) Anne Coulter, "High Crimes and Misdemeanors," pp. 142-143.

The FBI files affair raises serious questions. They deserve and require serious answers and real ones."[2]

Bill Clinton called Filegate a "bureaucratic snafu", but there was serious criminal activity going on here. *The New York Times of June 17, 1996 featured this editorial on Filegate:* "While it remains unclear whether White House aides were pursuing a political agenda in rummaging through the files, it is now apparent that there was a great potential for mischief. Both the White House and the FBI showed remarkably little regard for the privacy rights of Americans in their cavalier treatment of background files on more than 400 men and women who worked in recent Republican administrations...[The White House's] explanation has not been discredited, but it is looking shakier.[3]

Finally, Ann Coulter writes in her classic *High Crimes and Misdemeanors,* "Someone at the White House is responsible for hiring the men who implemented an unprecedented violation of nine hundred Americans' civil liberties. Someone at the White House is responsible for hiring the men who abused the powers of the executive branch to engage in political espionage against its presumed enemies, on a scale only dreamed of by the Plumbers, whose activities brought down Richard Nixon. According to this country's most recent precedent on impeachable offenses, that someone is the President.[4]

---

(2) Editorial, "Phantom Appointment," Washington Post, June 28, 1996.
(3) Coulter, p. 150
(4) Ibid., p. 154

So there you have it. To me, it looks as if Bill and Hillary have committed the equivalent of perjury, with respect to Filegate. They stonewalled and lied worse than Nixon ever did!

In a criminal trial, I feel Bill and Hillary would have been convicted of perjury, obstructing justice, and witness tampering. Possible prison sentence for criminal violations relating to Filegate for Bill Clinton- 2 to 3 years; for Hillary Clinton- 2 to 3 years.

Clinton Administration/White House Stories

The Clinton Staff

Bill Clinton was lent Air Force One by President George W. Bush for a flight from Washington D.C. to N.Y.C. on January 20, 2001. The Clinton people looted the plane! According to a story in the *Washington Times,* missing items from Air Force One included "the entire collection of Air Force One porcelain, china, silverware, salt-and-pepper shakers, blankets and pillow-cases- most of which bore the Presidential seal."[5]

At the Republican convention in Philadelphia in the summer of 2000, the Bush people gave the Republican House impeachment managers a very low profile, keeping them out of the media spotlight. An event to honor House Judiciary Committee Chairman Henry Hyde, who led the impeachment investigation into Bill Clinton, was held far away from the Convention Center. Amazingly, Rick Lazio, who was challenging Hillary Clinton in the N.Y. Senatorial election

---

(5) Carl Limbacher, Hillary's Scheme, p. 58

later that year, **was not permitted to address the convention!**[6] Basically, the Bush team didn't want to bring up anything to do with Bill Clinton.

Sadly, the Bush administration did nothing to go after Bill Clinton. Despite the fact that there was clear evidence of bribes paid to Roger Clinton and Hillary's brothers in order to get pardons from Bill Clinton, no legal action was taken against them. Similarly, nothing happened to Bill or Hillary over their involvement in pardoning the "New Square 4" (see pardons). And the Chinagate scandal, which indicated that Bill Clinton sold sensitive national security information to the Red Chinese in exchange for cash contributions to Bill Clinton's campaign, went nowhere. I am convinced that there was criminal conduct on the part of the Clintons- but George Bush simply called off the investigations.

Was there some sort of gentleman's agreement made between the Democrats and the new President Bush? **Bill O'Reilly,** host of "The Factor" and "The Radio Factor" seems to think so. He said on his radio show: "A very highly placed source- and I mean this guy knows what's going on in the Bush administration- told me about a month ago that when President Bush took office he had meetings with all of the Democratic leadership...One-on-one meetings in the Oval Office. The Democratic leadership made it quite clear to Mr. Bush that he would not get any cooperation- zero- on the part of the Democrats in the Senate and in the House if he pursued any kind of criminal investigation against Bill Clinton.

---

(6) Ibid., p. 59

"Basically, they said look, if you embarrass us- by us we mean the Democratic Party- if you, Bush-Ashcroft, indict Clinton on bribery of go after Hillary or any of this- we're gonna shut you down. We're not gonna do anything. You're not gonna get any [legislation] passed in four years."[7]

O'Reilly didn't name the source, but said he was "very highly placed."

The Bush administration did nothing to aid the victims of the Clinton political hit machine: people like Billy Dale, Gary Aldrich, Linda Tripp, and Dennis Sculimbrene. All of them had served in the White House going back to the days of George H.W. Bush. Aldrich, a decorated 30-year veteran of the FBI and Dale, former head of the White House Travel Office, both teetered on the brink of bankruptcy because of legal actions initiated against them by the Clintons. Linda Tripp also experienced tremendous emotional and financial hardships, after her efforts to expose Bill Clinton's lying and criminal behavior, resulted in her personal destruction.[8]

Hillary received a free pass to run for the U.S. Senate when the Republicans in the House Judiciary Committee failed to go after her husband with all the available criminal evidence against him. Because Clinton had a 60% approval rating in the polls and because the Clinton spin team had presented Clinton as someone who had "just lied about sex", he escaped criminal prosecution. The greatest crime in the Clinton impeachment is that Ken Starr didn't lock up the Clintons for life!

---

(7) Ibid., p. 61.
(8) Ibid., p. 62.

Though the lead House impeachment counsel David Schippers gathered reams of testimony from Kathleen Willey and Juanita Broaddrick, who both accused Clinton of sexual assault, Republican House and Senate leaders, mindful of mainstream media polls showing President Clinton's job approval well above 60%, were anxious to get the entire Sexgate imbroglio behind them.

Even though there was ample evidence of criminal behavior in Travelgate, Chinagate, Whitewater, abusive use of the IRS against Clinton enemies, enough mysterious deaths to keep a dozen coroners busy around the clock- Bill and Hillary Clinton pulled off the biggest hoax in American history as they walked away from one criminal act after another. To me, it is a commentary on the weakness of the American justice system that Martha Stewart is facing prison time, while Bill and Hillary Clinton are free to walk the streets!

All along the plan has been for Hillary to be President after Bill. Remember that. Hillary didn't want Howard Dean to run away with the nomination in 2004. Bill and Hillary did all they could to keep Al Gore out of the race. What Hillary wanted was a horserace among the candidates and a deadlocked convention. Then she could sneak in as the Democratic nominee in 2004. Bill and Hillary put their buddy Wesley Clark in the race just to cut into Howard Dean's and John Kerry's popularity.

Hillary Clinton is probably the dirtiest person in the history of American politics. She is consumed with her own ego and consolidating her own power base. She will stop at nothing to reach her goal of occupying the White House. Trust me.

According to Arkansas State Trooper Larry Patterson, Hillary Clinton used anti-Semitic slurs on "up to 20 different occasions."[9] At a meeting between consultant Dick Morris (a Jew) and Hillary Clinton, Morris was trying to negotiate a raise. In an obviously anti-Semitic slur, Hillary blurted out: "That's all you people care about is money."[10] Former Israeli Prime Minister Yitzhak Shamir felt that Hillary was a danger to the Jews. He said about Hillary: "She leans very closely towards the Arabs, and that is very dangerous…I view Hillary Clinton as a great danger to Jews if she is elected."[11]

Hillary hosted a reception for leaders of the American Muslim Council and the Council on American-Islamic Relations (CAIR). Salam al-Maryati, a backer of Hezbollah, chaired the event. CAIR's spokesman Ibrahim Hooper, who once said that Osama Bin Laden is no worse than Jerry Falwell or Pat Robertson, gave Hillary a Koran at that reception.[12]

And guess who the Clintons invited to the White House more than any other Chief of State? None other than the P.L.O.'s Yassir Arafat!

---

(9) Ibid., p. 95.
(10) Ibid., p. 96
(11) Ibid., p. 105.
(12) Ibid., pp. 106-107

Back in 1992, Hillary Clinton said to long-time supporter Linda Bloodworth-Thomason - "Eight years of Bill, eight years of Hill, that was the dream."[13]   There were signs in Hillary's office saying 'In the White House, Hillary 1996.'[14]

When Hillary ran for the Senate in New York, her original opponent was former N.Y. Mayor Rudolph Giuliani. Dick Morris felt that the Clintons were the ones who leaked the story of Giuliani's extra-marital affair to the media. After all, this was typical Clintonian behavior, collecting dirt on opponents to win races.   The Clintons were known for investigating the personal lives of their opponents.   They hired private investigators to attempt to destroy and intimidate any women who claimed to have had affairs with Bill Clinton.

Carl Limbacher, author of *Hillary's Scheme,* quotes an article that Dick Morris wrote for the *New York Post on* November 9, 2000:

"In almost all their campaigns and scandals, the Clintons hire investigators (in 1992, they even paid for them with Federal funds) to find ammunition to use their adversaries' private lives against them. Woman after woman has been demonized by their secret police- usually on orders from Hillary- and [these women] have had **their past dragged** through the mud and leaked to the press to discredit their accounts of the president's sexually predatory practices."[15]

---

(13) Ibid., p. 18
(14) Ibid., p. 18.
(15) Ibid., p. 22

Hillary got to know Robert Reich and Mickey Kantor when she worked with them at Yale Law School on the "Yale Review of Law & Social Action."[16] Hillary served as an editor of this publication. Editors make the final decision on what goes into the magazine, right? In one issue of Hillary's magazine, which focused on the Black Panthers (fall 1970), police are portrayed as "pigs" as they mutter "*niggers, niggers, niggers.*"[17] In a cartoon entitled "What is a Pig?" the caption reads: "A low natured beast that has no regard for law, justice, or the rights of people; a creature that bites the hand that feeds it; a foul depraved traducer, usually found masquerading as the victim of an unprovoked attack."[18]

That was Hillary Clinton's idea of what police and law enforcement represent. I hope that all of you who are police officers, or spouses of police officers, or children or parents of police officers will read that quote over and over again. Throughout this book, I will give you dozens of other examples of how little respect the Clintons have for police, Secret Service, State Troopers, and law enforcement in general!

Hillary's political philosophy at Yale was right in line with the basics of Leninism, a form of Communism. Amassing power was a cornerstone of Leninism, and if one carefully analyzes the political philosophy and activity of Hillary at Yale, one is left with the inescapable conclusion that Hillary is fundamentally an enemy of capitalism and a

---

(16) Barbara Olson, Hell to Pay, p. 59.
(17) Ibid., p. 60.
(18) Ibid., p. 60.

big fan of Communism, Leninism, Socialism, and its accompanying values.[19]

The Clinton Spin Control

The Clinton Administration was micro-managed by a group of political strategists, attorneys, public relations mavens, private investigators, and press agents, who monitored the scandals of the Administration on a daily basis. This group decided what stories got out to the press, and shaped the image of Bill Clinton's presidency, so that the average person was deceived into thinking that all was well in the White House.

Some call it "spin control"- I call it media manipulation and lying! Polls were taken on virtually every issue. If an unfavorable story was about to break, the spin people would go into action. For example, on April 14, 1997, the DNC was releasing over 10,000 pages of fundraising documents. This would be the perfect day to release data on 56 wealthy Democratic donors who rode for free on Air Force One. On that same date, it became known that Clinton had been pressing for Federal jobs for 60 top fundraisers, half of whom were actually hired. Because of Clinton administration press spinning, these stories were buried deep inside the morning papers.

Howard Kurtz's "Spin Cycle" is a fascinating account of the process of damage control, public relations and "spinmeistering" which characterized the scandals permeating the Clinton Administration. Thanks to people

---

(19) Ibid., p. 64

like Mike McCurry, Rahm Emmanuel, Lanny Davis, Joe Lockhart, James Carville, and George Stephanopoulos, the American people were systematically shielded from the truth about just about everything that went down. Through Whitewater, Paula Jones, the Lincoln Bedroom Scandal, Filegate, and Travelgate, the process of spin control was in place. Instead of presenting the facts to the American people, the issues were "parsed", "spun" and "homogenized" for the people's consumption. Basically, the overriding theme was that it was most important to protect the President at all costs. The truth, in effect, was secondary.

Bill Clinton knew back in November, 1996, that his campaign was involved in illicit fundraising. He figured that if he spoke about things in the media, the damage would be less than the harm from a Congressional investigation. Clinton had been auctioning off virtually everything connected to the White House- not just overnights in the Lincoln bedroom. If one contributed between $10,000 and $25,000, he got to attend a large dinner with Clinton. For $50,000- $100,000 you got a more "intimate" dinner with Clinton, or you got into a coffee with Bill Clinton. High rollers, who forked over more than $500,000 got to ride on Air Force One with Clinton, got to sleep overnight in the Lincoln bedroom, or got to play 18 holes of golf with Bill Clinton.[20]

The Clinton team employed lawyers like Lanny Davis to provide spin and damage control. Whenever a scandal would pop up, Lanny Davis would emerge from the sidelines and go on a talk show to defend Bill Clinton- at all costs- no matter

---

(20) Howard Kurtz, Spin Cycle, p. 52.

11

what Bill Clinton had done. During the midst of the DNC fundraising scandal, Davis was actively involved. And the DNC was as guilty of misleading the American people as was Bill Clinton. A DNC memo even advised those who might be guilty: "Don't lie- announce an internal investigation or 'white paper' to examine the matter. (in other words, stall). And when all else fails: "Impugn the source."[21]

December 16, 1996- It became known that Bill Clinton's Arkansas buddy Charlie Trie had tried to present $640,000 of checks to the Clinton Legal Defense Fund. Many of the checks seem to have been written in the same handwriting. Soon it turned out that Charlie Trie had contributed over $ 200,000 to Clinton throughout 1993 to 1995. Trie received a Presidential appointment to a trade commission 3 and ½ weeks after he presented the $640,000 to the defense fund. Trie had visited the White House 23 times, most recently at a White House Christmas party, in December, 1996.

What was Bill Clinton's reaction to Charlie Trie's generosity? "Shit, this guy comes through the line to me & Hillary, says 'I'm sorry Mr. President, I didn't mean to embarrass you' and he leaves."[22]

The Clinton White House engaged itself in lie after lie. One lie would simply be replaced with another lie, until eventually any objective reporter would just give up expecting to hear the truth about anything.

---

(21) Ibid., p. 61.
(22) Ibid., p. 65.

When Washington *Post* reporter Michael Weisskopf asked Press Secretary Mike McCurry about a list of wealthy donors who slept in the Lincoln bedroom, McCurry said no way: "This is President Clinton's private home, and what he does in his private home is not public business."[23] When Weisskopf inquired about wealthy Clinton donors who flew on Air Force One, McCurry said he couldn't provide any lists because "he was swamped with requests from the *Post* and other papers, but that no one else could help because he was the only official authorized to deal with these inquiries."[24] When Weisskopf brought up the fact that Chinese weapons merchant Wang Jun had been to a coffee with Clinton, McCurry replied: "There are Chinese here every day in the White House...What's the big deal?...The President had no idea who Wang was."[25] Subsequently, Bill Clinton said he remembered "literally nothing" about meeting with Wang Jun, after the Washington *Post* ran a front-page story outlining Clinton's illicit fundraising.

December 30, 1996- Alan C. Miller wrote in the *L.A. Times*:

"It is becoming increasingly evident as each week goes by that Bill Clinton was a major participant in the Democratic Party's efforts- some of it in violation of federal law prohibiting foreign contributions- to raise an enormous war chest for the 1996 presidential election campaign."[26]

---

(23) Ibid., p. 67.
(24) Ibid., p. 67.
(25) Ibid., p. 67.
(26) Ibid., p.61.

December 29, 1996- the Washington *Post ran this lead story:* "A network of Democratic fund-raisers and donors with foreign connections appear to have traded on their access to President Clinton to boost their business dealings, unchecked by a White House determined not to lose an election for lack of cash."[27]

The Book the Clintons Never Want You to Read!

Gary Aldrich, a 30-year veteran of the FBI, wrote a book called *Unlimited Access,* which the Clintons never wanted to see published. The Clinton spin team tried its best to discredit Aldrich and to keep him off TV.

As a result of pressure from the White House, Aldrich was pulled from shows such as "Larry King "(CNN), Dateline NBC, and Nightline (ABC). On "This Week", George Stephanopoulos called Aldrich "A pathological liar."

I believe Gary Aldrich's book is 100% accurate. He simply exposes the sordid, evil nature of the Clintons and their staff. Hillary wants you to believe that *everyone is lying about the Clintons.* Christopher Ruddy (whom I have known and trusted for years), Ambrose Evans-Pritchard, Ann Coulter, Howard Kurtz, Jerry Oppenheimer, Michael Isikoff, Peggy Noonan, James Stewart, Gail Sheehy, Joyce Milton, "Buzz" Patterson, Bernard Goldberg, and yours truly- Hillary would consider all of them to be liars, part of that "vast right-wing conspiracy."

This line of reasoning is preposterous. There has never been a more corrupt administration than the Clinton

---

(27) Ibid., p. 62.

administration. The mysterious deaths of Ron Brown, Vince Foster, the countless scandals, the intimidation and molesting of women by Bill Clinton, the dirty evil tricks used by Hillary- one of the meanest people in American history- have motivated me to write this book.

Remember, for most of my life, I was a Democrat. I am a Jew, who lives in Los Angeles. Go figure!

Gary Aldrich found striking differences between the White Houses of George H.W. Bush and Bill Clinton. While the Bush staffers wore suits and neckties, the Clinton staffers wore torn or dirty jeans, faded sweatshirts, and ponytails.
While the Bush staffers gladly submitted themselves to FBI screening, the Clinton staff resisted FBI security checks on a regular basis.

Aldrich once recalled seeing a group of "biker dudes', complete with earrings, ponytails, and in one case- even a red Lenin lapel pin. Aldrich told the "biker dudes" he was looking for the Clinton Advance Team. The 'biker dudes' told him:
"We *are* the Clinton Advance Team."[28]

Aldrich noted from the first day of the Clinton Administration that Bill and Hillary Clinton loved to fight it out. In fact, Bill and Hillary were late to the 1993 inauguration because they had a big fight over the West Wing office, which is traditionally reserved for the Vice President. Hillary wanted that space- she had made a deal with Bill

---

(28) Gary Aldrich, Unlimited Access, p. 10.

Clinton. As far as she was concerned, she *was* the Vice President!

Then, the Clintons broke with 200 years of Presidential transition history by inviting a couple of friends to the traditional tea between the outgoing and ingoing first couples. Hollywood producers Harry Thomason and his wife Linda Bloodworth-Thomason joined the Clintons and the Bushes. Right after Bill Clinton was sworn in, the Secret Service and Capitol Police heard Bill and Hillary yelling at each other. According to Aldrich, Hillary was screaming at Bill "with uncontrolled and unbridled fury."   Hillary was heard screaming at Bill: "You Fucking Asshole!"[(29)]

And the Clinton White House was a pigsty. Unlike the neat and organized atmosphere of George H.W. Bush's staff, the Clinton White House was a free-for-all. In the Clinton White House canteen, people simply ignored spilled coffee, dirty napkins abounded, and it was every man (and woman) for himself.[(30)]

And the Clinton staff was rude. This is how Gary Aldrich described the elevators in the Clinton White House.

"The elevator arrived, and the Clinton crowd rushed it like animals at feeding time, without giving people a chance to get off. People pushed, shoved, grunted, bumped, and swore, trying to sort it out. The men didn't give any

---

(29) Gail Sheehy, "Hillary's Choice", p. 223
(30) Aldrich, op. cit., p. 12

deference at all to the women, who were giving as good as they got. It looked like a sale at Macy's or worse."[31]

Frank Posey was the fellow responsible for posting photos and portraits around the White House for Presidents Reagan, Bush I, and Bill Clinton. For the first time in his career, there were no photos of the President and Vice President together in federal buildings and U.S. embassies. Bill Clinton ordered photos of either him alone or pictures of him with Hillary!

Al Gore should have seen this as a message back in January 1993 of things to come.

According to Aldrich, Hillary Clinton issued an edict that all women on the White House staff must wear underwear after a female staffer stuck her bare ass in Hillary's face![32] Furthermore, Hillary insisted that no one from the staff- particularly the interns- could look at her, talk to her, or bother her as she circulated around the White House.[33] Hillary made sure that White House Director of Security Craig Livingstone followed through to keep the commoners from bothering the First Lady.[34]

The Clinton staff had very little respect for police, FBI, Secret Service, or staff from George Bush Sr.

The Clinton people would call them "Mormons" or "straights". Police were referred to as "pigs."[35]

---

(31) Ibid., p. 13.
(32) Ibid., p. 37
(33) Ibid., p. 37
(34) Ibid., p. 37
(35) Ibid., p. 38.

There was a major problem of theft of White House laptop computers by interns, and GSA Supervising Carpenter Woody Di Guiseppe found 2 male Clinton staffers having gay sex in a White House office. It would be common for women to engage in lesbian sex in the White House showers in the ladies room on the main floor of the White House. According to a permanent staffer from the White House, "I walked in the door and heard the shower running. I noticed 2 forms in the shower stall together. They were both women and they were really going at it. One was standing and the other one was on her knees, and you can guess the rest!"[36]

And the Clinton staff were a bunch of slobs! According to a cleaning lady named Melba who had worked in the Clinton White House, the Clinton people were disrespectful and lacking in personal cleanliness. They behaved like savages in a jungle!

Melba told Gary Aldrich: "Mr. Aldrich, no harm intended, but these new people are terrible! Every day we go into their offices and clean up after them, and the next day it's as if we had never been there before. They're [the Clinton staff] messy people, Mr. Aldrich. These people are sloppy. Some are real slobs, sir! They throw garbage on the floor, or they throw cups of coffee and miss the waste can and it splashes all over the wall. And they don't clean up. It's as if they don't care, Mr. Aldrich, and I hate to say this, and you must never repeat this as long as I'm here, but sir, President Bush's people were much neater and much nicer to us. And that's the God honest truth, sir."[37]

---

(36) Ibid., pp. 39-40.
(37) Ibid., p. 40-41

P.S. Melba the cleaning lady took early retirement to avoid having to deal with the overindulged slobs in the Clinton White House.

Gary Aldrich found George Stephanopoulos to be "aloof and unfriendly" and felt Dee Dee Myers had a sewer mouth, once telling the press to: **"eat shit and die."**[38]

Marty Black, who had been a full-time White House executive secretary, also couldn't stomach the Clinton administration's behavior. Before she left the Clinton White House, she told Gary Aldrich: **"I just can't take these Clinton people anymore."**[39] Lillie Bell was the supervisor of the Mail Analysis Office. When Gary Aldrich encountered her in the White House, she was reduced to tears. She told Aldrich: "As a black Democrat, I prayed to God that I could end my career working for someone like Bill Clinton. And I got what I prayed for and now, I've just turned in my retirement papers. I am leaving early, Gary. These people are doing things that are so *wrong!*"[40]

Betty Dunn was a long-time employee of the White House Correspondence Office. When she told her elderly husband that she had just lost her job, her husband suffered a fatal heart attack. According to Aldrich, Dunn called her supervisor:
"This can't be happening. I'm losing my job and my husband on the same day!" When her supervisor begged

---

(38) Ibid., p.42
(39) Ibid., p. 44
(40) Ibid., p. 49

19

Marsha Scott (director of the Office of Correspondence) to give Dunn her job back, Marsha Scott refused- they needed the slots!

This was the Clinton White House. Products of the 60's. If it feels good, do it. They had morphed into the most ruthless, self-serving staff in U.S. history. Patsy Thomasson from the White House Communications office scolded Aldrich when he asked for a phone list of White House staff members. He told her it was for the FBI, and she said: **"Screw the FBI! To hell with the FBI! They're not getting this list."**[41]

The Clinton White House was firing people left and right. Two dozen people from the Office of Presidential Correspondence were fired. Mountains of mail piled up and, in many cases, it was just shredded and thrown out rather than being answered, as previous White Houses did. Bill Clinton didn't want to use IBM computers that the Bush White House had used. The training staff on the IBM computers were all fired.

Many of the Correspondence Office staff who were fired had been life-long Democrats.

Ellen Strickhartz was a life-long Democrat. The correspondence analyst said this after she was fired as the Clintons took over: "I voted for them. I can't believe they've done this to me. I'm a registered Democrat, I have a family

---

(41) Ibid., p. 46

to feed. A mortgage to pay. There are no jobs. What am I going to do?"[42]

The firing of the employees in the Correspondence Office is very similar to the firing of the White House Travel Office. The travel office firings have been linked directly back to Hillary- again they needed the slots!

Marsha Scott was a former girlfriend of Bill Clinton. The former hippie used to travel the country in a VW bus. Wherever the bus ran out of gas, it would become her home. In the Clinton White House, Scott earned $100,000/yr., and according to Aldrich, she would often wear "a very short skirt and- like Sharon Stone in the movie *Basic Instinct*- kept ostentatiously crossing and uncrossing her legs."[43]

And the Clinton people were even pigs at the White House canteen. It would be commonplace for the Clinton people to "double-dip" at the drink machines, even though the canteen was a very small business and ran on a tight profit margin. Worse, the canteen had a system where you paid for your food after weighing it on a scale. One guy took the biggest cup available, filled it with frozen yogurt, and ate the yogurt as he waited on line, just to avoid paying for the yogurt he took! Aldrich was not surprised to see where the "yogurt thief" worked- he had an ID badge from Hillary Clinton's Health Care Task Force![44]

---

(42) Ibid., p. 48
(43) Ibid., p. 48
(44) Ibid., p. 51

Gary Aldrich on the Death of Vince Foster

Gary Aldrich found it incredible that the FBI was not in charge of the investigation into the death of Vince Foster.[45] Aldrich brought up several key questions:

(1) Was Vince Foster a threat to Bill and Hillary Clinton?
(2) Was Vince Foster angry at someone in the White House?
(3) Was Vince Foster romantically involved with Hillary Clinton?
(4) Why were the Park Police placed in charge of the Foster death investigation?

Bill Clinton's Ego

All Clinton cared about was his own presidential legacy. In a discussion between Bill Clinton and Dick Morris, Clinton asked Morris how he thought his presidency would be evaluated by future historians. Morris and Clinton had arbitrarily divided 18 of the 41 Presidents into 3 tiers, one being the highest and three being the lowest. Where, Clinton wanted to know would Morris place him? In the third tier, responded Morris. Clinton asked Morris: "What do you think I need to do to become first tier?" Morris answered that Clinton couldn't be 1st tier "unless unanticipated historical forces put him there."

Clinton responded: "Like a War."[46]

---

(45) Ibid., p. 77
(46) Dick Morris, "Off with their Heads," p. 69

There it is—proof of the real Bill Clinton's overriding concern for his Presidential legacy over all else. Besides, what more would you expect from a draft dodger who scorned and berated the military and law enforcement for his entire adult life?

Jeb Bush calls Bill Clinton 'Most Self-Absorbed Person' in U.S.

There is an unwritten law that says that former Presidents should not be publicly critical of sitting Presidents. This tradition stems from the concepts of class, respect, and decency, qualities Bill Clinton cares little about. Florida Governor Jeb Bush held nothing back when he went on the Sean Hannity Radio Show to discuss Bill Clinton's criticism of President Bush: "All I'll say is that Bill Clinton is the most self-absorbed person living in America. And the tradition of former presidents not being critical of their successors, I think, is a very good one. It's why we've had transitions since the beginning of the Republic. And almost all presidents have been very respectful of that. But President Clinton wouldn't view himself being critical of anybody because he's always thinking of himself. It's all about Bill."[47]

Clinton fires all U.S. Attorneys

Bill Clinton fired all the U.S. attorneys when he took office in January, 1993. This has never been done before in American history. Do you realize what this means? By

---

(47) Carl Limbacher Jr., "Newsmax Magazine," Aug. 2003

putting in all his choices as U.S. attorneys, Clinton could almost guarantee that he would never be investigated for breaking the law. By having a fraud like Janet Reno as Attorney General and a whole new staff of Federal prosecutors who were clones of Clinton, it was a done deal that nothing could ever happen to Bill Clinton. Even though he raped the country, literally and figuratively, Clinton would never pay the price for his crimes.

Chris Ruddy points out how one of the U.S. attorneys who got fired in Little Rock, Arkansas, was investigating Clinton's involvement in Whitewater and the defrauding of the Small Business Administration. And guess who the attorney's replacement was? A friend and former law school student of Clinton's, Paula Casey. How convenient for Bill Clinton! He was suddenly in the clear. He not only used the Justice Department to protect himself, he used the IRS and the FBI. By obtaining private FBI files on his enemies, having the IRS audit anyone he didn't like, and having the Red Chinese illegally contribute to his campaign for reelection, he did his best to destroy democracy.[48]

But good luck trying to call him out on his crimes. Anyone who criticized him gets audited or killed mysteriously.

If you believe Bill Clinton, everyone who criticizes him is also a liar. Paula Jones was just "trailer trash". Kathleen Willey made up her story. We all remember his famous "I did not have sex with that woman- Miss Lewinsky" charade.

---

(48) Chris Ruddy, "Clinton Ends his Presidency as he Began It," Newsmax.com, Jan. 19, 2001

Elizabeth Ward Gracen, Dolly Kyle Browning, Sally Perdue, the Arkansas state troopers, and all the journalists who have documented the trail of crimes, scandals, and assorted transgressions committed by the Clintons. According to Bill and Hillary, all of these people are members of some vast right-wing conspiracy, which is out to get them!

Hey Bill and Hillary- listen up! For my whole life, until you two came along, I was a Democrat. I was brought up on Long Island- in the very Jewish section known as the Five Towns. Yet I am convinced that the two of you belong in prison. Bill and Hillary- you must think that American people are really gullible!

On the contrary, I feel that all these people have been telling the truth all along. It's about time we recognize Bill and Hillary Clinton for what they are- a pair of power-hungry whores who will use anybody and any cause to realize their main goals- enriching their power base and their pocket books. Conversely, ask yourself, what do all these men and women gain by accusing Bill Clinton? I want you, the reader, to make the ultimate judgment. Just do me two favors- keep an open mind and keep reading!

For Sale- Clinton White House

Bill Clinton sold practically everything at the White House to the highest bidder- rides on Air Force One, seats on foreign trade commissions, golf and jogging outings with Bill, burial plots at Arlington National Cemetery, tours of the White House, state dinners, you name it- and the Clinton White House had it for those who could afford it.

The White House was pimped out like an escort service. The more you paid, the more you got. For $10,000 you might get to go to a dinner with President Clinton, or maybe just go to a coffee. For $100,000, you could sit at a table with Bill Clinton. In one of the most brazen acts of political extortion, Bill Clinton charged a wealthy donor $1.5 million to "fly with Clinton to meet Pope John Paul II at Newark Airport."

The Clinton administration sold seats on Department of Commerce foreign trade missions for $50,000 a pop. Ron Brown, the late Secretary of Commerce under Clinton, was unhappy with the arrangement. Right before his death, he told his partner Nolanda Hill, "I'm a motherfucking tour guide for Hillary."[49]

John Huang and Johnny Chung were both involved in using their connections with China to bolster the bank accounts of the Democratic Party. Chung visited the Clinton White House more than 50 times, and 21 times he was allowed in by Hillary's office. Huang worked with the influential Riady family, whose Lippo group had billions of dollars invested in Red China.

Chinagate wasn't an easy scandal to track, unlike so many of the others that infected the Clinton administration. To be sure, John Huang had access to sensitive CIA files related to technology transfers. Ask yourself, what would Chung, Huang, or the Chinese government expect to get in return for their donations to Bill Clinton and the Democratic National Committee? Were they possibly receiving classified American nuclear codes and technology?

---

(49) Barbara Olson, "Hell to Pay," pp. 287-288

Brother, Can You Spare Some Bone China?- Gifts to the Clintons!

Jewish people are notorious for having beautiful sets of China, but probably no Jewish family in Beverly Hills or Great Neck has a collection of china in any way comparable to that of Bill and Hillary Clinton! As the Clintons approached the twilight of their co-Presidency, the gifts started rolling in. Hillary actually had the chutzpah to register with fancy retailers, as if she were some impoverished bride from the slums of Brooklyn! In fact, Clinton Chief of Staff John Podesta admitted to "Meet the Press's" Tim Russert that friends of Hillary were soliciting wealthy Democrats, imploring "Would you please buy this silverware, these gifts for Mrs. Clinton for her new houses?"[50]

And did they give! Steven Spielberg (overnight guest in the Clinton White House from the world of Arts and Letters and Sports) and his wife Kate Capshaw gave china valued at $4,920!. Mary Steenburgen ("Arkansas Friend" who slept over in the Clinton White House) and Ted Danson (overnight Clinton White House guest a la Spielberg) gave china valued at $4,787.[51] Over and over again, the names Ron and Beth Dozoretz pop up! Let's find out who they are...

Beth Dozoretz was a major fundraiser for the Clintons. Besides hosting a fundraiser at her Washington estate that raised $1 million for the Democratic National Committee

---

(50) Olson, "Final Days," p. 64
(51) Ibid., p. 64

(DNC), she pledged to raise another $1 million for the Clinton Library.

Basically, the Dozoretzes are a pair of wealthy people with too much time and money on their hands. Beth came from money- her father was a successful dentist in Worcester, Mass. Beth was formerly President of Clyde's Sportswear, pulling down a hefty six-figure salary. Her husband Ron has been a navy psychiatrist, a former Senatorial candidate and vice chairman of the Virginia Democratic Party. Most recently, Ron Dozoretz was in charge of FHC Health Systems, Inc. a conglomerate of mental health care businesses. Beth has had a tough time holding on to her husbands- After three divorces, Beth married Ron in 1989![52]

Ron took Beth to the 1992 Democratic Convention, where they first met Bill and Hillary Clinton. Like so many others, this couple was conned and mesmerized by the "charm" and "charisma" of the Clintons.

As Beth recounted, in her own words "All of a sudden this beautiful woman comes walking by, and it was Hillary. Almost involuntarily, I jumped out of my seat and yelled 'You're fabulous'" Hillary thanked her. "Then Bill gave his speech and I'm jumping out of my chair."[53]

The Dozoretzes moved to the Washington area, where they purchased a mansion formerly belonging to Michael and Arianna Huffington for a cool $4 million. Immediately, they fell into the Bill and Hillary circle of friends, sleeping at the

---

(52) Ibid., p. 65
(53) Ibid., p. 64-65

White House, relaxing with them at Martha's Vineyard, Camp David, golfing, and overall partying. But they didn't stop there. The Dozoretzes named Bill Clinton the godfather of their newborn daughter, Melanne Rose. Even their rabbi, Rabbi Jeffrey Wohlberg, was taken aback by this. "I don't know whether in the back of their minds is the idea that, God forbid, anything happens to them, he [Clinton] would take over the moral education of the child."[54]

It is significant how many Jewish people backed the Clintons. The reason it is significant is because their wealth in many cases protected the Clintons from the arm of the law. I am Jewish, so I feel qualified to talk about Jewish people. I grew up in the Five Towns of Long Island, an area that is overwhelmingly Jewish. I graduated with a B.A. in Political science from Brandeis University, a predominantly Jewish university in Waltham, Mass. I have visited Israel 4 times, and I am fluent in Hebrew. If there is anything in this world on which I am an authority, it is Jews, Jewish people, and Jewish guilt and self-hatred!

I will happily identify the names of Jewish people that served as pimps and enablers for the Clintons over the years. Jews are usually not like me. Most Jews are liberals; many are socialists, communists, even anarchists. But I am a Republican, thanks to the behavior and actions of Bill and Hillary Clinton! Most Jews will support Bill and Hillary Clinton, simply because they are Democrats! And don't think the Clintons didn't know how loyal most Jews are to the Democratic party! I recently talked to Bob Kohn, the author of "Journalistic Fraud: How the N.Y. Times Distorts

---

(54) Ibid., p. 65

the News". He gave me a great quote, which he attributed to his mother Bertha Kohn.

"If Hitler ran for President on the Democratic ticket, most of the Jews would vote for him."

So, let the world know that Ron and Beth Dozoretz are both Jewish.

Steven Spielberg is Jewish. Barbara Streisand is Jewish. Monica Lewinsky is Jewish. What is it about Bill and Hillary Clinton and the Jews?

Marc and Denise Rich- both Jewish!

Marc Rich, as we all know, is the tax cheater pardoned by Bill Clinton. His wife, the former Denise Eisenberg, was a former lover of Bill Clinton and a multimillion dollar contributor to the DNC and the Clinton Library.

Denise Rich gave the Clintons 2 coffee tables and 2 chairs worth $7,375.[55]

Denise Rich, according to the "New York Times" of March 3, 2001- initially gave $350,000 to the Clinton Library. After she received an E-mail from Marc Rich's strategist, recommending that she talk with Bill Clinton, she pledged another $100,000. The money was given through Beth Dozoretz, finance chairwoman of the Democratic National Party. Denise Rich hosted a fundraiser for the Clintons that raised $3 million for them. On top of that,

---

(55) Ibid., p. 66

Denise gave at least $1 million to the Democratic party, and $10,000 to the Clinton legal defense fund.[56]

Remember now- Less than 6 weeks before this article appeared, Bill Clinton pardoned Denise's ex-husband Marc Rich, one of the biggest tax cheaters in American history!

Here is a list of some of the gifts the Clintons got as going away presents.[57]

- Ely Callaway, Carlsbad, CA, $499, golf driver
Robin Carnahan and Nina Ganci, St. Louis, MO, $340, two sweaters
Glen Eden Carpets, Calhoun, GA, $6,282, two carpets
Iris Cantor, New York, $4,992, china
    Dale Chihuly, Seattle, $22,000, glass sculpture
    Colette D'Etremont, New Brunswick, Canada, $300, flatware
    Dennis Doucette, Coral Gables, FL, $310, golf bag, clothing, book
    Martin Patrick Evans, Chicago, $5,000, rug
    Lee Flicks, Cincinnati, $3,650, kitchen table and four chairs
    Lynn Forester, NYC, $1,353, cashmere sweater
    Paul Goldenberg, La Habra, CA, $2,993, television and DVD player
    Barbara Allen, Belfast, Northern Ireland, $650, watercolor of the Clinton Ancestral homeland

---

(56) Ibid., p. 66
(57) "Final Days," pp. 66-68.

Georgetown Alumni, class of 1968, $38,000, Dale Chihuly basket set

Arthur Athis, L.A., $2,400, dining chairs

Dendez Badarch, Ulan Bator, Mongolia, $1,300, drawings of landscapes

Robert Berks, Orient, NY, $2,500, bust of Harry Truman

Bruce Bernson, Santa Barbara, CA, $300, golf putter

Mr. and Mrs. Bill Brandt, Winnetka, IL, $5,000, china

Ken Burns, Walpole, NH, $800, photo of Duke Ellington

Myra Greenspun, Green Valley, NV, $1,588, flatware

Vinod Gupta, Omaha, $450, leather jacket- Gupta slept over in White House!

Richard C. Helmstetter, Carlsbad, CA, $525, golf driver and balls

Hal Hunicutt, Conway, AK, $360, golf irons

Ghada Irani, LA, CA, $4,944, flatware

Jill and Kenneth Iscol, Pound Ridge, NY, $2,110, china & jacket- Iscols slept over in White House, along with children Kiva & Zack Iscol!

Mr. and Mrs. Walter Kaye, NYC, NY, $9,683, cigar travel humidor, china

Cabinet, and copy of President Lincoln's Cooper Union speech

David Kilgarriff, North Yorkshire, England, $300, golf driver

Steve Leutkehans, Morton Grove, IL, $650, golf driver

David Martinous, Little Rock, AK, $1,000, needlepoint rug

Steve Mittman, NY, $19,900, two sofas, easy chair, and ottoman

Katsuhiro Miura, Japan, $500, golf driver

Jay Munro, Sarasota, FL, $650, painting of New York City

Brad Noe, High Point, NC, $2,843, sofa

Margaret O'Leary, San Francisco, $595, pantsuit and sweater

Mr. and Mrs. Joe Panko, Concord, NC, $300, three putters

Mr. and Mrs. Paolo Papini, Florence, Italy, $425, Italian leather box (great for storing cocaine)

Mr. and Mrs. Morris Pynoos, Beverly Hills, CA, $5,767, cashmere shawl and flatware

Brian Ready, Chappaqua, NY, $300, painting of Buddy, Clinton's late dog

David Rowland, Springfield, IL, $500, check signed by President Truman in 1934

Stuart Shiller, Hialeah, FL, $1,170, lamps- Hillary loves lamps!

Mr. and Mrs. Vo Viet Thanh, Ho Chi Minh City, Vietnam, $350, framed tapestry.

Joe Tumpson, Miami, FL, $3,000, painting

Edith Wasserman, Beverly Hills, CA, $4,967, flatware

Mr. and Mrs. Allen Whiting, West Tisbury, MA, $300, painting "Oyster Pond"

James Lee Witt, Alexandria, VA, $450, cowboy boots

> Mr. and Mrs. Bud Yorkin, LA, CA, $500,
> antique book on George Washington.

In all, Hillary's loot totaled more than $50,000 in china and flatware alone!

Bill Clinton's Goals and Personality Traits

Bill Clinton's plan for 1992 was just to get some name recognition. George H.W. Bush had been a very popular President, and Bill Clinton's chances to beat Bush were slim. Bill Clinton told Arkansas newspaper publisher Garric Feldman (May '91) "I'm going for name recognition. I'm not going to win, but I'm going to get ready for 1996."[58]

Bill Clinton was known for his phenomenal memory, at least until he was impeached and couldn't remember a thing. As a young campaigner in Arkansas, Bill would have staffers write down the names of people he had met on the campaign trail. The next day each person would receive a personally-signed note from Bill himself! Amazingly, Clinton could recall individual details about the people he met, as indicated in these follow-up letters. Thousands of these letters were sent out.[59]

Bill Clinton helps to bring down Howard Dean's Campaign!

After Howard Dean starting taking the advice of Bill Clinton and former members of his Administration, his entire

---

(58) Jerry Oppenheimer, "State of a Union," p. 227
(59) Ibid., p. 137

organization tanked. In just the few short weeks that he started listening to the Clinton team, Dean went from Democratic front-runner to Democratic trivia question! Such national security nightmares as Anthony Lake and Susan Rice began advising Howard Dean in recent weeks. Bill Clinton has been giving Dean advice on the Israeli-Palestinian conflict. It is quite likely that Dean's comments about having an "evenhanded" policy with respect to Israel may have been out of the mouth of Bill Clinton.

Dean's highly irresponsible comments questioning George Bush's knowledge of 9/11 and his comments admonishing Americans "not to prejudge the guilt of Osama Bin Laden" seem to have the influence of the Clinton team behind them. Former Clinton Secretary of State Madeline Albright has also been advising the Dean camp.[60]

Bill Clinton, are you really a Democrat?

How Bill Clinton used the IRS Against his Enemies

It is really shocking how many people associated with the Clinton scandals were audited by the IRS. The individuals and organizations audited by the IRS during Clinton's Administration is a scandal in itself! Let's get right into it.

(1) Paula Jones was audited in 1997. Her income was $37,000, placing her statistically in the least likely category to be audited. Someone leaked confidential information about Paula Jones to a reporter at the *New York Daily News*. The writer, Lars-Erik Nelson, claimed the information about

---

(60) Newsmax.com Magazine, Feb. 2004, p. 46

how Jones treated her legal defense fund on her tax return had to have come from either someone who worked for the IRS, or someone in the Clinton White House.[61] Did Bill Clinton order an audit of Paula Jones? If so, that could have constituted not only impeachable, but also criminal conduct.

(2) Elizabeth Ward Gracen started receiving audit letters from the IRS, just a few weeks after having received a series of threatening, mysterious phone calls. The caller told her: 'You should really keep your mouth shut about Bill Clinton and your life. You could be discredited. You could have an IRS investigation.'[62]. These calls came weeks after Gracen had gone public to express her regrets over having had a sexual tryst with Bill Clinton. Gracen told *The Toronto Star:* "I think [Bill] Clinton is a very dangerous, manipulative man, and I've had to be very careful."[63] The audit letters were addressed to her parents' house, even though that address was not used in her previous tax returns. On December 3, 1999 Gracen's lawyer Vincent Vento told the Cox News Service that Gracen "pays her taxes, she's really square...She just feels it's completely unfair...The only person who would benefit would be the president of the United States, unless there's some other agenda out there."[64] Gracen told *The New York Post:* "I was physically scared... We are talking about the president of the country here, and between the friendly calls on one hand telling me to get out of town for my own good and then talking about smear tactics on the

---

(61) Carl Limbacher, "Hillary's Scheme," pp. 198-199
(62) Ibid., p. 203
(63) Ibid., p. 203
(64) Ibid., p. 204

others I got scared. Yes, physically scared."[65] Why did Elizabeth Gracen deny being raped by Bill Clinton? Was she in fear of her own life? Her agent Miles Levy was asked by Paula Jones case private detective Rick Lambert why Elizabeth Gracen wouldn't talk to her on the telephone. (Lambert had called Gracen, but Gracen pretended to be someone else and had hung up on Lambert.) Liz Gracen's agent told Lambert: "Look, that would be career suicide for Liz and you know it."[66] Suddenly, things started getting weird. Gracen and her boyfriend went off to St. Martin to escape the States for awhile. *While she and her boyfriend went for a jog on the beach, someone broke into her room. They didn't take a Rolex or $2,000, which was on the table in the room. But they did ransack the place. According to Gracen, the burglars were looking for tapes or other evidence that Gracen might have. Hotel workers noticed some men "in suits" outside her door at the time. They thought those men were friends of Gracen. They were not, but I think they were friends of Bill Clinton.*

(3) Juanita Broaddrick, the woman who claimed to have been raped by Bill Clinton, (her story appeared on Dateline NBC and in the Wall Street Journal), was audited for the first time in 27 years. The IRS audit came after Broaddrick's story became known to the nation. Broaddrick told Newsmax.com's Carl Limbacher, "In 27 years in business, I've never been audited." Broaddrick also told Limbacher "that there had been no change in the financial circumstances of her nursing home business that might have triggered IRS

---

(65) Ibid., p. 202
(66) Ibid., p. 201

scrutiny."[67] NBC lied to Juanita Broaddrick. Her story of being raped by Bill Clinton was supposed to air in late January, 1999, but Dateline NBC didn't run the story until *after Bill Clinton had been acquitted by the Senate. I am quite certain that many Democratic Senators would have voted to convict Bill Clinton if they had seen the story of Juanita Broaddrick's rape by Bill Clinton on Dateline NBC prior to the impeachment vote! Where's the outrage from the feminists?*

(4) Gennifer Flowers was audited by the Clinton IRS.[68]

(5) Billy Dale- 30 – year veteran of the White House Travel Office before being sacked by the Clinton White House (i.e. Hillary) was audited by the Clinton IRS.[69]

(6) Chinagate figure Johnny Chung, who spoke out against illegal fundraising in the Clinton White House, was audited by the Clinton IRS.[70]

Folks, what you have right here is a lot more than coincidence. It represents the wrath of Bill and Hillary Clinton. It is beyond my comprehension why no special prosecutor, attorney general, or member of Congress has looked into Bill and Hillary Clinton's criminal use of the IRS. I believe we see a pattern here- a pattern of abuse of power and an open-and-shut case of impeachable, even criminal behavior!

---

(67) Ibid., p. 213
(68) Ibid., p. 212
(69) Ibid., p. 212
(70) Ibid p. 216

One fact you may not have known is that Hillary's pal from Yale Law School and a 1992 Clinton campaign advisor, contributor, and member of the Clinton transition team, Margaret Milner Richardson, was the Commissioner of the IRS during the years of many of these audits.[71] Before she finally resigned in November, 1997, Billy Dale, Paula Jones, and Gennifer Flowers had been audited.[72] According to attorney and brilliant commentator Ann Coulter, IRS agents examining the taxes of Billy Dale were "aware" of Commissioner Richardson's link to Bill and Hillary Clinton from both Yale Law School and the 1992 campaign. Coulter claims that Richardson told White House attorneys "she was on top of it."[73] [Dale's audit]

According to Investor's Business Daily, "the IRS has hit some 20 conservative groups and several of Clinton's critics with audits, audit warnings, or delays in granting nonprofit status."[74]

Among others targeted by the Clinton IRS:

---

(71) Joyce Milton, "First Partner" p. 324
(72) Limbacher, op. cit., p. 216
(73) Anne Coulter, "Crimes and Misdemeanors, p. 132. Also see House Report 104-849: "Investigation into the White House Travel Office Firings and Related Matters": Report by Government Committee on Government Reform and Oversight, Sept. 26, 1996. The notes from a June 28, 1993 White House management interview of Beth Dolan and Cliff Sloan of the White House Counsel's Office reveal that William Kennedy has said this. The notes read: "PR [IRS Commissioner Peggy Richardson] on top of it. She said at a party IRS on top of it or something like that."
(74) Limbacher, op. cit., pp. 194-195

(1) Kent Masterton Brown – attorney who opposed Hillary's health care plan and filed lawsuits against the plan.[75]

(2) Shelly Davis- wrote a book sharply critical of the IRS[76]

(3) Patricia Mendoza- got in trouble with the IRS one month after yelling out at Bill Clinton "you suck" when Clinton tried to shake her hand. [Mendoza and her husband were kept in custody by the Secret Service for 12 hours over this.][77]

(4) Bill O'Reilly- host of Fox News Channel's "The O'Reilly Factor" and long-time critic of Bill and Hillary Clinton was audited.[78]

(5) *The National Review and the American Spectator-* conservative magazines that have criticized and exposed the Clintons- received scrutiny from the Clinton IRS.[79]

(6) The following conservative organizations have been audited by the Clinton IRS: Christian Coalition, Citizens for a Sound Economy, Oliver North's Freedom Alliance, the Heritage Foundation, the National Rifle Association, the Western Journalism Center, the National Center for Public Policy Research, Fortress America and Citizens Against Government Waste.[80]

---

(75) Milton, op. cit., p. 324

(76) Ibid., p. 324

(77) Ibid., p. 324

(78) Limbacher, op. cit., p. 195

(79) Ibid., p. 195

(80) Ibid., p. 195. See also *Washington Times*, June 8, 2000.

Inside the Clinton White House

In the Clinton White House, there was no dress code, unlike the White Houses of Ronald Reagan and George H.W. Bush. Clinton's people wore pony tails, spiked hair, and T-shirts. Ronald Reagan wouldn't even take his jacket off in the White House, out of respect for the White House and the institution of the Presidency.[81] The Clintons held the Secret Service in great contempt. Bill resented the fact that the Secret Service were always hovering around the White House living quarters. Secret Service agents were turned into baggage porters by the Clintons.[82]

Clinton Fundraiser Commits Fraud and Pleads Guilty

Most readers probably don't know the name of Aaron Tonken, and that's just how the Clintons want it.

He was a major Hollywood fundraiser who helped the Clintons get money from their Hollywood friends. In an *LA Times* article from 2003 it says that Mr. Tonken pled guilty to mail and wire fraud and allegedly misused Clinton charity funds. Prosecutors believed he siphoned at least $7 million worth of charity funds for his own uses.[83]

But that's not all! Remember Marc and Denise Rich, the criminals pardoned by Clinton on his last day of office? Tonken was all tied up in the Marc Rich-Clinton scandal, and

---

(81) Barbara Olson, "Hell to Pay" p. 234
(82) Ibid., p. 237
(83) *LA Times*, December 10, 2003

he has made several questionable deals with Denise Rich, not to mention questionable gifts to the Clinton library.

One of Tonken's celebrity charity events under investigation was a fundraiser organized by Tonken. Get this-it was called "A Family Celebration," and it was hosted by Carson Daly of MTV. Such celebs as Elizabeth Taylor, Britney Spears and Sylvester Stallone showed up. Hillary Clinton even did her part, sending a videotape praising "my good friend Aaron Tonken." Bill Clinton and Gerald Ford spoke at the event.

Then there was the gala Tonken spearheaded on the eve of the Democratic National Convention in 2000, intending to raise funds for Hillary's Senate race (for more info on Hillary's Senate donors see the appendix). This event was the subject of intense scrutiny by federal investigators. Everything about this Tonken guy is fishy! According to the *LA Times* article, Tonken was liable to face at least ten years in prison for fraud in connection to Clinton fundraising events. His case is still pending at the time of publication of this book- keep your eyes out for the latest information.[84]

Sometimes I wonder, do the Clintons have any friends who haven't ended up in jail?

Speaking of Hollywood...

In a recent article by Matt Drudge of the famous Drudge Report, Drudge wrote about a celebrity event organized by Laurie David, wife of Seinfeld co-creator Larry David, on

---

(84) *LA Times*, Saturday, November 15, 2003

December 2, 2003. This gala, described in a mass e-mail as a *"Hate Bush Rally,"* was organized to *"...Prevent the advancement of the current extremist right-wing agenda."* It goes on... *"Do not miss this meeting. This will be a high-level briefing to discuss the strategies to affect what happens next November."*

I wonder if these strategies will involve fraud and illegal fundraising?

The meeting, at the Beverly Hills Hilton, was chaired by Harold Ickes, former Deputy White House Chief of Staff, and Ellen Malcolm, founder of Emily's List. Emily's List is a group devoted to putting pro-choice women in office.

Check out the Hollywood limousine liberals who attended this "Hate Bush Rally":

- Julie Bergman, a producer who came up with the idea of the "silent protest" during the Oscars (a blue and green peace sign pinned onto the jacket)

- Scott Burns, the guy who produced the Arianna Huffington ad that linked SUVs with terrorism

- Steve Byrnes and Jamie Mandelbaum, agents representing Hillary Duff and Tori Spelling

- Ariel Emanuel, an agent who represents West Wing creator Aaron Sorkin; Naomi Foner, a lady who executive produced "Homegrown," a comedy about lovable pot farmers

- Cami Gordon, an author of children's books and member of Mothers for Natural Law

- Lyn Lear, Norman Lear's wife

- Michelle Kyd Lee, the Executive Director of the Creative Artists Agency Foundation

- Julia-Louis Dreyfus, from Seinfeld and Saturday Night Live fame, who is married to sitcom producer Brad Hall.

- Jay Sures, an agent for United Talent Agency who hosted a Wesley Clark fundraiser at his home in Brentwood.

- Marge Tabankin, the political guru to Barbra Streisand who headed the Hollywood Women's Political Committee[85]

Clinton's Speaking Gigs

A lot of people are probably wondering what Bill Clinton has been up to since he left the White House. He's been doing quite well, actually! He routinely demands exorbitant fees for speaking around the world. A Japanese Civic group in Mito, Japan, gave Clinton $400,000 to speak to 2000 kids in high school. What was the message of the speech? He told the kids to "have a dream." Don Walker of the Harry Walker Agency, who represents Clinton, has said that Clinton usually

---

(85) The list and information about the rally were provided by *www. DrudgeReportArchives.com*

gets $100,000-$125,000 for speaking in the U.S. When speaking abroad he usually gets much higher rates.[86]

In 2001 Clinton went to the United Kingdom where he received several thousand dollars for addressing the Jewish National Fund in Glasgow, Scotland. His topic of choice was the "Middle East Problem," a problem he himself failed to solve. I would love to hear his thoughts on the subject. He went on to give the Richard Dimbledy Lecture on "The Struggle for the Soul of the Twentieth Century," in England, as well as the Diana Princess of Wales Lecture on AIDS.[87]

This one is good: Clinton spoke at a company retreat for Morgan Stanley for somewhere between $100,000 and $150,000. So many shareholders and employees were offended by Clinton's presence that the CEO, Philip Purcell, sent a mass email apologizing for Clinton's "behavior as President." Some Clinton supporters dropped their accounts because they were offended by the apology.[88]

Then in March of 2002, Clinton visited Australia, earning a total of $1.175 million for giving 7 speeches in 5 cities. All in all, in 2002 Clinton took home $ 9.5 million for a total of 60 speeches. Martin Duberman said "I'm sure Clinton needs these speeches psychologically more than he does for financial reasons." Clinton's ego aside, he did begin the lectures as a result of his $4 million legal expenditures. And

---

(86) StraitTimes.com, June 18, 2003
(87) LewRockwell.com, Dec. 21, 2001
(88) News.com, Feb. 13th, 2001, Cecily Barnes

now Clinton is the "most sought-after speaker in the lecture industry," according to his agent.[89]

Check out these White House Guests![90]

During the Clinton Administration there were 404 friends and contributors to the Clintons who got to spend the night in the Lincoln Bedroom (or Camp David) as a special "thank you." The *New York Times* published a list of all of these lucky Clinton friends who bought a night at the White House. About 100 of them were donors to Hillary's Senate Campaign, but as Bill Clinton said in 1997, "The White House was never sold." Among the 51 "Arkansas friends" who spent the night in the White House, there are:

Diane Blair
Jim Blair
Kaki Hockersmith (Clinton's Interior Decorator)
Mary Steenburgen
Danny Thomason
Linda Bloodworth-Thomason

Officials and Dignitaries:
President Jimmy Carter
Amy Carter
Annette Carter
Chip Carter
James Carter
Jamie Carter
Jeff Carter

---

(89) *TheNation.com,* Humayun Akhtar
(90) John Broder and Don Van Natta, *New York Times*, "Senate Donors Among Guests at White House," Sep. 23, 2000

Jeremy Carter
Joshua Carter
Margaret Carter
Rosalynn Carter
Sarah Carter
California Governor Gray Davis
Sharon Davis
Rikki Kleiman
Eleanor McGovern
George McGovern

Arts Letters and Sports:
Jimmy Buffett
Chevy Chase
Caley Chase
Cydney Chase
Emily Chase
Jayni Chase
Betsy Cronkite
Walter Cronkite
Walter Cronkite IV
Ted Danson
Donna DeVerona
Danny DeVito
Kenny G
Max G
Quincy Jones
Alexis Kaplan
Rick Kaplan
Irena Medavoy
Jennia Medavoy
Mike Medavoy
Nicolas Medavoy

Rhea Perlman
Dennis Quaid
Meg Ryan
Will Smith
Jada Smith
Kyle Smith
Trey Smith
Steven Spielberg

Longtime friends:
The Rev. Floyd H. Flake
Terry McAuliffe
Jack McAuliffe
Mary McAuliffe
Sally McAuliffe
Terry McAuliffe
Linda Rosenbloom
Kate Rosenbloom
Alana Schulman
Haley Schulman
Kori Schulman Marc Schulman
Maureen Schulman
Carly Schuster
Elaine Schuster
Gerald Schuster
Heidi Schuster
Jessica Schuster
Lizzie Schuster
Mark Schuster

"Friends and Supporters":
Daniel Abraham
Elyssa Adler
Goldie Adler

Harry Adler
Mary Adler
Paul Adler
Rachel Adler
Sam Adler
Alan Cohn
Betsy Cohn
Martin Edelman
Michael Goldberg
Vinod Gupta
Jill Iscol
Kenneth Iscol
Kiva Iscol
Zack Iscol
David Kaplan
Linda Kaplan
Howard Kessler
Michelle Kessler
Chris Korge
Jim Levin
Mary Patricia Levin
Alan Patricof
Susan Patricof
Norman Pattiz
Mary Pattiz
Haim Saban
Cheryl Saban
Heidi Saban
Ness Saban
Tanya Saban

Melrose Larry Green

CHAPTER TWO

Reason Number Nine the Clintons Belong in Prison

Castle Grande- read the section on Castle Grande in the Arkansas chapter and you will see why I am convinced the Clintons were both guilty of perjury and fraud. It is amazing that the McDougals and David Hale went to prison for fraud in Castle Grande, and Bill and Hillary know nothing. I feel they both deserve 2-3 years in prison for their criminal conduct in Castle Grande.

Lies Told By the Clintons Part One

(1) Bill Clinton lied when he said he never attempted to kiss Kathleen Willey on the lips.

(2) Bill Clinton lied under oath when he said he did not attempt to touch Kathleen Willey's breasts.

(3) Bill Clinton lied when he denied taking Kathleen Willey's hand and putting it on his penis.

(4) Bill Clinton lied under oath when he denied telling Kathleen Willey: "I wanted to do that for a long time," after he allegedly touched her inappropriately and placed her hands on his penis.

(5) Bill Clinton lied when he denied having a sexual relationship with Gennifer Flowers.

(6) Bill Clinton lied when he told "60 Minutes", referring to Flowers' claim of an eleven-year relationship with Bill Clinton: "That allegation is false. She didn't tell the truth."

(7) Bill Clinton lied when he said "he had no specific recollection of meeting Kathleen Willey in the Oval

Office." Six months prior to his deposition, his lawyer relayed that information to Michael Isikoff of the *Washington Post*.

(8) Bill Clinton lied when he said there was "nothing sexual" about his sexual molestation of Kathleen Willey.

(9) Bill Clinton lied when he stated that he only saw Monica Lewinsky on 2 or 3 occasions in 1995, when she brought him some documents. The fact is there are at least 24 documented meetings of Lewinsky and Clinton, *many of which involved oral sex.*

(10) Bill Clinton lied when he said he "wasn't sure" if he ever talked to Monica Lewinsky about the possibility she might have to testify in the Paula Jones lawsuit.

(11) Bill Clinton lied when he said he never had an extramarital affair with Monica Lewinsky.

(12) Bill Clinton lied when he said he never had "sexual relations" or an "affair" with Monica Lewinsky.

(13) Bill Clinton lied when he said that Betty Currie set up Monica's job interview at the U.N.

(14) Bill Clinton lied when he said he couldn't remember giving Monica a specific gift he had given her. And if he wasn't lying, that shows how little Monica even meant to his sorry life.

(15) Bill Clinton lied when he denied asking David Hale if he was "going to help Jim out?" (Castle Grande loan- $300,000)

(16) Hillary Clinton lied when she said she did no work on Castle Grande-billing records that turned up at the White House proved she had billed 30 hrs. at $120/hour!

(17) Bill Clinton lied when he told Sidney Blumenthal (referring to Monica) "She came on to me and I didn't have sex with her." (This is actually 2 lies for the price of one!)

(18) Bill Clinton lied when he told Robert Siegel of NPR that "it's more important for me to tell the American people that there wasn't improper relations."

(19) Bill Clinton lied when he said he never met with Paula Jones.

(20) Bill Clinton lied on January 26, 1998, when he told the American people: "I did not have sexual relations with that woman, *Miss Lewinsky,* I never told anyone to lie, not a single time. Never. These allegations are false." [This lie has the record for the most lies within one lie- Five!]

Hillary Clinton

Thoughts from Barbara Olson, author of *Hell to Pay*

The late Barbara Olson tragically died on September 11, 2001. She had been a passenger on the plane that terrorists crashed into the Pentagon. But this brilliant attorney lives on through her 2 classic works *Hell to Pay and The Final Days.* I recommend these two books to anyone who has any doubts about the criminal conduct of Bill and Hillary Clinton.

Olson wrote: "I have never experienced a cooler or more hardened operator than Hillary Clinton. The investigators working for Independent Counsel Kenneth Starr found, as we did, that in one White House scandal after another, *all roads led to Hillary.* To investigate White House improprieties and scandals, the evidence necessarily led to *her* hidden hands guiding the Clinton operation."[1]

---

(1) Barbara Olson, Hell to Pay, p. 3.

Hillary Clinton claims to be innocent of all criminal wrongdoing. While she has not yet been indicted, that is a function of clever lawyers and Bill and Hillary's knowledge of the law. Throughout this book, I will tell you why I think the Clintons belong in prison, but I will never accuse them of being stupid! Bill and Hillary Clinton are two of the most calculating, devious, arrogant, self-serving, and intelligent lawyers on the face of the earth! The fact that the Clintons are not in jail simply means that they are better lawyers than the ones who should have indicted them!

Barbara Olson again: "The press discovered her [Hillary's] fingerprints, figuratively and sometimes, literally, on scandal after scandal- from the firing, smearing, and attempted framing of the White House Travel Office staff, to the ransacking of White House Deputy Counsel Vince Foster's office after his suicide, to billing records that materialized in the White House residence like a gift from the starship *Enterprise*. She began to look like an albatross, and lost clout, becoming the weakest member of the triumvirate."[2]

Hillary was once playing soccer back in high school. She encountered a player from the other team who didn't much care for Hillary. The other girl said to Hillary: "I wish people like you would freeze to death." When Hillary asked how the girl could say that without knowing Hillary, the girl responded. **"I don't have to know you to hate you."**[3] That pretty much sums up my opinion of Hillary Clinton- **I don't have to know her to hate her!**

---

(2) Ibid., p. 10.
(3) Ibid., p. 33.

At Yale, Hillary wasn't the best-looking co-ed on campus- she had "stringy hair and Coke-bottle glasses"[4]

She was a supporter of the Black Panthers, who saw rape of white women by black men as a justifiable act of protest against white racist persecution. The Panthers engaged in torture and murder, and they referred to police as "pigs." These were the people Hillary Rodham revered. Hillary was closely allied with Panthers' lawyer Charles Garry and Communists Robert Truehaft and Jessica Mitford.

Bill and Hillary Clinton had their first fight as a Presidential couple in inauguration day, 1993. On the steps of Blair House, Bill Clinton screamed at his wife: **"Fucking bitch!" Hillary's reply was: "Stupid motherfucker".**[5]

Hillary had known about Bill's womanizing for years. Even before they were married, Hillary once went through Bill's desk, tearing up girls' phone numbers that he had collected on the campaign trail.[6] But Bill and Hillary had a deal: the power would be shared- and the ultimate goal- a co-Presidency- had to be kept in focus. In many ways, Bill and Hillary each have the qualities the other lacks.

"It is Bill more than Hillary, who can engage people around a coffee counter or across the nation on television. She accepts him as he is, because he is willing to return the favor. He is the willing vehicle for her ideas and her quest

---

(4) Ibid., p. 54.
(5) Ibid., p. 66.
(6) Ibid., p. 68.

for power. And he could be the launch pad for a presidential candidacy of her own."[7]

Bill and Hillary were introduced to each other by Robert Reich at the cafeteria of Yale Law School. Years later, Clinton rewarded Reich with a cabinet appointment-Secretary of Labor. Hillary thought "makeup was superficial and silly. She didn't have time for it."[8] Bill and Hillary moved in together in a $75/month apartment in New Haven. In 1972, they worked on the McGovern campaign, where they met **Betsey Wright,** who was to go on to protect Bill Clinton from the media after he would get involved with one woman after another. It was Wright who coined the term **"bimbo control."**

Sometime in 1974, when they Clintons were living in Arkansas, Hillary started hiring private investigators to keep an eye on her husband Bill. Her objectives were not only to see who Bill was messing around with, but also to see if Bill's womanizing was a liability to her political aspirations.

Mary Lee Fray was in charge of controlling the traffic of women in and out of Bill Clinton's office, when he ran for Congress in Arkansas in 1974. Her job was to make sure that Hillary was never around when Bill's other girlfriends were in the office and vice versa. According to Mary Lee Fray: "Hillary had a weight problem and she wouldn't diet...She didn't have a body for a dress. So I told her to at least buy some nice underclothes."[9]

---

(7) Ibid., p. 68.
(8) Ibid., p. 70.
(9) Ibid., p. 87.

Dick Morris once asked Bill Clinton, if he could ask John F. Kennedy one question, what would it be? Not surprisingly, Bill Clinton replied: "I'd want to ask him, you know, how did you do it? 'How'd you get away with it?'[10]

When Hillary arrived in Arkansas, she wasted no time in intimidating and alienating many of the students who were volunteering to work for Bill Clinton. According to Marla Crider, an old girlfriend of Bill's, "She [Hillary] was very dictatorial. She literally came in and just turned everything around, changed everything. She didn't know how to deal with Southerners. We are very easy-going, laid-back, which drove her nuts. She would get furious if there was any frivolity. Furious. It was like- 'Have you forgotten what our goal is?' She unraveled. It was almost like she was angry the whole time."[11] According to Paul Fray, "None of those kids really liked her. She would come in, want to run the show, tell everybody what they were supposed to be doing."[12]

Ron Addington worked with the Clintons back in 1974. He remembered that the ladies in the office despised Hillary. "The girls just couldn't stand her, giving orders all the time."[13] Addington remembers Bill and Hillary would argue a lot. He could recall at least 15 to 20 big arguments the two of them had.[14]

---

(10) Ibid. p. 91.
(11) Jerry Oppenheimer, State of a Union, p. 141.
(12) Ibid., p. 141.
(13) Ibid., p. 142.
(14) Ibid., p. 144.

Radio talk show host Michael Medved actually attended Yale at the same time as Hillary. He recalls that there were 2 girls that everyone at Yale wanted to date; then there was a whole range of women that were possibilities to date. Hillary was in neither of those categories. She was heavy and "she wore those sweatshirts, socks and sandals, and big baggy black pants."[15] And what did Bill Clinton see in Hillary? Well says Medved, she was "an available female. You took what you could get."[16]

Let's Name our Daughter Laura!

According to Fox News Channel's Brit Hume, "Statistics from the Social Security administration show that no name has gone out of style in the U.S. more than the name 'Hillary' did after the Clintons moved in to the White House." Hillary had been a popular name for girls from the 1960's to the 1990's, having peaked at #136 in 1992. But right after 1992, the name "Hillary" dropped precipitously and by 1993, "Hillary" wasn't even ranked. Says Hume: "It took more than 3 times that long for Adolph, as in Hitler and Ebenezer, as in Scrooge, to fall off the charts." Hillary's spokesperson said the "comparison to Adolph Hitler is hardly fair and balanced."[17]

Hillary on the Warpath

During a speech at John Jay College of Criminal Justice in New York City (early 2003), Hillary Clinton bashed the

---

(15) Oppenheimer, "State of a Union," p. 7
(16) Ibid., p. 10
(17) Human Events, Sept. 22, 2003, p. 9

Bush administration and its Department of Homeland Security. Hillary called President Bush's homeland security plan a "myth" and said that "the country is only marginally safer than it was before September 11."[18]

What follows are excerpts of her speech to the students at John Jay- to me these comments border on treason and sedition and give comfort to the Al Qaeda terrorists!

"Our people remain vulnerable, nearly as vulnerable as we were before the terrorist attacks. Our vigilance has faded at the top, in the corridors of power in Washington, D.C., where the strategy and resources to protect our nation are supposed to originate, where leaders are supposed to lead... We have relied on a myth of homeland security- a myth written in rhetoric, inadequate resources and a new bureaucracy instead of relying on good, old-fashioned American ingenuity, might and muscle..."[19]

Hillary asked the students: Will "ending the dividend tax make air travel safer? Will it keep a dirty bomb out of New York Harbor? Will ending the dividend tax save one police officer or firefighter his or her job? In short, will it make America safer, more secure? Of course, the answer is no."[20]

Then Hillary, whose husband did nothing to stop Osama Bin Laden after he committed one after another atrocity and who turned down offers from the Sudan to turn over Bin Laden to the U.S., had the nerve to say that the Bush

---

(18) Ibid., Feb. 3, 2003, p. 17
(19) Ibid., p. 17
(20) Ibid., p. 17

Administration ignored warnings about Bin Laden from the outgoing Clinton administration![21]

In a radio interview, the shameless Senator from New York blasted the Bush administration. "I know that during the transition between the Clinton and Bush administrations that the outgoing administration told the incoming one that they would spend more time on terrorism and bin Laden than anything else. And that wasn't their priorities, their priorities were different."[22]

Republican Congressman Peter King (NY) was shocked. He felt that Hillary's comments only served to make our country more vulnerable to the terrorists.

"I just think it was a cheap shot," King said. "It just invites the enemy to attack again."[23]

But what is on Hillary's Website?

On Hillary's website **friendsofhillary.com,** donors to Hillary's 2006 Senatorial campaign can receive awards such as coffee mugs, "silver toned" bookmarks, pens, and "personally inscribed copies of her million-selling memoir "Living History." People who sign up to be one of "Hill's Angels" agree to send e-mails to 10 friends, and they receive a membership card with a "giant-winged "H" emblazoned on the front."

---

(21) Ibid., p. 17
(22) Ibid., p. 17
(23) Ibid., p. 17.

On its first day, the website had so much traffic that it crashed. The website has policy positions, photographs, and ways "to help re-elect Hillary."[24]

Sister Frigidaire

Coincidentally, Hillary Clinton grew up in the same town as Henry Hyde, the Chairman of the House Judiciary Committee, the committee that would impeach her husband. That town was Park Ridge, Illinois. In Hillary's high school newspaper, it was once written that she would likely become a nun. Her nickname was **"Sister Frigidaire."**[25]

During the 60's, Hillary embraced a magazine called *Motive* which promoted lesbianism, sanctioned terrorism, and condoned those who took part in the race riots of America. This magazine was subsidized by the United Methodist Church and featured articles by SDS' **Carl Oglesby.** Hillary kept a file of these magazines in her dorm room at Wellesley. Oglesby's main rap was: **'What would be so wrong about a Viet Nam run by Ho Chi Minh, or a Cuba by Castro?"**[26]

During her freshman year at Wellesley, Hillary was elected president of the Young Republicans Club.[27] She was known as a "Goldwater Girl", named after the late Sen. Barry Goldwater (AZ), who was the far right-wing Republican candidate for President back in 1964.

---

(24) Ibid., Aug. 4, 2003, p. 16.
(25) Joyce Milton, The First Partner, p. 18
(26) Ibid., p. 26
(27) Ibid., p. 27

Although former Clinton Labor Secretary Robert Reich is credited with first introducing Bill Clinton to Hillary Rodham on a cafeteria line at Yale Law School, they first talked to each other in the law school library. In a classic story, Bill stared longingly at Hillary, before she broke the ice by telling him: "Look, if you're going to keep staring at me and I'm going to keep staring back, we might as well introduce ourselves."[28] On their first date, Bill took Hillary to an art exhibit. When he discovered that the museum was closed, Bill sweet-talked the janitor into opening the museum by offering to help the janitor dump the trash.[29]

When they first met, Bill was a little overweight and sported a beard. And Hillary wasn't the best-looking girl at Yale. According to one fellow student, she belonged to the **"look like shit school of feminism."**[30]

Bill Clinton referred to Hillary as "Hilla the Hun."[31] In December, 1977, Gennifer Flowers discovered she was pregnant. Bill Clinton was about to run for governor of Arkansas. The last thing he needed was a love child, so he gave Gennifer Flowers $200 in cash to get an abortion.[32] When Gennifer Flowers first met Hillary Clinton, she saw Hillary "as a fat frump who was behaving oddly, laughing too loud and drawing attention to herself."[33]

---

(28) Ibid., p. 48
(29) Ibid., p. 48
(30) Ibid., p. 50
(31) Ibid., p. 94
(32) Ibid., p. 94
(33) Ibid., p. 95

Susan Henley was a student at Ouachita Baptist University, near Arkadelphia, Arkansas, who fell in love with her professor James McDougal. She became Susan McDougal, and has been rumored to have been a lover of Bill Clinton.[34]

When a political supporter once presented Hillary with a gift of earrings with the Arkansas razorbacks logo, Hillary was most ungrateful. Not only did she not try them on, she commented: **"This is the kind of shit I have to put up with."**[35]

Hillary Clinton turned a **$1,000 investment into $99,500 by investing in cattle futures.** Her broker, Robert "Red" Bone was a former Tyson chicken executive, who had been accused of manipulating the market in egg futures. Hillary said of her incredible skill in the commodities market: **"I was lucky."**[36] According to Caroline Baum and Victor Neiderhoffer, who examined Hillary's trading records in the "National Review", it looks as if Hillary's broker engaged in an illicit form of trading called **straddling.** Basically, straddling involves allocating profitable trades to particular clients and charging losses to less favored clients. Brown and Niederhoffer's analyses indicated that one Refco client had trades of over $1 million assigned to his account. He then lost all his equity on a margin call, having been charged with a loss of $100,000! The original records of 2 of Hillary's most successful trades are missing.

---

(34) Ibid., pp. 96-97
(35) Ibid., p. 97
(36) Ibid., p. 108

Just to show you what special treatment Hillary received, consider this fact. By December 11, 1979 (3 months into her account's existence), when she had just $6,000 on deposit with Refco, **Hillary controlled contracts with a value of $2,300,000!** Hillary claimed to have learned about commodities trading from reading the "Wall Street Journal", but on 3 of her most significant trading dates, **she had been involved in day-long activities with Legal Services Corporation!**

Hillary's account was a non-discretionary account.[37] It was illegal for her friend Jim Blair or Red Bone to trade for her.

I feel that Hillary should have gone to prison for her role in her cattle futures trading back in 1979! Factually, her case is a lot more criminal that the facts surrounding Martha Stewart.

Bill Clinton raised the car license fee in 1978. It soon became public knowledge that Hillary didn't renew her tags for her Fiat in 1977 and 1978, Bill blamed this on an aide in his office who forgot to renew Hillary's registration.[38]

Besides the customary staff of cooks and maids, Bill Clinton had lots of perks as governor. The salary was only $35,000/year, but the legislature authorized all sorts of extras. In addition to the typical pensions and health care benefits, Bill had a 12-man detail of state troopers at his beck and call. They would drive him around in a Lincoln Town car.

---

(37) Ibid., p. 108
(38) Ibid., p. 112

Although Clinton's perks amounted to over $750,000, he only paid taxes on his $35,000 salary.

"During Clinton's first term one aide, Russ Perrymore, clocked so many miles on his state-issued car running personal errands for the governor and the first lady that legislators threatened to order an investigation. Hillary took state business into the Rose Law firm and asked state troopers to deliver personal items to her at work, including Tampax- a chore they saw as an attempt to humiliate them. By the late 1980's, she would be criticized for dispatching convicts who did yard work for the Governor's mansion to take care of the outside chores at a Little Rock condo owned by her parents."[39]

Those Democrats Just Love Hillary!

According to a Time/CNN survey conducted in early 2004, Hillary Clinton had a 73% favorability rating, which was 35 points ahead of any of the Democratic Presidential hopefuls. Similarly, her impeached husband, who was demonstrated to have been a liar, received a 71% approval rating.[40] **And you want to know why I want nothing to do with the Democratic Party?**

American Airlines Flight waits on tarmac for 90 Minutes until Hillary boards her flight!

According to an article in "Human Events", Hillary Clinton was the cause of an American Airlines jet waiting on

---

(39) Ibid., pp. 112-113
(40) Human Events, Apr. 2004

the tarmac for 90 minutes. Hillary was en route to a book signing for her new book, and apparently she and her people were running late.

The N.Y. Post got the scoop: "The flight out of JFK the other night sat on the tarmac without explanation until an hour and a half after the scheduled departure time." A passenger in first class soon discovered the reason for the delay when an "unapologetic Hillary Clinton and her entourage of flunkies and bodyguards hurried onto the plane so she could make it to a book signing for *Living History.*"[41]

According to Newsmax.com, the host of MSNBC's "Hardball, **Chris Matthews,** was on a plane when he encountered Hillary and her entourage. **Do taxpayers pay for Hillary's entourage? Inquiring minds want to know!**

Hillary is a Role Model in Communist China

The director of the press and media institute at Beijing's Academy of Social Sciences, Yu Quanyu, selected Hillary Clinton as "a shining example of a successful manipulative orator, for apparatchiks to follow." Her ability to win over public opinion with "little or no reasoning" has been recommended as role model for the Communist Party soldiers. This honor to Hillary appears in an article in *Ideological and Political Work Studies*, in 1998.[42] What impressed the Communist Chinese was how Hillary discredited all her opponents by branding them as members of a vast right-wing conspiracy.

---

(41) "Human Events," Feb 3, 2003, p. 17
(42) Ibid., August 4, 2003, p. 16

Hillary Disses the American Legion!

Hillary had been invited to a ceremony honoring 5 American soldiers who died in the Korean War. The ceremony, sponsored by the Queens County Committee of the American Legion, was held in June, 2003. One of Hillary's people told the Legion that Hillary couldn't attend the event, but she would issue a "Senate proclamation honoring our fallen members." Well, a month went by and no proclamation was received by the American Legion chapter. According to Korean war vet and American Legion service officer Dan O'Sullivan: "It was an insult…[Hillary's] actions toward our organization, veterans and the families of foreign war heroes, are an utter disgrace."[43]

P.S. O'Sullivan sent two letters of protest to Hillary's office at the Senate, but he received no reply to either letter.

Bill and Hill- still working as a team, even after Monica!

According to Sidney Blumenthal, author of *The Clinton Wars, even after* Hillary knew all about Bill and Monica, they still communicated as a team. Blumenthal had been listening in to a phone conversation between Bill and Hillary during the days right after August 15, 1998. According to Blumenthal, "They were still working as a team."[44]

Hillary- the TV Movie is Coming to A&E!

A&E will be airing a 2-hour made for TV movie on Hillary Clinton. The movie will be based on Gail Sheehy's

(43) Ibid., January 26, 2004, p. 27
(44) Ibid., Aug. 18, 2003, p. 21

book *Hillary's Choice.* According to *Human Events,* producers have approached Sharon Stone about playing the role of Hillary. The movie "will focus on Hillary's quest to fulfill her high hopes and ambitions as she repeatedly faces humiliating personal setbacks." According to Robert DeBitetto, A&E's senior vice-president of programming, "It's a fascinating story and one that has captured the imagination of the public."[45]

Sean Hannity Praises 'Hillary's Scheme' by Carl Limbacher

"Of all the books that have been written about [Hillary Clinton], this one is the definitive book that probably the Clintons will fear the most." That is what Fox News Channel's Sean Hannity said about Limbacher's expose of Hillary Clinton on his show, "Hannity & Colmes."

Said Hannity: "This is a terrific read and a great book-and it lays it all out. If you look at the polls, she's the most popular Democrat. She beats all nine other no-names."

Limbacher contends that Hillary will run for President, almost definitely in 2008 and *perhaps in 2004!*
Notes Hannity: This book reminds us of everything this woman is involved in...I don't think it misses a beat in pointing out every lie, every inconsistency, straight on down the line."

According to author Carl Limbacher, who has written extensively for Newsmax.com, "Hillary's Scheme"

(45) Ibid., Aug. 18, 2003, p. 21

Is a "clarion call for conservatives and Republicans" to start preparing for a Hillary Presidential run in 2004.[46]

Hillary "Very Grateful" to have grown up in 'White Suburbs'

In a recent speech carried on C-Span, Senator Hillary Clinton told an audience that she was grateful that she grew up in a white suburb. Most of the mainstream media did not report her remarks, which are as offensive to members of the African-American community as were Trent Lott's recent comments about the late Strom Thurmond.

Hillary said the following: "There are just a lot of things that happened in the 20th century that some people apparently couldn't get over...exactly what was that golden age that they want to go back to?...Is it back to the 1950's white suburbs for family life, which I grew up in and write about in my book- and *am very grateful for*- but didn't exactly describe the universal experience in America?"

Rev. Jesse Peterson, head of the Los Angeles-based Brotherhood Organization of a New Destiny was shocked.

"Where's the outcry from the mainstream media and Democrats about Hillary's statements? These people were all over Trent Lott calling him a racist and accusing him of being nostalgic about the Jim Crow era...This is a double standard.

Niger Innis, spokesman for the Congress of Racial Equality agreed that Hillary was given special treatment.

---

(46) Ibid., August 11, 2003, p. 17

"If it had been a Republican, they'd be crucified!"[47]

Hillary's Book Sales May be Overstated by over 1 Million Copies!

Hillary Clinton's book "Living History" came out in June, 2003. According to her publisher, Simon & Schuster, Hillary has sold "more than 2.25 million copies" in 2003. But, according to Nielsen Bookscan figures, Hillary has sold 1,084, 520 copies of her book. Bookscan tracks purchases to such outlets as Barnes & Noble, Borders, and Costco; it reaches approximately 75% of total sales. Factoring in the other 25% of sales, it still leaves Hillary at 750,000 copies below the 2.25 million figure![48]

Hillary's zeal for promoting the book has become so intense that many have seen political aspirations behind it. Hillary herself claimed to have personally autographed more than 20,000 books, signing until her hands can move no longer. She has taken to wearing a wrist support and soaking her hand in ice so she can keep going, and she has been all across the United States and over to Paris, London and Amsterdam in a nonstop quest for higher book sales. Apparently her promotion has paid off, because the book has become the number one bestseller in markets that do not usually pay attention to American political memoirs, such as England, Germany, France, and Ireland. Hillary fans have been getting up before dawn to form lines stretching around city blocks just to see her and shake her hand. All this despite

---

(47) Hannity on "Hillary's Scheme", Newsmax.com Magazine, October, 2003 p. 10
(48) Newsmax.com Magazine, October 2003, pp. 10-11

the warnings of critics that her book is self-serving and lacks substance. I guess they are all too blinded by their love for Hillary to notice.[49]

Is She or isn't She? Does Hillary Go Both Ways?

For years, rumors have circulated about Hillary Clinton's sexuality. Long-time lover of Bill Clinton Gennifer Flowers once confronted Bill, telling him: "There's something you need to know. I've been hearing tales around town that Hillary is having a thing with another *woman*." Bill burst out laughing, and Gennifer wanted to know what was so funny. Bill replied: "Honey, she's probably eaten more pussy than I have."[50] Two favorite nicknames Bill had for Hillary were "The Sarge" and "Hilla the Hun."[51]

Martin Mawyer, president of the **Christian Action Network,** wrote an open letter to Hillary back in October, 2000 in which he challenged her to reveal her sexual orientation. For years, there have been rumors of moonlight swims at Camp David with groups of women. Mawyer wanted Hillary to release the names of all women who have been invited to Camp David. Mawyer told the *Star:* "We've heard reports that some very shameful lesbian going-on have taken place at Camp David with Hillary's knowledge, and sometimes her participation. That information about who was there and when may have been deliberately kept out of

---

(49) New York Times, July 26, 2003
(50) Gennifer Flowers, Passion and Betrayal, p. 41
(51) Gennifer Flowers, "Passion and Betrayal," p. 41

the official logs. We want to see all of those guest lists- not just the ones the White House has released."[52]

Mawyer felt that "wealthy gay supporters of the Clintons are said to have used Camp David for lesbian trysts- with the first lady in attendance."[53]

People such as Secret service agents, cooks, and groundskeepers have leaked information "that Hillary used Camp David as a meeting place for her lesbian friends."[54]

On one occasion, a witness was making a security round "when he saw Hillary and a brunette woman frolicking in the pool."[55] Hillary shouted "Who's there?", as she and the young woman hurriedly exited the pool.[56]

On another occasion, a group of rowdy lesbians arrived at the gate at Camp David and "berated the guards when they had to wait until their security clearance was OK'd."[57]

"Some of them had apparently been drinking before they arrived and they were bitching loudly that they were kept waiting. One of them said: *'Don't you know that we are friends of Mrs. Clinton?'*[58]

---

(52) Star, October 17, 2000, p. 18
(53) Ibid., p. 18
(54) Ibid., p. 18
(55) Ibid., p. 18
(56) Ibid., p. 18
(57) Ibid., p. 18
(58) Ibid., p. 18

Hillary arrived an hour later and was driven to a VIP cabin named Red Oak, where several of the lesbians were lodged.

According to the Star's confidential source, "Hillary ordered her Secret Service detail not to hover around the area unless they were summoned." "Hillary left about midmorning the next day, at which point the remaining women sunbathed on the cabin's patio and snuggled in ways the agents deemed 'extremely inappropriate.'"[59]

Mahatma Gandhi, Hillary wants $10 on pump # 1!

Speaking to a group of Democrats at a fundraiser in St. Louis, Hillary Clinton told a shocked audience: "Mahatma Gandhi ran a gas station down in St. Louis." Now I ask you, why does Trent Lott have to resign over his "racist" remark, while Hillary Clinton is – as usual- given a free pass by the media for an obviously *demeaning and racist comment?*

Could it be because the media overwhelmingly backs anything connected to Bill or Hillary Clinton? As Bernard Goldberg has often pointed out, 89% of the White House Press pool voted for Bill Clinton. One top leader of a center devoted to the study of Gandhi found the remarks "stereotypical and insensitive."

Hillary immediately apologized, saying "I have admired the work and life of Mahatma Gandhi and have spoken publicly about that many times. I truly regret if a lame attempt at humor suggested otherwise."[60]

---

(59) Ibid., p. 18
(60) Human Events, Jan. 12, 2004, p. 43

Folks, just think what the media would have been saying if Bill Frist, Dick Cheney, or George Bush made this kind of insulting remark! They would all be calling for the resignation of the offending Republican.

Naturally, the frauds from the liberal community ran to Hillary's defense. The administrator of the M.K. Gandhi Institute said "I don't think she was, in any way, trying to demean Mahatma Gandhi."[61]

You Cannot be Serious!

In the annual Gallup poll, Hillary Clinton was voted as the woman most admired by Americans.

Hillary received 16%, Oprah Winfrey got 7%, Laura Bush and Condoleeza Rice tied at 4%, and poor Barbara Bush got only 2%.

There is no accounting for the stupidity of the American public!

Hillary's Philosophy

Hillary Clinton is a radical feminist who believes that marriage is an enslaving institution. In one of her early writings (Harvard Educational Review), she compared marriage to slavery and the Native American reservation system.

---

(61) Ibid., p. 43

"The basic rationale for depriving people of rights in a dependency relationship is that certain individuals are incapable or undeserving of the right to take care of themselves and consequently need social institutions specifically designed to safeguard their positions. It is presumed that under the circumstances society is doing what is best for the individuals. Along with the family, past and present examples of such arrangements included marriage, slavery, and the Indian reservation system."- Hillary Clinton, writing in the Harvard Educational Review.[62]

Perhaps this explains why Hillary tolerated all of Bill's cheating on her. To her, marriage is an institution which represses people. It seems as if Hillary's radical feminist background gave Bill Clinton a free pass to mess around. What kind of a marriage is it anyway?

After Bill lost his re-election race for Governor in 1980, Hillary took the defeat really badly. A friend heard Hillary yelling at Bill: "Wake up! People believed it was wrong! Can't you see that?"[63]

Hillary's temper was legendary. According to her friend Carolyn Huber, "the person on the receiving end of it never gets over it."[64]

Hillary could be sarcastic too. She once wrote: "Of course when I live in suburbia with my commuter husband and 2.5 children, there is always PTA, the Junior League and

---

(62) Barbara Olson, Hell to Pay, p. 107
(63) Gail Sheehy, Hillary's Choice, p. 139
(64) Gail Sheehy, "Hillary's Choice," p. 139

other distinguished ventures in which I could indulge."[65]   At Wellesley, Hillary was President of the Young Republican club. When she graduated Wellesley, neither her parents nor her 2 brothers attended Hillary's commencement exercises.[66]

During the summer of 1968, Hillary was a junior at Wellesley.   She began a three year love affair with a Georgetown University undergrad by the name of David Rupert. Rupert noted that he was attracted to Hillary despite her big, ugly glasses.   Rupert didn't "remember any mascara."[67]   Hillary and Rupert met during the summer of 1968- both worked as interns for Congressmen. According to Rupert, Hillary was never wild or out of control. Whenever they slept together, "we always used birth control."[68] Rupert said this about Hillary: "There was always the perfectionist, the drive, always the ambition." Why did they break up? "I never stated a burning desire to be President of the United States. I believe that was a need for her in a partner."[69]

On September 12, 1998, Hillary gave an interview in which she spoke of her experiences as an intern (Yes, even Hillary was once an intern) to Congressman Melvin Laird, back in 1968. "I have pretty good antennae for people who are chauvinistic or sexist or patronizing toward women."[70]

---

(65) Ibid., p. 60
(66) Ibid., p. 59
(67) Ibid., p. 64
(68) Ibid., p. 69
(69) Ibid., p. 74
(70) Ibid., p. 64

Just 3 days later, Bill Clinton was deposed in the sexual harassment lawsuit of Paula Jones.

Hillary's Legal Skills

During the inquiry into the impeachment of Richard Nixon, Hillary worked as a lawyer on the House Judiciary Committee. According to William Dixon, a member of the committee staff, Hillary "paid no attention to the way the Constitution works in this country, the way politics works, the way Congress works, the way legal safeguards are set up."[71]

Jerome Zeifman was the Democratic counsel to the House Judiciary Impeachment Inquiry in 1974. Hillary Clinton worked for Zeifman. This is what Zeifman wrote about Hillary in his job evaluation of her performance: Zeifman "could not recommend her [Hillary] for any future position of public or private trust. A number of the procedures she recommended were ethically flawed. And I also concluded that she had violated House and committee rules by disclosing confidential information to unauthorized persons."[72]

In 1995, Zeifman wrote a book, *Without Honor: the Impeachment of President Nixon and the Crimes of Camelot.* He cites specific examples of Hillary Clinton's dishonesty. In one instance, Zeifman characterized Hillary as "unworthy of

---

(71) Investor's Business Daily, Dec. 6, 1990
(72) R. Emmett Tyrrell, Jr., Madame Hillary, p. 78

either public or private trust."[73] In another, Zeifman feels that Hillary had a tendency towards "misleading, if not deceiving Congress."[74]

Hillary felt that any impeachment of Richard Nixon should not be limited to criminal offenses. In her Judiciary Committee report, she wrote: "to limit impeachable conduct to criminal offenses would be incompatible with the evidence concerning the constitutional meaning of the phrase...and would frustrate the purpose that the framers intended for impeachment."[75]

Wait a minute, Hillary. Let me get this straight. For Richard Nixon, it is wrong to limit the impeachment to just *criminal* offenses. But for your husband Bill, the conduct *had to be criminal to be impeachable.* It sounds like a double standard for me. How ironic it would be, that 25 years after Hillary argued for Richard Nixon's impeachment on matters *of a non-criminal nature,* Bill Clinton's lawyers would be arguing just the reverse- that Bill Clinton's crimes *had to be criminal to be impeachable.*

Aren't liberal Democrats something?

The Black Panthers and Hillary

During her days at Yale, when Hillary was a big supporter of the Black Panthers, she became friendly with

---

(73) Ibid., p. 79 This quote originally appeared in the New York Post, Aug. 16, 1999.
(74) Ibid., p. 79 See also Jerome Zeifman, Without Honor, p. 123
(75) Barbara Olson, Hell to Pay, p. 124

Panther attorney Charles Garry. Garry had a private investigator, Jack Palladino, who worked for him on the Panther case involving the torture-murder of Alex Rackley. Years later, Hillary and Palladino would work together in controlling "bimbo eruptions." These were well-orchestrated attempts to discredit and destroy the accounts of Bill Clinton's girlfriends. At Yale Law School, Hillary Clinton and Bill Lann Lee both organized demonstrations in support of the Black Panthers. Years later, Bill Lann Lee would be the chief of the Department of Justice's Civil Rights Division, under Bill Clinton.[76]

Several Black Panthers in New Haven had been accused of the murder-torture of one of their own members, Alex Rackley. These animals didn't just kill Rackley with one gunshot. "Before he died, his Panther brothers had clubbed him, burned him with cigarettes, scalded him with boiling water, stabbed him with an ice pick, and *finally* shot him twice. Police found his mutilated body floating in the Coginchaug River, twenty-five miles north of New Haven.[77]

During the time that Hillary was associate editor of the *Yale Review,* she prepared and edited an entire issue devoted to the Black Panthers. The editorial cartoons pictured policeman as "pigs."[78] One "pig" in uniform is called a "fascist." Another has been decapitated. In the cartoon, the police were depicted as thinking: "Niggers! Niggers!

---

(76) Carl Limbacher, Hillary's Scheme, pp. 132-133.
(77) Carl Limbacher, Hillary's Scheme, pp. 132-133.
(78) David Brock, The Seduction of Hillary Rodham, p. 32

Niggers!"[79] This particular drawing has the caption "Seize the Time", which was the rally cry of the Panthers.

I am sure many of you are surprised to hear of Hillary's links to the Black Panthers. Very few outlets of the mainstream media ever reported on Hillary's past at Yale, when she embraced the tactics and views of the Panthers. Thanks to such well-respected sources as the late Barbara Olson and writers Jerry Oppenheimer and Gail Sheehy, I have been able to give this information to you.

Inside the Hillary Clinton Camp

People such as Harold Ickes and Susan Thomases were at the core of the inner circle of Hillary's operations. These two are not nice people. They will stop at nothing to get their way. Another key person on the Clinton team was James Carville. You know him, he's the bald guy on CNN who just won't shut up! James Carville is one of the reasons I left the Democratic Party. A Clinton insider once said about Harold Ickes: "He has done more single-handedly to destroy the Democratic Party than anyone else."[80] Ickes leans far to the left. According to Barbara Olson, Ickes is "driven and choleric, a born hater and intriguer."[81] Susan Thomases was the New York lawyer who loved to control things. Hillary placed Thomasses in charge of controlling Bill Clinton's schedule. Thomasses, a typical angry New York leftist, left her influence on Hillary. Writer Camile Paglia put it this way: "But her "steely soul remains, the butch substrate that

---

(79) Ibid., p. 32
(80) Olson, op. cit., p. 207
(81) Barbara Olson, Hell to Pay, p. 207

can be seen in the baleful, bloodless face of lawyer Susan Thomasses."[82]   Susan Thomases and Harold Ickes were instrumental in getting Hillary to run for the Senate. Harold Ickes is involved in the movement to destroy and discredit President George Bush.

What does it require to be in the inner sanctum of Hillary's political team? A former White House staffer told Gail Sheehy, a prerequisite "is to show a balls-out, go-to-the-mat mentality about taking on their enemies. Anybody who has a hang-up about fairness is cast out as part of the enemy camp."[83]

Things Involving Hillary That Dan Rather Never Told You

Another shocking incident which received little or no media coverage occurred on October 14, 2001, at Westchester County Airport, outside of New York City. A Ford van carrying Senator Hillary Clinton blew past a security checkpoint at 35 miles per hour, seriously injuring police officer Ernest Dymond. Dymond was unavailable to return to work for weeks, as he had sustained serious injuries to his hand and elbow. Because of restrictions imposed by his police department, Dymond was unable to comment on the incident, but, according to Newsmax.com writer Carl Limbacher, "Dymond did note, however, that neither Hillary Clinton nor her staff had contacted him to inquire about his condition or apologize for the accident in any way."[84]

---

(82) Ibid., p. 208
(83) Ibid., p. 209
(84) Limbacher, op. cit., p. 135

This incident occurred just one month after September 11, and Dymond feared that perhaps there could be terrorists in the van. As he was clinging to the back of the van, Dymond yelled to the van driver: "What the hell are you doing?" Limbacher reports: "Only after the Westchester cop threw his shoulder into the vehicle and began banging on its side did Clinton's car come to a halt, about 100 yards beyond the checkpoint...[Dymond] described Senator Clinton's driver as 'quite agitated' when he was stopped and ordered to produce identification...Two weeks later Dymond was still unable to return to work, suggesting the encounter with Clinton's van left him in much worse shape than the hospital had let on."[85]

Almost two months after the incident, Dymond was still hampered by the injuries he had suffered. When asked for a comment, Dymond's wife told *The National Enquirer:* "Not that we wouldn't like to talk. But none of us are allowed to."[86]

Now compare and contrast the previous incident with what happened to former Congressman J.C. Watts (Republican/ African-American) when he got into an argument with a policeman at Will Rogers Airport in Oklahoma. Watts was given a parking ticket while he was assisting his wife with her bags. He felt that officer Edward Stupka had ticketed his car unfairly. Unlike Officer Dymond, who was kept quiet, Officer Stupka demanded and received a written apology from Congressman Watts! And,

---

(85) Ibid., p. 134
(86) Ibid., p. 135

though the Dymond story, involving Hillary the Democrat received virtually no media coverage, the incident with officer Stupka and J.C. Watts the Republican was picked up by "print coverage from coast to coast."[87]

Barbra Streisand and the White House[88]

In 1996, Hillary's father Hugh was lying on his deathbed in Scranton, PA. Hillary rushed back to Washington, when she heard that Bill had been wining and dining Barbra Streisand at the White House. Babs had slept in the Lincoln bedroom and had been escorted by Bill Clinton to the annual Gridiron dinner. There he serenaded the crowd on the saxophone, offering up the Coasters' hit "Yakety Yak." Hillary was furious when she found out that Bill was partying with Streisand. She and Bill got into a big fight, and Hillary ended up the winner, causing a long scratch on Bill's face. The White House spin was that Bill had cut himself shaving, a story which White House spokesperson Dee Dee Myers later indicated was totally false.

Probably the only thing Hillary Clinton and Monica Lewinsky ever agreed upon was their mutual hatred for Barbra Streisand. Monica said "She's soooo annoying." Miss Lewinsky suspected that Bill had carried on an affair with the diva.

Bill Clinton wasn't exactly a stud during his Oxford days. He was a bit overweight, was a bad dresser, and according to his good friend Mandy Merck, "he had crap in his beard a

---

(87) Ibid., p. 135
(88) Gail Sheehy, Hillary's Choice, p. 234

good deal of the time...He wasn't real good-looking...I just thought of him as someone who was going into politics, and who was a plump, funny guy."

Clinton has a strange sense of humor, even during his Oxford days. Once, after hugging Many Merck, he said to her "Did you know I was the fastest fuck in the world?" 'What?', she asked.. Clinton replied "You didn't feel that did, you?"[89]

Bill Clinton and Hillary Rodham met at Yale Law school. From the outset, it was a mutually beneficial relationship. Bill was always the outgoing schmoozer, who couldn't seem to manage time or organize his life. Hillary, on the other hand, was a focused, no-nonsense woman, who had evolved from being a Goldwater girl in high school to a feminist/activist at Wellesley College, before meeting her partner in crime in the law library at Yale.

During his days at Yale, Bill Clinton was known for his voracious appetite. Radio talk-show host and former Yale classmate Michael Medved remembers how Bill would eat a potato. "I specifically remember him showing off swallowing those potatoes. "'Look, Ah'm gonna make this potato disappear.' "It was almost a macho thing with him, like look how much I can eat, look how manly I am. People talked about it behind his back- did you see what Bill Clinton ate?[90]

---

(89) Jerry Oppenheimer, State of a Union, p. 124-125.
(90) Ibid., p. 12

Bill and Hillary were a hot sexual couple at Yale. At Yale in the 70's there were very few women. According to Michael Medved, "You took what you could get."[91] Bill and Hillary were all over each other, often displaying affection publicly. It was as if they were telling all of Yale Law school- "look we have a relationship. "According to one female classmate, when they moved in together "they shut that door and didn't come out for a year. They fucked each other's brains out."[92]

At Yale, Bill and Hillary were totally different in their approach to their studies. Hillary was always well-prepared for class. Bill typically would put off studying until the night before an exam and would frequently grab his neighbor's notes on the way out the door. Hillary was the logical, concise human computer. She would often chastise Bill for babbling, rambling, and not getting to the bottom line. Often Hillary could be heard "telling him to get to the point, give it a break, or even, occasionally, just plain shut up."[93]

On October 11, 1975, Bill Clinton and Hillary Rodham got married. Hillary picked out a wedding dress off the rack of a store on the day before the wedding. She decided to keep her own name, which caused a furor among many of Bill's friends. In 1974, young Bill Clinton was a candidate for U.S. Congress from Arkansas. One of his earliest affairs was with co-worker **Marla Crider**. Hillary was insanely jealous of Marla. At one point, Hillary sent her father and her kid brother Hugh Jr. down to Arkansas to "keep an eye"

---

(91) Ibid., p. 10
(92) Ibid., p. 13
(93) Ibid., p. 14

on Marla Crider. Speaking of Hillary's brother, Crider said "Hillary had assigned him to me. He walks in and says 'You must be Marla.' Here we go. His assignment was to occupy all of my time that I would allow him to occupy. According to long-time Clinton co-worker Paul Fray, "Hughie Rodham went after that girl with both barrels. Hillary sent him to do the bidding for her, to get her ass gone."

Hillary Clinton was a "plain Jane", compared to most of the women who had been Bill's girlfriends. When Clinton family friend and campaign staffer Paul Fray, first set eyes on Hillary, he was shocked. Taking in Hillary's bad hair, ugly glasses, and unshaved legs and underarms, Fray thought "My God, Bill Clinton, you son of a bitch- you could have any woman on the face of the earth, and you brought one (Hillary) that looks like the south end of a mule going north."[94] "She had these whisky-jigger-bottom glasses, thick lenses, and she had on a prairie league dress."[95]

When Fray's wife Mary Lee tried to entice Hillary into their house, with offers of ice tea and lemonade, Hillary stayed put in the car outside. In a letter she wrote to her mother, Mary Lee Fray described Hillary Rodham. "Mother, she's very plain, to the point you could call her homely. She could mix well in certain parts of Arkansas, where they wear long clothes and no makeup."[96]

When Hillary went to visit Virginia Kelley, her future mother-in-law, she was poorly groomed. Bill Clinton's

---

(94) Ibid., p. 113
(95) Ibid., p. 114
(96) Ibid., p. 114

mother was taken aback by Hillary's dirty feet, unkempt hair, stinky clothes, and hairy armpits- this was the girl her son Bill called his main squeeze.[97]

Before her death, Virginia Kelley eventually reconciled with Hillary Clinton, but she never really bonded with Hillary in any meaningful way.

In 1974, Bill Clinton was unsuccessful in his virgin run for Congress from the 3rd district in Arkansas. At the Fayetteville headquarters, Hillary got into a heated argument with campaign manager Paul Fray. At one point, she called him "A fucking Jew bastard!"[98] This comment was witnessed and confirmed by Mary Lee Fray and campaign worker Neil McDonald. Two decades later, Arkansas state trooper Larry Patterson told Newsmax.com that Bill and Hillary Clinton regularly hurled anti-Semitic epithets such as "Jew bastard" and "Jew motherfucker" at each other.

Bill Clinton was fascinated at tales of Lyndon Johnson's sexual escapades on the floor of the White House. According to Clinton buddy Cliff Jackson, "Bill thought it was so neat that LBJ could get away with something like that."[99]

When Clinton ran for Congress in 1974, women were drawn to him. According to one office worker, "They'd write down their names, their phone numbers, their addresses on a napkin or on whatever was handy, and hand it to him."[100] This became the modus operandi for the next 20

---

(97) Ibid., p. 114
(98) Ibid., p. 153
(99) Ibid., p. 123
(100) Ibid., p. 124

years of Clinton's political career. Literally hundreds-perhaps thousands – of women were procured for Clinton by state troopers, bodyguards, and other people who were in complicity with the pervert-in-chief!

Bill's affair with Marla Crider ended in a most unfortunate way. Marla felt she was being followed as she left her office. She received an inordinate number of "hangup" phone calls. She always suspected that Hillary was behind this.

When Hillary arrived in Arkansas, she wasted no time in intimidating and alienating many of the students who were volunteering to work for Bill Clinton's 1974 Congressional campaign. According to Marla Crider, Hillary just didn't know how to deal with the Southern mentality. "she would get furious if there was any frivolity. It was like 'have you forgotten what our goal is?'[101] It was almost as if she was angry the whole time. Paul Fray noted that few of the kids from Arkansas cared for Hillary. "She would come in, want to run the show, and tell everybody exactly what they were supposed to be doing."[102] Clinton friend Ron Addington said "The girls just couldn't stand her giving orders all the time."[103] He recalled that on at least 15 occasions Bill and Hillary had drag-out shouting sessions, and Hillary had a sewer mouth like a drunken sailor.

And Hillary was never known for her sense of tact, either. When University of Arkansas law school assistant dean Steve

---

(101) Ibid., p. 141
(102) Ibid., p. 141
(103) Ibid., p. 141

Clark told Hillary Rodham back in 1974 that he might run for Arkansas attorney general, this is the campaign advice Hillary offered up to her friend: "Well then do me a favor. You need to lose a little weight. Because it is a little embarrassing to vote for my little fat friend Steve."[104]

Brian Snow was amazed at just how selfish Hillary could be. On one occasion, he and Hillary were walking down a New Orleans street when they encountered a street person who collapsed right in front of them. The pathetic guy lost consciousness and started frothing vomit from his mouth. Snow said that this guy needed mouth-to-mouth but who would do it? Hillary said to Snow "Not me- you're going to do it." Eventually, paramedics came and delivered aid to the man in distress. Snow turned to Hillary and told her "Hillary, this deprived us of the chance to save someone's life." Hillary responded "Oh no, it didn't…It deprived **you** of a chance to save someone's life."[105]

This was the essence of Hillary Clinton. Everything was about her.

Bill Clinton once confronted a political writer who couldn't stand Hillary. Bill explained his affinity for the future first lady and U.S. senator. "She's a remarkable person, she's so smart, she can figure things out, and she's the smartest person I've ever known." The writer noted how little love, passion, or emotional bond existed beyond this level, in the strange marriage of Bill and Hillary Clinton.

---

(104) Ibid., p. 165
(105) Ibid., p. 166

Great quotes from the mouth of Hillary Clinton[106]

"He's a great human being."- Hillary describing James Carville; from a column by Ann Coulter - Townhall.com- 9/26/02

"Goddamit Bill, you promised me that office!"- Hillary yelling at Bill on the morning of the inauguration- Jan. 20, 1993. Hillary wanted the office usually assigned to the Vice-President; "Bill & Hillary: The Marriage", p.258; by Christopher Anderson, William Morrow & Co., 1999.

"For God 's sake Bill, don't be an asshole. If you want to lose this election because you're too chickenshit, then go ahead!"- Hillary's advice to Bill as he was seeking political office in Arkansas, ibid., p. 145.

"Where is the goddamn fucking flag? I want the goddamn fucking flag up every fucking morning at fucking sunrise." - Hillary addressing the governor's staff at the Little Rock mansion; "Inside the White House", p. 244, by Ronald Kessler, Pocket Books, 1995.

"My personal, trained Pigs!"- Hillary and Bill's description of their Secret Service guards; "Unlimited Access", p. 90, by Gary Aldrich, Regnery Publishing, Inc., 1996.

"We have to destroy her." - Hillary referring to Gennifer Flowers, who revealed the details of her 11 year-old affair with Bill Clinton during the 1992 Presidential primaries-"The

---

(106) The Deck of Hillary, Newsmax.com.

Final Days", p. 13, by Barbara Olson, Regnery Publishing, 2001.

"You fucking Jew Bastard!"- Hillary yelling at campaign manger Paul Fray, after Bill lost his Congressional election in 1974, "The State of a Union", p. 153, by Jerry Oppenheimer, Harper Collins Publishing, 2000

Hillary's Book Deal

On December 15, 2001, one month before she was sworn in as U.S. Senator from New York, Hillary received an $8 million dollar advance from Simon & Schuster to write her official memoirs. Because Simon & Schuster's parent company Viacom had substantial influence in Washington politics, the advance was immediately causing controversy in the Senate. Typically, Senators may accept book advances that are "usual and customary". Is $8 million dollars "usual and customary?"

According to the Congressional Accountability Project, the advance was "gargantuan" and presented all sorts of possible conflict-of-interest problems. But leave it to the shifty Clinton White House to find a legal escape hatch for Hillary. Because the advance was signed before she was sworn into the Senate, she was not bound by the Senate rules. She wasn't covered by the ethics rules applicable to White House employees, either. Hillary wasn't a White House employee, she was simply a first lady. So the $8 million went into her hands, no questions asked.[107]

---

(107) Barbara Olson, "The Final Days," p. 42.

Press Secretary Jake Siewert stated "I think obviously, everyone wants their spouse to do as well as possible, and the President's no exception to that rule."[108]

When Newt Gingrich originally was to receive $4.5 million for his book deal, the Democrats screamed bloody murder and Gingrich's advance was reduced to $1. Yet no Democrats protested Hillary's $8 million. According to Clinton's spokesman Jake Siewert, "There was also some question about whether Gingrich's story was really worth $4.5 million, whereas no one doubts that Mrs. Clinton's story is worth any amount of money."[109] Jake, I do!

According to a top official in the Arkansas state government, Hillary was the actual governor for ten years: "She is one very professionally tough bitch", says the official.[110]

Years earlier, Hillary was at the forefront of the radical feminist movement. During her college days, she served as an intern for forever Communist lawyer Robert Truehaft. Truehaft and his wife Jessica Mitford were both Stalinists and staunchly pro-Soviet. Even the Black Panthers were intimidated by them.

It is very important to remember that Hillary had two Stalinists as mentors from early on in her career. **I maintain that both Bill and Hillary are basically anarchists at heart, who are both strongly influenced by Stalinism and the entire Communist ideology.** Just as no opposition was

---

(108) Barbara Olson, "The Final Days," p. 42.
(109) Ibid., p. 45.
(110) Ibid., p. 46.

tolerated by Stalin or the other Communists, anyone who says anything against the Clintons is part of "the vast right-wing conspiracy." Anyone who finds fault in the sordid methods used by the Clintons has an agenda. They, on the other hand, are always right and never wrong. Give me a break. It's about time the Clintons were exposed for who they really are- a bunch of cons who belong in federal prison!

Hillary panders to the naïve Jewish community in New York. I am a Jew who moved from Long Island to Los Angeles over 20 years ago. If there is anything I know about, it is Jews. Jews tend to be very naïve, very liberal, and often very self-hating. Hillary must have known how easy it would be to con the Jewish community in New York. Let's go back a few years, to the congressional race in Arkansas in 1974. Bill Clinton lost his first political race. Hillary went up to the campaign manager Paul Fray and called him a fucking Jew bastard." Furthermore, Arkansas State Trooper Larry Patterson insists that Bill and Hillary would often call each other "Jew bastard" and "Jew motherfucker" whenever they were mad at each other.[111]

More Words of Wisdom from Hillary Clinton!

"Fuck off! You don't tell me where to go." - Hillary to state troopers and bodyguards, after they tried to tell her she would be late for her next appointment - Christopher Anderson, op. cit., p. 205.

"Stay the fuck back, stay the fuck away from me! Don't come within ten yards of me, or else!"- First Lady Hillary

---

(111) Ibid., p. 37.

Clinton to her Secret Service detail; Gary Aldrich, op. cit., p. 139.

"Come on Bill, put your dick up. You can't fuck her here." - Hillary to Bill, after catching him trying to make contact with a woman at a political event; Kessler, op. cit., p. 243.

"I was lucky"- Hillary describing how she turned a $1000 investment in cattle futures into $100,000, in approximately one year; "The First Partner: Hillary Rodham Clinton", p.108, by Joyce Milton, William Morrow & Co., 1999.

Hillary Booed at 9-11 Benefit Concert

On October 20, 2001, Hillary Clinton appeared at a benefit concert at Madison Square Garden for the victims of 9-11. In the audience were hundreds of New York City firefighters and police officers, along with family members of those who perished in the World Trade Center collapse.

This concert had been organized by Paul McCartney and was aired on VH-1. As soon as Hillary walked onstage, she was loudly booed! The audience shouted "Get off the stage! We don't want you here!" Twenty seconds later, Hillary abruptly left the stage.

When VH-1 re-ran the concert on December 25, 2001, the boos and negative audience comments were digitally erased and "replaced with cheers and applause." In fact, this new revisionist version of the concert is what can be heard on the DVD version of the concert.

Tammy Bruce, in "Death of Right and Wrong" points out the irony that Viacom- the same company that owns VH-1 also owns Simon & Schuster, the publishing house that gave Hillary Clinton her $8 million book deal![(112)]

MORE Hillary Quotes!

"Gentlemen, I have looked at your proposal, and it's pure bullshit. Now you've had your meeting! Get out!"- Hillary talking to health insurance executives- "Unlimited Access", p.88, Gary Aldrich, Regnery Publishing, Inc. 1996.

"Where the fuck have you been?"- Hillary yelling at Governor Bill Clinton, after he returned home to the mansion in the middle of the night, after a romp with one of his girlfriends in Little Rock. - "Bill & Hillary: The Marriage" p.202, by Christopher Anderson, William Morrow & Co., 1999.

"That'll teach them to fuck with us!"- Hillary talking to her staff after making her "vast right-wing conspiracy" charge on the Today show- "The Case Against Hillary Clinton, p. 162, by Peggy Noonan, Regan Books, 2000.

"I just don't have any memory of that"- Hillary testifying under oath with respect to a memo stating that she wanted the White House Travel Office employees fired and replaced with her own people. "You Don't Say: Sometimes Liberals Show their True Colors," p. 141, by Fred Gielow, Freedom Books, 1999.

---

(112) Tammy Bruce, "The Death of Right and Wrong", pp. 247-248.

"Who is going to find out? These women are all trash. Nobody's going to believe them." Hillary commenting on all the women who claimed to have had affairs with Bill Clinton. Anderson, op. cit., p. 220.

"Goddamn it Bill, how long do you expect me to put up with this shit?" - Hillary to Bill, after one of their many arguments over Bill's infidelities. Anderson, op. cit., p. 202.

"I mean you've got a conservative and right-winged press presence with really nothing on the other end of the political spectrum."- Hillary kvetching about the right-wing press, despite the fact that 89% of White House press corps went for Bill Clinton in 1992- C-Span.

"The media misunderstand me. I am actually very traditional in most of my beliefs, especially social issues."- Hillary speaking to Clinton staffer David Gergen.- "Eyewitness To Power", p. 267-268, David Gergen, Simon & Schuster, 2000.

"I'm sorry. I don't recall."- One of 50 times Hillary said this before a Congressional committee investigating Whitewater and the Rose Law firm billing records- "A Few of Hillary Clinton's Hits, The Progressive Review, 2/24/99.

"Bill and I worked hard at our marriage with a great deal of mutual respect and deepening love for each other."- "It Takes a Village", p.43, by Hillary Rodham Clinton, Simon & Schuster, 1996.

Hillary's Book Advance vs. Newt Gingrich's Book Advance

Back in 1998, when former Speaker of the House Newt Gingrich (Republican) received a book deal of $4.5 million, journalists such as Dan Rather were highly critical of the deal. On his CBS news, Rather said "More tonight about whether Australian-born- and-centered communications billionaire Rupert Murdock is trying to buy influence with politically connected authors." At the time, Murdoch's company Harper Collins was dealing with regulatory issues in the U.S. Other journalists joined Rather in criticizing Gingrich's book deal. Other CBS reporters such as Eric Engberg and Rita Braver questioned Gingrich's ethics in receiving the book advance, which subsequently turned out to be roughly half of the amount of Hillary Rodham Clinton's whopping $8 million from Simon & Schuster!

Yet when Hillary Clinton received her $8 million advance from Simon & Schuster in late 2000, barely a word of protest was heard from the media. The major networks didn't question the deal. Yet Newt Gingrich had to give up his $4.5 million book advance! On CBS's Face the Nation, host Rita Braver said this about Gingrich: "You don't think he'll be called 'The Four-and-a-half Million-Dollar Man' any more?"[113]

Now, granted I am an intelligent guy, with degrees from good schools like Brandeis and Cornell Universities. But I can't compete with outfits like CBS. CBS' parent company, Viacom, includes VH1, MTV, Nickelodeon, Paramount

---

(113) Tammy Bruce, "The New Thought Police", pp. 190-191.

Pictures, Paramount TV, Infinity Broadcasting, Showtime, BET, and Simon & Schuster, Hillary's publishing house.

Interestingly, the Senate has not adopted the same strict ethics rules that the House has with respect to conflict-of-interest over its members' book deals. Newt Gingrich had to give up his book advance. Hillary Clinton won't even allow her fellow senators to review her book deal![114]

Hillary's Temper

Ron Addington worked on Bill Clinton's campaign for Attorney General. After he tried to get reimbursed for a roll of stamps used in a campaign mailing, Hillary read him the riot act. "Who authorized you to buy stamps? You don't have the authority to spend campaign money!"[115]

Addington said this about Hillary: "It's the way she treats people. I have friends who are state troopers and they've told me some godawful stories, when she was first lady in the governor's mansion. The way she treated the troopers, the staff- she was awful. Usually being appointed to the governor's staff is a plum job. They considered it punishment. They had to put up with her. They had to put up with him, too, having to hide his activities, being out all

---

(114) Tammy Bruce, "The New Thought Police," pp. 190-191. Rita Braver addressed her question to Bob Dole. Ironically, it was Braver's husband who put together Hillary's blockbuster $8 million book deal some 6 years later.
(115) Oppenheimer, op. cit., p. 173.

night long, no routine or family life. But the real reason they did not want to be there was because of Hillary."[116]

Little-known Facts About Hillary, Bill, and the family

Hillary's brother Tony used to be a repo man in Chicago.[117]

In September 1999, Hillary's brothers Hugh and Tiny were involved in a nutty (no pun intended) scheme to import hazelnuts from Russia.[118] This deal had been arranged through people connected to the Russian mafia.[119]

Bill Clinton would stop for "quickies" with women during his morning jogs.[120]

According to Gennifer Flowers, Bill Clinton told her Hillary had "eaten more pussy" than he had![121]

While the first cat, Socks, was at the vet, the doctor opened a door to find Hillary Clinton and another woman "locked in a passionate embrace."[122]

Hillary's Tortured Past

Hillary Clinton was a Goldwater girl back in high school. For those of you too young to remember Barry Goldwater, he

---

(116) Ibid., p. 174.
(117) Ibid., p. 209.
(118) Ibid., p. 209.
(119) Ibid.,, p. 209.
(120) Ibid., p. 209
(121) Flowers, op. cit., p. 41
(122) Oppenheimer, op. cit., p. 218.

was the ultra-right wing Senator from Arkansas who ran for President in 1964. Hillary, at the age of 17, **was a Goldwater girl!** Now it becomes clear where all her hatred for "the vast right wing conspiracy" comes from. It comes from her own tortured past!

Hillary attended college at Wellesley College, located just down the road from my alma mater, Brandeis University, in Waltham, Massachusetts. During Hillary's days at Wellesley, one of her biggest goals was to someday own a **yellow Jaguar XKE!**[123]

Over the years, Hillary built her own career plans, parallel to those of Bill. She worked for the House Judiciary Committee investigating Richard Nixon, back in 1973-1974. How ironic that her own husband would be investigated and actually impeached by the same committee some 28 years later! Hillary joined the Rose Law firm, where she befriended and worked with people such as Webster Hubbell and Vince Foster. Yet throughout it all, she and Bill Clinton were the ultimate law partners! Bigger than the State House in Arkansas and bigger than the Rose Law firm were the Bill and Hillary partnership!

Hillary was really Bill's alter ego and Bill's # 1 adviser over the years. Bill, in turn, was a philanderer who cheated on his wife Hillary thousands of times over his years as Arkansas Attorney General, Arkansas Governor, and President of the United States. In Hillary's mind, they were co-Presidents. In Hillary's twisted mind, when the people "elected" Bill Clinton to the Presidency in 1992, they also

---

(123) Barbara Olson, "The Final Days," p. 61

"elected" Hillary. It is very important to remember these basics as you analyze the plethora of lies, scandals, and dead bodies that lay in the wake of Bill and Hillary Clinton.

Both Bill and Hillary Clinton had their idols in mind, when they arrived in the White House. Bill Clinton tried to look and walk like his idol John Fitzgerald Kennedy. When he would walk with his head down and hands in his coat pockets, he reminded former Presidential speech-writer Peggy Noonan of JFK in the Jamie Wyeth portrait.[124] And Hillary thinks she is Eleanor Roosevelt. In the White House, Hillary Clinton had a shrine to Eleanor Roosevelt. She often summoned the spirit of Eleanor, with the help of a psychic.[125] But Eleanor Roosevelt stood for something- helping the poor, curing the sick, and aiding the downtrodden. **Hillary cared about one thing- Hillary.**

Barbara Olson, who perished in the plane that crashed into the Pentagon on September 11, 2001, was an attorney for the Department of Justice, a general counsel in the Senate, and a Congressional investigator. Her first book "Hell to Pay" offers some amazing insight into the criminal mentality of Hillary Clinton.

"I have never experienced a cooler or more hardened operator than Hillary Rodham Clinton. The investigators working for Independent Counsel Kenneth Starr found, as we did, that in **one scandal after another, all roads led to Hillary.** To investigate White House improprieties and

---

(124) Peggy Noonan, "The Case Against Hillary Clinton," pp. 8-9.
(125) Ibid., p. 9

scandals, the evidence necessarily led to her hidden hands guiding the Clinton operation."[126]

It was Hillary who initiated the use of private investigators and smear artists. It was Hillary who assembled the "secret police" who, according to adviser Dick Morris, was employed in a "systematic campaign to intimidate, frighten, threaten, discredit, and punish innocent Americans whose only misdeed is their desire to tell the truth."[127]

- Hillary was directly involved in the firing and smearing of the White House travel office

- Hillary, long rumored to have had an affair with Vince Foster, has been linked to the illegal ransacking of Foster's office immediately after his death.

- Hillary one day "discovered" the missing Rose Law firm billing records after she "discovered" them next to her bed in the White House.

- Hillary was obviously involved in all sorts of criminal activity with respect to the White House pardons. She perjured herself many times, and she "had no knowledge", "couldn't recall", and "couldn't remember" much of anything with respect to the flood of pardons that Bill Clinton handed out on January 20, 2001.

During her years at Yale, Hillary was actively involved in defending the "plight" of the Black Panthers, a racist

---

(126) Barbara Olson, "Hell to Pay," p. 3
(127) Ibid., p. 5

organization which justified the rape of white women by black men. The Panthers considered police to be "pigs." Hillary was close to, both professionally and personally, avowed Communists Robert Truehaft and his wife Jessica Mitford.[128]

In Clinton's presidency, Hillary played a major role in staffing decisions. According to Howard Kurtz, the author of "Spin Cycle", Hillary was behind the hiring of former White House Press Secretary Mike McCurry. Hillary once told Dick Morris: "Every once in a while I'm able to bring someone good in here, like McCurry."[129]

Bill Clinton's womanizing was a always a major political problem for him. The reason people like James Carville, Rahm Emmanuel, Lannie Davis, John Podesta, Paul Begala, Betsy Wright, George Stephanopoulos, and so many others got jobs was to do one thing: **to lie and cover up for Bill Clinton!**

Bill Clinton would routinely use the Arkansas State Troopers as his personal dating service. Even after he was elected President, Bill Clinton used the Arkansas governor's mansion to procure sex. On at least four occasions, State police guarded the door of the basement as Bill Clinton rendezvoused with a female Arkansas Power & Light executive. Meanwhile, Hillary and Chelsea were upstairs.[130]

---

(128) Ibid., p. 57
(129) Howard Kurtz, "Spin Cycle," p. 22
(130) Olson, "Hell to Pay," p. 212

Hillary's management of the campaign was really the main reason Bill Clinton became the 42nd President of the United States. She guarded Bill Clinton all the way. It was Hillary who rescued Bill after he lost the governorship years earlier in Little Rock. It was Hillary who taught Bill Clinton how to fight back against his enemies in Arkansas. After Clinton spoke for way too long at the 1988 Democratic Convention, it was Hillary who sat down and advised him how to give a speech.

In Hillary's mind, the presidency was half hers. She considered herself to be the co-President. According to Barbara Olson, "Hillary had almost single-handedly brought Bill Clinton from the brink of obscurity to the White House, and now it was time to collect."[131]

Bill and Hillary's arguments were overheard by both the Arkansas State Troopers and, later on, the Secret Service. On their way to a fundraiser, Hillary had a big fight with Bill. She capped it off by exclaiming, **"Goddammit you bastard, it's your fucking fault."**[132] And then there was the time Marine One (the Presidential helicopter) had to return to the ground because **Hillary had left her sunglasses in her limo!**[133]

For years, rumors have existed that Hillary Clinton is a lesbian, or at least a bi-sexual. Her husband Bill has often

---

(131) Ibid., p. 216.
(132) "Dereliction of Duty," Patterson, p. 68
(133) Ibid., p. 71

referred to the fact that **she has eaten more pussy than I have!.**"[134]

It has been reported that wealthy gay supporters of the Clintons have often used Camp David for lesbian rendezvous. On at least one occasion, Hillary was observed "frolicking in the pool" with another woman at Camp David, during a midnight swim. On another occasion, a limo full of lesbian activists showed up at Camp David. They were upset that they had to wait at the gate, while the guards approved their security clearances. One of them whined, **"Don't you know that we are friends of Mrs. Clinton?"**[135] An hour or so later, Hillary was whisked into Camp David and driven straight to Red Oak, a VIP area where many of the lesbians were staying. Hillary left around 11 a.m. the next day, while the remaining women sunbathed and snuggled in a way that Secret Service agents deemed "extremely inappropriate."[136]

The story of how Hillary turned a $1,000 investment into $100,000 reflects the dishonesty so characteristic of everything involved with Hillary Clinton. Her broker on the cattle futures deal, Robert L. "Red" Bone of Refco was a corrupt guy who was guilty of "straddling", and he had his license to trade pulled for one year.[137] Several commodities

---

(134) This exact quote was given to me from former Clinton political hit man Larry Nichols, who has worked with Bill and Hillary Clinton for years. It has also appeared in numerous tabloid and internet sources.

(135) "Star," October 17, 2000, p. 18.

(136) Ibid., p. 18. The sources for this story were Secret Service agents, cooks, and groundskeepers at Camp David.

(137) Olson, "Hell to Pay," pp. 140-141.

traders suspected that Hillary was guilty of allocated trading, which is a totally illegal form of financial trading. Shortly after Hillary reaped her bonanza, Hillary's broker "Red" Bone was disciplined by the Chicago Mercantile Board for "serious and repeated violations of record-keeping functions, order-entry procedures, margin requirements, and hedge procedures."[138]

The Clinton White House was saturated with an atmosphere of paranoia.[139] Hillary and Bill Clinton were so upset with the Secret Service leaks to the media that at one point **they considered replacing the Secret Service with private security guards![140]**

At one point, even the cooks and the gardeners at the White House had to answer detailed questionnaires, questioning their political affiliations. Bill Clinton had Marsha Scott, his former girlfriend from the hippie days, and present White House director of correspondence fire the women in the White House correspondence office. These were women who had been working there for decades. Many were approaching retirement age. Of course this meant absolutely nothing to the Clintons. Mail piled up all over the place; reports surfaced that boxes of mail were simply thrown out.[141] But, like the fired travel office staff (see **Travel Office- Billy Dale)**, the Clintons had to get their people in.

Several White House chefs were fired, as was long-time Presidential barber Milton Pitts, who had trimmed the locks

---

(138) Ibid., p. 142.
(139) Ibid., p. 238
(140) Ibid., p. 238.
(141) Ibid., p. 239

of Presidents dating back to the Kennedy White House. Hillary Clinton had White House usher Chris Emery fired for having placed a personal phone call to former First Lady Barbara Bush. Emery, who lost his job over one harmless phone call, had a wife and an eight year old daughter. I guess kids don't matter to Hillary Clinton, if their dad knows the Bush family![142]

Why are the Clintons so obsessed with privacy and control? According to Barbara Olson, the Clintons had a long history of using private investigators and political dirty tricksters to gain information on others. Bill and Hillary Clinton will do whatever it takes- including murdering someone- to get their way! Nothing stops the Clintons!

That is why I am writing this book, so that the Attorney General, the President, and the FBI will work on prosecuting and locking up the Clintons!

The Clintons' firing of the White House travel office resembled a Stalinist *putsch*, or perhaps a page out of the Bolshevik Revolution. The Clintons had to get rid of the old staff and bring in their own people. Billy Dale, who had served the White House travel office for over thirty years, along with his staff, were given an hour to clean out their offices, after which they were driven out of the travel office in a "windowless van under the watchful eyes of uniformed Secret Service."[143]

Hillary was known for her temper tantrums. She would often explode like a volcano at the slightest thing. It is

---

(142) Olson, "Hell to Pay," pp. 240-241
(143) Ibid., p. 243.

reported that Hillary once threw a Holy Bible at a Secret Service agent for driving the limo too slowly. Many reports surfaced in Washington about the Clintons scolding the Secret Service, with fits of profanity and general verbal abuse.

It would be common for the Clintons to show up quite late for events. They came two and one-half hours late to a reception for the U.S. Holocaust Museum. As if it wasn't bad enough that Lech Walesa and the Speaker of the House were stood up, **elderly Holocaust survivors had to wait in the rain for hours until Bill Clinton finally showed up!** Barbara Olson recounted how the King and Queen of Norway were waiting for the Clintons at a "landing of the White House on a frigid night, a scene that played over and over again on Norwegian TV." Olson pointed out, "In a sense the Clintons allocated their time shrewdly. How many electoral votes does Norway have?"[144]

---

(144) Ibid., p. 235.

CHAPTER THREE

Reason Number Eight the Clintons Belong in Prison

Bill and Hillary's Abuse of the IRS to Intimidate Women and Political Enemies. See the section on the Clintons and the IRS- I feel the Clintons committed perjury, witness tampering, obstruction of justice, and abuse of power. It is unbelievable that there wasn't criminal prosecution brought against the Clintons for their role in sicking the IRS against Bill's girlfriends, his rape victim Juanita Broaddrick, Billy Dale from the Travel Office, and the dozens of conservative political organizations that were *audited by the Clinton IRS*. I feel that both Bill and Hillary Clinton deserve at least 5 years in jail each for their roles in abusing their authority with respect to the IRS. If this is not abuse of power, then *nothing* is.

Here are More Lies From Bill and Hillary Clinton

(20) Bill Clinton lied when he said he had sex with Gennifer Flowers only once- in 1977.

(21) Bill Clinton lied when he told PBS's Jim Lehrer "I did not ask anyone to tell anything other than the truth. There *is* no improper relationship.

(22) Bill Clinton lied when he said he forgot about his draft notice, back in the 60's.

(23) Bill Clinton lied when he told Mort Kondracke of *Roll Call* that his relationship with Monica Lewinsky was "not sexual."

(24) Bill Clinton lied when he said he didn't have any recollection of even seeing Paula Jones.

(25) Hillary Clinton lied when she said: "There is a vast right wing conspiracy against my husband."

(26) Bill Clinton lied when he said he never coached Betty Currie to say that she had never seen him alone with Monica Lewinsky. I guess it depends what the meaning of "alone" is. If Betty Currie was in the same room as Monica and Bill for even one second, one could literally argue that Clinton and Lewinsky were not alone. Besides, how would Betty Currie know Clinton and Monica were alone, without her having been there? (Think about how ridiculous Clinton's lying became.)

(27) Hillary Clinton lied when she said she played no role in the firing of the White House Travel Office, According to David Watkins, and Chief of Staff Mack McLarty, Hillary *was* behind the decision. ("We need the slots.")

(28) Bill Clinton lied when he said, about the fired Travel Office, "I had nothing to do with any decision, except to save the taxpayers and the press money. That's all I know."

(29) Hillary Clinton lied when she said the spent an entire week at Ground Zero (World Trade Center)

(30) Hillary Clinton lied when she said she didn't know who Craig Livingstone was.

(31) Bill Clinton lied when he developed a false affidavit cover story with Monica Lewinsky.

(32) Bill Clinton lied when, in speaking to Lewinsky about how she got her job, "Well, you could always say that the people in Legislative Affairs got it for you or helped you get it."

(33) Bill Clinton lied to the grand jury when he said he couldn't remember calling Monica on December 17, 1998 at 2 a.m. to discuss her being a witness in the Paula Jones case.

(34) Bill Clinton led when he said he didn't remember what he said and "to whom he said it" with respect to comments he made to the Secret Service about their keeping quiet about the affair.

(35) Bill Clinton lied when he claimed not to remember his conversation with Secret Service Captain Purdie.

(36) Bill Clinton lied when he claimed not to recall Vernon Jordan's telling him about a meeting between Jordan and Monica Lewinsky.

(37) Bill Clinton lied when he testified that Monica Lewinsky brought him gifts "once or twice."

(39) Hillary Clinton lied when she dismissed her thank-you letter to the American Muslim Council as being "a typical thank- you letter."

(40) Hillary Clinton lied when she said she didn't sign the letter thanking the American Muslim Council for its $50,000 donation to her Senatorial campaign.

Monicagate and the Impeachment Farce

The Farce of the Clinton Impeachment

In his best-selling book "Sellout", David Schippers, Chief Investigative Counsel for the House Judiciary Committee, outlines what a sham the whole Clinton impeachment was.

It is Schippers' contention that the House Judiciary Committee had only a weak desire to see Bill Clinton removed from office or even impeached! Trent Lott, the Senate majority leader at the time exclaimed to Henry Hyde, Chairman of the House Judiciary Committee, "Henry, you're not going to dump this garbage on us."[1] At a Joint House

---

(1) David Schippers, "Sellout", p. 9.

and Senate conference, Senator Joseph Biden said to Henry Hyde "we make our own rules."[2]   When Henry Hyde indicated to a group of Senators that his committee had clear and convincing evidence of Bill Clinton's having raped Juanita Broaddrick, Senator Ted Stevens (R-Alaska) said: "Henry, I don't care if you prove he (Clinton) raped a woman and then stood up and shot her dead- you are not going to get sixty-seven votes!"[3]

Schippers recounts the fraud he uncovered in the "Citizenship USA" (CUSA) program, under which the Clinton administration bent the rules on naturalization for more than 1 million aliens, so that the Democratic vote count in states like California, Illinois, New York and New Jersey could be inflated.

- According to an audit prepared by KPMG Peat Marwick in 1996, more than 75,000 new citizens had arrest records when they applied for citizenship!
- 155,000 citizens had fingerprints that were unclassifiable and never resubmitted
- 61,000 people were given citizenship with no fingerprints submitted at all![4]

If Schippers had been given enough time, he might very well have recommended the CUSA fiasco as an impeachable act based on an abuse of power. But remember the polls! Bill Clinton was hovering around a 68% approval rating. The economy and the stock market were booming. So what

---

(2) Ibid., p. 17.
(3) Ibid., p. 23.
(4) Ibid., p. 45.

if the President had broken the law? No one is perfect! And besides, people had more cash in their pockets than ever. Throughout the country, there were all sorts of rationalizations and preposterous defenses for Bill Clinton's totally unacceptable and disgraceful behavior. "Hey every President does it...Bill Clinton just got caught!", "I like Bill Clinton. He's just a normal guy!", or my favorite "Everyone is entitled to a little head!"

But Bill Clinton did a lot more than get "head". He engaged in a massive pattern of lying, cover-up, intimidation, witness tampering, and obstruction of justice, which should have sent him to Federal prison for hundreds of years!

The impeachment of Bill Clinton was destined to fail from the outset. The scope of the inquiry was sharply limited by the leadership of the House Judiciary Committee. Senators Trent Lott, Ted Stevens, and Arlen Specter- all Republicans- were less concerned with convicting Bill Clinton for his many acts of treachery than they were with the expediency of the polls. David Schippers, the chief Investigative Counsel of the House Judiciary Committee and his staff wanted to impeach Bill Clinton over Chinagate. They wanted to investigate and possibly bring impeachment charges in connection with Bill Clinton's rape of Juanita Broaddrick. Schippers and his staff of lawyers wanted to bring up the molestation of Kathleen Willey by President Bill Clinton. In all these cases, Schippers felt that Bill Clinton was guilty of obstruction of justice, witness tampering, and perjury.

Bill Clinton had been hitting on Kathleen Willey on several occasions, before the famous groping incident in November, 1993. On one night in early December 1992

Clinton called her at home asking Willey if she could come up to the White House and spend some time with him. On an earlier occasion, he had called Willey and told her he could make sure the Secret Service would not be around. This was the Williamsburgh, VA meeting I alluded to earlier.

After the groping incident, the Clinton lawyers went into action. They wanted Kathleen Willey to sign a statement indicating that Bill Clinton never sexually harassed her. Willey ignored the lawyers. In August, 1997, a major financial backer of Clinton called Willey. He encouraged Willey to avoid giving a deposition if she was subpoenaed in the Paula Jones case. The donor, who my research reveals to have been **Nathan Landow,** reminded Willey that it was just Bill Clinton and her in the room that day at the White House. He told her: "All you have to do is deny it, too." Or she could say "I can't remember; it's none of your business." Clinton's lawyers offered to get Willey the finest legal counsel, and it wouldn't cost her a cent.[5]

Now the Clinton goon squad really stated making things ugly for Kathleen Willey. Willey was about to give her deposition on January 10, 1998 in the Paula Jones case.

Just days before she was to give her deposition, Willey woke up one morning to find all four tires of her car were flattened. Her mechanic said to her: "Who the hell did you tick off? Your tires were flattened with a nail gun."[6]

Things got worse. Kathleen Willey started getting threatening, anonymous phone calls. One day her cat

---

(5) Ibid., pp. 114-115.
(6) Ibid., p. 116.

disappeared and it may have been killed as an act of intimidation against Willey.

On the morning of January 8, 1998- two days before Kathleen was to give her sworn testimony, she met a very strange man who jogged by her, as she was walking her dog. This stranger knew entirely too much about the personal life of Kathleen Willey. The following is a transcript of the exchange that took place between the jogger and Kathleen Willey on that morning:

Jogger: Good morning. Did you find your cat?
Willey: No, we haven't found her yet.
Jogger: That's too bad. Bullseye was his name, wasn't it?
   (This shocked Willey, because she hadn't revealed the name of her cat to anyone).
Jogger: Did you ever get those tires fixed?
Willey: They're fine (She starts to edge away and look around for help).
Jogger: So,____ and ____ (Willey's children's first names)?
   (Kathleen walks faster toward her house).
Jogger: And our attorney, Dan, is he okay?
Willey: He's fine
Jogger: I hope you're getting the message.

At this point, Kathleen Willey was terrified, and justifiably. This stranger knew the name of her children, her lawyer, knew all about her flat tires, even her missing cat. As Kathleen turned and ran, the jogger yelled at her: **"You're just not getting the message, are you?"**[7]

---

(7) Ibid., pp. 116-117. Nathan Landow, whose name keeps popping up in connection with trying to keep Kathleen Willey

Folks, you must understand that this was the *modus operandi* of the Clinton goon squad over the years, dating back to Arkansas. **Paula Jones** had been threatened with bodily harm from anonymous callers. Sally Perdue was threatened that her "pretty little legs might be broken" if she spilled the beans about her affair with Bill Clinton.[8] Karen Parks, Monica Lewinsky, the late Ron Brown, Gennifer Flowers and Linda Tripp have one thing in common- they have all expressed the opinion that the Clinton hit team will do anything to intimidate anyone who dares to cross or expose Bill Clinton.

Kathleen Willey was supposed to be a witness in Bill Clinton's impeachment trial, but things never got that far. Likewise, the numerous scandals of Chinagate, where there was a clear trail of Clinton and the Democrats receiving incredible amounts of cash contributions in exchange for the

---

from talking, hired private investigators to research the background of Kathleen Willey. When Landow was called before a federal grand jury, he pled the 5th amendment, and his lawyers would not turn over documents relating to his snooping into Kathleen Willey's personal life. Even more shocking, a private eye named Robert Miller, who had done work for Landow's attorney Saul Schwartzbach, is alleged to have told Rockville, Md. Private eye Jared Stern about undertaking a comprehensive examination into the private life of Kathleen Willey. The investigation would include what medications she was taking, an examination of her trash, and a check of her phone records. Stern turned down Miller's request. When he asked where it was coming from, Miller allegedly replied "from the White House."- Michael Isikoff, "Uncovering Clinton", footnote 5, pp. 380-381.
(8) Coulter, "High Crimes and Misdemeanors," p. 81

Clinton White House selling nuclear secrets to the Red Chinese, never made it into the impeachment hearings. **Dolly Kyle Browning was all** ready to testify against Bill Clinton in the impeachment trial, but that too was eliminated because of time pressures. The Republicans in the Senate wanted to get the trial over as soon as possible. In fact, many of them were as duplicitous as the Democrats!

To be sure, Dolly Kyle Browning's testimony alone could have subjected Bill Clinton to charges of perjury, witness tampering, and obstruction of justice. Remember, she was once told by Clinton's people: "If you cooperate with the media, we will destroy you."[9] Schippers said this about the incriminating nature of Dolly Kyle Browning's testimony:

"Browning's interview was possible further evidence of the President's willfully providing perjurious, false, and misleading testimony to a grand jury. As with his deposition testimony, he flatly denied...an improper relationship with Browning."[10]

Additionally, David Schippers felt that there was credible evidence that Bill Clinton was guilty of witness tampering and perjury with respect to the actions of staffer Marsha Scott. "We had thus uncovered evidence of blatant perjury on the President's part and witness tampering with Marsha Scott- all in the President's own handwriting. Had there been a real trial in the Senate, the American people would have heard all of this."[11]

---

(9) Schippers, "Sellout", p. 120.
(10) Ibid., p. 124.
(11) Ibid., p. 125.

So there you have it. The Clinton spin team won out again. It's amazing what a bunch of crooked lawyers can do when they put their heads together.

Bill and Hillary wanted the American people to believe that Monica Lewinsky was an aberration- a mistake, a one-time mistake and lie that must be forgiven. In reality, it was just part of a pattern of abuse, molestation, pandering, that should have resulted in the prosecution and incarceration of Bill Clinton. It is beyond me that this guy Clinton has not yet been indicted!

I have concluded that there is a consistent pattern of lying, deceit, manipulation, and perjury that has permeated the entire political careers of Bill and Hillary Clinton. They lie about everything, and their attitude is like that of actor Leonard diCaprio in a recent movie role, "Catch Me if you Can." It is my opinion and the opinion of David Schippers, Chief Investigative Counsel for the House judiciary Committee that Bill Clinton should have faced impeachment charges over Chinagate, his lies and tampering with Kathleen Willey, his lies and tampering with Juanita Broaddrick, and his lies, intimidations and tampering with Dolly Kyle Browning.

I'll go one step further. I think one day soon Bill and Hillary will be locked up for a long, long time.

And one more thing, Hillary. David Schippers is a Democrat, from your home town- Chicago.

Three and one-half weeks after the House Judiciary Committee sent Bill Clinton a detailed questionnaire, he answered the committee. His answers given on November 27,

1998 were vintage Bill Clinton- indirect, convoluted, and parsed to fit the meaning he found beneficial to him- basically anything but the truth!   Clinton wouldn't even admit he was the chief law enforcement officer of the country, according to David Schippers.[12]

Here's what Bill Clinton told the committee, when they asked him if he was the chief law enforcement officer: "The President is frequently referred to as the chief law enforcement officer, although nothing in the Constitution specifically designates the President as such."

And Clinton couldn't remember anything. He couldn't remember whether he discussed Monica Lewinsky's affidavit in the Paula Jones case with Vernon Jordan. He couldn't remember what the gifts were that he gave to Monica Lewinsky.   He couldn't remember the statements he allegedly made to White House appointments secretary Betty Currie (i.e., "Monica came on to me, and I never touched her, right?" and "You were always there, right? We were never really alone.") Bill Clinton couldn't remember how many times he talked to Betty Currie.   Bill Clinton couldn't remember when he talked to Betty Currie.   In short, whenever something came up that incriminated Clinton, that showed him to be guilty, he forgot. By forgetting, he made it virtually impossible to *prove he was guilty of perjury. This technique is known to all lawyers- they teach it in law school.*

In response to seven detailed questions from the Committee about Clinton's denying having a sexual relationship with Monica Lewinsky in conversations with

---

(12) David Schippers, "Sellout", p. 194.

Sidney Blumenthal, Erskine Bowles, John Podesta, Harold Ickes, and others, Clinton issued the same response:

"As I have previously acknowledged, I did not want my family, friends, or colleagues to know the full nature of my relationship with Ms. Lewinsky. In the days following the January 21, 1998 "Washington Post" article, I misled people about this relationship. I have repeatedly apologized for doing so."[13]

Clinton simply didn't answer the committee's questions. He just gave the answers *he wanted to give.*

The chairman of the House Judiciary Committee Henry Hyde was in a rush to conclude the impeachment process. For example, Chief Investigative Counsel David Schippers wanted to call Dolly Kyle Browning to testify against Bill Clinton, but there was no time! Hyde wanted the Judiciary Committee to conclude its work and take a vote on articles of impeachment by Friday December 11. He wanted to finish up in the 105th Congress; funding might not be re-authorized in the 106th Congress. Besides, witnesses would require rebuttal and all this would take time, Dolly Kyle Browning flew to D.C. on her own dime, but Hyde's House Judiciary Committee wouldn't let her testify![14]

On Thursday December 10, 1998, David Schippers appeared before the House Judiciary Committee to air his report on Bill Clinton. The Chief Investigative Counsel for the Impeachment Committee- this Democrat from Chicago-

---

(13) Ibid., p. 199.
(14) Ibid., p. 200.

stressed that, contrary to public opinion, this impeachment was not "just about sex." He stressed: "It is about multiple obstructions of justice, perjury, false and misleading statements, witness tampering, and abuses of power, all committed or orchestrated by the President of the United States."[15]

In his statement to the House Judiciary Committee, David Schippers made a brilliant point. When, on November 15, 1995, Monica Lewinsky flashed her thong underwear at Bill Clinton, why didn't he simply report her behavior to her superior and let her know that such behavior would not be tolerated in the White House? Perhaps because that is the *response of a normal person to this situation.* Instead, Bill Clinton, the perv that he is, took full advantage of the situation. So what if she was an intern in his office? So what if he was the President of the United States, the most powerful man on earth! So what if she was young enough to be his daughter!

This was free hot piece of ass! (Author's comment).

Clinton and Lewinsky started an affair, largely consisting of oral sex, **in the Oval Office.** From the outset, the relationship was predicated on lies. The alleged purpose of Lewinsky's visits to the White House was to "visit Betty Currie." This lie is at the crux of later perjuries and obstruction of justice charges.[16]

Bill Clinton didn't want problems with the Secret Service. Clinton told the Secret Service Watch Commander

---

(15) Ibid., p. 203.
(16) Ibid., p. 204.

Jeffrey Purdie: **"I hope I can count on your discretion."**[17] Purdie, in turn, instructed several of his officers not to talk about the Lewinsky affair to anyone.

When Clinton testified about his comments to the Secret Service, he said: **"I don't remember what I said and I don't remember to whom I said it."**[18] As far as Captain Purdie's testimony, Clinton swore: **"I don't remember anything I said to him in that regard. I have no recollection of that whatsoever."**[19] Clinton's testimony was filled with half-truths and legalese. Did Clinton remember calling Monica at 2 a.m.? **"No sir, I don't. *But it is quite possible that that happened.*"**[20]

Janet Reno's Evasion

There was a lot of shady stuff going on with the DNC and Red China throughout the Clinton administration. The FBI under Louis Freeh and prosecutor Charles LaBella felt there was enough evidence of impropriety in this area to create an independent counsel. Attorney General Janet Reno was against that. Reno didn't want to release reports written by Freeh and LaBella to a Congressional committee. Facing a contempt of Congress citation, she eventually released the reports with dozens of relevant passages deleted- sometimes 20 blank pages at a time. Still, Republican Senator Orrin Hatch said she had adequately protected herself from contempt of Congress.

---

(17) Ibid., p. 209.
(18) Ibid., p. 210.
(19) Ibid., p. 210.
(20) Ibid., p. 214.

David Schippers said to Reno: "Well, you dodged that bullet. At least you won't be going to the slammer today."[21] Contrast this little known story to the brouhaha made over the redacted 20 pages in the 911 report. Schippers wanted all files relating to Johnny Chung, Charlie Trie, John Huang, and Mark Middleton, including transcripts, depositions, tape recordings, logs, and notes of interviews. But the House Judiciary Committee changed the subject matter of the subpoenas. In effect, the House Judiciary Committee stonewalled the impeachment of Bill Clinton. The subpoena to Reno was drastically altered. David Schippers was on the verge of resignation at this point.[22]

The Demonization of Ken Starr

One of the most disgusting things the Democrats did during the Clinton era was the way they demonized Ken Starr, the Independent Counsel.

Who was Ken Starr? Unlike most of the slimebags that pimped for and enabled Bill Clinton to repeatedly flaunt the law, Ken Starr was an ethical, almost squeaky clean lawyer. Not only was he an international scholar in constitutional law and a former Solicitor General, but Starr had also been the recipient of 6 honorary doctor of law degrees from 6 different universities. Starr had argued many cases before the Supreme Court, and he was asked to take the Independent Counsel position. This is very important: he never sought out the position.

---

(21) David Schippers, "Sellout", p. 136.
(22) Ibid., p. 145.

Yet the shifty Clinton administration pursued Starr as if *he* were the criminal, and *Bill Clinton* was the victim. Folks, in fact, the reverse was true. Ken Starr was an honest, ethical brilliant guy who was simply trying to do a job he had been hand-picked to do.

Now keep in mind the White House could unleash whatever it wanted against Ken Starr. According to the White House spin, Bill Clinton was the victim of a vicious right-wing nut named Ken Starr. Starr was the guilty party; Bill Clinton was the innocent party who Starr was unfairly trying to target and destroy. If any of you believe that scenario, I have a nice bridge in Brooklyn, which I would love to sell to you.

Fact: By law, Starr couldn't respond to the allegations of the James Carvilles, Hillary Clintons, and Lanny Davises, and they all knew that and took advantage of that! If Starr did respond, it might have revealed confidential grand jury information.

Fact: Ken Starr was hand-picked by Democratic Attorney General for his job as Independent Counsel!

Fact: Ken Starr's work resulted in lots of indictments and was anything but a waste of money!

According to David Schippers, "He [Starr] couldn't use the press against the President the way the White House attack machine was using it against him."[23] And the polls

---

(23) Ibid., p. 158.

destroyed Ken Starr's image- Clinton's approval rating was in the 60's; Starr's approval rating hovered around 15%.[24]

The majority of the American people, including many of my friends, drank the White House kool-aid. According to the carefully crafted spin, everyone- the judges, all the Republicans in Congress, the independent counsel and the prosecutors- were part of this big conspiracy against an innocent, great President. The whole process was a witch-hunt against a popular President, who never did anything wrong.

Yet, many, many people such as I were totally disgusted by the Clintons, Furthermore, I was shocked the way the Democratic party- to this day- has stood behind this totally corrupt, immoral, power-hungry couple. **Bill Clinton** was invited to appear before the Independent Counsel at least **6 times!** Besides, Starr's office had amassed considerable evidence to indict Monica Lewinsky and others guilty of all sorts of criminal behavior. There is a myth that Monica Lewinsky was "seized", "held against her will" or "captured" by Starr's office. Nothing could have been further from the truth. Monica was treated with professionalism and courtesy by the office of Ken Starr. She was never held incommunicado or held against her will for one second!

But there was perjury, witness tampering, and obstruction of justice committed by Bill Clinton- with respect to Monica Lewinsky, with respect to Kathleen Willey, with respect to Dolly Kyle Browning, and with respect to Juanita

---

(24) Ibid., p. 158.

Broaddrick. In a court of law, **Bill Clinton could have faced many, many years in Federal prison!**

Bill Clinton was given the option of reading a specially prepared statement at the outset of his testimony. According to Schippers, whenever a tough question was asked to Clinton which might involve his perjuring himself, he would simply re-read the statement, thereby taking up precious committee time.

And whatever Ken Starr did was portrayed by the Clinton defense team as the wrong thing. Whatever the Republicans proposed in the House was opposed by most of the Democrats. As David Schippers noted: It was "unfair" to investigate beyond the referral, vote against the Democrats' amendments, interview prospective witnesses without the President's lawyers, keep the secure room closed to the public, release more material, not release more material, ask for witnesses before the committee, not present witnesses before the committee, invite Judge Starr to testify, not invite Judge Starr to testify, and many more accusations."[25]

A Book You Must Read

Sellout by David Schippers, Regnery, 2000.

After you have read David Schippers book *Sellout*, you will know why Bill Clinton belongs in prison. But you must get the book. It is in the current affairs section of Barnes & Noble. Get the book. Read the book. Before I get into the facts, let me tell you a little about David Schippers. First,

---

(25) Ibid., p. 164.

Schippers is an attorney. Second, he is a trial attorney with over 40 years of experience. Schippers worked in Bobby Kennedy's Justice Department, leading the Justice Department's Organized Crime and Racketeering Unit. He prosecuted mafiosos such as Sam Giancana and Sam Battaglia. Third, Schippers was Chief Investigative Counsel to the House Judiciary Committee, investigating the impeachment of Bill Clinton. Fourth, DAVID SCHIPPERS IS A DEMOCRAT!

Throughout the impeachment process, Bill Clinton lied and lied and lied. According to Schippers, Clinton used his office to commit witness tampering, perjury, and obstruction of justice. Clinton tried every legal maneuver to conceal his lying: he would parse words, he would conveniently forget incriminating events, and when he wasn't out and out committing perjury, he just "forgot" or "could not recall" key facts and events. What were some of the things Bill Clinton forgot?

According to Secret Service watch commander Jeffrey Purdie, Clinton stated to him "I hope you use your discretion" or "I hope I can count on your discretion." White House secretary Betty Currie told some members of the Secret Service that if they shut up about Monica Lewinsky, no one in the Secret Service would be fired or disciplined. Conveniently, Bill Clinton did not remember a thing about his statements to the Secret Service. Bill Clinton told the grand jury, under oath: "I don't remember what I said and I don't remember to whom I said it."[26] What about the account of the Secret Service agent, Bill? Clinton responded:

---

(26) David Schippers, Sellout, p. 210.

"I don't remember anything I said to him in that regard. I have no recollection of that whatever."[27]

Of course Clinton would claim this. What Clinton did was to prevent himself from being nailed for obstruction of justice, perjury, and witness tampering. How amazing that a guy like Bill Clinton, a Rhodes Scholar, a graduate of Yale Law School, a guy known for his encyclopedic mind and quick recall of the facts, suddenly has developed a memory problem! When it came to remembering things that could have convicted him and resulted in his doing some prison time, Bill Clinton had a memory problem.

Bill Clinton called Monica Lewinsky at 2 a.m. on December 17, 1998, to inform her that she was on the witness list in the Paula Jones case. When asked by the grand jury, if he remembered that call, Bill Clinton responded: "No sir, I don't. But it would- it is quite possible that that happened."[28]

It is very difficult to summarize the Impeachment of Bill Clinton in just a few pages. But let me try to do it. The House Judiciary Committee voted out 4 articles of Impeachment against Bill Clinton. Article I, which alleged that Bill Clinton committed perjury before a grand jury passed 228-206. Article II, accusing Bill Clinton of perjury in a civil lawsuit, failed 229-205. Article III, alleging Bill Clinton committed obstruction of justice, passed 221-212.

Article IV, charging Bill Clinton with abuse of power, failed 285-148. In the Senate, where the case was tried,

---

(27) Ibid., p. 210.
(28) Ibid., p. 214.

Article I failed, with 45 "yes" votes to 55 "no" votes. Article III failed, with 50 "yes" votes to 50 "no" votes.

For Bill Clinton to be thrown out of office, a vote of 67 "yes" votes (2/3 of the Senate) was required.

The reason Bill Clinton wasn't convicted was simple: plain old 2nd grade arithmetic! The Senate was made up of 45 Democrats and 55 Republicans. *Every Single Democrat voted against convicting Bill Clinton! On Article I and Article III not one Democrat voted to convict Bill Clinton. The vote among Democrats was 0 −45, meaning that every Democrat sided with Bill Clinton!* So the Democrats voted strictly along Party lines, with not one vote of crossover to the other side.

Yet an analysis of Republican votes in the Senate shows a totally different picture. *10 Republican Senators voted against convicting Bill Clinton on Article I. 5 Republican Senators voted against convicting Bill Clinton on Article III. In both cases, Republicans crossed over to the other side.*

Schippers points out that when the evidence from Ken Starr's office arrived in the "secure" room in Congress, *5 Democrats from the House Judiciary Committee never even signed in to review the evidence! Barney Frank (Mass.) said: "There's no evidence, there's no evidence." The other 4 Democrats who never signed in to the evidence room were Howard Berman (CA), Rick Boucher (VA), Jerrold Nadler (NY), and Melvin Watt (NC)*[29]

---

(29) Ibid., p. 60.

Who were the 10 Republicans that voted with the Democrats in Article I? They were Senators Shelby (AL), Stevens (Alaska), Snowe and Collins (Maine), Specter (PA), Chafee (RI), Thompson (TN), Jeffords (VT), Warner (VA), and Gorton (WA).[30]

Who were the 5 Republicans who voted with the Democrats in Article III? Senators Snowe and Collins (Maine), Specter (PA), Jeffords (VT), and Chafee (RI).[31]

Only 1 Democrat from the House of Representatives voted on *all four articles to impeach Bill Clinton.*
That was Representative Taylor (Mississippi). Four Democrats voted to impeach Bill Clinton on Articles I, II, and III but voted "no" on Article IV. Those Congressmen were McHale (PA), Hall and Stenholm (Texas), and Goode (VA).[32] Many Republicans voted against impeaching Clinton, especially on article IV. So, it appears that, if anything, the Republicans are a lot more open-minded and non-partisan than the Democrats!

Bill Clinton spoke about how he conned the American people through the impeachment process, in remarks he made in April, 2000.

"On the impeachment, let me tell you, I am proud of what we did there because I think we saved the Constitution of the

---

(30) LexisNexis Congressional, Senate vote on impeachment that President Clinton committed perjury
(31) Lexis Nexis Congressional, Senate vote on impeachment alleging that President Clinton obstructed justice
(32) Washingtonpost.com, The Impeachment Vote

United States. I am not ashamed of the fact that they impeached me. That was their decision, not mine. And it was wrong. As a matter of law, the Constitution, and history, it was wrong. And I'm glad I didn't quit, and I'm glad we fought it."[33]

I'm sorry, Mr. Clinton, the U.S. Congress was not wrong. We live in a Democracy and you raped the country. You lied, murdered, raped, molested, and conned the American people. Some day you and your wife will be caught. It took a long time to catch Al Capone, but he eventually went to prison.

The common myth circulated by the Clinton team was that Bill Clinton's behavior was "just lies about sex." Nothing could be further from the truth. In reality, Bill Clinton engaged in witness tampering, obstruction of justice, perjury, abuse of power, and- some say- treason and murder! I used to be a Democrat- I voted for Bill Clinton in 1992- and I then I found out all about the background of Bill and Hillary Clinton. I am no longer a Democrat, and I will have nothing to do with a party that embraces the likes of Bill and Hillary Clinton. And I won't stop until the Clintons are where they belong- in a prison cell- the same prison cell that Webb Hubbell, Jim Ray Tucker, Jim and Susan MacDougal were in.

Why did Vince Foster really die? What did he know about Bill and Hillary's lawbreaking? Why did Ron Brown die? What did he know about Bill and Hillary's sale of

---

(33) Schippers, op.cit., p. 3.

secrets to the Red Chinese in exchange for political contributions?

David Schippers and his staff were all ready to bring up impeachable offenses that had *nothing to do with Paula Jones and Monica Lewinsky- Chinagate, Bill Clinton's rape of Juanita Broaddrick, etc. but he could not because "the politicians lost their nerve and severely limited the scope of the inquiry."*[34]

The House Judiciary Committee submitted an 81-question questionnaire to Bill Clinton. His answers were vague, misleading, and often deceptive. It certainly looks as if Bill Clinton coached his appointments secretary Betty Currie, back on January 18, 1998, when he told her:

(1) I was never alone with Monica, right?
(2) You were always there when Monica was there, right?
(3) Monica came on to me and I never touched her, right?
(4) You could see and hear everything, right?
(5) She wanted to have sex with me, and I cannot do that.

All of these statements are lies. Right there, Bill Clinton has perjured himself, committed witness tampering, and obstructed justice.

On January 17, 1998, President Bill Clinton was deposed under oath in the case of Jones v. Clinton. Clinton, when

---

(34) Schippers, op. cit., p. 4.

asked if he ever discussed with Monica Lewinsky the possibility that she would testify in the Paula Jones case, responded "I'm not sure." When Bill Clinton was asked under oath, if he was ever alone with Monica Lewinsky, he answered "I don't recall."[35] Bill Clinton had to say this, to avoid perjuring himself.

Bill Clinton couldn't recall the facts of a meeting that was held between Vernon Jordan and Monica Lewinsky, even though Jordan recalled meeting with Clinton that same day and relayed all that transpired to Clinton.

David Schippers points out that Clinton's testimony was peppered with "false and misleading statements to the federal court, the grand jury, and the Congress of the United States."

Clinton engaged in doubletalk, so no normal person could even keep track of his lies. For example, Clinton couldn't remember giving any gifts to Monica, when he testified before the grand jury. He gave a pathetic excuse for this lie.

"I think what I meant then was that I don't recall what they were, not that I don't recall whether I had given them."[36]

Bill Gets Confessional

Independent counsel Ken Starr was confident that Bill Clinton had committed up to 11 impeachable acts, involving obstruction of justice, witness tampering, perjury, and abuse

---

(35) Schippers, op. cit., p. 215.
(36) Schippers, op. cit. p, 218.

of power. So now Bill Clinton went into a confessional mode. At a prayer breakfast at the White House on the eve of the release of the Starr report, a tearful Clinton told a room full of clergymen: "I have sinned."

Yes he had! Clinton asked for everyone's forgiveness. Pandering to the Jews, he quoted from a passage from the Gates of Repentance, a Yom Kippur prayer. Clinton had been given this prayer by a Jewish friend of his.

On December 11, 1998, the House Judiciary Committee voted out 4 articles of impeachment against the 41st President of the United States, William Jefferson Clinton. On December 16, 1998, Clinton coincidentally ordered massive air strikes against Iraq, citing Saddam Hussein's failure to allow in U.N. inspectors to search for weapons of mass destruction.

On February 13, 1999, the Senate acquitted Bill Clinton.

Ann Coulter's Take on Clinton

In her book "High Crimes and Misdemeanors", Constitutional law attorney Ann Coulter concludes that Bill Clinton "has lied repeatedly, openly, and directly to the American people. He does not even seem to care whether there is a plausible sense in which his lies might be justified as half-truths- so long as he can get away with the lie, even temporarily...It's impossible even to keep track of all the lies he has told."[37]

---

(37) High Crimes and Misdemeanors, Ann Coulter, pp. 16-17.

Democratic Senator Bob Kerrey said this of Bill Clinton: "Clinton's an unusually good liar. Unusually good. Do you realize that?"[38]

At a press conference on April 30, 1998, ABC's Sam Donaldson asked Bill Clinton a really good question.

"Now you deny wrongdoing, I understand, but as a standard for presidents what do you think: Does it matter what you do in private moments, as alleged? And particularly does it matter if you have committed perjury or in another sense broken the law?"[39]

This was Bill Clinton's response:

"Well, since I have answered the underlying questions, I really believe it's important for me not to say any more about this. I think that I'm, in some ways, the last person who needs to be having a national conversation about this."[40]

In effect, Bill Clinton has put himself above the law. He has no comment as to whether or not he is a felon, or if Presidents should be subject to the laws of ordinary people. And so it begins...

There are so many books about Bill and Hillary Clinton, but if you want a book with the most meat- the most facts- I recommend "High Crimes and Misdemeanors" and "Treason", by Ann Coulter. Coulter doesn't hold back. She

---

(38) Ibid., p. 17.
(39) Ibid., p. 17.
(40) Ibid., p. 17.

is a brilliant attorney with a razor-sharp mind. Her facts on the Clintons are irrefutable and thoroughly documented.

According to Coulter, the "crimes" of Richard Nixon are nothing compared to those of Bill Clinton:

"From the 900 FBI files in the White House to a pattern of IRS audits of Clinton's enemies to selling the Lincoln bedroom, Clinton had already done things Nixon only dreamed about."[41]

Says Coulter: "Other presidents weren't vulnerable because other presidents weren't such pigs...The rules that apply to all other Americans just don't apply to President Clinton."[42]

At a press conference on February 6, 1998, CNN's Wolf Blitzer asked Bill Clinton a question: "Mr. President, Monica Lewinsky's life has been changed forever- her family's life has been changed forever. I wonder how you feel about that and what –if anything- you'd like to say to Monica Lewinsky at this minute?"

Bill Clinton paused, smiled and said: "That's good. [He laughed along with the reporters] that's good, but at this minute I'm going to stick with my position in not commenting."[43]

---

(41) Ibid., p. 27.
(42) Ibid., p. 27.
(43) Ibid., pp. 27-28.

In essence, Bill Clinton considered the Presidency to be a big joke- telling the truth didn't matter. Basically, the American people could fuck off. He was about to prove that he was above the law.

Paula Jones and the Impeachment

On May 8, 1991 Paula Jones was working at a state-sponsored conference in Little Rock, when State Trooper Danny Ferguson gave her a note with a hotel room number attached: "the Governor would like to meet you." Thinking nothing of it, Paula Jones went up to Bill Clinton's hotel room. According to the complaint of Jones v. Clinton, filed 5-6-94-

"After some small talk in which Clinton informed Jones that her boss was Clinton's 'good friend', Clinton began praising Jones' "curves", kissed her, slid his hand up her culottes, and "lowered his trousers and underwear exposing his erect penis and asked Jones to "kiss it".[44] As Jones quickly left Clinton's room, Clinton reminded her that he was friendly with her boss. *(For more details on the Paula Jones story see the chapter on Clinton's Women.)*

Right there folks is a classic example of sexual harassment. Whether you Clinton supporters see it as such is your problem: Paula Jones cost Bill Clinton $850,000 and paved the way for Kathleen Willey and Monica Lewinsky to step forward.

---

(44) Ibid., p. 29. Also Complaint, Jones v. Clinton, No. 94-290, at para. 20-21 (May 6, 1994)

In January 1997, Paula Jones' lawyers received an anonymous phone call. The caller said: "I had a similar thing happen to me." That caller was Kathleen Willey.

Linda Tripp had been a secretary to Vince Foster in the White House Counsel's office. Like Monica Lewinsky, she was transferred from the White House to the Pentagon, as they were both too hot to handle in the Clinton White House. Linda Tripp felt that Vince Foster had been murdered; the whole thing just didn't make sense. Linda Tripp was in fear of her life, and didn't like being called a liar by Bill Clinton's lawyer. That's what led her to tape her conversations with Monica Lewinsky.

Monica proudly referred to herself as "Special Assistant to the President for Blow Jobs."[45] And to those who think this was only about sex, consider this. It sure looks as if Bill Clinton's golfing buddy lawyer Vernon Jordan went out of his way to get Monica Lewinsky a job in New York City. Monica signed a false affidavit (a felony) denying a relationship with Bill Clinton. In exchange for Monica Lewinsky's lying in her affidavit, Vernon Jordan would help her with her job prospects in New York City. Monica Lewinsky was committing one felony after another. She asked Linda Tripp to lie about the sexual trysts described on the tapes. According to Coulter, "Lewinsky is on the tapes asking Tripp to lie under oath about what Lewinsky had told her. That's suborning perjury."[46]

---

(45) Ibid., p. 33.
(46) Ibid., p. 34.

On January 12, 1998, Linda Tripp stopped by Ken Starr's office. The next day she had lunch with Monica at the Ritz Carlton, in Pentagon City, VA. On January 14, 1998, Linda Tripp retained a new lawyer, Jim Moody, and on January 15, 1998, Ken Starr presented evidence to Attorney General Janet Reno concerning the role of Vernon Jordan and Webb Hubbell in altering Monica Lewinsky's testimony.[47]

To reiterate, Richard Nixon did maybe 1% of what Bill Clinton did. Nixon told one lie and invoked executive privilege on 1 occasion. Although Nixon contemplated using the IRS to conduct political audits, those audits were never carried out. Bill Clinton, on the other hand, lied repeatedly-under oath- used the IRS to audit and intimidate his enemies and walked away scot-free. As Ann Coulter writes, "If Nixon telling 1 lie, not under oath, constituted the creation of an "Imperial Presidency" demanding the president's impeachment, what has Clinton created by telling repeated lies not only to the public, but under oath?"[48]

Phone Sex at 6:30 A.M.

On one occasion, Bill Clinton called Monica Lewinsky for phone sex at 6:30 a.m. According to Monica's FBI statement, "Clinton exclaimed 'good morning'...after having orgasm."

In one deposition, Monica Lewinsky indicated that most of her episodes of "oral" with Bill Clinton were "quickies." Clinton did not disrobe- he simply unzipped the First

---

(47) Ibid., p. 36.
(48) Ibid., p. 15.

Trousers! Once, when Monica was servicing the President in a hallway, someone came into the Oval Office. Clinton "zipped up really quickly and went out and came back in...I just remember laughing because he had walked out there and he was visibly aroused, and I just thought it was funny...It wouldn't necessarily be noticeable...but it was just funny to me."[49]

At first, Monica wasn't sure that the stain on her blue dress was Bill Clinton's semen- the first semen! She thought it "could be spinach dip or something."[50]

How did Monica Lewinsky describe her phone sex with Bill Clinton? "He's taking care of business on one end, and I'm taking care of business on another. "[51]

Lewinsky observed Bill Clinton masturbating, including one time in the office of aide Nancy Hernreich.[52]

Lewinsky claimed that Bill Clinton engaged in oral-anal contact with her.[53]

An anonymous tipster who worked on the Clinton impeachment investigation told sources at Newsmax.com that it is quite likely that there were other rapes committed by Bill Clinton, besides the one against Juanita Broaddrick.

---

(49) Ruddy and Limbacher, "Bitter Legacy", pp. 54-55.
(50) Footnote 443, Part I, Starr Report
(51) Footnote 837, Part I, Starr Report
(52) Footnotes 25 and 31, Part II, Starr Report
(53) Footnotes 28 and 35, Part II, Starr Report

One case is of a 14-year-old girl who claimed to be raped by Bill Clinton at a cocaine party. Rick and Beverly Lambert, who worked as investigators for Paula Jones, were told about the woman's claim. "Rick Lambert traced the woman, now in her twenties, to California but was unable to locate her."[54]

But wait! Bill Clinton also may have cheated on his *own mistress*!

Eleanor Mondale is the daughter of former Vice-President Walter Mondale. One day Bill Clinton was having a private meeting with Eleanor Mondale in his White House office. At that very moment, Monica Lewinsky had a slew of gifts she wanted to give to Bill Clinton- a mug, an antique cigar holder, a book, and a necktie.

Since Bill Clinton was already with a woman at the time, Monica was kept waiting at the northwest gate guard booth. Personal secretary Betty Currie sent word to Monica that Bill Clinton was unavailable, and a Secret service agent told her the President was meeting with Eleanor Mondale. Monica stormed away in a jealous rage, as she perceived Eleanor to be a rival for Bill Clinton's affections.

Clinton, in turn, got mad at the Secret Service agent for telling Lewinsky about Eleanor Mondale. After smoothing things out with Monica, Clinton invited her back to the Oval office that afternoon. When Monica complained to Clinton about Vernon Jordan's failure to help get her a job, Clinton responded: "Oh, I'll talk to him. I'll get on it."[55]

---

(54) Ruddy and Limbacher, op. cit. p. 45
(55) Michael Isikoff, "Uncovering Clinton," p. 246

So, the President who could have been dealing with terrorism, Saddam Hussein, homelessness, the Mideast, or any of a hundred different issues affecting the nation was cheating on the intern who aspired to be "assistant to the President in charge of blow jobs."[56]

Ken Starr- A Clinton's Best Friend

According to Christopher Ruddy, investigative reporter and chief CEO of Newsmax.com, Ken Starr decided from the outset not to indict the Clintons or any other White House officials. It was the Clinton "spinmeisters" who painted Starr as "the tough mean prosecutor out to get the President."[57] In reality, it is quite possible that Ken Starr had cut some sort of deal with the Clintons.

Starr was basically soft on Webster Hubbell, when he cut him a plea agreement. Hubbell did not have to cooperate with Starr in the Judge's investigation of the Clintons. This happened twice with Hubbell, once when he had admitted misleading federal investigators and back in 1994 when he admitted to fraudulent billing practices at the Rose Law firm and tax evasion. Although it is quite possible that Webb Hubbell could have fingered the Clintons and had them locked up, Ken Starr failed miserably by not seeking Hubbell's cooperation in the investigation.[58]

---

(56) Coulter, op. cit., p. 33.
(57) Christopher Ruddy and Carl Limbacher, "Bitter Legacy," p. 65
(58) Ibid., p. 64.

Chris Ruddy points out several basic flaws in the performance of Ken Starr. Starr had a double standard when it came to issuing indictments. It would take more evidence for a Bill or Hillary Clinton to be indicted than you or me, under Starr's formula. According to Ruddy, "This is nothing less than a grant of titles and nobility for government officials, which is expressly prohibited by the Constitution."[59]

Starr investigated Monica Lewinsky, only at the urging of Janet Reno. Why did Ken Starr tarry for eight months before signing a plea agreement with Monica? According to Ruddy, the whole Monica Lewinsky thing was a smoke-screen to cover the much more serious crimes of Bill Clinton. Ruddy points out: "Clinton would never be removed from office over a sex scandal."[60]

Ruddy's theories are nothing short of brilliant.

Is it possible that Ken Starr was in some way under the control of the Clintons? Ruddy seems to think so. Ruddy goes on to describe the irony inherent in that those who cooperated with Starr got worse treatment than those who "stonewalled." For example, 2 key Whitewater witnesses-David Hale and James McDougal- both went to prison, but Webb Hubbell and former Arkansas governor Jim Ray Tucker, who failed to cooperate, got off easy! Ruddy concludes "Because of Kenneth W. Starr's complicity, the most corrupt administration in the history of the country continues with no end in sight."[61]

---

(59) Ibid., p. 67
(60) Ibid., p. 68
(61) Ibid., p. 68

Ruddy points out several questions surrounding the death of Vince Foster. Why did Miquel Rodriguez, Starr's lead prosecutor in the death of Vince Foster, resign?

Did Rodriguez have knowledge of a cover-up in the death of Foster? Why were the Arkansas State Troopers, who knew of the death of Vince Foster several hours before the White House knew, not deposed?[62]

Clinton's Possible Oedipus Complex

One thing many people do not know is that Monica Lewinsky is a mirror image of Bill Clinton's mother Virginia Kelly. In fact, it you look at pictures of both of them at the age of 23, you can see the striking resemblance. Clinton is so messed up, that on top of all his other sicknesses, he might also suffer from the *Oedipus Complex, in which the boy is sexually attracted to his mother!* Clinton favorably compared Monica to his mother, saying that she, like his mother was "full of piss and vinegar." Charming, I guess.[63]

At the time Clinton met Monica, he was at an emotional low point. The marriage between Bill and Hillary was just a sham at this point. But Bill Clinton really liked Monica Lewinsky. What did Bill Clinton like so much about Monica Lewinsky?

Was it that she was young enough to be his daughter? Was it that she was an intern, making her "forbidden fruit?" Was it that, unlike his own *shikse Hillary, Monica was a high*

---

(62) Ibid., p. 67
(63) Oppenheimer, "State of a Union," p. 255

class Jewish girl from Beverly Hills? Was it that Monica looked so much like Bill's own mother?

It seems that Monica Lewinsky fulfilled *all* the sick sexual fantasies in the perverted mind of Bill Clinton! He could fantasize forbidden sex with a young Jewish girl who reminded him of his mother! As my grandfather used to say: "Nothing to Beat!"

Monica gave Bill Clinton "head" while he spoke on the phone to members of Congress and world leaders. Not being totally selfish, Bill Clinton returned the favor by *inserting a high-quality cigar into Monica's vagina and then tasting the cigar! According to President Bill Clinton, the cigar he had just inserted into the 23 year-old intern's vagina, in the Oval Office, "Tasted good."*[64]

When the White House staff had Monica Lewinsky fired on April 5, 1996, Bill Clinton was bummed out. He moaned to her: "Why did they have to take you away from me?" Clinton told Monica the he would return her to the White House when he won reelection that November. He would get her any job she wanted. Monica asked if she could be "assistant to the President for blow jobs." Bill Clinton replied: "I'd like that."[65]

And was this guy Clinton ever hooked on Monica. A sample of their middle-of-the night phone conversations shows just how really far gone President Clinton was.

---

(64) Ibid., p. 255
(65) Ibid., p. 256

"All I think about is you and your job. I'm obsessed with you and finding you a job. I wake up in the morning and it makes me sick thinking about it. My life is empty except for you and this job search. All I have is my work and this obsession. I'm on your team."[66] (Bill made this particular call on what happened to be his 22nd wedding anniversary-October 11, 1997!)

Mind you, folks. This comment is from a guy who *didn't have a relationship with that woman- Miss Lewinsky.*

Monica gets an Abortion

After her affair with Bill Clinton was over, Monica became pregnant from an affair with another older man. She had to borrow money from her aunt to pay for the abortion, as her ex didn't want to help her.[67]

It is possible that the Israeli government blackmailed Bill Clinton during the Lewinsky scandal. In his book "Gideon's Spies", Gordon Thomas claims that the Israeli secret police-the Mossad- taped over 30 hours of Bill Clinton having phone sex and used that to convince Clinton to end an FBI investigation into a Mossad spy, code-named MEGA, inside the White House. This new became public in April, 1999. If this were true, it could have been the grounds for opening a second impeachment of Bill Clinton. But the sad truth is that Trent Lott didn't want to go after Bill Clinton again.[68]

---

(66) Ibid., p. 256-7
(67) Ibid., p. 257
(68) Ruddy and Limbacher, "Bitter Legacy," p. 37-8.

Monica Lewinsky Tidbits

Monica's mother didn't want Monica to work at the United Nations. Her mother complained that there were **"a lot of Arabs working there...it's no place for a Jewish girl."**[69]

Monica once said that lying wasn't a big problem, because she was **"brought up with lies all the time."**[70]

When Monica's parents were divorced, she would make up stories to get money from her father.[71]

---

(69) Isikoff, "Uncovering Clinton," p. 219
(70) Ibid., p. 251
(71) Ibid., p. 251

Melrose Larry Green

CHAPTER FOUR

Reason Number Seven the Clintons Belong in Prison

Campaign Fundraising - This scandal didn't get the coverage it demanded, but the Clintons basically used *extortion and racketeering to get money from wealthy Democrats.*

By turning the White House into one big garage sale, the Clintons violated the law over and over again. The way the Clintons raped the Democratic Party is grounds right there for campaign finance reform. See the sections on *Democrats who Rode on Air Force One for $$$$, Democrats Who Slept in the Lincoln Bedroom for $$$$.* I feel bad for the naïve Democrats who threw their money away to make Bill and Hillary Clinton wealthy, and to keep them out of prison. I feel that Bill and Hillary Clinton, along with Terry McAuliffe must be investigated by an independent counsel for bribery, extortion and racketeering, perhaps under the RICO Act. In many ways, the Clintons committed robbery too. I think they both deserve at least 10 years in prison for their criminal activity connected to illicit fundraising.

Even More Lies told by Bill and Hillary Clinton

(41) Hillary Clinton lied when she said she didn't sign the letter thanking the American Muslim Council for its $50,000 donation to her Senatorial campaign.
(42) Hillary Clinton lied when she said she never read the plaque from the American Muslim Council which thanked her for participation in the group's activities.

(43) Hillary Clinton lied when she told Tim Russert of "Meet the Press" that "the record is clear that Bill Clinton spent an enormous amount of time" fighting terrorism.

(44) Hillary Clinton lied to Tim Russert when she claimed "there's quite an extensive record of the Clinton administration's efforts against terrorism."

(45) Bill Clinton when he said that Dolly Kyle Browning had made up her claims of a long-standing sexual relationship between Clinton and Browning. In fact, a relationship between the 2 of them had gone on over a 32-year period.

(46) Hillary Clinton lied when she denied ever calling Paul Fray "a fucking Jew Bastard". (There were at least 2 eyewitnesses who hear her say it!)

(47) Bill Clinton lied when he told the N.Y. Times: "In 29 years, my wife has never uttered an ethnic or racial slur against anybody, ever. She's so straight on this, she squeaks."

(48) Bill and Hillary Clinton lied when they said they had no idea that their siblings were involved in seeking pardons for friends and business partners and received substantial compensation for their efforts.

(49) Hillary Clinton lied when she said, after converting a $1,000 investment in cattle futures into $99,537: *"I got lucky."*

(50) Bill and Hillary Clinton lied when they denied James McDougal's assertion that he arranged for his S&L to pay the Rose Law firm a monthly retainer, *as a favor to Hillary and under pressure from Governor Bill Clinton.*

(51) Hillary Clinton lied in 2 federal investigations when she said she hadn't performed any legal work on Castle Grande. When her Rose Law Firm billings turned up in the White House, it proved she had been lying- she had billed several hours to the project!

(52) Hillary Clinton lied when she told a crowd in 1982, "I don't have to change my name...I've been Mrs. Bill Clinton." Actually, at that time she was calling herself Hillary Rodham!

(53) Hillary Clinton lied in the "60 Minutes" interview when she said, in effect, that there had been a rough period in their marriage that was now behind them. In fact, Hillary has known to this day that her husband has constantly preyed on women, day and night.

(54) Bill Clinton lied when he claimed to have cut the White House staff by 25% by Oct. 1, 1993. In fact, the staff actually *increased by 10%*

(55) Bill Clinton lied when he claimed never to have read the law school writings of Attorney General nominee Lani Guinier.

(56) Hillary Clinton lied when she said she is not in favor of big government.

(57) Bill Clinton lied under oath when he said he never had a sexual relationship with Dolly Kyle Browning.

(58) Bill Clinton lied when he said he never had a sexual relationship with Sheila Lawrence.

(59) Bill Clinton lied when he said he remembered "literally nothing" about meeting with a Chinese weapons official in the White House. All such meetings are written down, and the President's convenient forgetting is just another expression of the lie.

(60) Hillary Clinton lied when she said she had no role in the clemency granted to the New Square 4, and she lied when she said she had no opinion about the clemency.

The Clinton Pardons

The Unbelievable Story of Marc and Denise Rich- FBI Fugitive Pardoned by Bill Clinton after ex-wife gives millions plus herself to Clinton!

The greatest novelist or screenwriter in Hollywood could not come up with a more amazing scenario than the incredible story of Marc Rich and his ex-wife Denise Rich. Let me try to fill you in...

Marc Rich fled to Switzerland in 1983, after he was convicted by a U.S. Court of evading *more than $48 million in taxes!*

Marc Rich made his fortune by lying, cheating, and defrauding people. In short, he was a perfect candidate for a pardon by Bill Clinton.

- Rich lied to the Nigerians by telling them he was selling their oil to Spain when he was actually selling it to South Africa. He sold 11 million tons of oil to South Africa between 1979 and 1990. On top of that, he bribed the Nigerian government to the tune of $1 million.

- Rich broke the American law by trading with an enemy nation- Iran! Rich and his partner Pinchus Green masterminded a $200 million oil deal with Iran. Payment for the oil came in the form of rockets and automatic weapons which Ayatollah Khomeini used in his war against Iraq.

- Rich broke U.S. law by trading with the Libyans-, who were designated sponsors of international terrorists. Rich bought Libyan crude oil through 3rd parties and illegally shipped soybeans and barley to Libya.

- Rich developed sugar and metals trading deals with the dictatorship of Fidel Castro's Cuba.[1]

All of these deals could have put Marc Rich in prison for many, many years. But he lived dangerously and constantly thumbed his nose at the authorities. Morris "Sandy" Weinberg prosecuted Marc Rich back in the 1980's. He said "Mr. Rich and Mr. Green have apparently made vast sums of money over the past twenty years by trading with virtually every enemy of the U.S."[2]

Rich was guilty of "daisy chaining", a process of fraudulently relabeling old oil as new. This enabled Rich to sell oil which could have legally been sold at $6/barrel for $25-$40/barrel! In addition, Rich was guilty of a practice called "calving", a fraudulent method companies use to artificially inflate prices and evade income taxes.

The U.S. Attorney's office handed down a 51-count indictment to Marc Rich, part of it based on the Racketeer Influenced and Corrupt Organization (RICO) statutes.

Attorney Weinberg told a committee of Congress in 1991 "the evidence was absolutely overwhelming that Marc Rich,

---

(1) Barbara Olson, "The Final Days", pp. 130-131.
(2) Ibid., p. 131.

in fact, committed the largest tax fraud in the history of the United States."[3]

Marc Rich at first tried to ship out of the country two steamer trunks filled with incriminating evidence against him, but Sandy Weinberg's men intercepted a Swissair 747 before Rich could smuggle out the data! Subsequently, Rich put together a high-powered team of lawyers to defend him- a team consisting of Edward Bennett Williams, prestigious New York and Washington law firms, Swiss law firms, and even Michael Tigar (he defended the Chicago Seven and the Seattle eight.)

According to the late Barbara Olson, Edward Bennett Williams offered Sandy Weinberg $100 million to settle the Rich case. Weinberg declined the offer, so Rich and his buddy Pinchus Green left the country.[4]

First, Marc Rich became a citizen of Spain on July 26, 1982. On July 18, 1983, he became a citizen of Israel. He changed the name of his company from Marc Rich International to Clarendon, Ltd. Incredibly, **his firm sold close to $1.3 million in** nickel and $4 million of copper to the United States Mint, a division of the same Treasury Department that Rich had defrauded out of $48 million![5]

I would say that Marc Rich lived like a king in Switzerland, but I doubt if any king had the life of luxury that this FBI fugitive had! Rich has a Swiss mansion filled with

---

(3) Ibid., p. 131.
(4) Ibid., p, 132.
(5) Ibid., p. 132-133.

original Picassos! He owns a villa in St. Moritz and a $10-million home in Marbella, which is located on the Spanish coast. Rich, who reportedly raked in $7 *billion in 2000,* crisscrosses the world in his own jet, naturally.[6]

There was one thing this man who had everything lacked- a pardon!

Marc Rich embarked on a comprehensive program of lobbying for his pardon- a program that involved influential Jews, members of the Israeli government, leaders of American Jewish organizations, and —last but not least- his ex-wife, a *very, very, very close friend of Bill Clinton!*

Marc Rich lined up an all-star team of Jewish people to speak out on his behalf- author Elie Wiesel, former Israeli Prime Ministers Ehud Barak and Shimon Peres, Abe Foxman (executive director of ADL), and Abner Azulay, a former top leader of the Israeli secret police, the Mossad (and also a director of the Rich Foundation).[7]

Why did all these Jewish dignitaries and politicos rally to the defense of the U.S.'s largest tax cheat? Perhaps because Marc Rich's Foundation, the Rich Foundation, gave $2.6 million to the Tel Aviv Museum of Art. Perhaps because the Birthright Israel received $5 million from the Rich Foundation. Perhaps because the Israel Philharmonic also received a small fortune from the Rich Foundation.[8]

---

(6) Ibid., p. 134
(7) Ibid., p. 135
(8) Ibid., p. 134

If the American Jewish Congress (AJC) would write a letter to Clinton on Marc Rich's behalf, he would donate $100,000 to them. Rightfully, the AJC turned Rich down. But Abe Foxman over at the Anti-Defamation League of B'nai Brith wasn't quite so moral as the folks at the American Jewish Congress- he accepted Rich's donation of $100,000 in exchange for ADL's writing a letter to Clinton supporting Rich.[9]

Marc Rich hired lawyer Jack Quinn, who had represented Bill Clinton and Al Gore. Quinn tried all sorts of legal maneuvers to try to defend Rich's criminal actions, but the government would buy into none of them. The U.S. Attorney Otto Obermaier actually flew to Switzerland to try to settle with Marc Rich, but "although he was willing to pay staggering sums in fines, Rich refused any deal that would involve surrendering to federal authorities and submitting to the U.S. justice system."[10]

And now to the rescue comes Marc Rich's ex-wife and part-time girlfriend of Bill Clinton- Denise Rich!

Abner Azulay put it in an E-mail. The member of the Israeli Mossad wrote: "The present impasse leaves us with only one other option: the unconventional approach which has not yet been tried and which I have been proposing all along...sending "DR on a personal mission to No. 1 with a well-prepared script."[11]

---

(9) Ibid., p. 135
(10) Ibid., p. 136
(11) Ibid., p. 136-7.

Oh yes DR is Denise Rich and "No. 1" is Bill Clinton!

Denise Rich

Denise Rich, the ex-wife of international fugitive Marc Rich, was a girlfriend of Bill Clinton. According to Bill, she reminded him of Gennifer Flowers. Denise visited the White House dozens of times to spend time alone with Bill Clinton. She was given access to the Oval Office and the living quarters. A top Washington socialite told the "National Enquirer": "Of course Bill slept with Denise."[12]   Among White House insiders, it was common knowledge that Bill and Denise were an "item". Denise used to brag to her friends about her sexual exploits with Bill Clinton.[13]

Denise Rich was a very wealthy woman. Depending on whom you believe, Denise Rich walked off with either $350 million[14] or $500 million[15] in her divorce deal with Marc Rich. Denise lives in a 25,000 square-foot three-story apartment in Manhattan, summers at *2 homes in the Hamptons,* and vacations with fellow liberals at her Aspen, Colorado retreat. To get between her homes in New York, she travels by helicopter. Over the years she has had several plastic surgeries, which make her look a lot younger than 59 years of age.

---

(12) "National Enquirer," March 13, 2001, pp. 48-49.
(13) Ibid., p. 48
(14) Ibid., p. 49
(15) "Globe," Feb. 13, 2001, p. 5

According to the New York Times, Denise Rich gave $450,000 to the Clinton library.[16] The final $100,000 of that donation arrived 2 months after Abner Azulay's E-mail had been written.

Most of the $1 million she donated to Bill Clinton's campaign came during the time that Jack Quinn was working on her ex-husband's pardon.

In addition, Denise Rich donated $100,000 to the Democratic National Committee, $109,000 to Hillary Clinton's Senatorial campaign, paid $40,000 for entertainers to play at Hillary's birthday on October 25, 2000, and $25,000 to the Gore-Lieberman Recount Committee.[17] I guess counting chads costs money!

As if that weren't enough, Denise Rich gave the Clintons over $7,000 worth of furnishings for their housing *after they left the White House.* And last but not least, Denise presented Bill with a gold saxophone at a cancer benefit she threw in November, 2000.[18]

The lawyers went into fifth gear. Jack Quinn and Abner Azulay E-mailed each other about phone conversations Democratic fundraiser Beth Dozoretz had with Bill Clinton about the pardon of Marc Rich. According to a letter from Jack Quinn, "POTUS (short for President of the United

---

(16) "New York Times," March 3, 2001- "Donors and the Rich Pardon."

(17) Barbara Olson, op. cit., p. 138

(18) Ibid., p. 138

States) 'wants to do it' and was doing all he could 'to turn around the WH counsels'."[19]

Now Marc Rich met with former Israeli Prime Minister Ehud Barak. Three times Barak called Bill Clinton on the phone to discuss the pardon of Marc Rich. Clinton told Barak he was "working on" the Rich pardon and not to share that information with others.[20]

When Arthur Levitt, chairman of the Securities and Exchange Commission was told about the impending pardon of Marc Rich, he said to a White House official: "The man's a fugitive...This looks terrible."[21]

Jack Quinn, Denise Rich, and Marc Rich prevailed over the U.S. Department of Justice. Marc Rich, the biggest tax cheat in U.S. history- Marc Rich- who was on the FBI's most wanted list for International fugitives received *his pardon from William Jefferson Clinton on January 20, 2001.* Just one day earlier, Bill Clinton copped his own plea bargain with special prosecutor Robert Ray, so it just must have been the season!

Former Mayor of New York Rudy Giuliani couldn't believe that Marc Rich had been pardoned. Giuliani, who had been the U.S. Attorney in charge of the Rich prosecutions heard the news while attending the inauguration of President George W. Bush. Giuliani told an aide to "Check again". Perhaps "they must mean Michael Milken."

---

(19) Ibid., p. 139
(20) Ibid., p. 139
(21) Ibid., p. 140

Giuliani even asked his aide to spell out "Marc." He said it was "impossible" that the President would pardon a fugitive like Marc Rich.[22]

One lawyer who had handled many of the applications for pardon told "Newsweek" that "I think Clinton wanted to pardon all of them" and that "he just can't stand law enforcement."[23]

What did Marc Rich have to say about his pardon? This is the statement that his p.r. agency in Tel Aviv released: "I do not consider the pardon granted by President Clinton as an eradication of past deeds- but as the closing of a cycle and a humanitarian act...The indictment against me in the United States was wrong and meant to hurt me personally- the pardon granted by President Clinton remedied this injustice eighteen years later."[24]

How was Denise Rich able to get Bill Clinton to pardon her ex-husband Marc Rich? No doubt her millions donated to the Clintons was a big factor. But also it was Bill Clinton's "special relationship" with Denise Rich that helped close the deal to pardon one of America's biggest tax cheats!

According to one person who knew them both, "Bill once vowed to get her (Denise) into the sack...She's incredibly sexy. The way she totters around on impossibly high stiletto heels, almost falling out of her tight little suits, used to drive Clinton wild. When he's around her, you can almost see his

---

(22) Ibid., p. 141
(23) Ibid., p. 141
(24) Ibid., p. 141

tongue hanging out. He's like a big ol' hound dog around a juicy ham bone. Denise always knew Clinton had a thing for her and she played it to the hilt. Around him, she wears short skirts and low-cut tops that make his eyes pop."[25]

I find it incredible that the Congress never investigated Bill Clinton for all the shenanigans surrounding the pardon of Marc Rich. The Democratic Party needs to be investigated too. To me it looks like a *quid pro quo. If The story of the Marc Rich pardon is not a quid pro quo or a bribe, nothing is, folks!*

Harvey Weinig- This one is unbelievable. Weinig was serving time for taking part in one of the biggest drug money-laundering cases in New York's history. What did Harvey Weinig do? He aided the Cali drug cartel and was involved in a kidnapping. When Bill Clinton commuted his sentence to 270 days served, the Department of Justice and the U.S. Attorney in New York were amazed. Even Colombian governmental officials called Clinton's commutation of Weinig "sordid."

How did Weinig get this commutation? It turns out he was related by marriage to a former Clinton staffer. And his attorney knew the right people. Weinig's lawyer bypassed the normal channels and went directly to John Podesta, Bruce Lindsey, and White House Counsel Beth Nolan.

And- alas- **Harvey Weinig was an attorney!**[26]

---

(25) "National Enquirer," March 13, 2001, p 48-49.
(26) Olson, op. cit., p. 162-3.

Former Colombian President Ernesto Samper was outraged. He called Weinig's clemency "repugnant". Samper argued: "What would happen if, with just a few days left in my presidency, I had set free several drug traffickers, arrested in Bogota, and if those same people were found to be helping people in my government?" Colombian anti-drug czar Rosso Serrano also couldn't believe the Weinig commutation. It "sent the wrong message to the anti-drug struggle, because it negates the suffering of all the families who died to fight trafficking."[27]

William Sterling Anderson- Anderson had been sentenced to 14 months in prison for a fraud conviction related to his mobile home business. The former South Carolina speaker pro tem had doctored customer credit records. Anderson was pardoned by Bill Clinton on January 20, 2001.[28]

David Marc Cooper- Cooper was convicted in 1992 of fraud in a case related to installing faulty brake shoes for army jeeps. Cooper was pardoned by Bill Clinton on January 20, 2001.

William Dennis Fugazy- Fugazy was a bigshot in the limousine business who was guilty of perjury and creditor fraud. Fugazy was pardoned by Bill Clinton on January 20, 2001.

Charles D. Ravenel- Ravenel was involved in Savings & Loan fraud with Citadel Federal Savings Bank, one of the

---

(27) Ibid., p. 163.
(28) Ibid., p. 163, along with the following 2 pardons.

largest bank frauds in South Carolina's history. Ravenel was once a Democratic senatorial candidate. Ravenel was pardoned by Bill Clinton on January 20, 2001.[29]

Christopher V. Wade- Wade was a real estate agent connected to Whitewater. He was guilty of concealing assets in a bankruptcy proceeding and fraud not related to Whitewater. Wade was pardoned by Bill Clinton on January 20, 2001.

Stanley Pruet Jobe- Jobe was convicted of check kiting. Jobe was pardoned by Bill Clinton on January 20, 2001.

Stuart Harris Cohn- Cohn was found guilty of commodities fraud back in 1979. Cohn was a brother-in-law of former Democratic representative Sam Gedjenson. Cohn was pardoned by Bill Clinton on January 20, 2001.

William Arthur Borders- Borders was convicted of bribing a judge. Borders was pardoned by Bill Clinton on January 20, 2001.

Richard Pezzopane- Pezzopane was convicted of bribing a judge. Pezzopane was pardoned by Bill Clinton on January 20, 2001.

Michael James "Jimmie" Rogers- Rogers, a county sheriff, had pled guilty to taking bribes from organized crime interests involved in illegal gambling.

---

(29) Ibid., p. 164, as are the following 9 pardons.

Leonard Browder- Browder was guilty of Medicaid fraud and illegally dispensing controlled substances. Browder was pardoned by Bill Clinton on January 20, 2001.

Robert Michael Williams- Williams was found guilty of fraud related to foreign securities. Williams was pardoned on January 20, 2001.

Joseph A. Yasak- Yasak was a Chicago police sergeant who was convicted of lying to a grand jury. Yasak was pardoned by Bill Clinton on January 20, 2001.

Billy Wayne Warmath- Warmath was guilty of minor credit card fraud. He had committed credit card fraud in the amount of $123.16! Warmath actually served a year and one day in jail for this act! Yet Marc Rich, who also got a pardon from Clinton, defrauded the government of $27 million in taxes and never served a day in jail! Warmath was pardoned by Bill Clinton on January 20, 2001.[30]

Lies told by Hillary- Braswell Pardon

When Hillary Clinton said she did not know of her brother Hugh's influence in obtaining the pardon of embezzler Almon Glenn Braswell, she simply lied.

Bill Clinton, Hillary Clinton, *and* Hugh Rodham were all at the White House on the very day the pardon was signed- January 20, 2001. *Two days after Braswell received his pardon from Bill Clinton, he wired $200,000 to Clinton's*

---

(30) Ibid., p. 165

brother-in-law (Hillary's brother) Hugh Rodham, in payment for his help in arranging the pardon.

A top source in the Justice Department told the "National Enquirer":

"Hillary knew that her brother was involved in trying to get pardons from the President. And this wasn't the first time Hugh was involved trying to get a pardon from his brother-in-law...Hugh Rodham was in the White House and Oval Office when the President was signing pardons on Friday, January 19, and again on the morning of January 20...I've been told Hugh Rodham actually delivered the pardon petition for Glenn Braswell, which was made out by lawyer Kendall Coffey, directly to the President."[31]

Miami attorney John B. Thompson was so outraged by the conduct of Hugh Rodham and the Clintons that he filed a grievance against Hugh Rodham with the Florida Bar. According to Thompson, "If she (Hillary) knew what Hugh was doing, Hillary could be considered a co-conspirator in a felony- her brother charging tens of thousands of dollars an hour, which in effect is a bribery rate!"[32]

Hillary's comment on the role her brother played in the pardons:

"I did not know my brother was involved in any way in any of this."[33]

---

(31) National Enquirer, March 13, 2001, p. 48-49.
(32) Ibid., p. 48-9.
(33) Ibid., p. 48-9.

Salim B. Lewis

Lewis was pardoned by Bill Clinton on January 20, 2001. This white-collar criminal who pled guilty to stock manipulation was represented by Bill Clinton's former classmate and roommate from college, Douglas Eakley.[34]

Edward Downe, Jr.- was found guilty of insider trading. Downe had been a donor to Hillary Clinton's Senatorial campaign. The S.E.C. was highly critical of Bill Clinton's pardon of Downe.[35]

Charles Morgan III- convicted of conspiracy to distribute cocaine. Pardoned by Bill Clinton on January 20, 2001. Morgan received legal assistance from former associate counsel and Rose Law firm partner William H. Kennedy. [36]

David C. Owen- a Republican who had been convicted of filing a fraudulent tax return. His final day pardon came after assistance from attorney James Hamilton, who had been Vince Foster's lawyer and an adviser to Bill Clinton. Hamilton received notoriety for refusing to reveal his final conversations with Foster to the independent counsel.[37]

Susan McDougal- former partner with the Clintons in Whitewater and alleged part-time girlfriend of Bill Clinton (according to her late husband) was pardoned by Bill Clinton

---

(34) Barbara Olson, "The Final Days," pp. 159
(35) Ibid., p. 159.
(36) Ibid., p. 159.
(37) Ibid., p. 159

on January 20, 2001. McDougal went to jail for 18 months for refusing to give sworn testimony against Bill and Hillary. This despite the fact that she had been ordered to testify by a federal grand jury from Arkansas![38]

Stephen Smith, who had been convicted in the Whitewater investigation and had been an aide to Governor Bill Clinton received a final day pardon.[39]

In all, Bill Clinton pardoned 24 people from Arkansas. Of all of Clinton's pardons, 47 were granted without being reviewed by the office of the pardon attorney of the Department of Justice. The pardons of Henry Cisneros, Susan Mc Dougal, and Roger Clinton were in that group.

Convicted spy Jonathan Pollard felt betrayed that he didn't receive a pardon. He told the Israeli newspaper Yediot Aharanoth that he was wrong in "waving the flag of Israel." He said "I should have waved a dollar bill in front of them and convinced them that I had a lot of money."[40]

Musician Ry Cooder had been fined $25,000 by the Treasury Department in 1999 for not obtaining the proper permit to travel to Cuba. Cooder applied for a legal permit in August, 2000. In September 2000 he gave $10,000 to the Senate campaign of Hillary Clinton. He received his permit on January 17, 2001.

---

(38) Ibid., p. 160
(39) Ibid., p. 160.
(40) Ibid., p. 166.

Naturally, Hillary and Cooder denied there was any link between the permit and the $10,000 he gave her campaign.[41]

The Pardons and Influence Buying- Why has no one brought up bribery charges?

I have already mentioned that Hillary's brother Hugh Rodham received $200,000 for his help in getting Bill Clinton to pardon Almon Glenn Braswell. Convicted drug dealer Carlos Vignali also paid $200,000 to Rodham for help with his pardon. We'll get to Vignali in a little while, but suffice it to say that he was a big-time drug dealer. He was busted for the sale of **500 pounds of crack cocaine!** And make no mistake about it. Worms like Vignali ruin the lives of hundreds of thousands of our vulnerable young people, who for some misguided reason see drug running as a quick way to score lots of quick cash.

One of the greatest myths circulated by the left is that drug usage is a "victimless" crime. That is total nonsense. I have seen drugs ravage members of my family and close friends. In my opinion, dealers of drugs like cocaine and heroin are about as evil as anyone out there. They prey on vulnerable people, make them into addicts, and slowly drag the life out of their victims.

Yet Bill Clinton had no problem pardoning one of the biggest drug dealers in the Federal prison system, just because his daddy was a big contributor to the Democratic party!

---

(41) Ibid., p. 167

(In fact, after the details of the Vignali pardon became known to me, I immediately left the Democratic party). The acts of Hugh Rodham with respect to Braswell and Vignali were so foul that Miami attorney John B. Thompson filed a grievance with the Florida Bar. "The fact that that these are clearly excessive fees to Mr. Rodham, wholly insupportable, apparently, by the hours spent, increases the likelihood that these were not fees but rather bribes. If Hillary knew what Hugh was doing, **Hillary could be considered a co-conspirator in a felony- her brother charging tens of thousands of dollars per hour, which is in effect a bribery rate!**"[42]

Another of Clinton's conquests in the bedroom was Denise Rich. Her ex-husband, Marc Rich, was probably the most outrageous of all the people to receive a pardon. This fugitive from American justice was wanted for bilking the U. S government of $48 **million in taxes!** Rich was also involved in illegal arms trades with countries such as Iran. The billionaire lived the life of a king in Switzerland, as he thumbed his nose at the American authorities who wanted to prosecute him. In short, Marc Rich, who made the FBI's Most Wanted List for International Fugitives, was a perfect candidate for a pardon from the scumbag Bill Clinton!

But wait, it gets much more interesting. Denise Rich was a frequent visitor to the White House. According to one insider, Denise Rich visited the White House scores of times as a guest of the President. She had access to the Oval office and the private living quarters. Often, Rich and Bill Clinton were observed kissing and holding hands. It was common

---

(42) National Enquirer, March 13, 2001, pp. 48-9.

knowledge among staff at the White House that Bill and Denise had a much closer relationship than "just good friends." She actually boasted to friends about her escapades with Clinton.

Denise Rich was certainly not the only sexy lady who visited the White House when Hillary was out of town. But as one Washington socialite stated: "Of course Bill slept with Denise." Bill told a friend that Denise reminded him a little of Gennifer Flowers.[43]

Anyone who says anything against the Clintons is part of the "vast right-wing conspiracy." Anyone who finds fault in the sordid methods used by the Clintons has an agenda. They, on the other hand, are always right and never wrong. Give me a break. It's about time the Clintons were exposed for who they truly are - a bunch of cons who ought to be making our license plates!

The Terrorists Pardoned By Bill Clinton!

Bill Clinton gave pardons to members of a Puerto Rican terrorist group- FALN- who were responsible for bombings and killings in Chicago, New York City, and D.C. At least 6 people were killed in the bombings, and scores more were injured!

Yet intense lobbying on the part of Puerto Rican legislators such as Jose Serrano (D-NY) turned these terrorists- no different from the Al Qaeda- into political prisoners. Furthermore, it is quite likely that the clemency Bill Clinton granted to these terrorists may have been linked

---

(43) Ibid., pp. 48-9.

to Hillary Clinton's desire to woo the Puerto Rican vote in her November 2000 Senatorial bid.

U.S. Attorney **Joe DiGenova** spoke about Bill Clinton's actions with respect to the Puerto Rican terroroists. "Let me just say, categorically, the Puerto Rican terrorists were pardoned because they were a political benefit to the President's wife. Make no mistake about it. There is no justification for these pardons.[44]

There were so many final day commutations and pardons by Bill Clinton (176 in all) that it is very easy to pass some of them by. But let me tell you about the commutation of **Susan Rosenberg.** Sue Rosenberg was an active participant in a violent leftist group called the **Weather Underground.** In October 1981, her group held up a Brink's truck in Nanuet, NY, killing guard Peter Paige and two police officers Edward O'Grady and Waverly Brown (an African-American policeman). Rosenberg drove the getaway car and escaped.[45]

The Weather Underground was part of a group of related splinter groups that predominated throughout the 60's, 70's and 80's throughout the country. Groups such as the Weather Underground, the Black Liberation Army, the Red Guerrilla Resistance, and the May 19th Communist Organization comprised "the Family."

The Family was responsible for the bombing of the U.S. Capitol on November 7, 1983. Other targets of "the Family" included the South African consulate in New York City, the

---

(44) Barbara Olson, "The Final Days," p. 19.
(45) Ibid., p. 21-23.

Naval War College at Fort McNair, the Washington Navy Yard's computer center, the Israeli Aircraft Industries Center, and the Patrolmen's Benevolent Association in New York.[46]

Sue Rosenberg was involved in aiding the escape from prison of Joanne Cheismand, who was given a life sentence for murdering a State trooper from New Jersey. In 1984, police apprehended Rosenberg unloading 640 pounds of explosives at a Cherry Hill, New Jersey warehouse. Rosenberg referred to the explosives as "combat material." In addition, she was found to own 14 firearms, an Uzi submachine gun, and fake ID!

In short, Susan Rosenberg was a terrorist! **T-E-R-R-O-R-I-S-T!**[47]

I am not interested in the whining defenses of the spoiled brats of the 60's and 70's who went on their killing sprees. The wives and children of Peter Paige, Edward O'Grady, and Waverly Anderson are not in any way consoled by Sue Rosenberg's "struggle" against apartheid in South Africa! As far as I am concerned, none of these terrorists who killed totally innocent people should be looked at as anything but cold-blooded killers!

Yet Susan Rosenberg claimed to be a "political prisoner". Consider the T-shirts Rosenberg wore during her trial: "Support New African Freedom Fighers" and "What is a Nation Without an Army?" Rosenberg claimed she was a "revolutionary", not a criminal. Throughout her trial she invoked the "struggles" in the Middle East and Central

---

(46) Ibid., pp. 21-23.
(47) Ibid., p. 21-23.

America. Rightfully, a jury with some common sense sentenced this beast Susan Rosenberg to 58 years in prison![48]

The late Barbara Olson outlines the details of Sue Rosenberg's crime spree in her book "The Final Days". According to Olson, after Rosenberg was sentenced she proclaimed "Long live armed struggle. By taking up action to attack South Africa, the United States military, the war profiteers, and the police, we begin to enact proletarian internationalism."[49] Olson pointed out that Rosenberg signed her letters from jail "Venceremos" (We will conquer.)

Over the years, Sue Rosenberg became a hero for the Left. Morons such as Noam Chomsky and William Kuntsler lobbied for her release. Super liberal and Clinton buddy Congressman Jerrold Nadler (D-NY) went on "60 Minutes" arguing for the release of Sue Rosenberg.[50] And it worked-Bill Clinton commuted the sentence of cop-killer Susan Rosenberg on January 20, 2001.

You might ask: what kind of a home did Susan Rosenberg come from? Was she from the working class? Was she impoverished? Did she ever have to struggle for anything in her life? Did she go to public high school and state universities? If you answered "yes" to *any* of the previous questions, you would be wrong. Susan Rosenberg grew up in an upper-middle class Jewish home. Her father Emmanuel Rosenberg was a successful dentist on the upper

---

(48) Ibid., p. 22-23.
(49) Ibid., p. 23.
(50) Ibid., p. 23.

Westside of Manhattan. Susan Rosenberg attended the Walden School (a private school) and Barnard College!

After Barnard, she worked with the Young Lords and the Black Panthers in a drug counseling program.

Susan Rosenberg, who received clemency from Bill Clinton, was also known as "Barbara Grodin." She once proudly stated: "I rob banks with black people."[51]

Some politicians were outraged by the special treatment given to terrorist and cop-killer Susan Rosenberg. Former New York City Mayor Rudolph Giuliani and my old friend, the senior U.S. Senator from New York Charles Schumer were shocked by Clinton's actions. Kathy Boudin, another terrorist, recently won her freedom from prison.

To this day, I am waiting for an apology to the families of the victims from Susan Rosenberg. To this day I am waiting for one word of remorse on her part. Let me know if you hear anything.

There is a direct link between the Sue Rosenbergs of this world and the Bill and Hillary Clintons of this world. Like Sue Rosenberg, Hillary Clinton went to a top private college (Wellesley). Like Sue Rosenberg, Hillary Clinton worked for and sympathized with the cop killers in the Black Panthers. And like Sue Rosenberg, Bill and Hillary Clinton grew up in that generation that said to the world: "If it feels good, do it...Cops are pigs- free the people."

Unfortunately, I graduated from two top universities – Brandeis and Cornell- during that era, and I went to school

---

(51) Ibid., p. 22

with the Sue Rosenbergs, the Hillary Clintons, the Bill Clintons, and the Jerrold Nadlers. They are nothing but a bunch of frauds, and I am embarrassed by their fake political ideologies!

My condolences to the victims of the crimes of Sue Rosenberg, the Weather Underground, and the Black Panthers. Shame on you, Bill Clinton, for freeing this terrorist!

Reaction to the Clinton Pardons

Former President Jimmy Carter said this of the pardons: "I think President Clinton made one of his most serious mistakes in the way he handled the pardon situation the last few hours he was in office...A number of them were quite questionable, including about 40 not recommended by the Justice Department." Speaking of the Marc Rich pardon, Carter said: "I don't think there is any doubt that some of the factors in his pardon were attributable to his large gifts. In my opinion, that was disgraceful."[(52)]

DNC member Paul Goldman was head of the Virginia Democratic party. He said of the Clinton pardons: "Mr. Clinton didn't just take the White House china; he took its soul and flushed it down the toilet."[(53)]

California Senator Diane Feinstein said: "I certainly believe that in the case of criminal pardons a president should vet those pardons, not only with the Department of Justice,

---

(52) Ibid., p. 169.
(53) Ibid., p. 170.

with the line prosecutor, with judges, with victims- and we saw that in the Puerto Rican case where none of the victims were consulted, and there was broad concern about those pardons. I have concerns not only about the Rich pardon but with a number of the criminal pardons."[54]

Another Democratic Senator, Charles Schumer (NY) said: "To my mind, there can be no justification for pardoning a fugitive from justice. It does not matter that the fugitive believed the case against him was flawed or weak. It does not matter that the fugitive was enormously philanthropic. Pardoning a fugitive stands our justice system on its head and makes a mockery of it. One of the great strengths of our criminal justice system is that it is just that, a system. By allowing someone to opt out of that system by fleeing and then opt into that system to get a pardon perverts the system entirely."[55]

In his sworn testimony, pardon attorney Roger Adams testified that he was told Marc Rich was "living abroad"; he had no idea Rich was under indictment and a fugitive from justice.[56]

Even superliberal Democratic Congressman Henry Waxman was sharply critical of Bill Clinton and his last minute pardons. "The failures in the pardon process should embarrass every Democrat and every American. It's a shameful lapse of judgment that must be acknowledged...[57]

---

(54) Ibid., p. 183.
(55) Ibid., p. 183-184.
(56) Ibid., p. 184.
(57) Ibid., p. 189

Bill Clinton Defends his Pardons

In a disgraceful op-ed piece in the "New York Times" of February 18, 2001, Bill Clinton presented his case for the wholesale round of pardons to the coke dealers, swindlers, and international fugitives that he pardoned. In a shocking essay, Clinton somehow justified Rich's pardon based on the significant influence that Rich had in the American and world Jewish community! This is exactly how the final reason for pardoning FBI fugitive Marc Rich was justified by Bill Clinton:

"Many present and former high-ranking Israeli officials of both major political parties and leaders of Jewish communities in America and Europe urged the pardon of Mr. Rich because of his contributions and services to Israeli charitable causes, to the Mossad's efforts to rescue and evacuate Jews from hostile countries, and to the peace process through sponsorship of education and health programs in Gaza and the West Bank...[58]

The fact that Marc Rich had donated millions to Israeli causes and Denise Rich had donated $1.2 million to the Democratic National Committee, $75,000 to Hillary's Senatorial campaign, and $450,000 to the Clinton Library had nothing to do with Marc Rich's pardon. Of course Bill had to say this, to keep himself out of prison. To me, the Rich pardon is a simple case of bribery, and Bill and Hillary Clinton both belong in prison for their acceptance of cash, in exchange for pardoning one of the FBI's most wanted international fugitives!

---

(58) Ibid., p. 172-173.

Naturally, Bill claimed he knew nothing and was totally innocent of any wrongdoing. "The suggestion that I granted the pardons because Mr. Rich's former wife, Denise, made political contributions and contributed to the Clinton library foundation is utterly false. There was absolutely no quid pro quo."[59]

Hillary on the pardons: I was So Disappointed and I Know Nothing

Hillary's comments in the wake of the pardons were a joke. Here is a woman who controlled virtually every millisecond of her husband's Presidency and she knew nothing about anything. Conveniently, Hillary had no knowledge of her brothers' taking money to arrange pardons. Of course Hillary had to say this to stay out of prison. Hillary had to deny any involvement in her brothers' affairs; her ass was on the line!

Here is a transcript of Hillary's comments on the pardons:

"Well I was **very disappointed** and saddened by this whole matter. You know, it came as a surprise to me, and it was very disturbing. And **I'm just very disappointed** about it," Hillary whined in a news conference. "With respect to any questions about the pardons or the president's handling

---

(59) Ibid., pp. 172-173. This lie from the same character who told America: "I did not have sex with that woman Miss Lewinsky." Why is this lie any different than any of the of the thousands of lies from the perverted mind of Bill Clinton?

178

of the pardons, you'll have to ask him or his staff about that."[60]

"You know, I did not have any involvement in the pardons that were granted or not granted, you know, and I'm **just very disappointed** about my brother's involvement."

"You know, as I have said in the past, when it became apparent around Christmas that people knew that the president was considering pardons, there were many, many people who spoke to me or, you know, asked me to pass on information to the White House Counsel's Office. I've already said that I did that, and I did. There were many, many people who had an interest, a friend, a relative, but it was all passed on to the White House Counsel's Office, and they, along with the president, made the decisions."

"If I had known about this, we wouldn't be standing here today. **I didn't know about it,** and I'm very regretful that it occurred, that I didn't know about it. I might have been able to prevent this from happening. And I'm just **very disappointed** about the whole matter."

"**I don't know anything** other than what has now come out, and I did not learn about that until very recently."

"**I did not know** my brother was involved in any way in any of this. I learned that there were some press inquiries, of a vague nature, last week sometime."

---

(60) Ibid., p. 176-179. All of the following quotes are from Olson's "The Final Days."

"I did not know any specific information until late Monday night. I was actually in a movie theater, and I was called and told that my brother had been involved and had taken money for his involvement...As soon as I found out, I was very upset about it, and **very disappointed** about it."

[My brother] was a frequent guest at the White House. You know, he's my brother. (Author's note: **unlike the song, in this case he *is* heavy!"**) I love my brother. I'm just **extremely disappointed** in this terrible misjudgment that he made."

"As soon as we found out Monday night, I was heartbroken and shocked by it, and, you know, immediately said that this was a terrible misjudgment and the money had to be returned. And that's what we worked on."

"I was reacting as someone who was **extremely disappointed** in this whole matter. This was a very sad occurrence to have happen. And I wanted to be sure that the money was returned, and it has been."

"Let me use my own words, and my own words are that **I'm very disappointed**, I'm very saddened, and I was very disturbed when I heard about it."

"[It's] very regrettable, and it shouldn't have happened. And if I'd had any knowledge or notice of it, I believe I might have been able to prevent it. I don't think we'd be standing here talking about it. But I did not."

"You know, **I'm very disappointed** about what's gone on for the last weeks. It is certainly not how I would have preferred or planned to start my Senate career, and I regret deeply that there has been these kinds of matters occurring."

"I have my hands full being a senator, learning the ropes, you know, working with my colleagues, and I love doing it. I'm having a really good time doing it, but, of course, **I'm disappointed** and saddened that, you know, these matters are up."

"Obviously, I wish that the last weeks had unfolded differently, and I'm very sorry that they have not. But all I can say is now I've got a position and a responsibility that I'm going to do my very best to fulfill to the very best of my ability. And people will have to judge me at the end of my term based on what I do, and that's what I'm going to ask people to do."

"I really think that everything has to be put in context. And I know that that's often difficult to do, but I feel that our country is stronger and better because of the Clinton administration."

"You know, I don't have any memory at all of ever talking to my brother about this. You know, that's my best memory. But I have to say, and I will repeat once again, information was coming to me, information was passed on. So, you know, if I said information came, people wanted to look at, I might have said that. I just don't remember anything other than that."

I knew nothing about my brother's involvement in these pardons. I **knew nothing** about his taking money for his involvement. I had no knowledge of that whatsoever."

"You know, I mean, I've said that I think my brother made a terrible misjudgment."

"I personally don't have any information."[61]

Denise Rich had spoken with the White House about Marc Rich's pardon. Jack Quinn and Beth Dozoretz were in on getting the Rich pardon. But Hillary knew nothing, didn't say a word about pardons to anyone. This from a loud-mouthed obnoxious woman who got into everyone's face at every opportunity. Suddenly she knew nothing and remembered nothing about anything she might have known.

According to Hillary, she never knew Marc Rich. She knew nothing about Rich's pardon. When asked about future problems from the pardons, Hillary "didn't have any information." Hillary said that the fact that her brother received $400,000 had nothing to do with the Braswell and Vignali pardons arranged by Bill Clinton. "There was no connection...But again, with respect to any of these decisions. You'll have to talk with people who were involved in making them, and that leaves me out. I don't know enough to answer your questions. And I don't want to say anything that leads you to believe that I either know something or don't know something, because I don't. And so you'll have to ask people who were involved in them."[62]

The editorial staff of "The New York Times" didn't buy into Bill Clinton's justification for the pardons.. The Times

---

(61) Ibid., p. 176-179.
(62) Ibid., pp. 179-181.

was concerned that "Mr. Clinton was discussing Mr. Rich's case with major contributors to his party while he kept the Department of Justice in the dark about his consideration of a pardon for one of the nation's most famous tax fugitives." The Times did not believe Bill Clinton's claim that there was 'absolutely no quid pro quo' with respect to the Rich pardon. There remained a "tangle of lobbying, public relations and legal activities depicted in E-mails among Ms. Rich, Beth Dozoretz, a former finance chairwoman of the Democratic National Committee, and Jack Quinn, the former White House counsel who became Mr. Rich's lawyer."[63]

According to the "New York Times", "the story of this pardon begins and ends with money and the access afforded by money."

Journalist Michael Kelly was hardly a conservative. He had closely covered Bill Clinton in the 1992 campaign and wrote for the "Atlantic Monthly." In the "Washington Post of February 21, 2001, Kelly called Bill Clinton's defense of the Rich pardon **"in almost every important way a lie."** True, other Presidents had issued controversial pardons, but no one had ever opened the doors to the prisons like Bill Clinton did! Speaking of the other Presidents, Kelly wrote: "None sought to corrupt the pardoning process on a wholesale basis. None set up a secret shop to bypasss his own government and speed through the special pleas of the well connected and the well heeled. None sent the Justice Department dozens of names for pardon on inauguration

---

(63) Ibid., pp. 173-174

morning, too late for the department to run even cursory checks."[64]

Beth Dozoretz had been a prodigious fundraiser for the Clintons. She pledged $1 million dollars to the Clinton Library. She held a fundraiser at her mansion where she raised $1 million for Bill Clinton. Beth had been speaking with Bill Clinton and knew all about Jack Quinn's E- mails which said the President **"wants to do it"** and urged Denise Rich to speak to Bill about Marc Rich's pardon!

Denise Rich knew all about the pardon of her ex-husband Marc Rich. Denise had contributed millions to the Clintons. She had been in touch with Bill Clinton on an ongoing basis right up to the day that Bill pardoned her ex, who had been wanted by the FBI for years!

So when the House Committee on Government Reform, which was investigating the pardons, sent Denise a list of 14 questions, she pled the 5th Amendment rather than admit her criminal wrongdoing in cahoots with Bill Clinton. **Denise refused to answer the following questions posed by the Committee:**

- Were all political contributions made by you between 1992 and the present made with your own money? (Author's note: A truthful answer might have indicated criminal acts by Bill Clinton, Marc and Denise Rich, and others)

- Were you ever provided with money by any individual so that you could make a political contribution?

---

(64) Ibid., p. 175.

How much money have you given or pledged to the Clinton Library?

Describe all contacts you have had with President Bill Clinton regarding your former husband, Marc Rich.

Did you ever discuss a pardon for Marc Rich with President Clinton? If so, describe the substance, place and time of such discussions.

Please list all gifts that you have given either to former president Clinton or to Senator Hillary Rodham Clinton.[65]

Denise Rich, one of the most knowledgeable people in the Democratic Party, who knew Bill Clinton intimately and was involved in the DNC for years, suddenly knew nothing about anything!

Denise Rich didn't even show up for the hearing investigating the dirty deeds surrounding Bill Clinton's pardon of her ex. Beth Dozoretz showed up, but she too pled the 5th to all the Committee's questions.

Similarly, Hillary Clinton knew nothing about anything. Hillary "never knew about Marc Rich at all." Hillary "knew nothing about the Marc Rich pardon until after it happened."
Hillary, a brilliant woman, graduate of Yale Law School, almost 20 years experience as an attorney, knew nothing…"I don't have any information…I don't know enough to answer your questions…And I don't want to say anything that leads

---

(65) Ibid., pp. 185-186.

you to believe that I either know something or don't know something, because I don't. And so you'll have to ask people who were involved in them."[66]   *(Author's note: provided those people don't plead the 5th amendment or somehow forget everything they knew!)*

Folks, now is a good time to scream!

---

(66) Ibid., pp. 180-181.

CHAPTER FIVE

Reason Number Six the Clintons Belong in Prison

(6) Travelgate- The firing of the White House Travel Office was a crime, masterminded, concealed, and denied by Hillary Clinton. The travel office people had been there in the White House for decades- Billy Dale had served for 30 years, prior to meeting the wrath of Hillary Clinton. The "crimes" alleged against Billy Dale were immediately thrown out by a jury of his peers, when he was acquitted. I think Hillary committed perjury, obstruction of justice, abuse of power, and quite possibly extortion and racketeering, prosecutable under the RICO act. I think Hillary Clinton deserves 3-5 years in prison for her criminal activity in Travelgate.

The Clinton Women

Bill Clinton and the Women

Some people call Bill Clinton charming.

I find him to be repulsive and disgusting. Bill Clinton is not just a womanizer- he is a sexual molester, a sexual criminal, a sexual predator, and - yes- a rapist!

Let's get right into it!

Clinton had a eleven-year affair with Gennifer Flowers. This affair was denied by Clinton, when Flowers went public with the details. There were audiotapes of Clinton and

Flowers talking about how to deny the affair. Clinton told her "All you got to do is deny it and hang tough…As long as everybody hangs in there, we're in the clear."[1]

Clinton's history with women is filled with examples of the behavior of a sexual predator. Going back to Paula Jones for a second, one can see what a sicko this guy Clinton was. According to Deborah Ballantine, another friend of Paula Jones, this was anything but a consensual act. Paula told her friend "Debbie, he pulled his pants down and asked me to suck his dick."[2] Upon running into State Trooper Danny Ferguson at a Little Rock restaurant, Paula Jones stressed to Ferguson that her story was 100% truthful. Said Ferguson: "I know it's all true, but everybody else doesn't. And he always gets away with it."[3]

Clinton has standard pickup lines with the women. And there were hundreds- perhaps thousands- of women that Clinton picked up over the years! One of Clinton's favorite approaches to women would be to go up to a woman reading a book- any book- and say "I can't believe you're reading this! This book changed my life!"[4] According to one of the troopers that procured women for Clinton, this line worked with lots of women. Many of the women Clinton hit on never became household names like Paula Jones. Take "Washington Post" reporter Laura Sessions Stepp, for example. At the Gridiron Dinner on March 23, 1994, Clinton hit on her. He wouldn't let go of her hand, even as she tried

---

(1) "Uncovering Clinton", by Michael Isikoff, p. 56
(2) Ibid., p. 42
(3) Ibid., p. 44
(4) Ibid., p. 24

to remove it. All of you ladies reading this know how uncomfortable this behavior can be. "You really have to come see me in Little Rock", Clinton told the attractive young journalist.[5] Stepp felt that Clinton was definitely coming on to her. She said she had shaken enough politicians' hands to know that this guy Clinton was different from the normal guy.

The Clinton campaign hired well-known private investigator Jack Palladino to help control "bimbo eruptions." It was decided that the Clinton White House would launch a comprehensive program of attacking and destroying the claims of any and all women who claimed to have been molested, attacked, or consensually involved with President Bill Clinton. Paula Jones was denounced as "trailer trash".

There was more than $100,000 in Clinton campaign money paid to Palladino. The initial payment of $ 28,000 was laundered through a Denver law firm, before being paid to Palladino's San Francisco detective agency. That fee was listed on the disclosure statements of the Federal Elections Committee as "legal fees."[6] It was Palladino's job to get to the many women who claimed to have had affairs with Clinton, before the tabloids did. Palladino would try to have these women sign affidavits denying any romantic involvement with Clinton. If the women didn't cooperate, he would try to destroy their credibility or question the woman's mental stability.[7]

---

(5) Ibid., p. 29-30
(6) Isikoff., p. 32
(7) Ibid., p. 31

Melrose Larry Green

Let's briefly consider Sally Perdue, whose name will pop up several times later on this book. Sally was a former Miss Arkansas, who had an affair with Bill Clinton back in 1983. Palladino killed a "National Enquirer" story about the affair by submitting to the tabloid signed statements by a couple of angry "associates and estranged family members" questioning her veracity. During the 1992 Presidential campaign, she was promised a Federal job if she would keep quiet about her affair with Bill Clinton. A witness who overheard the job offer also overheard this threat: "We can't guarantee what will happen to your pretty legs", if she declined the job offer.

When Clinton had an encounter with Connie Hamzy at a Little Rock pool party, the circumstances were very similar to those of the Paula Jones incident. Once again, a State Trooper approached the woman and acted as Bill Clinton's pimp. When Hamzy recounted the incident 7 years later in "Penthouse", Hillary Clinton said "We have to destroy her story."[8] A crooked lawyer named Michael Gaines was involved in trying to discredit Conny Hamzy. Gaines signed an affadavit saying that Hamzy's account was "fictional". Hamzy complained to Independent Counsel Ken Starr that Gaines received a nomination to serve as Chairman of the U.S. Board of Paroles as a reward for falsely discrediting Hamzy. Regrettably, Starr did no follow-up to this. Previously, Gaines was Governor Bill Clinton's attorney in charge of state pardons.[9]

---

(8) Ibid., p. 47
(9) Ibid., notes, p. 362

I want to briefly mention Kathleen Willey at this point, but don't worry, we will go into a lot more depth about her later on. Kathleen was a devoted supporter of Bill Clinton. She was groped by Bill Clinton, and she felt totally violated by America's 41st President. His advances were unwelcome, to say the least. As usual, the Clinton legal team and the Clinton spin machine went into action! According to Clinton attorney Robert Bennett, Clinton had a "very dim memory" of consoling Willey after her husband's death. Said Bennett: "It is preposterous to imagine that the President of the United States would make an improper advance toward this woman at the time he was consoling her about her husband's death."[10]

Mr. Bennett, you should have checked your calendar. Bill Clinton molested Kathleen Willey on November 29, 1993. Her husband's dead body wasn't discovered until November 30, 1993.

As far as Bill Clinton knew, Kathleen Willey's husband was very much alive on the evening of November 29, 1993, when he groped and molested Ms. Willey.[11]

Clinton's lawyer begged Michael Isikoff not to write about the Kathleen Willey incident in *Newsweek*. "Don't write this story. Don't write it. The punishment is too great. The president doesn't deserve this."[12]

Mr. Bennett, I think he does deserve it!

---

(10) Ibid., p. 159
(11) Ibid., p. 159
(12) Ibid., p. 160

P.S. - ABC, NBC, CBS, CNN, "Washington Post" and "The New York Times" all ignored the Kathleen Willey story at first.[13]

Paula Jones

Paula Jones alleged that when Bill Clinton invited her to his room in a Little Rock hotel, he "lowered his trousers and underwear, exposing his erect penis, and asked Ms. Jones to "kiss it." This is how Paula Jones described the First Penis: it was "five to five and one-half inches, or less, in length…a circumference of the approximate size of a quarter, or perhaps very slightly larger"…it was "bent or crooked from Mr. Clinton's right to left, or from an observer's left to right, if the observer is facing Mr. Clinton."[14]

After the Lewinsky affair became public knowledge, Bill Clinton sank to an emotional low point. Hillary wasn't speaking to him. Bill would talk to Buddy the dog and confide his innermost thoughts to him. According to a close friend, Clinton's eyes were red from crying, he was quite possibly suicidal, and the White House was a very tense place.[15]

A close friend of Clinton said: "We all feared for the worst. If he had been in jail, there would have been a suicide watch. There's no doubt the Secret Service guys were

---

(13) Ibid., p. 161
(14) Oppenheimer, p. 259
(15) Ibid., p. 263.

ordered to keep a tight guide on him, to watch for any acute signs."[16]

Why don't we do it in the bushes?

Back in 1980, Bill Clinton had a fling with a former campaign volunteer. According to long-time acquaintance of the Clintons Peach Pietrefesa, "He [Bill] was fucking a married woman in the bushes in the summer of 1980. He'd go jogging and meet her. She was a former campaign volunteer who wasn't getting along with her husband. Bill would come home and talk about her to Hillary: 'Don't you think she's fabulous? She is such an incredible...Hillary knew what he was doing and got pissed."[17]

After Bill would cheat on Hillary, he would feel remorseful and penitent. Until the cycle repeated itself and he cheated again. Bill always promised that was the last time, until the next girl came along.

According to state trooper Captain Larry Gleghorn, Hillary was rude and inconsiderate with the security detail. "She never offered us a cup of coffee. She was like a robot. Her actions were that way to anybody who wasn't on her level. You were just in her way."[18]

Hillary had a mouth like a sewer. Back in 1974, she was telling Bernie Nussbaum, her buddy from the Watergate days, about how Bill was going to be President someday.

---

(16) Ibid., p. 263
(17) Gail Sheehy, "Hillary's Choice," pp. 149-150.
(18) Ibid., p. 154.

Nussbaum felt it was ridiculous that Hillary would say her boyfriend Bill would become President of the U.S. Hillary's response: "You asshole, Bernie, you're a jerk. You don't know this guy. So don't pontificate to me. He is going to be president of the United States."[19]

She was right.

One of Bill Clinton's flings during his failed campaign for Congress in 1974 was with a young lady that everyone in the Fayetteville office called "the college girl." This woman was infatuated with Bill Clinton. Bill tried to get "the college girl" to back off. He told his campaign manger Paul Fray: "You need to get Mary Lee to get to know this girl. See what Mary Lee can do to slide her on off down the road. Do you think she could be your baby-sitter to keep her out of headquarters?"[20]

Paul Fray and his wife had lots of arguments over "the college girl." When Hillary would come in the front door, Fray would hustle the college girl out the back door. Once Paul Fray confronted Hillary over the rumor that she was a lesbian. Hillary told Fray: "It's nobody's goddamn business. Fuck this shit!"[21]

State trooper Larry Patterson recalls the morning of Labor Day, 1991. Hillary drove out of the Governor's mansion in her blue Olds Cutlass. Just a minute or two later, Hillary returned to the mansion, yelling at Patterson: "Where is the

---

(19) Ibid., p. 91
(20) Ibid., p. 111
(21) Ibid., p. 112

goddamn fucking flag? I want the goddamn fucking flag up every fucking morning at fucking sunrise."[22]

Not to be outdone, there was the time a state trooper wanted an autographed photo of Governor Bill Clinton. Bill Clinton's reaction: "I don't have time for that shit."[23]

Hillary wasn't the most popular person in town. When the Democratic State party convention was held in Hot Springs, Arkansas in 1974, the campaign did not reserve a hotel room for Hillary, and Bill's mother would not let Hillary stay at her house. Hillary was not really wanted in Hot Springs. Once she found a list of Bill's favorite girlfriends and she "tore it to shreds."[24]

Hillary Rodham was a "plain Jane", compared to most of the women who had been Bill's girlfriends. When Clinton family friend Paul Fray first set eyes on Hillary, he was shocked. Taking in Hillary's bad hair, bad glasses, and tacky wardrobe, Fray said: "I thought, my God, Bill Clinton, you son of a bitch- you could have any damn woman on the face of the earth, and you brought one who looks like the south end of a mule going north."[25] "She had these whiskey-jigger-bottom glasses, thick lens, and she had on a prairie league dress, stuff of this nature. I said in my own mind, well he's marrying him a hippie."[26]

---

(22) Ronald Kessler, "Inside the White House," p. 246
(23) Ibid., p. 246.
(24) Sheehy, op. cit., p. 112
(25) Jerry Oppenheimer, State of a Union, p. 113
(26) Ibid., p. 114

Mary Lee Fray wrote to her mother about Hillary: "Mother, she's very plain, to the point you could call her homely. She would mix well in certain parts of Arkansas where they wear long clothes, no makeup." When Hillary went to visit Bill's mother, Viginia Kelley- she was poorly groomed, with dirty feet, unkempt hair, dirty clothes.[27]

In 1982, Hillary hired a private investigator to run down Bill's many affairs with women.[28] His name was **Ivan Duda.** This would not be the last time she would be checking up on his philandering.

According to state trooper Larry Gleghorn, Hillary could be a real bitch. "She was a bitch day in and day out. She always screamed we were taking the wrong route when we drove her to an event. She was a die-hard anti-smoker and most of us smoked. She hated it when we wore cowboy boots, with our uniforms. It made her furious. On official trips, you'd go to her room and say to her 'We have to leave in 15 minutes' and she'd snap 'we know it.' They'd be late and they'd give us a good cussing."[29]

Bill Clinton had a thing about beauty queens who read the news. During the fall of 1980, Bill had a thing with **Lencola Sullivan,** an African-American hotty who had earned the title of Miss Arkansas. We'll never know what went on behind closed doors, but Lencola and Bill were seen

---

(27) Ibid., pp. 114-115
(28) Joyce Milton, The First Partner, p. 142
(29) Ibid., p. 119

partying together all over Little Rock, during the time she was working as a reporter for KARK-TV in Little Rock.[30]

As I mentioned, Ivan Duda was a private investigator whom Hillary had hired to dig up dirt on Bill. According to author Joyce Milton, Duda had identified more than 6 women who had been involved with Bill Clinton back in 1982. Among them was a woman who worked on the paralegal staff of Rose Law Firm. Hillary wanted someone who could keep an eye on Bill to minimize his negative exposure in future political campaigns.[31]

Once, Hillary and Duda were meeting in a car at a parking lot. They were stopped by 2 state troopers, who ran a check on Duda's driver's license. Subsequently, Duda was charged with carrying a badge, which was against state law. Strangely, the leader of the State Police unit that had stopped Duda, Sgt. Bill Eddins, was killed in a one-car accident. Eddins' family suspected foul play, but Duda never pursued the case as he was retired from the private eye game.[32]

Did Sgt. Bill Eddins carry a secret about Bill Clinton to the grave? Why did Bill Eddins die?

L.D. Brown: State Trooper takes you inside Bill Clinton's World

Arkansas State Trooper L.D. Brown worked for Bill Clinton for many years. He knew Bill Clinton personally,

---

(30) Ibid., p. 118
(31) Ibid., p. 142
(32) Ibid., p. 143

and his book *Crossfire – Witness in the Clinton Investigation-*(Black Forest Press, 1999) is a fascinating read. It outlines the corruption and duplicity of Bill and Hillary Clinton, and it confirms what I have always felt- the Clintons belong in prison!

When L.D. Brown first met Hillary Clinton at the Arkansas State House, he had no idea who she was. Brown was confronted by a woman with "coke-bottle thick glasses, no makeup, and an awful fright-wig of a mop matched by a stinky scowl that shot bullets right my way."[33] At the time, the doors were all kept open, so the movers could transport the personal effects of the Clintons into the Governor's mansion. Hillary bellowed: "And this door here was open too, and by God I want to know why." Brown said to his co-worker: "Barry, who the hell is that bitch with the thick glasses in the breakfast room?" Barry replied: "L.D., you have just met Ms. Hillary Rodham."[34]

According to Brown, Bill Clinton would habitually pick his nose and wipe his snot on the seat of Brown's police car-("He [Bill] had an awful habit of, well, picking his nose and wiping it on my seat. I took care to make sure my unmarked car was kept clean since Bill and Hillary would be riding in it."[35] In addition, Bill Clinton would regularly release *"elephant farts"* right in the front seat of Brown's car. It didn't matter to Bill if female staffers were right there! ("Even when female staffers would be in the car with us traveling to an event, Bill would read and treat them like they

---

(33) L.D. Brown, Crossfire, p. 19
(34) Ibid., p. 19
(35) Ibid., p. 24

weren't there. If the nose picking wasn't bad enough, he would let out what could only be described as elephant farts right there in the front seat. I would crack the window and the staffer would just cringe. The eruption would sort of wake him from his reading trance and he would mumble something like, "What was that?")[36]

Bill Clinton gave away lots of memorabilia to L.D. Brown. One thing he gave Brown was a book Bill and Hillary used in Studying for the Bar Exam: the Nacrelli Bar Review School Book. Interestingly, the passages describing the legal definitions of "bribery", "adultery", "treason", "conspiracy", and "partnerships" were all highlighted or underlined by the Clintons. The statement: "As a general rule, no person can be compelled to be a witness against himself" was highlighted in red ink.[37]

There was only one section of the Bar Review book that was totally devoid of even one mark or highlight- The section on legal ethics! (For the skeptics, L.D. Brown has photocopies of the bar review book in the Appendix to "Crossfire.")[38]

Bill Clinton had the hots for Susan McDougal. He told L.D. Brown: "L.D. she looks good in those riding pants doesn't she? Tell you what, she looks even better out of them!"[39] According to Brown, Bill bragged of his sexual trysts with Susan McDougal, while dismissing her husband

---

(36) Ibid., p. 24
(37) Ibid., pp. 26-28
(38) Ibid., p. 28
(39) Ibid., p. 29

James McDougal as "one goofy son-of-a-bitch…but he sure is a cash cow."[40]

At one party in Little Rock, Bill Clinton had his eyes on a cute girl named Elizabeth, who had been a cast member of the TV show "Hee Haw." When Governor Bill Clinton found out that his Attorney General Steve Clark had moved in on the woman Bill wanted that night, Clinton said of his Attorney General: **"That son-of-a-bitch!"**[41]

There has been considerable talk about the unusual curvature of Bill Clinton's penis. State Trooper Brown recalled that when Bill Clinton would "take a leak" in the restroom at the guardhouse of the Governor's mansion. Then a very strange thing happened. "While leaving the door open, he would start to urinate when all of **a sudden the 'lid'** would fall and he would yell, "Damned L.D., I just ah, well ah I just spilled water on myself!"[42] Brown noted that as Clinton walked back into the room "he would be wiping the fluid from his pants and asking me if you could still see the stain."[43]

Bill Clinton once tried to seduce Brown's wife Becky. "He slouched down next to Becky and offered her a beer. Incredibly, he began his 'I'm so bad' routine with Becky! I had seen him use it time and time again to try to get a woman to comfort him- comforting which he would then manipulate into eventual sex. Becky got out of there in a hurry. When

---

(40) Ibid., p. 29
(41) Ibid., p. 32.
(42) Ibid., p. 34
(43) Ibid., p. 34

she told me of the incident, I wanted to take Bill out and administer the punishment to him that he has escaped from so many of the 'significant others' of the women he has used over the years."[44]

Sally Perdue

Bill Clinton had a steamy four-month affair with Sally Perdue back in 1983, when he was Governor of Arkansas. Perdue, a former Miss Arkansas, is now 62 years old. She told her story on the Sally Jesse Raphael Show. According to Perdue, Bill Clinton called her "Long Tall Sally" and played his saxophone as she sang to him "He's Just My Bill." Perdue claimed that Clinton ran around in her nightgown and did lines of cocaine.[45]

Perdue posed for Penthouse. Clinton private investigator Jack Palladino used his muscle to keep Sally Perdue quiet. In fact, she was warned by Clinton's political hit team not to talk to any media about her affair with Clinton. After she was summoned to testify against Clinton in the Paula Jones case, Perdue avoided giving sworn testimony by moving to China.

According to Ann Coulter, author of "High Crimes & Misdemeanors", Palladino called all of Perdue's relatives and friends. Finally he found one relative who had negative things to say about Perdue. Palladino made that relative available to the press, in an attempt to discredit Perdue's

---

(44) Ibid., p. 43
(45) "Globe," March 27, 2001, "All the President's Women-Where are they Now?" p. 37

prior claims about an affair with Bill Clinton. Except for her July 1992 appearance on "Sally Jesse Raphael", Perdue was basically ignored by the print and broadcast media.

Then things started to get scary for Sally Perdue. The Clinton hit team started intimidating and threatening Perdue. Suddenly, she started receiving strange phone calls, visits, and written communications. On August 19, 1992, a man visited her and told her that "keeping her mouth shut would be worthwhile".[46]

Perdue said: "If I was a good little girl, and didn't kill the messenger, I'd be set for life: a federal job...I'd never have to worry again. But if I didn't take the offer, then they knew that I went jogging by myself and he couldn't guarantee what would happen to my pretty little legs."[47]

Perdue did not take the federal job, but she was soon fired from her position in the office of admissions in Lindenwood, Missouri.

Bill Clinton would often find women at political fundraisers. After one such event, Hillary chewed Bill out in the limousine afterwards: Hillary's typical line was: "Hell Bill, why didn't you just go ahead and fuck her right there!"[48]

State trooper Larry Patterson maintains that Hillary had a similar line- at fundraisers, she would say to Bill: "Come on

---

(46) Anne Coulter "High Crimes and Misdemeanors," p. 81
(47) Ibid., p. 81
(48) L.D. Brown, op. cit., p. 44

Bill, put your dick up. You can't fuck her here."[49] Bill once asked Larry Patterson to bring the wife of a prominent judge to a going away ceremony at the Little Rock airport. As soon as Hillary saw the woman, she said to Patterson: "What the fuck do you think you're doing? I know who that whore is. I know what she's here for. Get her out of here."[50]

And let's not forget the time Larry Patterson was sitting in the guardhouse at the governor's mansion when he heard Bill and Hillary arguing on the audio monitor. Hillary told Bill: "I need to be fucked more than twice a year."[51]

One girl Clinton had his eyes on was very young- about 21. It turned out she was the daughter of the Clinton's county coordinator who had sponsored this particular fundraiser for Bill! Hillary never hesitated to publicly make a fool out of Bill. Once Bill asked Hillary: "In lawsuits against the states, who has original jurisdiction, Hillary?" Hillary responded: "Goddam it Bill, the Supreme Court, Bill!!!"[52] According to L.D. Brown, Hillary warned Bill never to ask such a dumb question around Brown ever again.

According to L.D. Brown, Robin Dickey, a statuesque brunette beauty queen, had been a lover of Bill Clinton's. Dickey was a married woman with three kids. Bill would sneak Robin into the Governor's mansion whenever Hillary was out of town. Bill would give instructions to L.D. Brown to bring Robin Dickey in through the back door and the back

(49) Ronald Kessler, Inside the White House, p. 245
(50) Ibid., p. 245
(51) Ibid., p. 245
(52) Brown, op. cit., p. 44

gate of the mansion. Eventually, Robin Dickey left her job as the Mansion Administrator, as soon as Hillary got wind of the affair. Like Monica Lewinsky, Robin Dickey ended up working at the Pentagon.[53]

Governor Bill Clinton would go out at night and behave like a rock star. Dumb women would flock around him at clubs. His standard pickup line was communicated to the eager ladies through trooper Brown: "Ask that one if she wants to dance with the Governor of Arkansas."[54]

If Clinton scored with a woman, he would give the State Troopers the 'high sign': "which consisted of an index finger pointing upward making a circular motion. That meant, 'Get the car, I'm ready to go, I've scored!'[55]

Bill didn't only abuse women- he mocked Hillary's two brothers, Hugh and Tony. The brothers were a little overweight; Bill called them "Huey and Louie", after the Disney duck characters.[56]

L.D. Brown felt that Vince Foster and Hillary Clinton were romantically linked with each other. Brown recalled one night at the Little Rock Chinese restaurant of Charlie Yah Lin Trie, where Vince and Hillary were together. According to Brown, "Vince and Hillary were looking like they were in the back of a '57 Chevy at the drive-in, Hillary

---

(53) Brown, op. cit., p. 46-7.
(54) Brown, op. cit., p.52.
(55) Brown, op. cit., p. 53.
(56) Brown, op. cit., p. 55

was kissing Vince like I've never seen her kiss Bill."[57] Other state troopers saw Vince and Hillary "French-Kissing" and saw him place a hand on her breasts and on her behind."[58] The state troopers took Hillary to meet Vince at a retreat maintained by the Rose Law Firm in Heber Springs.[59] That was their weekend getaway spot.

One of the most significant women in Bill Clinton's life was Beth Coulson. L.D. Brown described her as a 'kewpie doll with brains'.[60] She was a real soul mate for Bill Clinton. Beth Coulson was married (no kids) and lived in the fashionable Heights section of Little Rock, not even 15 minutes from the Governors' mansion. Hillary once said to L.D. Brown "I know personally that we have to get some things from other people that we cannot get in our own marriage."[61] She was referring to Bill's relationship with Beth Coulson. Often Bill Clinton would go to see Beth for a "mental or physical fix."[62]

When Hillary found out that she and Bill had been invited to George H.W. Bush's summer house in Kennebunkport, Maine, Hillary bellowed: "Fuck him Bill...He's Reagan's goddam Vice-President!"[63] L.D. Brown showed Hillary a photo of the trooper with Nancy Reagan. Seeing the picture

---

(57) Brown, op. cit., p. 63.
(58) Kessler, op. cit., p. 245
(59) Ibid., p. 245
(60) Brown, op. cit., p. 61
(61) Ibid., p. 64
(62) Ibid., p. 62.
(63) Ibid., p. 69.

of Trooper Brown and Ronald Reagan's wife, Hillary said: "You ought to burn the goddamned thing, L.D."[64]

I hope that every member of the law enforcement family reads this next account! After State Trooper Louis Bryant had been gunned down by a white supremacist, Bill Clinton attended the officer's funeral in Texarkana, Arkansas. A large group of law enforcement officers had gathered at a reception at the Ramada Inn after the funeral. L.D. Brown asked Bill Clinton if he wanted to express his condolences to **the law enforcement** officials, who had just lost one of their own. Bill Clinton's response was: "Fuck those ignorant sons-of-bitches, I don't want to go in there."[65]

Many a time L.D. Brown would pick up manila envelopes filled with cash from convicted cocaine dealer Dan Lasater's office in downtown Little Rock. The packages would be taken directly to Governor Bill Clinton. Often, Brown would pick up packages for Bill Clinton at the Little Rock Air Center or Central Flying Service. In all cases, the the manila package concealed what Brown "knew to be money. The same look, the same feel."[66]

One time actress Mary Steenburgen visited the Governors' mansion with her former husband Malcolm McDowell. According to L.D. Brown, Malcolm looked and acted weird: "he didn't speak, even when spoken to, and

---

(64) Ibid., p. 69
(65) Ibid., p. 73.
(66) Ibid., p. 76

looked to be in a daze." Bill Clinton turned to L.D. Brown and said: "Don't let that son-of-a-bitch near Chelsea."[67]

According to L.D. Brown, Hillary "could cuss like a sailor and the levels of her attacks knew no bounds."[68] One trooper, Mark Allen, was actually reduced to tears after suffering verbal abuse from Hillary Clinton. Many state troopers asked to be transferred to highway duty after just 1 day of being around Hillary! If Hillary didn't like a driver, she would beg L.D. Brown to keep "that fuckin' idiot away from her."[69]

And Hillary had nothing but contempt for the plain folks from Arkansas. Once Hillary was at a country fair with Bill, and they were pressing the flesh with the "common" people. Hillary said to L.D. Brown: "Goddam L.D., did you see that family right out of *Deliverance? Get me the hell out of here!*"[70]

It would be common practice for Bill Clinton to deliver shopping bags of cash to black preachers throughout Arkansas. That way they would be sure to get out the vote for Bill Clinton. "Cash money was placed in the hands of black ministers charged with making sure black voters reached the polling booth knowing how to vote and who to vote for. The preachers would even pass out what I called 'crib sheets' with 'Bill Clinton' on them for the illiterate

---

(67) Ibid., p. 79.
(68) Ibid., p. 84.
(69) Ibid., p. 84.
(70) Ibid., p. 85.

voter to use in finding the correct lever to pull, a sort of voting 'match game.'[71]

Speaking of Jim McDougal, who went to prison for his buddy Bill Clinton, Bill Clinton said: "L.D., He's one goofy son-of-a-bitch, but he's sure good for a lot of money."[72] Charming. This is how Bill Clinton talks about his business partner from Whitewater, a guy whose wife he banged on the side. One can only imagine what words Bill Clinton had for backers such as David Geffen, Steven Spielberg, and Jeffrey Katzenberg, if his remarks about Jim McDougal are any sort of guide.

Reverend Jesse Jackson once showed up at the Governor's mansion. Bill Clinton was far from happy to see Jesse. He told L.D. Brown: "Listen, L.D., I know this guy's an ass, but would you mind making some coffee for him and meeting him at the front door since there's no one else here?"[73]

A Mysterious Phone Call

Michael Isikoff received a chilling phone call from a woman who described what Bill Clinton once did to her in the same hideaway office in the White House where he groped and fondled Kathleen Willey. After the two chatted in his office, Clinton started grabbing her breasts and was trying to kiss her, as he did with Willey. She pulled back and tried to resist him. According to the woman, she finally

---

(71) Ibid., p. 87
(72) Ibid., p. 89
(73) Ibid., p. 91.

pushed Clinton away and "he finished the job himself" (i.e., he masturbated himself).

As the woman left the White House, Clinton acted as if nothing had transpired.

Yet Clinton kept calling the woman at work. Clinton would call her just to make small talk. This woman was married to a man who was a major figure in the Democratic party. The woman said:

"I haven't had a man take advantage of me like that. I haven't felt that way since high school." This woman knew of another woman who was also molested by Clinton. This 2nd woman was also afraid to come forward.[74]

Michael Isikoff, author of "Uncovering Clinton" was a seasoned journalist. Having written for "The Washington Post", "Newsweek", and "The N.Y. Times", Isikoff was definitely not a member of the "vast" right-wing conspiracy. He wondered "Who was this guy Clinton? What demons possessed him? And how many more of them were out there-women too terrified and too smart to open their mouths?"[75]

Clinton and Paula Jones

Paula Jones was working as a secretary-typist at the Arkansas Industrial Development Commission when she had her chance encounter with Governor Bill Clinton. Paula Jones was approached by Arkansas State Trooper Danny Ferguson, who had a message for Paula from the governor. "The governor said I made his knees knock."

---

(74) Ibid., Isikoff, p. 162-163.
(75) Ibid., p. 163

The year was 1991. The place was the Excelsior Hotel in Little Rock, Arkansas, where the Quality Management Conference was being held. Governor Bill Clinton summoned Paula Jones to his hotel room. According to Jones, this is what happened.

Clinton reached over and slipped his hands up her culottes. Jones was stunned. "What are you doing? What is going on? He was trying to nibble on my neck, and I was trying to back off. I said…I don't want to do this."[76]

Clinton said to Jones: "I was just noticing you downstairs. I was looking at your curves and the way you walked around the front of the table, and I love the way your hair came down your back, the middle of your back and your curves."[77]

According to Jones, Clinton's pants were down to his knees. He was fully erect and was pleading with her to give him a "blowjob" (a.k.a. "head", "oral").[78] I want it bad, said Clinton. At one point, he asked Paula Jones to "kiss it."[79] Jones stated that Clinton's face turned beet red.

Bill Clinton felt that oral sex was the safest sex because the stomach acids would interact with swallowed semen to kill the AIDS virus.[80] My, the President had such concern

---

(76) Isikoff. p. 22
(77) Ibid., p. 22
(78) Ibid., p. 22
(79) Ibid., p. 22
(80) Ibid., p. 24

and compassion for the women who were the receptacles of the first semen!

As Clinton's pants were down to his knees, he reassured Paula Jones that he didn't want to make her do anything she didn't want to do. Jones' reaction was "Oh wasn't that sweet of him? Asshole. That one little sayin' in there I guess will get him off the hook."[81]

When Paula Jones claimed that Bill Clinton tried to make her give him some head in that hotel room in Little Rock, the White House denied the story. According to George Stephanopoulos, Clinton did not even know Paula Jones. Said the White House aide "It's not true...it's just a cheap fundraising trick."[82]

According to a blistering, convincing piece in the November 1996 issue of "American Lawyer", Paula Jones' case was a strong one. Attorney Stuart Taylor (who graduated 1st in his class from Harvard Law School), wrote that Jones' claim of "predatory, if not depraved, behavior by Bill Clinton is far stronger than the evidence supporting Anita Hill's allegations of far less serious conduct by Clarence Thomas."[83]

Paula Jones had been an outstanding employee. Her supervisors praised her for being "anxious to please", having good "calligraphy skills", and a "cheerful personality on the phone." She had earned three pay raises and a job promotion

---

(81) Ibid., p. 23
(82) Ibid., p. 15
(83) Ibid., p. 103

(her salary had risen from $10,270 /year to $12,800/ year).[84] She went up to Clinton's room for one reason- she hoped it might result in her getting a raise. Paula Jones had bills to pay. She was a member of the working class- the people who years later would overwhelmingly vote to put George W. Bush in the White House.

Bill Clinton began his lying years ago. An examination of Clinton's experiences dodging the draft over 30 years ago gives you a revealing picture of just how devious and selfish a young Bill Clinton was. Clinton graduated from Georgetown University in 1968. At this time, the U.S. was heavily involved in the Vietnam war, which sharply escalated during the Democratic administration of President Lyndon Baines Johnson. Bill Clinton joined ROTC, to avoid being drafted. Clinton surrendered his ROTC status in 1969 and became "1-A" (eligible to be drafted) after pulling # 311 in the draft lottery. A high number like 311 almost guaranteed that Clinton would not be drafted to serve in Vietnam.

According to Clinton, he simply went through the draft lottery and got lucky by not having been called to military service.

Fact- Bill Clinton lied about his history with the draft. He claimed in an interview with Washington Post political reporter Dan Balz, that he was never drafted by the Selective Service. Clinton claimed that he expected to be drafted while at Oxford, but he never was.[85]

---

(84) Ibid., p. 45
(85) Ibid., p. 26

Fact- the Associated Press discovered William Jefferson Clinton's draft induction notice, dated April, 1969. So we have caught Clinton in a lie. When asked about this notice, Clinton responded his draft board told him it was a "routine notice" and he wouldn't have to report until that fall after he returned from Oxford. Clinton said "It just never occurred to me to make anything of it one way or the other." David Broder, noted "Newsweek" columnist, said "That's bullshit-nobody forgets their draft notice."[86]

Clinton enrolled in ROTC only after he had been classified 1-A. His sole purpose in joining ROTC was to avoid having to serve his country. Graduate school deferments had been eliminated, so ROTC seemed to be a convenient way for Clinton to avoid having to fight for his country in Vietnam. Clinton claimed that he gave up his ROTC status and became 1-A because he felt guilty that four of his classmates from high school had perished in Vietnam. So he asked to be put in the draft. In fact, Nixon had begun major troop withdrawals by the fall of 1969. The war was winding down. Clinton had drawn a very high number in the draft lottery (311), making his chances of being drafted very slim. So those two factors propelled Clinton to give up his ROTC deferment. Clinton left the ROTC program, because it served his interests. Two days after he drew that high lottery number, Clinton wrote a letter to Col. Eugene Holmes, director of the University of Arkansas ROTC program, thanking him for "saving me from the draft."[87]

---

(86) Ibid., p. 29
(87) Ibid., p. 28

So, as he would often do later on his career, Bill Clinton rewrote history to serve his own interests. If Clinton really cared about his country, he would have honored his ROTC commitment, like millions of other American men and women have done over the years. Likewise, if he really felt bad about his dead classmates who had perished in Vietnam, why didn't Bill Clinton simply enlist at that point?

David Broder put it well. "That's when the lightbulb went off- that this is a guy who reconstructs his own history to suit his needs."[88] It should be noted that both the "Los Angeles Times" and "Wall Street Journal" reported that Bill Clinton used the influence of his mentor U.S. Senator William Fulbright to influence the local draft board back in 1968.[89]

Clinton and the State Troopers

Throughout his years as governor of Arkansas, Bill Clinton used a group of Arkansas state troopers to procure women for him. Larry Patterson, who had spent twenty-six years on the force of the Arkansas state police said "We were more than bodyguards…We had to lie, cheat, and cover up for that man."

In signed affidavits, Patterson and trooper Roger Perry alleged that Clinton was engaged in lying and deceit on a daily basis as he had affairs with hundreds of different women over the years of his term. Gennifer Flowers called Clinton often, and the troopers would routinely re-route her

---

(88) Ibid., p. 29
(89) Ibid., p. 27

calls to the troopers' guard house adjacent to the Governor's mansion. That way Bill Clinton could talk to Hillary without Hillary's knowing about the calls.

Clinton had a stable of half a dozen "steadies", girlfriends that he could count on for sex 2 or 3 times per week. According to the troopers this group consisted of "the wife of a prominent judge, a Clinton aide, a local reporter, and a department store clerk."[90]

In addition, the troopers served as Clinton's personal escort service, as they would round up any additional women who might catch the young governor's fancy! Basically the routine went like this: Clinton would notice a woman and alert the troopers, who would give the woman Clinton's telephone number and/or hotel room number. Clinton would instruct the troopers to tell the woman something complimentary about how smitten he was with her looks. Sometimes, there would be sex "on the spot."

Sometimes the troopers set aside hotel rooms in advance, just in case Bill Clinton got lucky with a woman. Shockingly, one of Clinton's favorite lines was that he needed to take a phone call from former President Ronald Reagan, when in reality Clinton was retiring to a room with the female catch-of-the-day.[91]

Clinton instructed the troopers to call him if Hillary was coming over to the governor's mansion while Bill was fooling around with other women. Often Clinton would sneak out of the mansion at night to meet up with women.

---

(90) Ronald Kessler, "Inside the White House," p. 242
(91) Ibid., p. 242

Typically, he would borrow one of the state troopers' cars, to avoid being recognized. Once, Hillary woke up at 2 a.m. and discovered that Bill had left the state house. A state trooper located Bill at one of his "steady's" apartments. Bill yelled "God! God! God!" when he realized Hillary had caught him. After speeding back to the mansion, Bill engaged in a big fight with Hillary. The next morning Trooper Perry "found a kitchen cabinet door hanging from its hinges. Debris was all over the kitchen floor."[92]

Bill Clinton would receive "head" from the department store clerk in her pickup truck. On at least one occasion, the truck was parked in a remote area of the governor's mansion's parking lot. Trooper Patterson could observe Bill Clinton getting "head", as he watched from a 27-inch security TV screen. On one occasion, Chelsea's baby sitter was driving by at the exact moment that Bill Clinton was receiving "head" from the department store clerk. Trooper Patterson managed to direct the baby sitter away from the pickup truck where Clinton was being serviced, by telling her that there was a security problem on the grounds.

When Patterson later recounted this close call to Bill Clinton, the governor responded to Patterson "Atta Boy". Patterson remembered one day when Bill Clinton was being orally serviced by the same woman, as Bill Clinton was waiting to pick up young Chelsea Clinton at Booker Elementary School. Said Patterson: "I parked across the entrance and stood outside the car looking around, about 120 feet from where they parked in a lot that was pretty well lit. I could see Clinton get into the front seat, and then the lady's

---

(92) Ibid., p. 243

head go into his lap. They stayed in the car for 30 to 40 minutes."[93]

Bill Clinton and Connie Hamzy

Bill Clinton had a fling with Connie Hamzy at a North Little Rock hotel, back in 1984. Hamzy was approached by a friend who told her that "the Governor wanted to meet me in the lobby". According to Hamzy, "We ended up in an alcove, making out like crazy! He was kissing me, and his hands were all over me. Finally, he asked for my phone number."[94]

Connie Hamzy passed 3 lie detector tests, but she never saw Clinton again after that one quickie.

Marilyn Jenkins

Another girlfriend of Bill Clinton's was Arkansas Power & Light executive Marilyn Jenkins. Clinton would pretend to go for a 5-mile run, but in reality he would cut short the run to meet up with this particular woman. Then, to make it look as if he had worked up a sweat running, "Clinton would use the troopers' bathroom so he could splash water on his face to make it appear as if he had been sweating."[95]

In February 1990, reporters in Little Rock started to investigate the cell phone records of Bill Clinton and the calls made on behalf of him by the state troopers. Trooper

---

(93) Ibid., p. 243
(94) National Enquirer, Feb. 28, 1997, pp. 24-25.
(95) Kessler, op. cit., p. 244

Patterson claimed that his boss- "Buddy" Young- "told Patterson that he would have to claim he made the calls that Clinton placed to the woman."[96] The records revealed that Clinton had called the woman's home and her office extension fifty times between 1989 and 1991. On July 16, 1989, the records showed 11 calls to the woman's home. Two months later, phone records revealed that Clinton called the woman's home for 94 minutes at 1:28 a.m., while Clinton was on an official trip to Charlottesville, VA. He called the same woman at 7:45 a.m. the same day and spoke with her at her home for 18 minutes. According to White House counsel Bernard Nussbaum,: "This president calls lots of people."[97]

After Clinton was elected President in November, 1992, state troopers sneaked the same woman into the governor's mansion on at least three occasions. At times they sneaked her in as early as 5:15 a.m. "Dressed in a baseball cap and trench coat, she would use her maiden name and tell Secret Service agents she was a staff member coming in early."[98]

Hillary was keen to what Bill was up to with all the women. If Bill seemed inordinately interested in a particular woman at an inopportune time, Hillary would say: "Come on Bill, put your dick up. You can't fuck her here." Remember the judges' wife? On Clinton's last day in Little Rock, he asked the State troopers to bring the judges' wife to an airport ceremony. Trooper Patterson brought the woman to the ceremony, only to be confronted by Hillary, who told Patterson: 'What the fuck do you think you're doing. I know

---

(96) Ibid., p. 244
(97) Ibid., p. 244
(98) Ibid., p. 244

who that whore is. I know what she's here for. Get her out of here.'[99]

According to Patterson, Bill Clinton just shrugged his shoulders and looked at him; Patterson followed Hillary's commands and dropped off the woman at the Holiday Inn Center City.

Belinda Stronach

Bill got together with this Canadian billionaire beauty in Aspen, CO while on a skiing trip on January 2004. Hillary was furious about the hookup and threatened divorce when she heard that Bill planned another rendezvous with Stronach in Switzerland. It seems that Bill was advising Stronach on her own political career in Canada, planning her ascent to the top of the Canadian Conservative party. Hillary told Bill that he was not to see her again and to stop advising her, or else she would seek divorce. But Belinda is both younger and better looking than Hillary, at 37 years old and in the prime of her career. Bill has always been attracted to beautiful, intelligent and ambitious women, so it's easy to see why the hookup took place. But Bill heeded Hillary's warning, because he hasn't seen Stronach since. And he needs to stay with Hillary if he wants a chance to live in the White House again.[100]

---

(99) Ibid., p. 245
(100) Globe, Feb. 17, 2004, p. 41

Did Bill Clinton father a black child?

According to Little Rock prostitute Bobbie Ann Williams- an African-American- she and 2 other prostitutes had a wild night of sex with Bill Clinton at his mother's cabin near Hot Springs, Arkansas, back in 1986. She claimed to have become pregnant that night from Bill Clinton- the child Danny Williams is now 17 years old.

According to Williams, "When my baby was born, he was as white as any white child...I told myself, this is Bill Clinton's baby because he's the only white man I slept with that month."[101]

Williams claimed that Bill Clinton paid her for sex 13 times! Williams passed a lie detector test, but when her sister went to the governor's office to talk about her nephew's impoverished upbringing (Williams was in jail at this time), Bill Clinton's office totally rebuffed her!

If you look at the picture of Danny Williams on p. 41 of the "Globe" of March 27, 2001, you can see for yourself the face of Bill Clinton on the photo of young Danny Williams.

Hillary's Frustrated Plea

State Trooper Patterson was once sitting in the guard house at the mansion, as he overheard Hillary complaining to Bill on the audio monitor: "I need to be fucked more than twice a year."[102]

---

(101) "Globe," March 27, 2001, p. 41
(102) Kessler, p. 245.

Obviously, Hillary had a mouth like a sewer. Once, Patterson witnessed a shouting match in the mansion between Bill and Hillary. "She has a garbage mouth on her, and she was calling him 'mother fucker', 'sucker', and everything else. I went into the kitchen, and the cook, Miss Emma, turned to me and said, 'The devil's in that woman.'[103]

Sharon Stone and Bill Clinton

According to Dick Morris' mistress Barbara Pfafflin, Sharon Stone has always fantasized about being with Bill Clinton. Dick Morris told Pfafflin: "I'm sure they had a liason during a Presidential trip...Bill Clinton is really, really hot for Sharon Stone." When Pfafflin asked Morris if he thought the liason was sexual, he responded "With Bill Clinton, everything is sexual."[104]

One of Stone's friends told the "National Enquirer" that if Bill weren't married to Hillary, Sharon Stone would be in bed with Bill Clinton. Said the friend: "She thinks the ultimate aphrodisiac would be to sleep with the President. And she has said that one of her all-time fantasies is to visit the White House and run from room to room 'twirling Bill Clinton's boxer shorts above my head.'"[105]

After reading that, I have to throw up.

---

(103) Ibid., p. 246
(104) National Enquirer, Feb. 17, 1998, pp. 24-25.
(105) Ibid., pp. 24-25.

The Flag Incident

Then the famous flag incident. It was Labor Day, 1991. Hillary had left the mansion in her blue Cutlass. Within a couple of minutes, she pulled back into the mansion. Patterson thought something was wrong, so he rushed out to her. According to Patterson, Hillary screamed: 'Where is the goddman fucking flag?' It was early and we hadn't raised the flag yet. And she said, 'I want the goddamn fucking flag up every fucking morning at fucking sunrise.'[106]

Once when a trooper requested an autographed photo from Governor Clinton, Bill Clinton is quoted as having said: "I don't have time for that shit."[107] Furthermore, according to Patterson, Clinton promised all the troopers that guarded him they would get jobs in his White House. That didn't pan out, but Buddy Young, head of the Clinton security detail received a $92,300/ year job as a regional director of the Federal Emergency Management Agency (FEMA). Patterson said: "We lied for him (Clinton) and helped him cheat on his wife, and he treated us like dogs."[108]

Clinton never actually denied the troopers' claims. He simply said that the charges had been dealt with during the campaign. In a radio interview, Clinton actually said: "We...we did, if, the, I, I, the stories are just as they have been said," and after this unintentional confirmation of the

---

(106) Kessler, p. 246.
(107) Ibid., p. 246
(108) Ibid., p. 247

troopers' allegations, Clinton blurted "They're outrageous, and they're not so."[109]

In the final pages of "Inside the White House", Ronald Kessler offers his final assessment of the Clinton presidency:

"In the same vein, Clinton's compulsive philandering while governor of Arkansas suggested immaturity, insincerity, poor judgement, and arrogance that can now be seen in the immaturity of the staff he selected and his own indecisiveness and lack of convictions and values......[110]

"From the inadequate vetting of Dr. Henry Foster, Jr., before his nomination as surgeon general, to the burgeoning number of criminal investigations into Clinton appointees, the Clinton White House continued to demonstrate its lack of competence, if not its lack of ethics. From Bosnia to Cuba, Clinton continued to zig and zag, As in the movie "Dave", Bill and Hillary continued to emerge from the Marine helicopter holding hands, only to begin screaming at each other or ignoring each other once they got inside the White House. All the show could not hide the fact that Clinton was a shallow man with poor judgment and no real convictions."[111]

Markie Post and Bill Clinton

According to an insider, Bill Clinton and "Night Court" star Markie Post were very, very good friends. Right after

---

(109) Ibid., p. 249
(110) Ibid., p. 262
(111) Ibid., p. 265

Bill Clinton got into the White House, in January, 1993, he started seeing Markie Post in private meetings at the White House.

Recounts the insider: "Word came down Clinton wanted to see the buxom actress. On one occasion Markie received a call telling her to be in a certain hotel at a certain time. These secret get togethers in California hotels happened several times. Clinton was clearly smitten with Markie. She's exactly what Bill likes in a woman- blonde, beautiful, bubbly, and big-chested."[112]

Bill Clinton first met Markie Post through his famous Hollywood friends, producers Harry Thomason and Linda Bloodworth-Thomason. Harry Thomason wanted to get his people in the White house Travel Office- he was instrumental in having Hillary Clinton fire the staff of the White House Travel office. Markie was at the White House with the Thomasons as guest of the Clintons, the night after Bill and Hillary took up residence at 1600 Pennsylvania Ave. That was the night the famous photo of Markie Post and Linda Thomason jumping up and down on the Lincoln bed (in the Lincoln bedroom) was snapped. Looking like a couple of 6 year-olds, "Markie began jumping up and down on the bed like a wild child, yelling 'We made it! We're in the White House now!'"[113]

The insider continued: "Linda joined her on the bed. The husbands stood by and watched in awe. It was truly an incredible scene.

---

(112) National Enquirer, Feb. 17, 1998, pp. 24-25.
(113) Ibid., pp. 24-25.

According to a key member of the White House Historical Society, Mike Melton,: "The White House is a designated museum. We would definitely not want someone jumping up and down on the Lincoln bed."[114]

And you wonder why I have no respect for Bill Clinton and his Hollywood crowd?

As if that were not enough, the Congressional committee investigating the firing of the Travel Office by Bill and Hillary Clinton subpoenaed the White House to turn over "all documents relating to 'contacts and communications' dealing with Markie Post.[115]

Barbra Streisand and Bill Clinton

Of all of Bill Clinton's lady friends, no one made Hillary Clinton madder than Barbra Streisand. Barbra came to the White House to "comfort" Bill Clinton while Hillary out of town at the bedside of her dying father. As soon as Hillary heard that Babs was hanging out with her hubby, she left her father's bedside and confronted Bill at the White House. First, Hillary gave Streisand a life-time ban from the White House, then he refused to talk to Bill for 2 days.[116]

Denise Rich and Susan McDougal

These former lovers of Bill Clinton were given favors on Clinton's last day in office- by way of pardons. Denise

---

(114) Ibid., pp. 24-25.
(115) Ibid., pp. 24-25.
(116) Ibid., pp. 24-25.

Rich's fugitive husband Marc, suspected of racketeering and conspiracy, was pardoned by Clinton as a favor. And McDougal, who went to jail for refusing to comply with the grand jury investigation of the Whitewater scandal, was pardoned by Clinton to return the favor of taking the fall for him.[117]

Marsha Scott

Marsha Scott has been a friend of Bill Clinton's since the late 60's. She boasted to her boyfriend Danny Dwyer "I've had sex with Bill Clinton every Christmas for 30 years, ever since we were in our early 20's in Arkansas. It's my annual Christmas present to him!"[118] According to Dwyer, Marsha Scott went to visit Bill Clinton every Christmas when he was Governor of Arkansas.

Scott was given a plum job in the Clinton White House-assistant to the President in charge of correspondence.[119] Her affair with Clinton continued after she moved to D.C.

Sheila Lawrence

Sheila Lawrence was the wife of Larry Lawrence, the late Ambassador to Switzerland and owner of the historic Hotel del Coronado. According to former U.S. State department foreign service officer Christina Marie Alexandre, in exchange for Larry Lawrence getting his ambassadorship,

---

(117) "Globe," Feb. 13, 2001, pp. 4-5.
(118) National Enquirer, Feb. 17, 1998, p. 28
(119) Ibid., p. 28

Bill Clinton got to have sex with 36 year-old Sheila Lawrence.

Alexandre told the "National Enquirer": "Sheila's sexual intimacy with President Clinton was an an open secret among the staff at Larry Lawrence's Hotel del Coronado in San Diego- and among his embassy staff in Switzerland. He wanted to be an ambassador and he asked Clinton for Switzerland as his reward for political support, and he got it. The tit for tat was that Larry would allow the President to be intimate with Larry's wife Sheila and not make a fuss over it."[120]

According to columnist Arianna Huffington, "Larry [Lawrence's] greatest leverage was having turned a blind eye toward Clinton's affair with his own wife."[121]

After Sheila Lawrence was deposed by Paula Jones' attorneys, she released the standard Clinton spin control denial: "I have never had a sexual or romantic relationship of any type with President Clinton."

No doubt, this is the work of the same writer who wrote Clinton's now famous "I did not have sex with that woman... Miss Lewinsky" speech a few years later!

Incidentally, Larry Lawrence was a big donor to the Democratic Party, having donated more than $10 million dollars to that cause. Lawrence faked his military record- he was not wounded in combat- resulting in his remains being

---

(120) Ibid., p. 28
(121) Ibid., p. 28

dug up from Arlington National Cemetery. Golly, it seems like Democrats lie about everything!

Kathleen Willey

In a lot of ways, the Kathleen Willey incident is one of the scariest of all. It involves the mysterious death of her husband, lies by Bill Clinton, cover-ups, and according to several legal experts, criminal and impeachable behavior by Bill Clinton.

First of all, you should all understand that Kathleen Willey was a Democrat- and a long time supporter of Bill Clinton. Second, she never wanted to be drawn into all this Clinton stuff, even though Bill Clinton definitely molested her in the White House on November 29, 1993. It was the Paula Jones legal defense team that subpoenaed Kathleen Willey's sworn testimony to bolster their case against Bill Clinton!

Now, I want you all to re-read the previous paragraph three times before continuing on!

Here are the facts: At first, Kathleen Willey didn't want to go public with the indignities she suffered at the White House at the hands of Bill Clinton. But the Paula Jones lawyers wanted her testimony to bolster their own case of harassment against Bill Clinton. Willey's lawyer, Dan Gecker, tried to have Federal judge Robert Merhige, Jr. throw out the subpoena forcing her to testify. Remember, it was the Paula Jones lawyers who wanted Kathleen Willey to testify.[122]   Apparently, the mainstream media and folks like James Carville forgot this simple fact!

Clinton's lawyer Bob Bennett tried to inquire what Willey might say if she were asked to become a witness. Was Willey sexually harassed?   Bennett wanted to know if Willey felt that Clinton's sexual advances were unwanted? According to Willey, it was "unexpected- and unwanted."[123]

So what could be any clearer? I am so sick of the defense that anyone who criticizes the sexual molestations of Bill Clinton is part of some "vast right-wing conspiracy!"
I am a Long Island Jew who lives in Los Angeles, who voted strictly Democratic until Bill and Hillary Clinton reared their ugly heads! If you looked at me, you would see that I look nothing like a redneck, a right-wing conservative, or a "good old boy." Yet I am proudly all of the above!

And is Michael Isikoff, respected journalist from the "Washington Post" and "Newsweek" a member of that "vast right-wing conspiracy?" According to the Clintons, anyone who questions their actions and criticizes their behavior is ip so facto guilty as charged. Give me a break!

Nathan Landow, former head of the Maryland Democratic Party (another Liberal Jew) and a big contributor to the Democratic party tried to encourage Kathleen Willey to shut up and not talk about Bill Clinton to anyone. According to Willey's sworn testimony, Landow told her

---

(122) Isikoff, Uncovering Clinton, p. 226
(123) Ibid., p. 227

"don't say anything." As long as she said "nothing happened", they couldn't prove anything.[124]

Ann Coulter makes a brilliant point in "High Crimes and Misdemeanors". Kathleen Willey was compelled by the court to give testimony in the Paula Jones trial. Unlike a sexual harassment or rape trial, this was not a "he said/ she said" issue; it was a "He said/They forced me to tell the truth under oath" issue.[125]

It is an established fact that Bill Clinton molested Kathleen Willey in the Oval Office around 3 p.m. on November 29, 1993. He grabbed her hand and placed it on the fully erect First penis! Around 5 p.m. that same day, her husband Ed Willey committed suicide with a single shot to the head in a wooded area of Richmond, Virginia. Was there a connection between Willey's being groped by Bill Clinton and her husband's suicide? Is it possible that Kathleen Willey phoned her husband after 3 p.m. and before 5 p.m. to inform him about what Bill Clinton had done to her? Ed and Kathleen's son, Patrick Willey thought so. When his mother's name hit the papers, he phoned home and asked his mother: "Did Dad know?"[126]

Ed Willey had at one time been a very successful real estate lawyer. He made a lot of money during the boom years of the 80's, and by 1992, both Ed and Kathy Willey had jumped on the Bill Clinton for President bandwagon. On the walls in their home, they proudly displayed a dozen framed

---

(124) Coulter, op. cit., p. 83
(125) Ibid., p. 84
(126) "Star," March 31, 1998, p. 4-5.

autographed photos of the future 41st President of the United States.

Kathleen Willey had a crush on Bill Clinton, to be sure. She took him by the arm and proudly introduced him to other influential Democrats at receptions. Bill Clinton couldn't care less that Kathleen Willey was a married woman. That never stopped him in the past, why should it now? After one political function, Bill phoned Kathy and told her if she could drive up to meet him and bring him some chicken soup for a sore throat he was nursing, Clinton could make his Secret Service guard scarce.[127]

Willey's friends knew that Bill Clinton wanted a lot more than chicken soup. Said one of them: "How couldn't we? Every time Clinton called her or smiled at her across a room, she'd talk about it for weeks. The way Kathy told it, she and the President had a flirtatious relationship from the get-go. Ed was a big Clinton supporter- he'd even brag, 'Did you see who my wife was kissing?' But he was no dummy."[128]

Concurrently with all this, Ed and Kath's marriage began to fall apart. A lot of it was due to financial pressure he was experiencing.   Ed Willey was $1 million in debt, and $300,000 of that amount was clients' funds that he never remitted to the client.

The financial problems were too much for Ed Willey. Before his death, he and Kathleen had a tremendous argument. The friend continues: "Ed finally owned up to the

---

(127) Ibid., pp. 4-5.
(128) Ibid., pp. 4-5.

trouble he was in. He had a deadline to pay back the $300,000 and he needed Kathy to sign a promissory note...It turned into a huge fight. She ordered him out of the house and told him she was moving to Washington, that Bill would take care of her. The next morning he packed a bag and left." When Willey went to the White House on November 29, "she told the president she wanted out of Richmond and out of her marriage."[129]

According to a "well-informed source", "the White House was in a panic when they heard Ed killed himself. At the very top, there was fear that Kathleen had phoned her husband and told him something about Clinton. They were deathly afraid he'd left a note blaming the president."[130]

Soon we will discuss the mysterious suicide of Vince Foster. Why are all these people connected to the Clintons killing themselves, or getting killed in car accidents, plane crashes, and other strange ways? Keep reading, as we connect the dots......

Gennifer Flowers

Before there was ever a Paula Jones or a Monica Lewinsky, there was Gennifer Flowers. Clinton carried on a long love affair with Gennifer Flowers; according to her claims, she and Clinton were together over a period of 11 years. They dabbled in everything: phone sex, rubbing food on each other (especially milk and ketchup), a little bondage, and lots of sex. They even made up names for their sex

---

(129) Ibid., pp. 4-5.
(130) Ibid., pp.4-5.

organs. Hers was called "the precious". His was called "the Willard".[131] Although Bill often wanted Gennifer to engage in threesomes, she wasn't into that scene.

Gennifer made no secret of the hatred she had for Hillary Clinton. In her book "Passion and Betrayal", Flowers described Hillary as "a fat frump with big thick glasses, an ugly dress, and a big fat butt." According to Flowers, even Bill had a few choice nicknames for Hillary: "Hilla the Hun" and "Sarge."[132]

Bill Clinton had gotten Flowers a job as an administrative assistant at Arkansas Appeal Tribunal, the state board that oversees disputes relating to unemployment claims. In sworn testimony, Flowers stated that she was "instructed not to be honest by Bill." Even though Flowers got her job through her relationship with Bill Clinton and not based on her competence or qualifications, Clinton instructed her to "tell them that I found out about it through the newspaper, and that's exactly what I did."[133]

In the fall of 1999, Gennifer Flowers gave a revealing interview to the "Hannity & Colmes" show on Fox News Channel. Flowers indicated that Clinton used drugs in her presence when he was Attorney General and Governor of Arkansas. Said Flowers:

"He [Clinton] made it very clear that if I ever wanted to do cocaine that he could provide that. And he also told me

---

(131) Flowers, op. cit., p. 71.
(132) Ibid., p. 41
(133) Isikoff, Uncovering Clinton, p. 225

that that he did so much cocaine at parties that his head would itch. And that he would be standing there trying to talk to people and he would feel like a fool because all he wanted to do was this [Flowers imitates Clinton scratching his head][134]

How nice! So the President was a cocaine user. We'll talk more about Bill's cocaine usage later on. Flowers went on in the interview to indicate that Bill clearly knew that Hillary was bisexual. In her 1995 book "Passion & Betrayal", Flowers quoted Bill Clinton as saying that "Hillary has eaten more pussy than he has."[135]

Juanita Broaddrick- Biting the lip is typical of rapists

When Bill Clinton allegedly raped Juanita Broaddrick, he bit her lip, and the biting almost tore one of her lips in two. Newsmax.com was contacted by a former rape investigator with the New Orleans Police Department who gave this scary account of this common technique among rapists.

"The reason rapists bite is because, even with the full weight of her attacker on top of her, the woman is often able to resist the parting of her legs by locking her ankles. The rapists arms are busy keeping her pinned down. The only weapon the rapist has left is his teeth, which he uses to bite

---

(134) Ruddy and Limbacher, "A Bitter Legacy," pp. 39-40.
(135) Ibid., p. 39-40. My friends Chris Ruddy and Carl Limbacher cleaned up Flowers' language. Various sources, including Larry Nichols, have quoted Clinton many times as having used this standard line whenever people asked him if Hillary was upset with *his* womanizing!

while demanding she open her legs...the lips are very sensitive. Biting them is so painful it distracts the victim, allowing a rapist to overcome her resistance. The victim can only hold out for so long as the blood flows into her mouth. Some women are stronger than others and I've seen their lips half-torn from their faces before they give up."[136]

Response of National Organization of Women to Broaddrick rape allegations

Patricia Ireland, former head of the National Organization for Women (NOW), criticized those who brought up the rape allegations against Bill Clinton in the Juanita Broaddrick case. She said: "If they care about women's rights, they should stop wasting time on unprovable charges and start working to improve the lives of women."[137]

Newsmax.com so correctly poses the question: why then did NOW put so much energy into the unprovable charges involving Clarence Thomas and Bob Packwood? I guess "provable charges" only apply to Republicans. Democrats, especially Presidents like Bill Clinton couldn't possibly commit sexual molestation, harassment, and rape. Right. But the height of irony, is that Bob Packwood had to resign when he never **touched one** woman, while all Clinton ever did was grope, feel, molest, and attack. Not only did Clinton manage to keep his job, but he soon started making more than $10 million dollars annually on the lucrative public speaking circuit.

---

(136) Ibid., pp. 42-43.
(137) Ibid., p. 41

Bill Clinton persisted in calling Juanita Broaddrick, after he allegedly raped her in the Camelot Motel in Little Rock on April 25, 1978. Juanita told Clinton point blank to "stop calling me."[138]

Juanita Broaddrick- on being raped by Bill Clinton-

"Then he tries to kiss me again. And the second time he tries to kiss me, he starts biting on my lip. He starts to bite on my top lip. I tried to pull away from him. Then he forces me down on the bed. And I was just very frightened. I tried to get away from him and I told him no, but he wouldn't listen to me. I told him 'please don't'…He was such a different person at that moment. He was just a vicious, awful person…It was a real panicky, panicky situation, and I was even to the point where I was getting very noisy, yelling to please stop. And that's when he would press down on my shoulder and bite on my lip."[139]

Remember, unlike Paula Jones and Gennifer Flowers, who both sought out the media to tell their stories about Bill Clinton, Juanita Broaddrick was pursued by the media. Broaddrick told the Paula Jones investigative team: "I just don't want to relive that. You know, it was just a horrible thing for me and I wouldn't relive that for anything."[140]

The alleged rape of Juanita Broaddrick by Bill Clinton was discussed in the "Wall Street Journal" and "Washington

---

(138) Ibid., p. 50
(139) Ibid., p. 50
(140) Isikoff, "Uncovering Clinton," p. 226.

Post", and was broken on "Dateline NBC". Lisa Myers was the reporter.

Juanita Broaddrick sued the President Bill Clinton and Attorney General Janet Reno in January 2000, according to Newsmax.com. Broaddrick's suit accused Clinton and Reno's Justice Department of attempting to "smear and destroy her reputation" by maintaining a file on her in violation of federal privacy laws.[141] Said Broaddrick: "I just want my FBI file- you know, the White House has refused to turn it over, and I want to know what's in it. I want to know what information they have on me."[142]

Why was there an FBI file on Juanita Broaddrick? Why were there no investigations into her allegations? How can the President of the United States just simply rape a woman and get away with it?

If you're Bill Clinton, it's easy. Just lie your way out of everything, intimidate and threaten anyone who gets in your way, and steamroll over anyone and anything that gets in your way!

Bill Clinton and Cyd Dunlop

Cyd Dunlop was a woman from Arkansas whose first husband was a contributor to Clinton's gubernatorial campaign in Arkansas. Back in 1986, Cyd Dunlop and her ex-husband Daryl were at a reelection victory celebration for Bill Clinton, at the Excelsior Hotel in Little Rock. After a night of dancing and celebrating, she and her husband retired

---

(141) Ruddy and Limbacher, op. cit., p. 35
(142) Ibid., p. 35

for the night. In the middle of the night, at 2 a.m., the phone to the Dunlop's room rang.

"Cyd, it's Bill."

"Bill who?' Dunlop asked.

"Bill, the governor," replied Bill Clinton. Dunlop glanced at her clock radio- it was after 2 a.m. What could Clinton want at this hour?

"I just wanted to hear the sound of your voice again," said Clinton, "Can you get out of your room?"

(By now, Dunlop's husband woke up, and Cyd tried to placate him by telling him it was a wrong number.)

"No, I don't think so," she said "Daryl knows I wouldn't do that."

But Bill Clinton wouldn't let it go. "Just tell him you need to be by yourself and think for a while," Clinton told her.

She replied, "I can't do that."

Bill Clinton asked her: "Can you go for a jog with me in the morning?"

Cyd reminded Clinton that she only had her red dress shoes with her. Still, Bill Clinton persisted: "What time are you leaving in the morning? Can you meet me at the old statehouse in the morning at around six?"[143]

Just to placate the governor, Cyd Dunlop said OK and went back to sleep. The next morning Cyd and Daryl Dunlop joked about Clinton's phone call, as they had breakfast with the Mayor of her hometown West Helena and his wife. Michael Isikoff, well-known national writer from

---

[143] Isikoff, op. cit., p. 61-63. The Barbara Olson book "The Final Days" confirms the account of Cyd Dunlop.

"Newsweek" and author of "Uncovering Clinton" confirmed Cyd Dunlop's story with the Mayor's wife.

At this point in his career, 40 year-old Bill Clinton was in his third term as Governor of Arkansas, chairman of the National Governors' Association, and a potential Presidential candidate. Yet, as Isikoff points out, "There he was, acting like some oversexed adolescent, carousing in the early hours of the morning, badgering the wife of one of his campaign supporters for a date."[144]

Did Bill Clinton Suffer from a Rare Disease Which Affected his Penis?

According to Paula Jones, Bill Clinton's penis was "crooked." It is quite possible that Bill Clinton suffered from a rare disease, Peyronnie's Disease, a rare condition affecting about 1% of men between the ages of 45 to 60. This condition, was first described by noted French scientist Francois Gigot de la Peyronnie, in 1743. It is characterized by curvature of the penis and, at times, severe pain preventing intercourse.[145]

Bill Clinton's Speech to the Democrats- 1988

At the Democratic convention in 1988, Bill Clinton gave the nominating speech for Michael Dukakis. Clinton's speech ran long- he just wouldn't get off the stage. The

---

(144) Ibid., p. 63.
(145) Isikoff, op. cit., p. 184. News of this possible affliction affecting the First Penis also appeared on the "Don Imus Radio Show" and in the "Washington Times."

crowd was yelling: "Get off! Get off!" Delegates booed loudly at the Arkansas Governor. For some reason, Bill Clinton spoke for 32 minutes. When he finally said, "And now, in conclusion...", the convention hall broke into loud applause. Bill Clinton was furious. Backstage, he denounced Dukakis as "that little Greek mother-fucker."[146]

Hillary joined the corporate boards of Tyson Foods, Walmart, and TCBY. At about the same time, Hillary worked with Vince Foster on a $3.3 million lawsuit brought against Clinton buddy and convicted cocaine dealer Dan Lasater by the FDIC. Somehow, through some clever legal wheeling and dealing, Vince and Hillary settled the suit for $200,000! Hillary should have gone to prison for her role in that lawsuit, but again she beat the rap when the FDIC ruled in her favor in March, 1994.[147]

State Trooper Larry Patterson is a friend of mine. He witnessed Bill Clinton's philandering on a first-hand basis. According to Patterson, Bill Clinton had women day in and day out. For example, on the evening of his disastrous speech to the Atlanta Convention in 1988, Bill Clinton disappeared into a closed hotel room with "an attractive young woman", after Hillary had returned, alone, to their hotel. Hillary didn't want Larry Patterson to talk in public, because, said Hillary: "You sound like a hick."[148]

And Hillary didn't enjoy posing for photos. One day, a group of preschoolers from the HIPPY program were getting

---

(146) Joyce Milton, The First Partner, p. 187
(147) Ibid., p. 190
(148) Ibid., p. 192.

their picture taken outside the Governors' mansion. Hillary was overheard on the intercom telling an aide: "I want to get this shit over with and get these damn people out of here."[149] To say Hillary Clinton is self-centered is an understatement. Consider these facts:

(1) When Bill was sick to his stomach with a bad virus in 1986, the day before Bill was taking over as chairman of the National Governors' Association, friends of Bill asked Hillary how Bill was. Had she called a doctor or given him some medicine? Hillary's reply: *"I'm not his nurse."*[150]

(2) Hillary Clinton and Brian Snow- a friend from the '70's- were walking together in the French Quarter in New Orleans when they encountered a street person who lost consciousness and needed mouth-to-mouth resucitation. As fluid oozed out of the poor guy's mouth, Snow said: "One of us should probably do mouth to mouth...Who's going to do it?" Hillary said: "not me- you're going to do it." Well, luckily, paramedics came along and helped the guy. After they left, Snow said to Hillary: "Hillary, this deprived us of the chance to save someone's life." Hillary's reply: "Oh no, it didn't...It deprived *you* of a chance to save someone's life."[151]

During 1989, Bill Clinton was carrying on at least 5 affairs with women simultaneously.

---

(149) Ibid., p. 192.
(150) Ibid., p. 200
(151) Oppenheimer, State of a Union, p. 166

(1) A married woman who lived in the Heights, who visited Bill Clinton when her husband was out of town. This was Beth Coulson.

(2) A woman who lived in a condo in the Sherwood district, on the outskirts of Little Rock. This was Marilyn Jenkins.

Larry Patterson recalls driving Bill Clinton to Chelsea's elementary school, where Bill met up with one of his girlfriends. The woman worked in a Little Rock department store, selling cosmetics. Patterson "saw the lady's head go into his lap", an almost certain reference to Bill Clinton receiving *head* (oral sex). On at least one occasion, the woman drove a yellow and black pickup truck onto the property of the Governors' mansion, where Patterson observed Bill and the woman going at it again. This time it was caught on film on the security camera at the Governors' mansion.[152]

Patterson was working the graveyard shift at the Governors' mansion that night in the late 1980's, when the woman drove in. Hillary was out of town. According to Patterson, Bill called down to the guardhouse right before 11 p.m. and said: 'Larry, I've got a friend coming over.' What follows is Patterson's description of the evening's festivities:

"So a small Datsun [or] Toyota pickup came in, drove right into the parking area where normally Hillary's car was parked or just on the other side of it...[Bill Clinton] walked out. He got in the car with this lady. I remember it being extremely cold that night. The engine was running on the vehicle. [I] could see smoke coming out. They were sitting in the truck. It was getting past midnight. I had the back gate

---

(152) Milton, op. cit., p. 191

shut. The alarm went off at the back gate. I looked out, saw it was Melissa Jolley, [Chelsea's] babysitter...When she came in the back gate...she would be within 20, 25 feet of the vehicle that the governor was in. So I went out to the gate. I told her...'Melissa, we've got a security problem. We've had a report of a prowler on the grounds. I want you to go to your house.'

"In the back of the Mansion there's a security camera. It's a pan-tilt-zoom camera that would go almost around 360 degrees...You could project this image from this camera up on a 27-inch monitor, a TV. While this act was going on in the truck, I put the camera in that area, zoomed it in, and saw this lady performing oral sex on the governor. After the act was complete, he went in the house, stayed five, ten minutes [and] came out. He said 'Larry, what was that going on? What was that with the car coming?' I said, 'That was Melissa,' and I told him the story.

"So he pulled up a chair, and he propped his feet up on the desk and he wanted to visit awhile. He said, 'Larry, you're doing a good job. I really appreciate, you know-you're security-conscious, and you take care of me, you're my buddy."

According to Patterson, the woman who serviced Bill Clinton that night was a "very attractive" woman who worked at M.M. Cohn's department store in Little Rock.[153]

---

(153) National Enquirer, June 10, 2003, pp. 34-35. Larry Patterson's account was from his sworn testimony taken in November, 1997, in connection with the Paula Jones sexual harassment suit against Bill Clinton.

Troopergate and Paula Jones

Arkansas state troopers told the L.A. Times and CNN that they had procured more than 100 women for Bill Clinton during his years as Governor of Arkansas.[154]

Here are some key dates: May 8, 1991- Bill Clinton lowers his pants in a hotel room with Paula Jones at a governor's conference and asks her to "kiss it."[155]

January 1998- Bill Clinton gives sworn testimony in a deposition to federal judge Susan Webber Wright.

May 1997- Clinton's relationship with Monica Lewinsky ends.

January 26, 1998- Bill Clinton makes his famous finger-wagging speech. ("I never had sexual relations with *that woman,* Miss Lewinsky.")

According to Tommy Robinson, who was an official in Clinton's Arkansas administration, Hillary was the actual governor of Arkansas. Robinson said Hillary "is one very professionally tough bitch.."[156]

Brian Snow couldn't believe what he saw when he met Hillary Rodham in 1974- she had no makeup, unkempt hair, and bad glasses.

---

(154) Barbara Olson, The Final Days, p. 107.
(155) Ibid., p. 107
(156) Ibid., p. 46

Gennifer Flowers

Gennifer Flowers had an 11-year relationship with Bill Clinton. In her book, *Passion and Betrayal,* she tells all, in quite graphic detail.

Flowers worked as a nightclub singer and also was a television news reporter. Once Gennifer asked Bill about rumors that Hillary was having an affair with another woman. Bill burst out laughing and told Gennifer "Honey, she's [Hillary] probably eaten more pussy than I have."[157] According to Flowers, Bill told her that Hillary was pretty dull in bed. Hillary didn't like to try different positions- just the missionary position. She was not at all playful in bed. Flowers states that Bill used cocaine- "there were several occasions when he mentioned to me that he had gotten high on coke."[158] At one party Bill told Gennifer about, he got so high on cocaine that it made his scalp itch. Bill told her: "I got so fucked up on cocaine at that party."..."He felt conspicuous because he was talking with people who were not aware drugs were at the party, and all he wanted to do was scratch his head. He was afraid that if he continued to walk around, people would think something more serious than dandruff was going on with him."[159]

In December 1977, Gennifer Flowers got pregnant by Bill Clinton. He gave her $200 cash to get an abortion.[160]

---

(157) Gennifer Flowers, "Passion and Betrayal," p. 41
(158) Ibid., p. 42
(159) Ibid., p. 42
(160) Oppenheimer, op. cit., p. 192

One thing was for sure: Gennifer loved sex and so did Bill! "As a lover, Bill was great! Though not particularly well endowed, his desire to please me was astounding. He was determined to please me, and boy, did he! At times I thought my head would explode with the pleasure. This was more than just great sex, it was great everything. I was falling in love with Bill Clinton, inside and out."[161]

And could Bill last as a lover? "His stamina amazed me. We made love over and over that night, and he never seemed to run out of energy."[162]

Bill once sought a "quickie" from Gennifer Flowers, while an assembled crowd outside the mansion was waiting for him to address them with a political speech.[163]

During one of their meetings, this one at the Mockingbird Hilton in Dallas, TX, Bill wanted Gennifer to dress up as a man, in a business suit. He told her to pull her hair "up under a man's hat and put on a man's suit." Gennifer decided against the idea, because her big breasts would have given the ruse away.[164]

During one evening, Bill Clinton became very emotional and started crying and shaking. According to Gennifer, he just kept crying. Flowers thought that maybe Bill had some idea that it was wrong to have been cheating on Hillary with

---

(161) Flowers, op. cit., p. 32
(162) Ibid., p. 32
(163) Ibid., p. 72
(164) Ibid., p. 56

Gennifer. But he didn't tell Gennifer anything- he just cried. But true to form, "whatever it was, he got over it within a few minutes and came back to bed with me, ready and eager for oral sex."[(165)]

Bill had a whole routine worked out with Gennifer. Often, his driver would wait downstairs in the car for Bill, if he and Gennifer were having a "quickie." Other times, Clinton would jog over to Gennifer's place from the Governor's mansion. Gennifer lived at the Quapaw Tower, an easy run from the Governors' mansion. Gennifer would see Bill running over from her balcony.[(166)] Man, this guy had it all down!

Bill once tried to convince Gennifer to get it on with him *in the ladies room of the Governors' mansion.*[(167)] Gennifer vetoed that idea. Too risky. Hillary might walk in on them, if she had to go.

According to Gennifer, Hillary knew what Bill was up to with all the action on the side. "This was Arkansas and Bill was king. He had a network of "good ol' boys" that would go to great lengths to protect him."[(168)]

Gennifer Flowers speculates that Hillary may have been involved with Vince Foster *and Webb Hubbell.* "In the last couple of years, stories have circulated about her reported affairs with people like Vince Foster and possibly Webb

---

(165) Ibid., p. 62
(166) Ibid., p. 64
(167) Ibid., pp. 67-68.
(168) Flowers, p. 68

Hubbell."[169] For years, rumors like these have swirled around Arkansas. Larry Nichols once told me that he is convinced that Webb Hubbell and Hillary had a thing. I cannot help but notice the *striking resemblance between a young Webb Hubbell and Chelsea Clinton.* If you look at pictures of Webb Hubbell from his college years (check out his autobiography *Friends in High Places),* you'll see what I am talking about. Also, there is a picture of a young Bill Clinton and a young Webb Hubbell in the photo section of David Brock's book *The Seduction of Hillary Rodham.* Webb Hubbell looks like a male version of Chelsea. The eyes, the lips, the cheeks- you must see these pictures! Larry Nichols told me an amazing story that I could never prove in a court of law- a story concerning Hillary Clinton and Webb Hubbell, during the time that Bill was trying to raise money to run for Governor. I really want to tell you this story, but since I can't prove it to be true- let me just say that Webb Hubbell looks exactly like Chelsea. Larry Nichols once told me that there was a memo circulated around the Clinton White House that there be *no photo ops. of Chelsea and Webb Hubbell.* I know it sounds far fetched, but wouldn't it be something if the father of Chelsea were actually...One thing I've learned with the Clintons- anything is possible. P.S. This could explain why Bill has never released his medical records. Blood type information is contained in medical records.

Bill could settle the issue by submitting a sample of his DNA and comparing it with Webb Hubbell's and Chelsea's. Let's just leave it at that for now...Back to Gennifer Flowers...

---

(169) Ibid., p. 69

Bill and Gennifer had names for their private parts. Her vagina was referred to as "Precious". Bill's penis was referred to as "Willard." Bill liked the name "Willard"- he told her it was "Willard, for Willy!"[170] Gennifer's breasts were referred to as the "girls". Bill would say to her (in a public place) "how are the girls?" and Gennifer would come back with "how are the boys?" The "boys" were Bill's testicles.[171] Bill and Gennifer enjoyed phone sex, and they would mutually masturbate during phone conversations. On one particular occasion, Gennifer describes the time she applied makeup to Bill. "At first he demurred, but then agreed. I applied eye shadow, then some eyeliner and mascara. Before he could say no, I also put a little bit of blush on his cheeks. He was astonished at how different he looked and asked me to do it again the next time we were together. He was absolutely fascinated by how different he looked with makeup on. I wonder if now, when the makeup people prepare him for TV appearances, he remembers the times we put makeup on him in my apartment."[172]

On one occasion, Bill had Gennifer reenact what Sharon Stone did in "Basic Instinct" as she crossed and uncrossed her legs for him, while she wore a hiked up skirt and no underwear. It was Bill's fantasy for Gennifer and him to make love in his office in the State Capitol, while people were busy working outside the office.[173] Things got even kinkier. Bill would drip ice over Gennifer's naked body, "he

---

(170) Ibid., pp. 71-72.
(171) Ibid., p. 72
(172) Ibid., pp. 72-73.
(173) Ibid., p. 72

soon had me moaning with pleasure as he held the ice over my naked body, slowly letting the icy water drip onto my nipples and slide down to my stomach. As he continued, moving it back and forth, dripping it all over me, I got so excited I couldn't wait for him to make love to me. But he teasingly tortured me, making me wait until I couldn't stand it any longer, then entering me and slowly building the tension even further until we reached a climax beyond anything we'd ever experienced together."[174] Gennifer describes the first time Bill Clinton "came" in her mouth. ("I wasn't expecting it, and I guess the shock showed on my face."). Bill wanted Gennifer to drip hot wax on him, but she wasn't into that. However, she did "agree to spank him, and he [Bill] got a big thrill out of it. Bill would pour honey all over Gennifer's body and lick it off. They played a game where he would blindfold her, take her into the kitchen and experiment with different foods. Again, in Gennifer's words: I loved it when he would slowly pour juice into my mouth until it overflowed, and little streams of liquid would trickle down my naked body." They would exchange roles, and Gennifer would control the food fantasy. At times, they were both covered in ketchup or milk. Bill wanted to tie Gennifer up, but she wasn't interested. Always the compromiser, Gennifer agreed to *tie Bill up*. "He was completely at my mercy, and I took advantage of it. I teased him and played with him until he was almost out of his mind with excitement. It turned both of us on so much that we did it again several times. Bill, as always, wanted to take it a step further, so the next time I tied him to the bed, he asked me to use a dildo-shaped vibrator on him. It was exciting to see

---

(174) Ibid., pp. 73-74.

him getting so aroused, and I couldn't wait to untie him so he could use it on me."[175]

Folks, I am not making up this stuff; read Gennifer Flower's book *Passion and Betrayal for more juicy details of the 11 year-long affair of Bill Clinton and Gennifer Flowers.*

Two more great stories emerge from Gennifer's book. One concerns the time when she was doing many radio interviews (what we call "phoners"), and she had to, well, let's just say take a whiz. But let me have Gennifer Flowers, Bill Clinton's girlfriend, explain it for you: "During one interview, I had to go to the bathroom so bad I couldn't wait. But the show was only half finished, and I could hardly excuse myself right in the middle of it to go use the potty. Desperate for relief, I looked around the kitchen and got the brilliant idea *to use a bowl.* So as I continued to answer questions about Bill Clinton and me, *I proceeded to tinkle in the bowl Luckily it wasn't stainless steel, so it didn't make any noise.* If the listeners only knew what was going on while they were asking me all those serious questions! *But when nature calls...*[176] O.K., Gennifer, now you have told me more than I need to know. If you want to know more, read Gennifer Flower's classic masterpiece *Passion and Betrayal.*

The last thing I want to say about Gennifer Flowers concerns *Jerry Parks.* Do you remember Jerry Parks? He was the guy who had been head of security for the Clinton-Gore office in Little Rock who was writing a book about Bill

---

(175) Ibid., pp. 74-75.
(176) Ibid., p. 145.

Clinton and the Arkansas political scene. Sadly, Jerry Parks was mysteriously gunned down and killed while he was driving his car on a road in Arkansas in September, 1993. The tapes and notes he had compiled for his book disappeared. Gennifer was in fear of her own life.[177]

A little more about Jerry Parks. Right after Vince Foster's death, Jerry Parks told his son Gary: "I'm a dead man".[178] According to phone records, there were 12 phone calls made by Jerry Parks to the White House, during the months before Vince Foster died, *including at least four calls directly to Foster's office!* According to Gary Parks, his dad had been calling the White House because he was owed money by the Clinton-Gore campaign, and he wanted to be paid.

Gary Parks felt that Ken Starr should have indicted Bill Clinton, and he was puzzled that Starr never investigated the mysterious death of his father.[179]

Shocking Stories about the Clintons

Here is a preview of Bill Clinton's upcoming new book, which will earn him around $10 million. The book will have many shocking revelations, as Bill Clinton "comes clean" and will admit to having seduced upwards of 100 different women, in the course of being married to Hillary. This is what I have learned will be in Bill's memoirs:

---

(177) Ibid., p. 147
(178) Ambrose Evans-Pritchard, "The Secret Life of Bill Clinton," p. 233.
(179) Chris Ruddy, "Vortex," Nov. 1998, p. 5- "Parks' Son Demands Murder Inquiry."

(1) He will admit to more than 100 affairs and that he is a "sex addict."[180]

(2) He will admit that he on several occasions he fantasized about Hillary having gay sex with Monica Lewinsky.[181]

(3) He will admit that he feared Monica might have overheard things and might have tapped into secrets which could have affected national security.[182]

(4) He will admit that Hillary inflicted physical abuse *on him, and he contacted the Secret Service to protect him from Hillary.* [183]

(5) He will express his guilt for having screwed up Chelsea's life to the point that it drove her to drink.

Clinton will discuss the Monica Lewinsky affair in great detail. Monica was privy to confidential conversations concerning terrorism, the war in Bosnia, the bombing of the Federal Building in Oklahoma, and other areas. Clinton will discuss the famous incident when Hillary savagely clawed Bill's face, after Hillary discovered that Barbra Streisand had spent the night at the White House. The story was that Bill had cut himself shaving, but it was Hillary's actions that forced Bill to put on makeup to conceal his wounds.

An inside source told the following to the *Globe:* "Bill has decided to come completely clean about the sins of the past. He wants to rehabilitate his image and make a brand-new start. Under the guise of being the dutiful wife, Hillary

---

(180) Globe, Feb. 10, 2004.
(181) Ibid.
(182) Ibid.
(183) Ibid.

has given Bill plenty of advice about what he should- and shouldn't- include in the book. He knows that if he waffles and dodges the facts with fancy lawyer's language, people will only groan and turn away. Bill isn't going to hold back anything on his sexcapades. He is planning on telling all about his wild romps, the way athletes like Wilt Chamberlain did. He's not proud of his excesses and his inability to control himself, but he has come to believe, through counseling, that sex addiction is a medical condition. He also draws the line at full disclosure of his medical secrets. In an early draft of the book, he hints that he has paid a price for his sex obsession, contracting a mystery disease, but he stops short of going into detail. Clearly, that problem convinced Hillary to steer clear of his bed years ago, and apparently, it led her to seek out female companionship. When Monica was hiding in the secret little room off of the Oval Office- where they had sex- she had plenty of time to see his most private correspondence, his secret personal diary and to overhear conversations with his lawyers and closest aides."[184]

The source continues: "He has known since the earliest days of the scandal that Monica could be his real downfall. The semen-stained dress and all the rest of the nasty sex stuff is nothing compared to what she really knows. He has torn his hair out over the years trying to remember what pages may have been open and what whispered conversations he may have had while she was waiting in the shadows of that little office, her lipstick smeared and dress askew. He knows she could have heard about details of the old money scandals like Whitewater and where some of those skeletons were

---

(184) Ibid.

buried. Even more worrisome are bits and pieces she may have overheard about presidential issues, which, if repeated, could cause an international incident, embarrassing our allies or even potentially toppling a government. **Hillary has also thrown books and an ashtray at the president.**[185] Bill writes that seeing Chelsea falling down drunk in the wake of his scandals tore his heart out. But he says she is proud that she seems to have come to grips with her problems, and the two have reconciled. If Chelsea hasn't exactly forgiven him, she has at least come to accept him, and that's all he can ask." According to the source, Bill's book has a shocking ending. "He actually hopes that Hillary does not run for the presidency. First, because he fears she would become a punching bag for their enemies all over again- whether they divorce or not- and he can't imagine her surviving that. And he admits he has a selfish reason as well. He dreams of being appointed a Supreme Court justice, which is what JFK wanted to do, had he lived to complete his presidency."[186]

Bill's book is still untitled. It should hit the bookstores right around the Democratic convention, if not a few weeks earlier. I find it incredible that Bill Clinton is going to plead that he was a "sex addict", after he molested, raped, and otherwise had his way with over 100 women! That's like a robber going through a hotel, stealing 100 Rolex watches, and then telling the judge he was a *"Rolex addict!"*

---

(185) Ibid.
(186) Ibid.

255

CHAPTER SIX

Reason Number Five the Clintons Belong in Prison

(5) Whitewater- This failed real estate deal resulted in the criminal convictions of several people close to the Clintons: their partners in Whitewater, James and Susan McDougal, Webb Hubbell, and others. Bill and Hillary lied (perjury) throughout the Whitewater investigation. The lawyers did a terrible job, by not putting Bill and Hillary in prison over their fraudulent behavior. It is quite possible that Bill and Hillary broke the law by issuing misleading and inaccurate personal financial statements. I think the Clintons should have been found guilty of perjury, fraud, and obstruction of justice, with respect to their criminal behavior during Whitewater. Both Bill and Hillary should have received a *minimum of 2 years in prison for their role in Whitewater.*

Clinton in Arkansas

Background on Bill Clinton

In 1988, Governor Bill Clinton thought about running for President. All sorts of rumors began to surface about Clinton and extramarital affairs. Betsy Wright felt that Clinton had to confront this issue, if he wanted to become President. She had been covering up for him for years, while the Arkansas State Troopers frequently procured women for young Bill Clinton.

Wright actually met with Clinton and discussed a whole list of possible affairs, and she suggested to him that he not run in 1988. Clinton decided not to run, primarily because of the time commitments away from Chelsea that a nationwide campaign would demand.[1]

At the 1988 Democratic National Convention, Bill Clinton gave a long (32 minutes) boring speech nominating Michael Dukakis as the Democratic candidate for President. The crowd was howling for Dukakis throughout his speech, and the lighting in the hall remained on during Clinton's speech, thereby reducing its effectiveness. In short, Clinton's speech was so pathetic, it actually became part of one of Johnny Carson's monologues! Carson began his monologue by saying "in closing" (a reference to Clinton's way of ending his painful speech) and noted "noted that the Surgeon General had just approved Governor Bill Clinton as an over-the-counter sleep aid, and that Clinton's speech went over "about as big as the Velcro condom." Carson said that the drama in Clinton's voice was "right up there with PBS pledge breaks."[2]

Clinton's friends Linda Bloodworth Thomason and Harry Thomason, friends of Bill from Arkansas and big-time Hollywood producers, got Bill to appear on the "Tonight" show. Bill charmed Johnny and the audience as he played the saxophone for an audience larger than the one that had heard his awful speech at the 1988 convention in Atlanta.[3]

In 1989, Bill Clinton was in the midst of a torrid extramarital affair, about which everyone in the State house

---

(1) David Marannis, First in His Class, p. 443
(2) Ibid., p. 446
(3) Ibid., p. 447

was familiar. The Clintons were going through marriage counseling, and they contemplated divorce. But both Bill and Hillary wanted to save the marriage. Hillary had put in a lot of time with Bill Clinton, and his infidelities would not overcome her ambition to someday become co-President.

By 1990, Bill Clinton had become depressed and overly defensive, as he questioned where his political life was leading. He wasn't sure if he wanted to run for another term as Governor, and there was lots of talk around Little Rock that Hillary might be a candidate. At the last minute, Bill decided to run for re-election.

Bill Clinton was very cozy with Tyson Foods and its boss Don Tyson. According to David Maraniss, well-known Clinton biographer, Tyson Foods got $7.8 million in tax breaks from 1988 to 1990 in Arkansas. Bill flew on Tyson's private jet at least nine times, and he became allied with many big corporations in the Arkansas community. Likewise, Hillary kept moving up the financial ladder, joining the boards of two Arkansas corporate powerhouses, TCBY and Wal-Mart.[4]

In 1990, Bill Clinton and Dick Morris got into a heated argument. Clinton actually punched Morris, who was a head shorter than his boss. Often, Morris would lament "I can't believe Clinton hit me!"[5]

Hillary Clinton always had a lot of balls, especially for a woman! She once started screaming at one of Bill's political

---

(4) Ibid., p. 454
(5) Ibid., p. 455

opponents in the gubernatorial primary, as he was conducting a press conference. She questioned the candidate's record on several fronts- her outburst made all the print and broadcast media.

In 1990, my friend Larry Nichols announced that he would be suing Bill Clinton. He alleged that Bill Clinton maintained a slush fund, at taxpayer expense, to entertain at least five of his girlfriends.

Bill Clinton won re-election in November, 1990. A month later, Clinton called Gennifer Flowers and discussed Sheffield Nelson, his Republican opponent in the gubernatorial race. Clinton told Flowers **"I stuck it up their ass."** Speaking of Nelson, Clinton said. "I know he lied. **I just wanted to make his asshole pucker...**But I covered you."[6]

Bill and Hillary's Dirty Tricks and Private Investigators

Throughout their careers, the Clintons have employed private investigators and dirty tricks to destroy anyone who gets in their way. Nothing Richard Nixon ever did compared with the damage to people's lives that has been inflicted by the goons who worked for Bill and Hillary Clinton. In one of Bill's political campaigns for Governor in Arkansas, Hillary hired Investigative Group International (I.G.I.), an agency run by a guy named Terry Lenzer. Lenzer's name comes up again and again. He was the guy who you could count on to dig up the dirtiest stuff imaginable on any opponent of the Clintons. In this particular campaign, Lenzer went after two

---

(6) Ibid., p. 457

Republicans, Tommy Robinson and Sheffield Nelson. Hillary knew Terry Lenzer from the Legal Services Corporation (LSC), where both occupied top positions. Mickey Kantor, who is another long-time political buddy of the Clintons, knew Terry Lenzer from LSC.[7]

Scandals and Lawsuits Surrounding the Clintons

Larry Nichols knows Bill and Hillary Clinton inside and out. Until he became born again and found God, he had been as dirty as Bill and Hillary were. He has told me that. Larry Nichols is one of the bravest guys in the country for blowing the whistle on Bill and Hillary. I have read and re-read Larry's great book *The Genie is out of the Bottle*. Larry worked for an entity in Arkansas called the Arkansas Development Finance Agency (ADFA). Although this was supposed to be an organization to provide bond financing to work for the betterment of the State of Arkansas, Nichols was convinced that ADFA was simply "a money laundering scheme for Bill's donors, such as cocaine dealer Dan Lasater. Clinton forced Larry Nichols out of ADFA in 1989, using some trumped-up charges having to do with Nichols' using his state telephone to make unauthorized phone calls to people in Nicaragua.

In September, 1990 Nichols sued Clinton and the State of Arkansas, alleging that ADFA was nothing more than a slush fund to pay for Bill Clinton's parties with his many girlfriends. A couple of judges who had been appointees of Bill Clinton threw out the lawsuit, but the damage had been

---

(7) Joyce Milton, the First Partner, p. 196

done. Bill Clinton's abuse of power and misuse of the public trust had become public knowledge.[8]

Castle Grande- This is one of many scandals that preceded Monica Lewinsky, the impeachment, and the pardons. Castle Grande was a project formulated by James McDougal. With 1,000 acres of Arkansas land, McDougal's goal was to build one-half acre homes, primarily for working class families. Federal assessors described Castle Grande as "low and swampy" and basically undesirable.[9] Jim Mc Dougal had been the owner of Madison Guaranty Savings & Loan. The value of the land was $1,750,000; McDougal could borrow only $600,000 from his own lending institution, so he arranged for Seth Ward, the father-in-law of Webb Hubbell to become the "straw buyer". In effect, Ward borrowed $1.1 million dollars from Madison Guaranty that he did not have to pay back. (In accounting, this is called a non-recourse loan). Ward was guaranteed a 10% commission on every parcel that was sold. Hillary was directly involved in Castle Grande. She drafted an option agreement that gave allowed Madison Guaranty to buy 22.5 acres from Seth Ward for $ 400,000, even though Hillary had been warned by Madison Guaranty executive Don Denton that "the agreement was drawn in an manner that might be illegal."[10]

Unfortunately, it gets more complicated. Hillary didn't care much for Seth Ward, which may explain why she did the option agreement. Hillary sounds like she's talking about

---

(8) Joyce Milton, The First Partner, pp. 196-197.
(9) Ibid., p. 177.
(10) Ibid., p. 179.

herself or Bill when she describes Seth Ward as "a persistent, demanding client, someone who pushed very hard for lawyers to respond to him, to get his work done... someone who wasn't shy about showing up at your office unannounced and demanding that you give him all the time he wanted right then, no matter what else you were involved in."[11]

Now Governor Bill Clinton got involved. According to Judge David Hale and State Trooper L.D. Brown, Bill Clinton went up to David Hale on the steps of the Little Rock Capitol building and said to him, "Are you going to help Jim and me out?"[12]   Soon, David Hale did make a loan of $300,000 to Susan McDougal, who was the wife of Jim McDougal, a partner of Bill and Hillary's in the Whitewater deal, and rumored to be a flame of Bill Clinton's too. David Hale testified that he had met with Bill Clinton, and James McDougal at the Castle Grande office to discuss a bogus loan from his company to Susan McDougal. According to Hale, *Bill Clinton pressured him to make the loan.* James McDougal backed up Hale's story, before he, McDougal, died in prison.

Well, the bottom line of all this is: James McDougal was found guilty of fraud and went to prison, David Hale was found guilty of fraud and went to prison. Susan McDougal was found guilty of fraud and went to prison. Webster

---

(11) Ibid., p. 178.
(12) Jason D. Fodeman, How to Destroy a Village, p. 18. This is a great book. The author was a 17 year-old with the maturity of a 53 year-old. I recommend this book to all youngsters who want to know what criminals the Clintons are.

Hubbell was found guilty of criminal activity and went to prison. Bill and Hillary Clinton *should have been found guilty of fraud and perjury.* Bill Clinton and Hillary Clinton denied everything, forgot all incriminating details, and- like they would do again and again- used their clever legal skills they had picked up at Yale Law School to dodge the same prison sentences that the McDougals, their business partners, Webb Hubbell (Hillary's mentor from the Rose Law firm and perhaps a lot more), and David Hale were not able to escape.

Specifically, Hillary denied *under oath* doing any work on Castle Grande. (Lie #1). Years later, billing records showed up in the White House indicating that she had billed 30 hours at $ 120/hour to Castle Grande. Bill Clinton denied having anything to do with pressuring David Hale or having exerted any improper influence in getting Hale to provide the $300,000 loan to Susan McDougal (Lie #2).

Harold Ickes and George Stephanopoulos used spin to protect Hillary from all her lying in Castle Grande. Harold Ickes was quoted as telling Beverly Bassett Schaeffer (Arkansas securities commissioner) to get their stories straight: "If we fuck this up, we're done."[13] The Clinton White House called the whole Castle Grande affair a "failed-land deal" – it was "old news." Stepanopoulos had a great comment: "Perjury takes intent. Simply describing plots of land by a different name when both names were in common usage is not perjury by any stretch."[14]

---

(13) Barbara Olson, Hell to Pay, p. 166.
(14) Ibid., p. 167.

I don't know if George Stephanopoulos is a lawyer or not, but if he is, I don't want him representing me! Bottom line in Castle Grande: Bill should have gone to prison for perjury and obstruction of justice, at the very least. Hillary should have gone to prison for perjury, obstruction of justice, and fraud. At the very least, they should have each gotten 2 to 3 years in prison and both should have been disbarred over Castle Grande alone!

The Mysterious Death of Vince Foster

The death of Vince Foster, Hillary Clinton's law partner from the Rose Law Firm and Bill Clinton's White House Deputy Counsel (# 3 person in Justice Department) on July 20, 1993 could be the topic of another book. I consider Foster's death to be a murder. I feel there were dozens of reason the Clintons would not want Vince Foster around anymore. According to the official version, Vince Foster committed suicide- I reject that theory 100%. At the very least, the Bush Administration should re-open the investigation into the death of Vince Foster. Specifically, the role of Bill and Hillary Clinton, with respect to their relationship with Vince Foster, needs to be investigated. For a great account of Foster's Death, I recommend *The Strange Death of Vince Foster,* by Christopher Ruddy (Free Press, 1997). It is not a quick read- Ruddy is a brilliant investigative reporter, who spent years meticulously documenting his facts surrounding Fosters' death. If it were ever proven that Bill and Hillary Clinton had any role in the murder of Vince Foster, they would belong in the same prison cell as anyone else who was involved as an accessory to murder. I am not accusing the Clintons of murdering Vince Foster- I just think the government should reopen its investigation into his death and start deposing some people from the Clinton Administration.

Bill Clinton's Cocaine Use- Roger Clinton

Sharlene Wilson was working as a bartender and federal drug informant. She had sold cocaine to Roger Clinton, who gave the coke to Bill. At one party, according to Wilson, "the governor was so out of it that he slid down the wall, ending up slumped in a trash can."[15]

Bill's friend **Dan Lasater, a convicted cocaine trafficker,** helped out Roger Clinton, according to an FBI investigation of Lasater. Lasater gave Roger Clinton $8,000 to help pay off some angry drug dealers, who had threatened to kill Bill, Roger, and their mother if they weren't paid back the cash Roger owed them.[16]

In 1984, Roger was caught on tape doing coke with an informant and setting up a $30,000 kickback in exchange for enlisting Bill's help in arranging a sewer permit for a time-share project, owned in part by Dan Lasater. Roger boasted: "We're closer than any brothers you've ever known…There isn't anything he wouldn't do for me." When roadblocks to the bribe presented themselves in the form of one honest board member, Roger Clinton assured the informant "that Big Brother would find a way around the holdout."[17]

---

(15) Joyce Milton, The First Partner, p. 164.
(16) Ibid., p. 165.
(17) Ibid., p. 165.

And Roger was proud of his sexual escapades with women at Bill's mansion, both in the main residence and the guest house. "Oh, they love it!", said Roger.[18]

In April, 1984, Roger Clinton was speaking on tape to Hot Springs, Ark. Police detective Travis Bunn. After doing some lines of coke, he said on tape: "I've got to get some for my brother, he's got a nose like a Hoover vacuum cleaner!"[19] Most of Roger Clinton's 3 dozen late-night visits to the Governors' Mansion after spring, 1983, were made when Hillary was out of town. Visitors' logs confirm that fact, and often Roger had one or more women with him at his late-night "meetings" at the State House[20]

Roger was not a small-time dealer, either. He was involved with dealers in New York City who had connections to Colombian dealers. Roger **"had been dealing in quarter pounds, half pounds, and whole pounds of cocaine."** Roger's lawyer in his drug case, Bill Wilson, was rewarded with a judgeship by Bill Clinton some years later.[21]

Bill's mother, Virginia Kelley, was a nurse anesthetist. On two occasions she was sued for malpractice after two female patients died during procedures when she was delivering anesthesia.[22]

---

(18) Ibid., p. 165.
(19) Ibid., p. 165.
(20) Ibid., p. 166.
(21) Ibid., p. 167.
(22) Ibid., p. 168.

In the middle of 1985, Hillary confided to her closest friends that she was on the verge of filing for a divorce from Bill. But a long round of marriage counseling coupled with political expediency (a divorce would have killed Bill and Hillary's goals of becoming President) kept them together.[23]

I have not tried to avoid the Whitewater Scandal. It has been covered in so many other books, but let me just say that Bill and Hillary Clinton lied their way throughout that investigation. Susan McDougal and James McDougal went to prison for crimes related to Whitewater. Hillary did a very shrewd job of not remembering key details related to Whitewater. She denied having knowledge of practically everything that could have incriminated her, and that's what kept her out of prison. The simple fact is the Clintons work as a team; they are both a bunch of shyster lawyers who conned people along the way, from Little Rock, to Washington D.C., and now- to New York City!

Even though Hillary billed out 15 hours of legal time at $120/hour on a microbrewery project, Hillary denied having any knowledge of the project. As a lawyer, Hillary knew how to not get caught. Any time that she would be committing perjury, she would simply not recall the facts, or claim to have had no knowledge of a situation. Webb Hubbell, Hillary's law partner at Rose, went to prison for crimes related to Whitewater. You can't tell me that Bill Clinton's partners in Whitewater- the McDougals and Webb Hubbell were any less guilty than Bill and Hillary Clinton!

---

(23) Ibid., p. 169.

The Clintons just know how to work the legal system for their benefit! Hillary's other partner from Rose, Vince Foster, ends up dead in a mysterious death in July, 1993. And you want me to believe that Bill and Hillary Clinton are totally innocent bystanders while everyone around them is either getting killed or sent off to prison?

Webster Hubbell

The Clintons' Arkansas friend Webster Hubbell, who looks just like Chelsea Clinton, is a case study in the selfishness and arrogance of Bill and Hillary Clinton. Consider Webster Hubbell's background- he had been a senior law partner at Rose Law Firm, when a young Hillary Clinton joined the firm. After a power-packed legal and political career in Little Rock, he joined his buddies Bill and Hillary Clinton as associate attorney general in the first term of the Clinton presidency. Vince Foster went to prison for stealing hundreds of thousands of dollars from clients at the Rose Law firm. Bill Clinton did not pardon Webster Hubbell. For years, rumors have swirled around Little Rock and Washington D.C. that Webb Hubbell might be the biological father of Chelsea Clinton. Although I have no conclusive proof of this rumor, I have heard this allegation from several sources. Larry Nichols, who has known the Clintons for years, and who worked for governor Bill Clinton swears to me that the story is true.

The following account was told to me by Larry Nichols in one of the many phone conversations I had with him. I have no way of determining its validity- my guess is as good as yours. Nichols told me he was at a meeting with Attorney General Bill Clinton back in 1978. Nichols claims that young Clinton was meeting with some wealthy backers, when suddenly the meeting was interrupted. In walked a smelly beast of a woman, with "bad b.o., hairy legs, hairy armpits, bad hair, and real bad glasses." According to Nichols, this was how Hillary Clinton broke up the meeting. She yelled to Bill: "Bill what are you doing?" Bill replied, "Hill, I'm gonna run for governor!"

Hillary immediately replied (according to Nichols): "Well I gotta get in Rose...I'm gonna fuck Hubbell!"[24]

Personally, I found Larry Nichols story to be shocking. I present it to you as a rumor, not a fact. I am the first to admit that without DNA or bloodtype analysis, this story must unfortunately be considered an allegation, not a fact. I heard this allegation from many people. According to a woman who has worked for a Republican U.S. Senator for 18 years, the rumor has been around Capitol Hill for years. People who knew and worked with the Clintons in Arkansas have told me they heard the rumor. I am reminded of the maxim: "A picture is worth a thousand words." Look at the picture of Webb Hubbell in David Brock's book and judge for yourself.

---

(24) I have known Larry Nichols for years. He has been a frequent guest on my radio talk show, and he knows the Clintons like the back of his hand. I am throwing this story out to you the reader as a rumor. I believe that the story could easily be true. Back in 1978, everything was very different than now. If you want to see the incredible resemblance between Web Hubbell and Chelsea, just look at the picture in David Brock's 1996 classic "The Seduction of Hillary Rodham." Compare the picture of a young Webb Hubbell and a young Bill Clinton with any picture of young Chelsea before her extensive plastic surgery. You will be shocked by the identical appearance between Hubbell and Chelsea!

In Webb Hubbell's biography "Friends in High Places," there are 363 references to Hillary Clinton.[25]

Larry Nichols has been a guest on my radio show on many occasions. I totally believe him, and I see no reason in the world why he would be lying. He and Larry Patterson have told me lots of stuff about the Clintons, and I have been impressed with their sincerity. Besides, what would be their motives in lying? They are not the ones who seek to attain power over others. But, in typical Clinton fashion, the Clinton goon squad has tried to discredit Nichols and Patterson.

It is shocking to me that Webb Hubbell was not pardoned by Bill Clinton. But that's the pig Bill Clinton for you. He probably has nothing but contempt for Hubbell.

Furthermore, there is another rumor running around Washington that there was a confidential memo in the Clinton White House prohibiting photo ops of Chelsea Clinton with Webster Hubbell. But I wouldn't put it past Bill Clinton not to have pardoned one of his closest buddies, and one of Hillary's long-time friends.

Bill Clinton pardoned his former Secretary of Housing and Urban Development Henry Cisneros. Cisneros had been found guilty of paying $250,000 in hush money to his ex-mistress Linda Jones. Cisneros copped a plea- he admitted to lying. Clinton pardoned Cisneros and his mistress.[26]

---

(25) Webb Hubbell, "Friends in High Places," pp. 1-332.
(26) Olson, "The Final Days," pp. 160-1.

CHAPTER SEVEN

Reason Number Four the Clintons Belong in Prison

(4) The Impeachment- Bill Clinton perjured himself over and over again in his testimony. He committed witness tampering and obstructed justice. There was more abuse of power in the Clinton administration than in all the other Presidencies combined! It is a crime that Bill and Hillary were not indicted for their crimes related to the impeachment. I blame George Bush and John Ashcroft for not indicting the Clintons. I feel that if they had been indicted, Bill and Hillary would have received prison sentences of a *minimum* of two years each, as a result of their criminal acts during the impeachment.

Clinton and the Media

Bias in the Media

Bernard Goldberg's "Bias" is a book about the media's overwhelmingly liberal slant on the news stories they show on primetime network television. In the book Goldberg describes the problem as he came to see it during his 28 years as a reporter for CBS news. The straw that broke the camel's back was a story about conservative presidential candidate Steve Forbes. In the segment, which aired on CBS Evening News, reporter Eric Engberg discussed Forbes' proposed tax cut using phrases like "Forbes pitches his flat-tax scheme as an economic elixir." These are not just words, Goldberg says, these are subtle ways of attacking the conservative Forbes without actually analyzing the facts of his tax plan.

But that's not all. Engberg goes on to say that "Forbes' number-one wackiest flat-tax promise is that it will give parents "more time to spend with their children and each other." This language showcases the built-in prejudices that most reporters have against conservatives and the way they don't take conservative ideas seriously. Goldberg doesn't take issue with a reporter's personal political preferences, but he says there is a problem when it affects the way they report on serious ideas that could possibly benefit the country.

Something interesting happened when Goldberg wrote an op-ed piece for the Wall Street Journal decrying the bias of the major networks. Rather than taking an objective, serious look at his claims, most of his media friends simply cut off their friendships. They refused to consider the fact that they were not reporting the news fairly. When Goldberg told his close friend Dan Rather he had written an editorial attacking the news media Rather's reaction was unexpected. Dan Rather launched into a long soliloquy about how much he loved his country, and how he had come close to tears many times when reporting news on patriotic issues. Rather clearly assumed that he was being directly accused of being unpatriotic and totally missed the point of the article. He and Goldberg have not spoken since. Eric Engberg, whose story Goldberg attacked in his op-ed piece, told Goldberg he was full of shit and hasn't spoken to him since.

In general Goldberg's claims were met with rage and feelings of betrayal instead of a clear-headed investigation of his claims. And Goldberg, a lifelong democrat, was accused of having a *conservative* bias by people like Andrew Heyward, who said "Bernie is certainly entitled to his political views, and his politics have been known for a very long time." Engberg's boss Al Ortiz asked Goldberg "What in the world were you thinking when you wrote that piece?" It seems that no one got the point. Or they did but didn't see anything wrong with their biases infecting the news.

Goldberg claims that the media's liberal bias began in the eighties when liberals felt disenchanted and outnumbered by the Reagan-dominated government. This is when political correctness evolved and the media grew into a forum for combating conservatism in all its forms rather than reporting the news. And liberals saw themselves as middle-of-the-road, viewing all conservatives as extremists. This is the basis for everything Goldberg says about the liberal bias: Liberals don't see it as a bias. They see their own views and ideals as moderate, such as women's rights, abortion, affirmative action, unions and such. They see organizations like the National Organization for Women as middle-of-the-road while the Christian Coalition is identified as "conservative," full of right-wing nuts.

Goldberg has illuminating things to say about how homelessness has been reported in the past two decades. During the 80's the homeless were seen on TV news reports as families, hungry children and elderly victims of the system. Nevermind the reality of the situation which is that most homeless people are victims of their own drug and alcohol habits and have few people to blame other than themselves. Goldberg points out that the liberal media in the 80's created a victim culture to make us think that the homeless were just like us, and we could all end up that way. This kind of thinking was clearly politically influenced and unfair. As Goldberg points out, Candy Crowley on CNN warned that "Winter is on the way and three million Americans have no place to call home." In 1993 Jackie Nespral said on NBC, "Nationally right now, five million people are believed to be homeless...and the numbers are increasing." On CBS Charles Osgood threatened that "It is estimated that by the year 2000, nineteen million Americans will be homeless." If we look behind the words you can find a hidden, liberal "pity" agenda- we must provide government programs for these poor victims. However, when Clinton took office homeless stories on the news decreased dramatically. In 1995 there were nine stories about the homeless on the major networks- CBS, NBC, ABC, and CNN- versus the seventy-one stories on the homeless in 1990 when George Bush was president. One might think that Clinton had solved the homeless problem. That is, if you believe everything the news tells you.

AIDS stories took on a familiarly liberal slant during the 80's. In efforts to convince the general population that they were at risk of getting the virus, the media ignored the blatant facts that most people with AIDS had gotten it through intravenous drug use and gay butt-sex! Yet there were countless stories alleging that "The disease of *them* is suddenly the disease of *us,*" and "Cases rising fast among heterosexuals," and "The proportion of heterosexual cases...is increasing at a worrisome rate...The numbers as yet are small, but AIDS is a growing threat to the heterosexual population" as well as "Heterosexuals and AIDS: The second stage of the epidemic" and let's not forget an article from the Ladies Home Journal entitled "AIDS and Marriage: What every Wife Must Know." Clearly news organizations didn't feel that anyone would care about AIDS unless straight middle-class people could get it. And they tried to scare people into voting for costly AIDS prevention programs.

Racial issues were filtered through the liberal media machine as well. Goldberg tells a story of two reporters, Diana Gonzalez and Larry Doyle, who did a story on chain gangs in Alabama for CBS. The particular chain gang they interviewed and shot on tape was completely full of black prisoners. When they had finished the story and gotten back to New York the two received a reprimand from the producers for not showing more white prisoners. It wasn't politically correct to show so many black prisoners on television, even if it was the truth. This is how liberals distort the truth in the media: it gets sacrificed for political correctness and ends up not helping anyone. Instead of showing more successful, upstanding black families they reasoned that they should show more white criminals to offset the black ones. Goldberg shows the hypocrisy inherent in the politically correct ideals of the media- they'll refer to Jamaicans as "African-Americans" in a misguided attempt not to offend anyone, but they wouldn't give their jobs or their educational opportunities to black people.

Goldberg argues that the news is overwhelmingly supportive of feminist issues, not giving them the same criticism they give men. There are countless news stories about deadbeat dads, uneducated men, violent men, and none about the excesses of feminism or the problems women create. News reporters consistently go soft on feminists, even Sam Donaldson, who once said "I've been very careful about offending women. I'll challenge presidents any day, but taking on half the world is asking too much."[1]   Goldberg indicates that stories about the dangers of raising kids in a home with two working parents are not shown on primetime television. No one wants to offend feminists, so we ignore the elephant in the middle of our country- **kids are suffering because of working mothers!** Goldberg asks a scathing question. In his words: "Why have the evening newscasts tiptoed around the most sensitive of all issues involving children- the day-care issue- going out of their way to accentuate the positive and de-emphasize the negative?"[2]   I think we all know the answer is political.

In another section Goldberg writes that we have been so fascinated by stories like "Where's Chandra?" and "Who killed JonBenet?" that we have ignored stories about what happens to latchkey kids or children of the latest fad, *divorce*. Stories about divorce and the loneliness of children aren't mysterious, sexy or juicy enough to warrant our attention. That's what TV producers think. And the reaction from feminists to the plight of children is to call for more government spending on day-care. Instead of looking at the real symptoms of the excesses of feminism, they will put band-aids like "day-care" on the problem and blame everyone but themselves. And TV is complicit in this excuse, for following a liberal agenda and pursuing ratings over substance.

Even worse, the mainstream media considers liberal views to be *reasonable*. It is *reasonable* to be for affirmative action. According to liberals, it is the norm to be pro-choice

---

(1) Bernard Goldberg, Bias, p. 141
(2) Ibid., p. 172

and anti-death penalty. Goldberg further points out the hypocrisy of many TV anchors, when they describe **Republicans** as **"Conservatives"** but do not label **"left-wing Democrats" as "liberals."** On TV, the Christian Coalition is identified as a conservative organization, but the National Organization for Women is practically never identified as a **"liberal" organization.**

Hollywood actors such as Bruce Willis or Tom Selleck are identified as conservatives, but Barbra Streisand and Rob Reiner are not identified as liberals. Goldberg contrasts the label of "conservative" talk show host Rush Limbaugh with no corresponding (i.e., "liberal") adjective describing a host such as, say, an Al Franken. As recently as this morning (February 17, 2004), on "Good Morning America", nationally-syndicated talk-show host Sean Hannity was referred to by Charlie Gibson as "Conservative Sean Hannity". Hannity received the "Conservative" label no fewer than 5 times during the 8 minute interview!

Goldberg delivers a brilliant analysis of how ABC News Anchor Peter Jennings described the U.S. Senators signing the oath book at the impeachment hearings of Bill Clinton. In almost all cases, Republicans such as John McCain and Rick Santorum were described as **"conservative"** or **"leaning to the right",** while Democrats such as Barbara Boxer, Ted Kennedy, Barbara Mikulski, and Charles Schumer were **never described as "liberal" or "left-leaning."**[3]

---

(3) Ibid., pp. 62-64

This bias exists, Goldberg maintains, because in the minds of the mainstream media honchos, "that which is right of center is conservative. That which is left of center is middle of the road. No wonder they can't recognize their own bias."[4]

NOW is not identified as a liberal organization, because the Dan Rathers, Tom Brokaws, and Peter Jennings perceive them as being "middle of the road." Goldberg writes: "To mainstream media, these are major elements of the liberal agenda. But to the liberals in the media, these aren't liberal views at all. They're just sensible, reasonable, rational views, *which just happen to coincide with their own*."[5]

Understanding this bias is fundamental to explaining the free pass that the mainstream media has given to Bill and Hillary Clinton!

According to Goldberg, most TV reporters cannot think on their own. They have to consult newspapers such as the *Washington Post and the New York Times* before they can have an opinion.[6] Goldberg wrote a piece for the *Wall Street Journal* in which he sharply criticized a piece by reporter Eric Engberg of the CBS Evening News. The story was critical of Steve Forbes' proposal for a flat tax. Engberg referred to Forbes' plan as a *"wacky scheme."* Would he have used such language to describe a plan of Hillary Clinton or Teddy Kennedy? Never! Goldberg's op-ed piece roundly criticized the reporting of CBS News.

---

(4) Ibid., p. 65.
(5) Ibid., p. 67.
(6) Ibid., p. 24.

Goldberg likens the mainstream media to the mafia. "If CBS News were a prison instead of a journalistic enterprise, three-quarters of the producers and 100 percent of the vice president's would be Dan's bitches."[7] Dan, by the way, is Dan Rather. According to Goldberg, Dan Rather is the "The Dan"- he speaks his own language –"Dan-ish" and basically controls CBS News. "Bernie G opened his big mouth to the wrong people- and he got whacked."[8] In "Dan-ish", "it's all my fault" means "*it's all your fault*"..."no problem" means "*big problem*"... "don't worry, amigo" means "*worry a lot, you unworthy piece of crap!*"[9]

Goldberg claims that CBS used to have a VP, whose unofficial title was "vice president in charge of Dan Rather." His "main job was to make sure Dan was happy. This was a very important job."[10]

Bernie Goldberg got to know the real Dan Rather, the one "who operates with the cool precision of a Mafia hit man who kisses you on the cheek right before he puts a bullet through your eyeball." When Dan Rather told Goldberg, "Bernie, we were friends yesterday, we're friends today, and we'll be friends tomorrow", he knew he was dead. As Goldberg put it, "it was just a matter of time."[11]

---

(7) Ibid., p. 16
(8) Ibid., p. 16.
(9) Ibid., p. 16
(10) Ibid., p. 16
(11) Ibid., p. 18.

Goldberg's article in the *Wall Street Journal* was a cardinal sin, as far as Dan Rather was concerned. Goldberg "violated the code of *omerta,* the sacred code of silence that both wise guys and news guys live and die by."[12]

Why am I discussing Bernard Goldberg in a book whose underlying premise is that the Clintons belong in prison? Because the same media that destroyed Bernard Goldberg for his accurate and incisive observations has covered and protected Bill and Hillary Clinton for decades! Dan Rather, Peter Jennings, Tom Brokaw, Barbara Walters and Mike Wallace have one thing in common- they are all Manhattan millionaires who are cocktail party buddies of Bill and Hillary Clinton!

But let's leave the big names alone for awhile and talk about the everyday reporter. Goldberg knows about reporting- after all, he put in almost **30 years with CBS News!** Goldberg points out that a reporter can find any expert to pretty much confirm what the reporter is *advocating* in his story. He notes that "experts" are a dime a dozen.[13] Ask enough "experts" and the reporter will eventually get the results he is looking for. Goldberg knew that to Dan Rather, dissent was betrayal.

CBS News Executive Andrew Heyward considered Goldberg's WSJ piece to be "an act of disloyalty" and a "betrayal of trust." Though Heyward had agreed with Goldberg that, indeed, there ***was a liberal bias to the media, had Goldberg quoted Heyward in his piece, that would have***

---

(12) Ibid., p. 18.
(13) Ibid., p. 26.

been [in Heyward's words] *"like raping my wife and kidnapping my kids!"*[14]

Media people will gladly take on politicians, lawyers, the military, and organized religion- that's fair game. But when someone like Bernard Goldberg uses that same strategy against the media, *that's not fair!* **And what did Eric Engberg have to say to his colleague Bernie Goldberg? Engberg said: "Okay, Bernie, here's my response. You're full of shit."**[15]

Dan Rather stopped speaking to Bernard Goldberg. Reporters at CBS stopped talking to Bernard Goldberg. Rather attacked Goldberg, calling him a "political activist." **Rather** told a reporter from the *Dallas Morning News:* "If you want to see my neck swell and the hair on the back of my neck rise, you just try to tell me how to report the news. When anybody tries to intimidate me into reporting the news their way, my answer is 'Get lost.' I've never done it. I'm not going to do it now."[16]

The President of CBS News, Andrew Heyward, felt that Goldberg had caused CBS "a great deal of residual pain and suffering." Bob Schieffer, chief Washington correspondent for CBS told the *Washington Post:* "If this place is as ethically corrupt as he [Goldberg] seems to think, I think he'd have no alternative but to resign." **Tom** Brokaw of NBC piled on too. He said "it was inappropriate for [Goldberg] to

---

(14) Ibid., p. 34-5.
(15) Ibid., p. 35.
(16) Ibid., p. 38.

go to a newspaper like the Wall Street Journal [and] attack your own organization."[17]

The *New York Times, typically, did not even cover Goldberg's article!*

You want to know what a wacko Dan Rather is? Listen to this! Do you remember the bombing of the Federal Building in Oklahoma City, on April 19, 1995, when 168 innocent people (including 19 children) were killed? Well, according to Goldberg: "Dan Rather was so incensed that Connie [Chung] was on the air first and getting all the airtime that when he finally arrived in Oklahoma City, he spent *hours on the phone with TV writers, blasting Connie Chung as a second-rate journalist."* Dan Rather was more concerned with *his own airtime – and the fact that Connie Chung got on the air first- than anything else!* Dan had been on vacation, and Connie got the scoop!

P.S. One month later, Connie Chung was fired from the CBS Evening News. Chung had been Rather's co-anchor on the nightly news. Sure enough, in the *Boston Globe Dan Rather said this about his axed co-anchor:* "I'm a friend of hers. I was yesterday, I am today, and I will be tomorrow." What Dan really meant, says Goldberg was: "I am *not* a friend of hers...I'm glad they finally fired her so I can have more airtime for myself."[18]

Hundreds of people were killed and wounded, and Dan Rather is worried about his airtime.

---

(17) Ibid., p. 39.
(18) Ibid., p. 44.

When Goldberg was preparing a piece on liberal bias in the news for his show "Eye to Eye", the President of CBS News, Andrew Heyward, told him, "you can't ask Dan any tough questions."[19]   Yet Heyward once told Goldberg: "Look, Bernie, of course there's a liberal bias in the news. All the networks tilt left." Then the President of CBS News told Goldberg: "If you repeat any of this, I'll deny it."[20]

Not everyone in the mainstream media was opposed to Bernard Goldberg's opinions.   John Stossel, Bob Costas, Roger Ailes, and Andy Rooney all went on record as either commending Goldberg or agreeing with the gist of his thesis that there is a pronounced liberal bias to the news.

To show you how biased the media is, consider the following:

According to a 1996 survey conducted by the Freedom Foundation and the Roper Center of 139 Washington bureau chiefs and congressional correspondents:

(1) 89% of the journalists voted for Bill Clinton in 1992, compared with just 43% of the nonjournalist voters.
(2) 7% of the journalists voted for George Bush; 37% of the voters did
(3) 2% of the journalists voted for Ross Perot, while 19% of the electorate voted for Perot.[21]

---

(19) Ibid., p. 48.
(20) Ibid., p. 49.
(21) Ibid., p. 129.

And you wonder why the Washington media has been so kind to the Clintons? When you consider that 89% of the Washington press corps supports Clinton, you have your answer! Conversely, that's why they are so tough on every move that George Bush makes.

I don't want to leave anything out of this first book on the Clintons, and if I don't put this in right here I might forget it. You know that clown Paul Begala who appears on "Crossfire "(CNN)? Well, Begala was a strategist for Bill Clinton during the '92 and '96 campaigns. According to Bob Woodward, author of *The Agenda,* Begala told former Treasury Secretary Robert Rubin that his attitude toward people with money was: "Fuck them [the rich]."[22]

Rick Kaplan, Head of ABC Political Coverage

In June 2003, ABC hired a Clinton friend named Rick Kaplan to be the Senior Vice President of its political coverage. This means he is one of the main driving forces behind such shows as Nightline, World News Tonight, and This Week with George Stephanopoulos.

Why don't we examine Kaplan's political past?

In 1992, when he was executive producing ABC's Prime Time Live, Kaplan served as a media advisor to Bill Clinton, telling him how to handle a 60 Minutes interview and how to manage the messy Gennifer Flowers situation. He also got Clinton on the Don Imus show when he was having trouble

---

(22) Ibid., p. 25.

on the campaign trail, and arranged for that interview to be shown on Nightline.

In '93, he stayed in the Lincoln Bedroom and played golf with the President. Fast forward to 1997- Kaplan was producing a CNN special on campaign finance. He asked his staff to eliminate the word "scandal" whenever talking about Clinton's various controversial fundraising tactics. Not once in the entire broadcast did viewers hear the phrase "Clinton scandal."

In 1998, at the height of the Lewinsky *scandal*, Kaplan produced a special for CNN that basically savaged and attacked every Clinton critic. Victims included Rep. Dan Burton and Ken Starr.

In 2000 Kaplan stayed at the White House again, and his 21-year-old daughter Alexis was treated to a two and a half hour White House tour by Bill Clinton. Later that year Kaplan counseled Al Gore when he was preparing for a debate with Bill Bradley.[23]

Bias in the N.Y. Times Book Review

It is amazing how differently the *New York Times Book Review* describes its bestsellers, based on whether the book has a "left" or "right" perspective. Consider how the *Times* of July 20, 2003 described Hillary Clinton's book *Living History:* A memoir by the junior senator from New York and

---

(23) Mediaresearch.org, "Bill Clinton Lapdog is now ABC's top dog."

former first lady.[24] No words in the description of Hillary's book are put in "quotes", *as if Hillary's book were factual and the truth.*

Yet look how that same list treats more conservative books.

Ann Coulter's book *Treason* gets this description from the *Times.:* The lawyer and pundit dissects "liberal treachery from the cold war to the war on terrorism."[25] The *Times* supplied the "quotation marks", *as if to tell the reader that Hillary Clinton is credible, but Ann Coulter is not. That is totally unfair and inaccurate.*

Similarly, look how the *Times* describes Al Franken's book *Lies (And The Lying Liars who Tell Them):* A satirical critique of the rhetoric of right wing pundits and politicians. Again, Franken, the liberal- like Hillary- has his book described *without any quotation marks in the blurb, as if it were the fact.* Compare the Franken book description with that of Michael Savage's new bestseller.

Here's how the recent *Times* described Savage's book, *The Enemy Within:* The syndicated radio talk show host sets out to rebuff "the liberal assault on our schools, faith and military."[26] The 'quotation marks' are supplied by the *Times* for Michael Savage but *not for* Al Franken!

---

(24) New York Times Book Review, July 20, 2003
(25) New York Times Book Review, July 20, 2003.
(26) Ibid., Feb 22, 2003

Finally, let's compare how the *Times* described *Big Lies* by Joe Conason vs. *Dereliction of Duty by* Lt. Col. Robert (Buzz) Patterson and *Off with Their Heads* by Dick Morris. Typically, the book on the "left" is presented as the norm; the books on the "right" are presented with the 'quotation marks', as if they are *not possibly true!* Look:

Big Lies by Joe Conason: A journalist examines conservatives' use of rhetorical argument in modern political discourse.[27] Conason is an avowed leftist, it should be pointed out. No quotation marks for a lefty.

Dereliction of Duty, by Robert (Buzz) Patterson: A retired Air Force colonel who served in the White House contends that Bill Clinton "compromised America's national security."[28] The *Times* used those 'quotation marks' again. And they left out 2 words when they described Patterson: *nuclear football.* Lt. Col. Patterson carried the "nuclear football" for Clinton, he didn't just *"serve in the White House!"*

Off With Their Heads, by Dick Morris: The television analyst condemns what he describes as a widespread campaign "to oppose and impede the war on terror."[29]

As you can see, I have read Bernard Goldberg's books *Bias* and *Arrogance.* The liberal bias of the media kept the Clintons out of prison- so far. I hope all the liberals reading this book are steaming right now.

---

(27) Ibid., Sep. 7, 2003
(28) Ibid., July 20, 2003
(29) Ibid.

Media Bias in the New York Times

In the book "Journalistic Fraud- How The New York Times Distorts the News and Why It Can No Longer Be Trusted", Bob Kohn exposes the techniques used by the New York Times to slant the news. Basically, the Times would go to extra lengths to protect Bill Clinton if he did something wrong and make sure to blame George W. Bush if he made a mistake in foreign or domestic decision-making.

Kohn describes an article from the "Times" of September 19, 2002, which indicated that the administration in 1998 failed to heed warnings that terrorists were going to crash a plane in to the World Trade Center. In the article, the "Times" didn't use the word "Clinton", leading the reader who didn't see the date "1998" to think that this was the fault of the Bush Administration!

Here's how the story appeared in the "Times":

"U.S. Failed to act on Warnings in '98 of Plane Attack"

The United States was told in 1998 that Arab terrorists were planning to fly a bomb-laden aircraft into the World Trade Center, but the F.B.I. and the F.A.A. did not take the threat seriously, a Congressional investigation into the September 11 attacks found.

The 1998 intelligence report from the C.I.A. was just one of several warnings the U.S. received, but did not seriously analyze, in the years leading up to the September 11 attacks that were detailed today at a Congressional hearing.

The fact is that Bill Clinton refused to meet privately with CIA Director James Woolsey. Clinton dropped the ball on Al Qaeda, yet the article never once blamed Clinton or the Clinton administration.

Yet, if the "Times" had accurately written the article, it would have read:

Clinton Team Failed to Act on Warning of a Plane Attack

The Clinton administration was aware in 1998 that Arab terrorists were planning to fly a bomb-laden aircraft in to the World Trade Center, but the F.B.I. and the Federal Aviation Administration did not take seriously the threats reported by the Central Intelligence Agency, a Congressional investigation into the Sept. 11 attacks found.

The 1998 intelligence from the C.I.A. was just one of several warnings the Clinton administration received, but did not analyze, in the years leading up to the Sept. 11 attacks that were detailed today at a Congressional hearing.[30]

Similarly, the "Times" slanted a story about the botched arrest of Khalid Sheikh Mohammed in March, 1996. It was the Clinton administration that didn't follow the advice of the CIA, allowing Khalid Mohammed to flee Qatar. Again, manipulative writing avoided blaming Clinton for his ineffective policy against terrorism.

---

(30) Kohn, pp. 61-62

"The New York Times" treats political fundraising dinners of Democrats and Republicans in totally different ways. The tone of coverage for Republican activities was "disparaging" and "accusatory". Clinton, whose behavior and tactics were in many ways similar to those of Bush, was presented in a "favorable light." Bush "engineered" his election; Clinton simply won re-election.[31]

On May 22, 2001, The "Times" reported that when President Bush spoke at Yale University, he received "catcalls" and 'boos" from the crowd. This description was contrasted with the favorable treatment given Hillary Clinton, when she addressed the Yale graduates the day before.

"She did not draw the kind of negative reaction that Mr. Bush did on the decidedly liberal campus."[32]

The Times conveniently left out of its story that there was substantial, vocal conservative opposition to Hillary's speech at Yale. Students had been urged by luminaries such as William F. Buckley Jr. to be civil in their opposition and to allow Hillary her 1st amendment rights.[33]

Drudge Breaks the Willey Story

Matt Drudge was the one who released the Kathleen Willey story on his website. White House staffers were very interested in Drudge's website; they had logged onto it over 2,600 times. Clinton's lawyer Bob Bennett called Willey's

---

(31) Ibid., pp. 182-183.
(32) Kohn, p. 97
(33) Ibid

account of being groped by Bill Clinton "fucking horseshit."[34] When it became clear that Willey was about to be subpoenaed in the Paula Jones case, Press Secretary Michael McCurry told Washington Post reporter Peter Baxter, "I could subpoena you for cocksucking.[35] When it was revealed that Charlie Trie had secretly laundered contributions to the DNC, the story was eclipsed by news of Clinton's progress with the budget and the release of new, favorably low unemployment rates.

Michael Savage Comments on Bill and Hillary Clinton

If you've never listened to Michael Savage, you're missing something real good. I must thank my friend Bruce Smirnoff for turning me on to Savage. Now I never miss a show. He's on in L.A. from 5 to 7 p.m., and he holds nothing back. His most recent book *The Enemy Within (WND Books, 2003)* is already a New York Times bestseller. This is what Savage has to say about the Clintons. First, here's Savage on Bill Clinton.

On immigration: Savage feels that Bill Clinton's immigration policy was a disaster. "It wasn't give us your tired and your poor. No, under Clinton it was "give us your loafers and your free-loaders...Clinton, the most scandalous president in our history, let the dregs of humanity invade America."[36]

---

(34) "Spin Cycle", Howard Kurtz, p.237
(35) **Ibid., p. 238**
(36) Michael Savage, The Enemy Within, p. 4.

On Clinton's appointment of Ruth Bader Ginsburg to the Supreme Court: Savage calls her a "neo-Marxist."[37] "When Clinton appointed her to the highest court in the land, she was the chief counsel for the ACLU- that ultra-leftist group which believes, among other things, that virtual child porn is protected speech."[38]

On Clinton's role of expanding the number of mosques in the U.S. Military: "During the mid-90's, when Clinton was president, the Pentagon authorized the Norfolk naval base in Virginia to open the first on-base mosque for Muslims.[39]
"Acting in the spirit of inclusion under Bill Clinton, our military expanded the chaplaincy program to include Muslim clerics."[40]

On Bill Clinton's Concept of Truth: "Truth, as we learned from eight torturous years under Bill Clinton, is in the eye of the beholder. How else could that egomaniac place his hand on a Bible and swear to tell the truth?"[41]

Michael Savage on Hillary Clinton:

"Leading the carrion call for universal health-care is Madam Clinton. She's been at it ever since she chaired the subversive Task Force on National Health Care Reform behind closed doors in 1993. Since then, she has admitted, "We need to take step-by-step progress toward providing

---

(37) Ibid., p. 28.
(38) Ibid., p. 170.
(39) Ibid., p.91.
(40) Ibid., p. 93.
(41) Ibid., p. 138.

[health] insurance for every American." Savage points out that *you and I, not Hillary, will pay for it.* "Of course, illegal aliens and welfare bums rejoice whenever Hillary pushes "free" health care. These freeloaders really expect to get something for nothing."[42]

"Yet, such evidence doesn't stop Hillary and the gang on the Left from announcing plans to provide what amounts to socialized medicine in the U.S. A...They're putting one over on the American people because many of us don't understand what's at stake when we hear the phrase "universal health-care."[43]

On George Bush: "Like Ted Kennedy, rather than applaud the troops for putting their lives on the line, Hillary Clinton used the second 9/11 anniversary to vent. She griped on national TV that Bush squandered "the trust and credibility of our government at a time when we have to trust and rely on what they tell us."[44]

Melrose Larry Green recommended reading: Michael Savage, *The Enemy Within,* WND Books, 2003.

---

(42) Ibid., p. 53.
(43) Ibid., p. 54.
(44) Ibid., p. 77.

CHAPTER EIGHT

Reason Number Three the Clintons Belong in Prison

(3) Chinagate- Bill and Hillary Clinton sold sensitive American technology to the Chinese. There is ample evidence proving that the Chinese received American military secrets and encryption software, in exchange for cash. To me, this is *treason. Treason is punishable by death.* If it could be proven, that Bill and Hillary Clinton committed the crime of treason, and I believe they may have, they should suffer the same fate as Julius and Ethel Rosenberg.

<u>Clinton Foreign Policy and National Security</u>

How Bill Clinton Balanced the Budget by Destroying the U.S. Military

One fact you don't hear on the CBS Evening News with Dan Rather is that Bill Clinton balanced the budget at the expense of **decimating and weakening American military strength.** For the first time in history, thousands of military men and women had to apply for food stamps. Consider the following facts:

(1) Under Bill Clinton, the army's strength was reduced from 18 divisions to 12 divisions! The first Gulf War in 1991 required 10 divisions alone!
(2) Under Bill Clinton, the navy was cut from 546 to 380 ships, giving America the smallest naval force since before World War II!

(3) Under Bill Clinton, the Air Force was cut from 76 flight squadrons down to 50!

All of these cuts made America much more vulnerable to terrorist attacks, both on our soil and abroad. To be sure, Al Gore boasted about taking 305,000 people off the federal payroll. But did you know that of those jobs cut, **286,000 (90%) came from the Department of Defense!**

Bill Clinton froze military pay, and as a result over 80% of the military were earning under $30,000/year. Not only did morale suffer at all fronts of the military, but we became an increasingly vulnerable target to terrorists who could aptly perceive our weakness and vulnerability in military strength alone. Under Clinton, the government of the People's Republic of China was able to gain valuable American military encryption software. According to well-known foreign policy analyst Al Santori: "Former administration officials successfully lobbied for the lifting of restrictions on sales of powerful American made communications encryption software. This has enabled the Chinese military to operate its weapons-development projects and conduct military exercises at higher levels of secrecy. In the ultimate *coup de grace,* the administration transferred the responsibility for licensing sensitive military technologies from a cautious State Dept. to an accommodating Dept. of Commerce, which appeared to act as a fundraising arm of the Democratic National Committee."[1]

In 1991, the Clinton Administration approved the sale of a $9 million supercomputer to a Chinese national for the

---

(1) Buzz Patterson, Dereliction of Duty, p. 9.

amazingly low price of $30,000! Department of Energy officials called the sale "a significant national security concern", as the computer was directly designed to carry out national security missions. The man who bought the computer was an expert in exporting U.S. technologies to Red China.[2] Congressman Curt Weldon wrote to former Dept. Of Energy Secretary Bill Richardson, "Ironically, at the very time the Congressional Committee was investigating the transfer of sensitive technology, your employees were selling some of our most sophisticated systems to them at bargain prices."[3]

Like much of Bill Clinton's cabinet, Energy Secretary Hazel O'Leary was a total disaster. She single-handedly did more to compromise national security than all her predecessors and successors combined. First, she abolished the practice of wearing colored security badges at DOE headquarters and national nuclear laboratories, because the practice was "discriminatory." Second, O'Leary abolished the policy of restricting visits to DOE facilities of foreign nationals from countries such as Iran, North Korea, and China- to unclassified areas of the laboratories. Now, these nationals received no background checks. Everyone was welcome to tap into our military secrets. Iranians, North Koreans, and Red Chinese- Come on Down!

Former Green Beret Edward McCollum was a whistleblower who was fired by Hazel O'Leary's Dept. of Energy. He had questioned what Bill Clinton's administration had done to compromise our national security.

---

(2) Ibid., p. 11.
(3) Ibid., p. 11.

McCollum was Director of the DOE's Office of Safeguards and Security. McCollum testified before Congress in a most candid way, to a commission led by former Senator Warren Rudman. In a memo he wrote on January 27, 1993, he noted a disturbing trend that he had warned about in three preceding annual reports: "During the past year disturbing trends continued that resulted in additional budget restrictions, further diminishing technical resources, reducing mission training and undermining our ability to protect nuclear weapons, special nuclear materials, and other critical assets. This is occurring at a time of increased responsibilities resulting from the international transfer of nuclear materials and dismantling of U.S. nuclear weapons. It is becoming increasingly difficult to protect our nation's nuclear stockpile."[4]

5 Ways Bill Clinton Destroyed the FBI

1. **Pardongate**: A memo was sent to FBI headquarters in Washington from the Atlanta FBI office warning of the impending Bill Clinton pardons of international fugitives Marc Rich and Pinchus Green. The memo, written in August 2000, warned that the pardons would be issued during the final hours of the Clinton Administration. Accompanying the tip were "detailed allegations of financial payoffs to ensure the presidential actions."

Confidential sources had tipped off the Atlanta office of Clinton's criminal role in the pardons of 2 of the FBI's most wanted international fugitives. Yet the FBI would claim that the memo never existed, until the agent who wrote the memo

---

(4) Ibid., p. 12.

came forward in March 2001 and stopped the cover-up in its tracks![5]

2. **TWA Flight 800**: The Clinton FBI took over control of the investigation of TWA Flight 800 (July 17, 1996) from the National Transportation Safety Board. According to NTSB investigators, "overbearing FBI agents immediately took control and hampered a lot of things we did." The bureau sat on the investigation so as to not interfere with Bill Clinton's re-election in November, 1996. Substantial and credible evidence exists that FBI agents convinced dozens of witnesses who claimed to have seen a missile hit the jet to change their stories.[6]

3. **Death of Vince Foster**: The FBI should have been in charge of the investigation into the death of Vince Foster, but the Clinton White House had fired FBI director William Sessions, on the eve of Vince Foster's death! The Park Police, who know nothing about homicide or suicide investigations, were put in charge of the investigation. The Clinton White House "ordered the FBI out of the death investigation." A critical witness, Patrick Knowlton, one of the first to discover Foster's body in Ft. Marcy Park, sued the FBI. Knowlton felt that the FBI agents altered his testimony. Arkansas Sate trooper Larry Patterson, who claimed he heard news of Foster's death before the body was discovered in Ft. Marcy Park, "testified that FBI agents badgered him to change his story."[7]

---

(5) "The Disintegration of the FBI", Phil Brennan, Newsmax.com Magazine, July, 2002, p. 15.
(6) Ibid., p. 15.
(7) Ibid., p. 15.

4. **Filegate**: For some reason, the FBI turned over 1000 "confidential files on top Republicans" to Clinton and White House security boss Craig Livingstone. This act was totally illegal, and the no one in the FBI was ever held accountable for this criminal behavior on the part of the Clinton Administration and the FBI.[8]

5, **Travelgate**: The Clinton White House sicked the FBI on innocent people in the travel office, so Hillary Clinton could get her people into the White House Travel Office. In her words, "we needed the slots." The head of the travel office, who had served faithfully for 30 years, was harassed by FBI agents and "indicted on phony evidence" before being quickly exonerated of any wrongdoing and acquitted by a jury of his peers![9]

Catastrophe- Ruddy and Limbacher

Bill Clinton was a compulsive talker who would talk to anyone who happened to be around. Saul Finkelstein was riding his bicycle with his two sons when, by chance, he ran into Bill Clinton. Clinton started talking to Finkelstein about Osama Bin Laden. For 15 minutes, Clinton told a total stranger that his administration missed Bin Laden by about an hour. Clinton wanted Finkelstein to know that "what happened on September 11 could in no way be traced to some failure on his administration's part."[10] Finkelstein told Washington Post reporter Lloyd Grove that Clinton told him

---

(8) Ibid., p. 15.
(9) Ibid., p. 15.
(10) "Catastrophe," Ruddy and Limbacher, p. 42

"but it will not be that difficult to get Bin Laden [today] because unlike in 1998...the U.S. will have the cooperation of surrounding countries."[11]

Did the Monica Lewinsky scandal affect Bill Clinton's war against terrorism? Apparently so, according to former Clinton aide and Fox News Channel commentator/author Dick Morris. "My sense is that the affair made him passive and risk-averse...As a result, I think he was less inclined to interfere with the military or to order long-term involvement."[12] Morris told FNC's Rita Cosby that the Lewinsky scandal distracted Clinton from going after Bin Laden. Says Morris, "Clinton was distracted, disheartened, depressed, and not terribly focused."[13]

Dick Morris' Perspective on Bill Clinton

In his book "Off With Their Heads", syndicated columnist and political analyst Dick Morris contends that Bill Clinton left three ticking time bombs to George W. Bush: Al Qaeda, Iraq, and North Korea. Morris argues that Clinton failed miserably with all three.

Bill Clinton knew all about Al Qaeda. After all, during Clinton's watch, the first attack on the World Trade Center occurred (1993), two of our embassies were attacked by terrorists, U.S. military outposts in Saudia Arabia were hit, and the U.S.S. Cole was attacked- all acts of al Qaeda

---

(11) Ibid., p. 42
(12) Ibid., p. 42
(13) Ibid., p. 44

When the World Trade Center was bombed on February 26, 1993, six people were killed and thousands were injured. This was the first terrorist attack on U.S. soil in the modern era. Sadly, Bill Clinton never even paid his respects by visiting the attack site!

Amazingly, he didn't attend any of the funerals of he six who died. According to Morris, Clinton's biggest flaw was in the way he perceived terrorism: he treated it as a crime rather than as a foreign policy emergency. Clinton's objective was to find the perpetrators and bring them to justice in the appropriate court of law. Morris argues that this strategy was doomed to failure, and it undoubtedly lay the groundwork for September 11th.

The Clinton White House dropped the ball on fighting terrorism. According to former White House aide George Stephanopoulos, the White House's attitude under Clinton was one of avoidance of the issue: "It wasn't the kind of thing where you walked into a staff meeting and people asked, what are we doing today in the war against terrorism?"[14]

Morris points out that Bill Clinton blew several opportunities to fight terrorism as far back as 1993! It was clear, after the first World Trade Center bombing, that some sort of conspiracy was involved. Ramzi Yousef, the mastermind of the attack, arrived in the U.S. in the company of Ahmad M. Ajaj, a pizza delivery man in Houston. Ajaj was detained at the airport for carrying three fake passports and other fake identification. Amazingly, Ajaj also carried "a

---

(14) Dick Morris, "Off with their Heads, p. 74

letter of introduction recommending him for training in guerrilla warfare in Pakistan or Afghanistan!"[15]

Richard Bernstein wrote in "The New York Times": "Who wrote Mr. Ajaj's letter of introduction? Why would he have to travel to the Middle East to obtain it? Whom did he see in the United Arab Emirates and Saudi Arabia?" The Clinton White House did no follow up in any of these areas. Morris points out that a responsive White House would have been all over these questions[16]

Morris describes the findings of terrorism expert Steven Emerson, the author of "American Jihad". There was a group of Muslims living in Jersey City, New Jersey who followed the blind cleric Sheikh Omar Abdel Rahman (We all remember the blind dude with the sunglasses). That group was planning to blow up the Holland Tunnel, the Lincoln Tunnel, the George Washington Bridge, and the Federal Office Building in lower Manhattan.

After Sheikh Rahman and nine of his posse were arrested in June, 1993, Clinton did absolutely nothing to fight terrorism. Morris writes: "He [Clinton] gave no extra tools to the FBI. He never ordered any major shakeup of the anti-terror apparatus. No massive mobilization was declared. The government simply shrugged its shoulders; the bank robbers had been caught, after all; why make a fuss?"[17]

---

(15) Ibid., p. 78
(16) Ibid., p. 78
(17) Ibid., p. 79

In January 1995, Youssef was arrested in Pakistan. According to Emerson, Youssef said in his interrogation that he "hoped (WTC) Tower One would fall sideways into Tower two- knocking over both and killing 250,000 people."[18]

As if this wasn't bad enough, Youssef "also participated in a plan to blow up 11 American jetliners within 48 hours- a disaster that was only barely avoided by chance."[19]

So there we have it- in black and white. Bill Clinton had ample warning of the intentions of Al Qaeda, as far back as February, 1993, when the World Trade Center was first attacked! Clinton had almost eight years to do what George W. Bush has so wisely launched- an all-out war on terrorism! Even as the exact description of the events of 9-11 are given to the Clinton administration back in January 1995! Bill Clinton had lots of time to party in the White House! Bill Clinton had lots of time to molest, harass, grope, and fool around with all sorts of women. Bill Clinton had time to retain over 900 FBI files in the White House- he had time to start more conflicts than I can name. He had time to drastically cut our military and put our fighting men and women on food stamps. He had time for lots of phone sex at all hours of the day and night, along with the real thing.

But alas, Bill Clinton couldn't mobilize the FBI, CIA, and ATF to stop Al Qaeda! Clinton didn't even do anything to beef up airport security, despite all the previous examples of terrorism under his watch.

---

(18) Ibid., p. 79
(19) Ibid., p. 79

Dick Morris has had a long history of working with Bill Clinton, dating back to the campaigns for the State House in Arkansas. Few people know Bill and Hillary Clinton better than Dick Morris. And few people are as honest and outspoken about the Clintons as is Dick Morris. After working for Bill Clinton in Arkansas, Dick Morris did a two year stint in the Clinton White House, serving from late 1994 through late 1996. On at least seven occasions, Morris and Bill Clinton were engaged in long, private meetings, during which they addressed such key issues as law enforcement, gun control, and crime. Some of these meetings would last from two to three hours. According to Morris, never once did Bill Clinton mention terrorism or the World Trade Center bombing.

Writes Morris: "Simply put, Clinton had no time for terrorism. Notoriously unable to delegate responsibility, compulsive in controlling the actions of his subordinates, Clinton was too busy juggling other issues to address the threat terrorism posed during the opening years of his presidency."[20]

Incredibly, Bill Clinton and the director of the C.I.A. R. James Woolsey did not have any private meetings in all of 1993 and 1994![21] Needless to say, Bill Clinton had lots of time for one-on-one meetings with women during that time. Bill Clinton did nothing as North Korea illegally developed nuclear weapons during his administration. He simply left the problem to George W. Bush. Back in 1998, the

(20) Ibid., p. 81
(21) Ibid., p. 74

"Washington Post" had reported that North Korea was developing several nuclear bombs in clandestine underground locations. Clinton did nothing: he didn't want to jeopardize the 1994 agreements, under which the U.S. agreed to provide food and oil to the North Koreans in exchange for its agreeing to "internationally monitored containment and eventual rollbacks of its nuclear capability." Overwhelming evidence of North Korea's building nuclear weapons and nuclear facilities surfaced in the "N.Y. Times" and "Washington Post" during mid-August, 1998.

Writes Morris: "When prompt action could have headed off North Korean noncompliance, Bill Clinton willfully and deliberately did nothing, allowing the North to build its bombs in underground caverns."[22]

Morris had an idea to fight terrorism which Bill Clinton totally rejected. Morris wanted to link DMV data (expired license or unlicensed driver data) to Immigration and Naturalization Service (INS) computers. Had that been done, we would have deported at least three of the 9-11 hijackers prior to 9-11- Mohammed Atta, Nawaf Alhazmi, and Ziad Sami Jarrah had all been stopped for either speeding or driving without a license. George Stephanopoulos wrote that Morris's plan of "stopping brown-skinned people driving a car with a busted tail light...failed to consider my fears of potential abuse and political harm to our Hispanic base." Morris concludes that Bill Clinton's need for Hispanic votes outweighed his interest in deporting terrorists.[23]

---

(22) Ibid., p. 89-90.
(23) Ibid., p. 90

George W. Bush and Bill Clinton had totally different approaches toward the issue of terrorism. For Bush, it was a simple case of good vs. evil. For Clinton, we had to look deeply into the root causes, based on "race, religion, or sexual orientation."[24] In a speech at Georgetown University on November 7, 2001, Bill Clinton noted that America carried out terrorism against slaves and Native Americans.

Dick Morris pointed out how Bill Clinton would give emotional priority to empathy for the victim over anger at the perpetrators of terrorism.[25] For Bush, fighting terrorism was the #1 priority. For Clinton, it was one of many issues: civil liberties, budgetary matters, starvation of Iraqi and North Korean people, etc. And Clinton's staff were not seasoned experts in international relations. Clinton instructed Dick Morris never to give him foreign policy advice unless they were alone. When other advisers such as Sandy Berger stayed too long in the White House, Clinton and Morris had a game they played. Morris would pretend to leave, wait downstairs for an "all-clear" from Clinton and then return to meet with him alone."[26]

Dick Morris knew Bill Clinton like no one else. Morris felt that Clinton was a weak President. He didn't want to lead Americans into a war with casualties, since he himself was a draft dodger! Clinton was weak with respect to Iraq, North Korea and Al Qaeda. Morris notes that people like Janet Reno, George Stephanopoulos, Warren Christopher,

---

(24) Ibid., p. 123
(25) Ibid., p. 123
(26) Ibid., p. 125

and Tony Lake prevented Clinton from launching an all-out war against terrorism.

Morris claims that Attorney General Janet Reno prevented the FBI from communicating with the Internal Security Section of the Justice Department. This weakened the FBI's effort to go after the terrorists before 9-11. These rules had been adopted in 1994. In 1996, 3 attacks occurred within 32 days. Nineteen died and hundreds were injured in the Khobar towers bombing in Saudi Arabia on June 25, 1996. This was the work of al Qaeda. On July 18, 1996, TWA Flight 800 blew up in mid-flight, killing all 230 passengers. On July 27, 1996, the bomb went off in Centennial Park. The first was definitely terrorism, the second might have been terrorism, and the third may have been terrorism. We don't have know that for sure, but *we do know that Bill Clinton did nothing to solve the Khobar Towers bombing!*

The FBI's Investigation had been stonewalled by the Saudi government. Finally, almost 5 years later, on June 21, 2001, the Bush administration handed down indictments to 13 Saudis and 1 Lebanese for their participation in the bombing of Khobar Towers.[27] While Bill Clinton dragged his feet and paid lip service to the American people, George Bush's White House vigorously prosecuted the war on terrorism.

We all know what happened on September 11. But could it have been prevented if Bill Clinton had been more aggressive in his actions against Saudi Arabia? We all know that 15 of the 9-11 hijackers came from Saudi Arabia.

---

(27) Ibid., p. 108

Back in 1996, Dick Morris conducted a survey for Bill Clinton. Over 90% of Americans wanted X-ray screening of baggage at airports, federalizing airport security workers, and photo ID for all passengers. Yet Clinton implemented none of these changes. What did Clinton do? He commissioned a study! Clinton implemented several weak measures such as airline employee background checks and matching bags to passengers.

In February, 1997, Al Gore issued a study on airport security. The airline industry was against most of Gore's recommendations. In fact, the Air Transport Association (ATA) had 210 lobbyists who influenced Congress to delay or water down airport security reforms. They spent over $16 million in their efforts. Many of the lobbyists were former Congressmen (10), or former FAA officers (3).[28]

Clinton did very little to get rid of brutal dictator Saddam Hussein. What he did do was to enable Iraq to sell more and more oil. In November, 1998, American and British troops fired 400 cruise missiles and launched 200 aircraft attacks against Iraqi sites. There were no protests to Clinton's bombing. On November 2, 1998, Saddam stopped the work of U.N. weapons inspectors. In January, 1999, the U.S. lifted limits on Iraqi oil sales. In effect, Saddam Hussein won on all fronts- he could produce oil and re-arm for a war against the United States.[29]

---

(28) Ibid., p. 113
(29) Ibid., pp. 121-122.

Dick Morris is of the opinion that Bill Clinton was weakened in his fight against terrorism an Osama Bin Laden by the scandals of Paula Jones and Monica Lewinsky. All the energy he put into fighting the allegations and questions posed by Jones and Lewinsky was time he could have devoted to the upcoming role of al Qaeda in 9-11.!

Buzz Patterson on Clinton

The Clinton Administration's ignorance of foreign affairs was even more evident in his handling of the military. Buzz Patterson was the carrier of the "nuclear football" for President Bill Clinton. In his best-selling book "Dereliction of Duty", he outlines how Bill Clinton weakened the military and seriously compromised national security throughout the years of his administration.

Patterson worked in the Clinton White House for two years, from May 1996 to May 1998. He was appointed to be one of five Air Force Aides that assisted the President in various duties concerning our national safety. What he witnessed during his time in the White House convinced him that the Clinton administration seriously compromised the safety of the United States through its ignorant and dismissive attitude towards the military.

President Clinton compromised our national security by cutting funds to the army, putting many army families on food stamps. He had little respect for the military and a minimal understanding of how to use it. This is evident in the failed mission in Mogadishu, which culminated in the ambush many people saw in the movie *Black Hawk Down*. Clinton spread military forces out beyond their capabilities with not enough funds to support their many operations. He expanded the military's role in Mogadishu beyond the simple humanitarian mission it had had under Bush. The military suddenly found themselves in a nation-building mission with no obvious end in sight.

It was the same in Haiti with the Operation Uphold Democracy- the troops were sent there poorly informed, with no clear mission and under-supplied. Patterson points out how Clinton's first presidential action concerning the military was the "Don't ask don't tell" policy regarding gays, a policy which displayed his ignorance of military realities. Everything he did regarding the military ended up lowering morale and compromising our national security.

Another thing Clinton did (time and time again) was lie to the American public by saying in speeches that there was not a single nuclear missile pointed at a child in the United States of America.[30] This kind of attitude created a false sense of security which led to complacency among the public. Another lie Clinton told repeatedly during his first campaign was that his would be "the most ethical administration in history."[31] Not only did the president lie but the White House was a very uncoordinated, sloppy place. Evidence of this is in the time President Clinton lost the nuclear codes- codes that the president must have with him at all times in case of emergency. The most bothersome part was how little he seemed to care. After saying "I'll track (the codes) down, guys, and get them back to you" he went back to his desk work, in no hurry to find them. There was also the time that

---

(30) Patterson, Dereliction of Duty, p. 53
(31) Ibid., p. 54

he was separated from the nuclear football for about 30-40 minutes after leaving NATO's Fiftieth Anniversary summit in a rush.[32] An aide had to walk it back to the White House on the street, where anything could have happened to it. This just demonstrates the carelessness and lack of respect for rules and regulations of the Clinton administration.

Most people who have a bad job can take comfort in knowing that it wasn't as bad as working for the Clintons in the White House. Patterson describes his life working for the Clinton Administration as humiliating, infuriating, and unprofessional. Hillary Clinton's brothers, Hugh and Tony, were a frequent presence at the White House and treated the Military aides as their personal servants. In displays of racism, many of Clinton's colleagues and friends treated African-American staff members as personal servants, including Alexis Herman and even Jesse Jackson. Patterson also recalls how many times Clinton refused to take calls from his "friend" Jesse Jackson, making Patterson lie and say the President was unavailable. Hillary Clinton was also an impossibly tough boss to have. She always had to have things her way, constantly making demands and overstepping her role as first lady.[33]

There was the time during a trip to the Netherlands in 1997 when someone suggested that Clinton make a congratulatory phone call to Linda Finch, a woman who had just completed a 73-hour trip around the world in a Lockheed Elektra propeller-driven airplane. Patterson made the suggestion to the President, who put it off. Hours later, when

---

(32) Ibid., p. 56
(33) Ibid., p. 62

it was too late to reach Finch, the First Lady chewed Patterson out when she realized the phone call had not been made. "Damn it, that's unacceptable! Why didn't I know about this? We can't miss opportunities like this. You get her on the phone!" She commanded Bruce Lindsey to make the phone call, who told Patterson to do it and went to bed. Patterson went to bed himself, knowing that it wasn't his responsibility.[34]

As this suggests, Clinton's staff was so young and inexperienced that the military aides were often forced to take over the planning of simple events that were beneath their level of expertise and not in their job requirements. And the President himself acted in a manner that would have gotten him court-martialed in the military. One female aide complained of being groped by the President on Air Force One. The President later apologized, but the facts stand for themselves- the President had few morals and little decency, and his lack of military experience showed in his conduct.[35]

Patterson makes the case that the problem with the Clinton Administration was their fundamental understanding of what the military should be used for. They saw the military as an organization for social service, not for inflicting damage on the enemy and keeping America safe. This attitude became evident during a trip to Brazil. U.S. Coast Guard Lieutenant Commander Graham Stowe was riding in a van through the slums of Rio de Janeiro with John Podesta, White House Press Secretary Joe Lockhart and the first lady's chief of staff Melanne Verveer. Verveer, seeing the

---

(34) Ibid., pp. 69-71
(35) Ibid., pp. 86-87

terrible living conditions, remarked that Brazil's military should be doing something with the U.S. Military to alleviate these terrible conditions. Podesta and Lockhart unanimously agreed immediately. Graham Stowe said that the military existed for national security, not helping the poor in Brazil.[36] The discussion ended there. In this way the Clinton Administration tried to sacrifice the reality of the military for their social ideals, without ever serving in the military or understanding the nature of the institution.

During Clinton's time in office, the military was deployed to forty separate nations in what were mostly called "unanticipated missions." In everyday language we would call it "channel surfing." We could safely compare Clinton's foreign policy to a squirrel crossing the road, looking around, stopping, considering the options, and eventually returning to the place it came from, not having accomplished anything. This happened in Somalia, Rwanda, Haiti, Macedonia, Bosnia, Ecuador, East Timor, Kuwait, Liberia, Albania, Congo, Gabon, Sierra Leone, Afghanistan, Sudan, and Iraq.[37] Most policy decisions were not made based on principles of wrong and right, they were instead made after extensive polling to see how the public's perception of Clinton would be affected by a certain military action. And the military were not given clear goals when sent to these places. So very little was accomplished and much money was spent on fruitless missions.

Patterson mentions the time Clinton sent the USS *Harlan County* to Port-Au-Prince, Haiti to make a show of force. The

---

(36) Ibid., p. 99
(37) Ibid., p. 112

intent of the mission was to restore democracy and rebuild a disintegrating nation. This would affect the U.S. directly because there were thousands of Haitian refugees coming to America every month and that had to be stopped. American troops ended up staying in Haiti for five months, but without clear goals or a strategies, little was accomplished and the Haitian economy worsened. Clinton wanted Jean-Bertrand Aristide in office to restore democracy in the country, so the military reinstated him. Nevermind the fact that Aristide was an Anti-American socialist who vehemently denounced the United States![38]

Another time in the fall of 1998 the National Security Council had located Osama bin Laden and the Tomahawk crews were all ready to strike. But once again, Clinton was unavailable. Sandy Berger tried to call Clinton but there was no answer. When Clinton finally called back, he couldn't make up his mind! He wanted to talk to the secretaries of defense and state, unaware of the urgency of making a quick decision. But, as usual, he couldn't make up his mind without discussing it with as many people as possible. Eventually it became too late to organize a strike. The famously elusive Bin Laden slipped away. This also highlights another bizarre ideological facet of the Clinton Administration. They believed that terrorists were just misunderstood people with legitimate grievances that could be solved through negotiation and diplomacy.[39]

The Clinton administration showed weakness when dealing with another threat, North Korea. Patterson reminds

---

(38) Ibid., pp. 118-119.
(39) Ibid., pp. 130-132.

us of how Clinton made numerous concessions to North Korea in efforts to curb their nuclear arms program, even giving them nuclear reactors to appease them! When North Korea sent a submarine full of 25 terrorists into South Korean waters, all Clinton did was urge restraint on both sides. He didn't want to break the "framework agreement" originally initiated by Jimmy Carter. This was even after South Korea begged the Clinton Administration to restart the joint military exercises we had performed with them from 1976 to 1994 (which we stopped as part of the appeasement agreement).

By November, 1995 Bill Clinton reduced the active duty military force from 2.1 million down to 1.6 million. He pared the army's 18 divisions down to 12. Clinton reduced the Navy from 546 to 380 ships. The Air Force was cut from 76 flight squadrons down to 50.[40]

The date was September 13, 1996- Bill Clinton was in the midst of a re-election campaign, and the country was on the brink of conflict in Iraq. Saddam Hussein had invaded Kurdistan in August, and on September 2 and 3, Clinton had ordered the firing of 44 cruise missiles at southern Iraq... Once again Saddam Hussein survived this attack, as he massacred thousands of his opponents.[41] But how did Saddam Hussein survive? Well, according to Patterson, the U.S. military was poised to strike at the Iraqis and take out significant targets- but Bill Clinton was too busy to take a call from his National Security adviser Sandy Berger. What

---

(40) Patterson, Dereliction of Duty, p. 4
(41) Ibid., p. 27

was Clinton doing, that he was so preoccupied? ***Clinton was
watching a golf tournament!***[42]

National Security Council deputy director Sandy Berger
was trying to get approval from Clinton to order a strike on
Iraq on September 13, 1996. Everything was a go: the fighter
planes were in position, targets were identified, and our
military commanders were waiting for the go-ahead from the
President. But Clinton was playing golf with Vernon Jordan
in Lake Manassas, Virginia, and he couldn't be disturbed.

Buzz Patterson, military aide to Clinton at the time, said
to the President "Mr. President, Mr. Berger has called again
and needs a decision soon...We have our pilots in cockpits,
ready to launch, and we're running out of the protective
cover of nighttime over there." This was the second call
Berger had placed to Clinton in an hour. Clinton responded
to his military aide, Lt. Col. Robert Patterson: **"I'll call
Berger when I get the chance."**[43]

Fifteen minutes later, an agitated Berger called back.
Where the hell was President Clinton? What was going on?
Clinton was involved with the golf tournament and Vernon
Jordan. Our fighting men and women in Iraq could wait until
the golf match was over! Patterson went to Clinton, for the
third time in an hour. Finally, he got to Clinton in a VIP tent.
Clinton told Patterson: "Tell Berger that I'll give him a call
on my way back to the White House. That's all." Well,
folks, I am sorry to say that the operation in Iraq shut down,

---

(42) Ibid., p. 29
(43) Ibid., 28

as thousands of miles away at a golf course in Manassas, VA, Bill Clinton signed autographs and worked the crowd!

"Without word from the President, jet engines would shut down, and pilots would return to their squadrons or beds. Maintenance chiefs would put down their headsets and prepare their fighters and bombers for another day."[44]

Lt. Col. "Buzz" Patterson had served in the Air Force for 15 years before working as a military aide in the White House. Over the years, he served in Rwanda, Haiti, Bosnia, and Somalia. But serving under Clinton was different. For the first time, soldiers questioned the President's motives and sincerity. Clinton really had great contempt for the military. Remember, Bill Clinton was the guy who dodged the draft back in the '60's. Bill Clinton burned the American flag at anti- American rallies during the Vietnam era.

Patterson details how Clinton used and abused the military to keep his own personal scandals off the front pages of the N.Y. Times and the Washington Post.

"When his disdain for the military became almost immediately evident, when he cut the military budget to the point where families of soldiers were relying on food stamps and reserve units were ordered to more & more overseas missions of apparently nebulous value, the grumbling grew into real and deep discontent."[45]

---

(44) Ibid., p. 30
(45) Ibid., p. 38

During the midst of the Monica Lewinsky scandals, Clinton actually lost his nuclear codes- the secret card which gave the President the ability to defend this country in case of a nuclear attack.

"President Clinton looked up sheepishly and confessed: "I don't have mine on me. I'll track it down guys, and get it back to you." On at least one occasion, the President and the nuclear football were actually apart for a period of 30-40 minutes. Clinton was in a hurry to wrap up a NATO meeting in D.C. on April 24, 1999. He was in such a rush, he left his military aide and nuclear football behind.

"For 30 or 40 minutes, the President and the nuclear football were separated. The President had made that conscious decision and couldn't be bothered to wait the additional minute or to ensure that his entire entourage, especially the essential foreign policy element, could come along."[46]

The Rodham brothers were obnoxious, demanding, and arrogant. People like the Rodham brothers and Terry McAuliffe regarded the Clinton's success as "all about them and what they could get out of it."[47] And Clinton's staff often treated the key White House employees in a condescending, almost patronizing manner. Lt. Patterson recounted how then Secretary of Labor Alexis Herman (an African-American) was toward the enlisted African-American man who worked as a driver for the White House

---

(46) Ibid., p. 58
(47) Ibid., p. 60

Transportation Agency.[48] Though their normal job responsibilities included carrying presidential medical equipment and supplies, Herman and others such as Jesse Jackson would routinely ask these Navy officers to carry their bags and honor other inappropriate requests.[49]

"It seemed to be a habit among some of Bill's high profile friends and colleagues that when outside of public purview they reflexively treated African-American service members in a manner I found appalling."[50]

And then there was the sheer arrogance of the Clinton staff. Patterson recalled that Clinton was once on a campaign meet-and-greet at the team complex of the Tampa Bay Buccaneers (an NFL team). A senior female staffer preceded the President, looking for the head coach. She went up to an African-American man and said:" Can you tell me where the head coach is?" Patterson told the staffer "You're talking to him." **The senior advisor didn't even realize that this African-**American **was the coach of the Bucs, Tony Dungy.** The senior advisor was unaffected. Patterson noted that she walked away and didn't even apologize to Coach Dungy for her racial insensitivity.[51]

People had to walk on eggshells around Hillary Clinton. Generally, Hillary did not want to see the staff in the halls of the White House, except for key staffers. Lt. Patterson

---

(48) Ibid., p. 60
(49) Ibid., p. 61
(50) Ibid., p. 61
(51) Ibid., p. 62

recounts how people would duck into office doorways to escape Hillary's line of sight.

"I'd hear whispering- 'she's coming, she's coming'- she would come in and they would scatter. She was the stern school marm and the rest of us were expected to hide as though we were kids in trouble...Hillary could be harsh, difficult, and unpredictable. Wherever Hillary Clinton went, she had her plastic box of files. The files could only be handled by the military aide, in Hillary's presence. The file box had to be in a conspicuous location on Marine One (the Presidential helicopter). The file box had to be in a conspicuous location in her White House bedroom. "Make sure she sees you when you're moving them and she sees exactly where you leave them."[52]

What were these files? Were these the Rose Law firm billing records that might have implicated Hillary and Bill Clinton in some illicit activity? Were these files related to the travel office, an office that Hillary had fired just to get her friends in (her exact words)? Did these files have damaging information relating to the mysterious death of Vince Foster?

Bill Clinton had very little respect for the military. Lt. Patterson stresses that Clinton was totally unprepared to be Commander-in-Chief. Unlike George H.W. Bush, George W. Bush, Dwight Eisenhower, and even Al Gore, Bill Clinton never had a day of military service! "No commander-in-chief evoked so much outright and unexpected indignation from the ranks of the uniformed military than he did. And no President ever expressed such a

---

(52) Ibid., p. 64

callous disregard for the military as he did by deploying the military so recklessly, often while simultaneously compromising military capability and degrading military morale.[53]

Clinton's primary focus was on fundraising, not governing the country. Routinely, hundreds paid big money to sleep in the Lincoln bedroom. Politicians like Willy Brown and Gray Davis, and show biz celebrities like Tom Hanks, Steven Spielberg, Chevy Chase, Barbra Streisand, Ted Danson- to name just a few- were frequent overnight guests at the White House. There was bowling, popcorn, movies, and lots and lots of partying- **courtesy of you, the American taxpayer.**[54]

The Clinton's travel bill was unbelievable. Over his 8 years in office, Buzz Patterson estimated that Bill Clinton 's trips cost the taxpayers over **half a billion dollars!** Clinton's 133 trips to 74 countries were more than the number of trips of Presidents Eisenhower, Kennedy, Johnson, and Nixon **combined!** In 1998, at the height of the Monica Lewinsky scandal, Clinton made 20% of his 133 trips.[55] And when Hillary ran for the Senate in New York back in 2000, she routinely flew Airforce C-9A's or C- 20's. These planes cost about $3500/hour to operate.[56]

Clinton even capitalized on natural disasters and the losses suffered by others. Patterson recounts a helicopter

---

(53) Ibid., p. 88
(54) Ibid., p. 74
(55) Ibid., pp. 76-77.
(56) Ibid., p. 78

flyover done by Clinton and his staff at an area destroyed by a tornado in Florida. Although 40 people died in the tornado, Clinton, rather than observing the destruction, **spent most of the flight playing cards with Bruce Lindsey and White House press secretary Joe Lockhart!** Only when the press helicopter approached did Clinton look out the window to observe the devastation. "The President quickly peered out the window, feigning an interested and grief-stricken expression...This playacting by the President was something I never ceased to marvel at...he almost always knew what to do to impress his audience."[57]

And the Clinton staff was greedy in ways you could never imagine. In a Presidential visit to Holland in 1997, the Clinton staff received royal treatment from the their Dutch hosts, who put their guests up in the royal palace. Each room was fully stocked with food and drink. Yet the self-serving Clinton staff **took all the liquor, and they stole crystal and china, too!** These facts were recounted to Lt. Patterson by the Dutch military aide.[58]

Bill Clinton even lied about his golf game. Patterson often accompanied Clinton on his numerous golf outings. Often Clinton would lie about ball placement and take extra shots while involved in otherwise meaningless golf games. Patterson recounts how on at least once occasion Clinton had shot a 92, even though he told the media he had shot a 79.

---

(57) Ibid., 75
(58) Ibid., p. 83

Lt. Patterson, the carrier of the nuclear football, actually kept score that day![59]

Stories about the Clintons You Won't hear from Dan Rather

Lt. Col. Patterson received a call from the presidential pilot Mark Donnelly; a female enlisted member of the crew of Air Force One had complained of being *touched inappropriately by the Commander-in-Chief.* According to the pilot, this happened "In one of the galleys on Air Force One on a recent trip. Apparently, he just cornered her."[60] The woman didn't want to file charges. She didn't want any money or fame- *all she wanted was an apology from Bill Clinton. Patterson arranged for Clinton to personally apologize to the enlisted woman that he had molested.*[61]

Things about Bill and Hillary Clinton You Never Heard from Dan Rather

Lt. Col. Patterson confirms other's accounts of Hillary's sewer mouth: she would be heard yelling: *"Godammit," "you bastard",* or *"it's your fucking fault."*[62]

Patterson was once on a helicopter with Hillary, when she demanded that the craft be brought down to the ground, because *Hillary had left her sunglasses in the limo!* To

---

(59) Ibid., p. 51. See appendix C, p. 191 for the actual scorecard on the back 9 holes!
(60) Patterson, Dereliction of Duty, p. 86
(61) Ibid., p. 87
(62) Ibid., p. 68

Hillary, her sunglasses were more important than the inconvenience she was causing at the moment. Hillary didn't care if the Secret Service and White House communications people had already pulled up their equipment. She would not budge. "I need my sunglasses. We need to go back."[63] Eventually, reason prevailed and Hillary forfeited a pair of sunglasses.

Bill Clinton lied about how he avoided being drafted during the Vietnam war. After Clinton was classified 1-A, he enrolled in ROTC. Graduate school deferments had been eliminated, so ROTC seemed a convenient way for Clinton to avoid having to go to Vietnam. Clinton claimed that he gave up his ROTC status and became 1-A, because *he felt guilty that four of his classmates had died in Vietnam.* So he asked to be put back into the draft. *In fact, Nixon had begun major withdrawals, the war was winding down, and Clinton had virtually no chance of being drafted.*

Hillary Clinton once told a member of the NRA that she used to be a duck hunter. She was speaking to a group in Fort Ann, N.Y., when someone who was an NRA supporter asked Senator Clinton a question about gun control. It was at this point that Hillary indicated that *she had once hunted, saying "It was ducks and a long time ago."*[64] I found this gem in *Newsmax.com magazine,* which pointed out other pearls about Hillary. By the way, the entire quote was: "I've gone hunting. I don't have anything against guns if guns are

---

(63) Ibid., p. 71
(64) Newsmax.com Magazine, July 22, 2002

used by responsible people…It was ducks and a long time ago."[65]

Here are some other dubious claims of Hillary that I picked up from the Newsmax.com Magazine:

(1) Hillary claims to have tried to sign up for the army, *but they turned her down because she was too old.*

(2) During the campaign in 2000, Hillary suddenly became a fan of the New York Yankees.[66] On June 10, 1999 Hillary told *Today Show's* Katie Couric: "I've always been a Yankees fan, but I needed an American league team…so as a young girl, I became very interested and enamored of the Yankees."[67]

(3) She and Bill claimed that they were contemplating adopting a child, in 1996, *when Hillary was 49 years old.*

(4) Hillary claimed she was named after famous mountain climber Sir Edmund Hilary, even no one ever heard of the mountain climber (the 1st to climb Mt. Everest) until 5 years *after* Hillary was born![68] In 1996, Hillary Clinton said: "Before I was born, a man named Sir Edmund Hilary became famous for being the first person to climb Mt. Everest. My father named me after him as a symbolic message that I could achieve anything I wanted in life…that I could climb ANY mountain…"[69] According to Newsmax, Hillary was born 5 years *before* Edmund Hilary climbed Everest. In 1947, when Bill's

---

(65) Deck of Hillary, Newsmax.com.
(66) USAToday.com, 4-4-00
(67) Op. cit., Newsmax.com
(68) From "The Deck of Hillary," Newsmax.com
(69) OP. cit., Newsmax.com

Hillary was born, *Edmund Hilary was an obscure beekeeper!*

In the book *Bloodsport, by* James Stewart, Susan McDougal describes a time when Hillary was less than cordial to some people who had given her a gift of a pair of "razorback earrings" (shaped like a hog). They asked Mrs. Clinton to try on the earrings. After the female who gave her the earrings was out of earshot, Hillary said to Susan McDougal: "See, this is the kind of shit I have to put up with here."

Bill Clinton and Gennifer Flowers were once practicing what she would say to the press about their relationship. Gennifer said to Bill that she would say (speaking about Bill's ability at *cunnilingus)*
"You eat good pussy." Bill said:"What!" Gennifer: "I said I had to them you ate *good pussy* and you said, 'Well, you can tell them that- if I don't run for president.'"[70]

An African-American prostitute from Little Rock named Bobbie Ann Williams claimed to "have had sex with Bill Clinton *about 13 or 14 times in late 1983 and early 1984, on one occasion recruiting two other prostitutes to help him fulfill a fantasy of being with three women at once."[71]*) Bobbie Ann Williams claimed to have had a love child by Bill Clinton. The boy, Danny Williams, looked *like a light-skinned 13 year-old African-American Bill Clinton.* DNA tests failed to prove that Bill was the father of Danny

---

(70) "The Deck of Hillary," quote was originally from "CounterClintonLibrary.com."
(71) Joyce Milton, "The First Partner," p. 215

Williams, but you can look at p. 41 of the *Globe of March 27, 2001. There is a picture of Danny Williams. He looks like a spittin' image of Bill Clinton!* As my father used to say, "A picture is worth a thousand words."

The Clinton Administration rejected several offers from the Sudanese to capture Osama Bin Laden. Clinton's policy to fight terrorism was a disaster. When the Sudanese offered the Clinton administration *dossiers on hundreds of al Qaeda terrorists, the Clinton administration turned down the offer. Losing Bin Laden, by Richard Miniter, explains the whole story.*

Hillary marched in the West Indian Pride parade in Brooklyn, during the summer of 2003. As parade goers yelled to her: "Run for President, Hillary!", Hillary *upstaged Mayor Michael Bloomberg, as she began to walk in front of him!* It is traditional for the Mayor of N.Y. to lead the parade.[72] Similarly, it is traditional that when a former Senator dies, *the senior Senator from that state makes a short speech in the Senate honoring the deceased Senator.* In New York, the *senior Senator* is Charles Schumer. But that didn't stop Hillary Clinton from taking Schumer's traditional role. Schumer was livid. "Schumer was out of his mind... the family was very upset.", reported one staffer.[73] Another said "Clinton could barely contain herself with the news... She practically ran out the door to make the announcement."[74]

---

(72) Human Events, Sept. 15, 2003, p. 21
(73) R. Emmett Tyrell, Madame Hillary, p. 100
(74) Ibid., p. 100

According to R. Emmett Tyrell, Bill Clinton might have been involved with as many as 5 other interns *besides Monica Lewinsky.*[75]

Attorney Larry Klayman Believes Bill and Hillary "will be behind bars someday"

Larry Klayman is an attorney who has devoted years to exposing the criminal activity of the Clintons. His organization, Judicial Watch, has filed more than 100 lawsuits against people and organizations that abuse power, particularly with respect to the Clintons.

Klayman believes Bill and Hillary Clinton "will be behind bars someday."[76] One case Klayman spoke of concerned businessman Peter Paul, who gave $2 million dollars to Hillary's Senate campaign, "which she never reported." Says Klayman about the Paul case: "We've forced the Ashcroft Justice Department to investigate it. True to form, rather than indicting Sen. Clinton, they've indicted Paul. We're defending him because he wants to tell the truth and because he didn't do anything wrong, and also is willing to come forth and do whatever it takes to have Bill and Hillary behind bars."[77]

Furthermore, Klayton believes Bill and Hillary committed treason, with respect to selling sensitive American

---

(75) Ibid., p. 170
(76) "Klayman Predicts Bill and Hillary Will be Indicted," Wes Vernon, Newsmax.com Magazine, July 2002, pp. 26-27.
(77) Ibid., pp. 26-7.

positions to the Chinese Communists in exchange for campaign contributions to the 1996 Clinton campaign.

According to Klayman, "Yes, Clinton did commit treason, and so did Hillary."[78] The Clintons "were giving away strategic positions for campaign contributions." They "were selling very high technology to the Chinese and granting export licenses if they (the Chinese) gave [the Clintons] large campaign contributions. That was Hillary's scheme. She actually devised that."[79]

According to Klayman, Hillary was the mastermind of the plan "to sell seats on trade missions to the Chinese for campaign contributions." Bill and Hillary took "$600,000 in communist Chinese cash from Charlie Trie, which was laundered into their legal defense fund at the same time the White House was writing letters telling the Chinese that we were not going to be aggressive over disputes in the Straits of Taiwan between China and Taiwan. So we were giving away strategic positions for campaign contributions."[80] Klayman told Newsmax.com that he "can't understand why Bush would look the other way." According to Klayman, Bill and Hillary were "the equivalent of domestic terrorists."

Klayman considers the intelligence committees in the House and Senate to be a "sham" who "don't do anything."

Klayman noted: "We need committees that actually do their job." Instead, we have "thousand-dollar suits, gold

---

(78) Ibid., pp. 26-7.
(79) Ibid., pp. 26-7.
(80) Ibid., pp. 26-7.

cufflinks, and multicolored ties...[we have] Sodom and Gomorrah on Capitol Hill."[81]

In a related suit, Klayman asserts that the April 19, 1995 bombing of the Federal Building in Oklahoma City was coordinated by foreign agents of Saddam Hussein's Iraqi government. According to documents he filed, "the entire plot was, in whole or in part, orchestrated, assisted technically and/or financially and directly aided by agents of the Republic of Iraq. Plaintiffs assert that the involvement and complicity of Iraq can be proven by both direct and circumstantial evidence in classic application, i.e., means, opportunity, and motive."[82]

Klayman further asserts that Terry Nichols and Timothy McVeigh were closely connected to Iraqi terrorists.

The plaintiffs "believe that the attack was not as simple as has been portrayed by the United States government during the criminal trials of Timothy McVeigh and Terry Nichols."[83]

Gary Aldrich of KABC- Interview with Larry Elder

According to Gary Aldrich, Bill and Hillary Clinton tended to downgrade and sometimes even disregard national security. Aldrich, a 30-year veteran with the FBI, felt as if Bill Clinton treated him in a condescending manner. According to Aldrich, Bill Clinton blew 2 opportunities to apprehend Osama Bin Laden- one by killing him and the

---

(81) Ibid., pp. 26-7.
(82) Ibid., pp. 26-7.
(83) Ibid., pp. 26-7.

other by arresting him. Clinton did not have the requisite character or understanding of foreign policy to take out Osama Bin Laden.

We all know that Bill Clinton was a womanizer for years. Monica Lewinsky was just one of Bill Clinton's many girlfriends. Many of Clinton's girlfriends became part of the White House staff. Aldrich felt that Hillary knew all about her husband Bill's womanizing.

Hillary hired a female staff member who job was to alert her if Bill was showing special attention to any women in the White House. Hillary was angry at Bill's stupidity and lack of discretion. Bill Clinton was reckless and sloppy. Monica Lewinsky had tremendous power over Bill Clinton. Monica told 13 or 14 of her friends about her relationship with the President of the United States.

Aldrich's first book "Unlimited Access" sold over 1 million copies and was on the "New York Times" bestseller list. But Aldrich had a rough time getting on TV to promote his book. CNN's Larry King and Dateline NBC canceled Aldrich's booked appearances. When Aldrich did appear on ABC, George Stephanopoulos told the nation that, as far as the White House was concerned, Gary Aldrich was a "pathological liar." The networks caved under enormous pressure from the Clinton administration to keep Gary Aldrich off the air. In fact, to this day Gary Aldrich has never been on any program at CBS!

Aldrich was a model employee of the FBI for 30 years. He had been cited many times for his fine work throughout his long career, so Aldrich's credibility is impeccable. To be sure, the FBI wasn't happy with everything in "Unlimited Access". They wanted Aldrich to remove some of the material about the death of Vince Foster, but he stood fast on that. Aldrich's partner Dennis Sculimbrene backed Aldrich 100%. The FBI was unhappy with Aldrich's partner and they pulled him out of the White House. They assigned him to a meaningless do-nothing job outside of the White House.

Aldrich felt that Bill Clinton's arrogance would intimidate him. Aldrich, however, stood tall and was not affected or scared by Bill Clinton and his political hit squad. Throughout, Gary Aldrich never backed down against Bill Clinton. Yet the mainstream media has been very good to Bill Clinton.

Gary's new book "Thunder from the Left" centers around the theme that the Democratic party has been hijacked by the Hard Left. The party is no longer the party of Franklin Delano Roosevelt, maintains Aldrich. Aldrich has nothing but praise for news outlets such as Fox News Channel and Newsmax.com.

According to Aldrich, Clinton never had a war on terrorism. He only had an investigation of terrorism. He would send 100 agents to Yemen to investigate the U.S.S. Cole, but in reality Clinton was doing nothing to fight the terrorists. If anything, Clinton was pulling the rug out from under the feet of the FBI.

FBI Director Louis Freeh went to former President Bush and Bush helped launch an investigation of the Khobar Tower bombing in Saudi Arabia. Gary Aldrich believes that Bill Clinton will go down in history as a weak President; the terrorists got bolder and stronger every day, culminating in the catastrophic events of September 11th.

Janet Reno as Attorney General didn't help things along, either. She tied up the FBI in ridiculous investigations in the areas of abortion clinics and tobacco companies, diverting valuable resources from the Bureau's fight against Al Qaeda, Bin Laden, and the forces of terrorism.

How Bill Clinton Ignored 2 Warnings from Osama Bin Laden!

Bill Clinton and his administration had advance warning of Osama Bin Laden's plan to crash airplanes into buildings as far back as 1994. In that year a federal report "warned of possible terrorist strikes, including ways in which hijackers could use airliners to hit landmarks such as the Pentagon or the White House." This report, called "Terror 2000" was never released to the American people because "of State Department concerns that it would cause panic." According to a UPI story by Pentagon correspondent Pam Hess, the report was dead on it its predictive accuracy. "Terror 2000" states: "The targets such as the World Trade Center not only provide the requisite casualties but because of their symbolic nature provide more bang for the buck. In order to maximize their odds for success, terrorist groups will likely consider mounting multiple, simultaneous operations with the aim of overtaxing a government's ability to respond, as well as to demonstrate their professionalism and reach...The report was compiled in 1994 after the 1993 World Trade Center bombing, from research and interviews of 41 intelligence, government and private industry experts, including foreign governments such as Israel and Russia...

"Terror 2000" was distributed to the Defense Department, State Department, Federal Emergency Management Agency, intelligence communities and members of Congress on June 24, 1994, according to author Marvin Cetron.

At the State Department's request, the report was "scrubbed" of some details, including how to hit the Pentagon or White House by airplane using the Washington Monument as a landmark. It was never publicly released again, again at the request of State, according to Cetron: "They said: 'You can't handle a crisis before it becomes a crisis. It scares the hell out of people, and they can't do anything. It's like a person with cancer; some people don't want to know. Others want to know everything so they can fight it."

When you consider the facts that (1) Bill Clinton never met one-on-one with his CIA Director James Woolsey and that (2) Bill Clinton only held 2 cabinet meetings in *all of 1998 (one to lie to his cabinet about Monica Lewinsky in January and one meeting to admit his lie in August),* you really can't blame the CIA or Clinton's cabinets for his failures!

The second blown opportunity to get Bin Laden emanated from "Operation Bojinka." Bojinka was a 1995 plot started by an al Qaeda cell in the Philippines whose ultimate goal was to blow up 12 American airplanes and use them as weapons to crash into buildings! Philippine Police Chief Superintendent Avelino Razon uncovered the plot "to plant bombs in U.S. airliners and hijack others to crash them into buildings like the CIA headquarters." According to Reed Irvine, from Accuracy in Media, "Razon said the plot was found on the computer of Ramzi Yousef, the organizer of the

1993 bombing of the World Trade Center. He had fled to Pakistan, but his laptop was found in the apartment he shared with his accomplice, Abdul Hakim Murad. Razon said both were agents of Bin Laden." According to a report in Agence France-Presse, "Among targets mentioned [in Yousef's computer files] was the World Trade Center in New York... CIA offices in Virginia and the Sears Tower in Chicago.

According to an article in "The Washington Post", when a Filipino investigator observed the events of September 11, he exclaimed: "It's Bojinka. We told the Americans everything about Bojinka. Why didn't they pay attention?" The Clinton government did nothing. The Clinton FBI counterintelligence chief, Dale L. Watson, downplayed the significance of "Operation Bojinka" calling it only as a plot to blow up "numerous U.S. air carriers." According to Irvine, Watson "said that the FBI had identified a 'significant and growing organizational presence' of foreign terrorists in the U.S. He swore the bureau had them under control."[84]

Reason Number Two the Clintons Belong in Prison

(2) Rape and Molestation of Women- I believe that Bill Clinton raped Juanita Broaddrick. The story aired on Dateline NBC in late February, 1999, and NBC held the story until Bill Clinton's impeachment trial was over. Broaddrick had 5 witnesses who backed up her story. Usually, a rapist gets about 10 years in prison. I feel that Bill Clinton raped Juanita Broaddrick. Had he been tried and convicted of the rape, Bill Clinton would have received 10 years in prison.

---

(84) "Clinton Warned of Bin Laden Plot- Twice," Newsmax.com Magazine, July 2002, pp. 18-19.

Bill Clinton should have gone to prison for the rape of Juanita Broaddrick. There are countless other women that Bill Clinton groped, molested, or coerced into sex. On top of that, he lied about all his adulterous affairs. It wasn't just one or two- it was hundreds. Bill Clinton perjured himself, raped a woman, molested scores of women, and he certainly belongs in prison for at least 10 years for the crime of rape alone!

Even More Lies Told By the Clintons

(61) Hillary Clinton lied when she claimed it was attorney Richard Massey, not Hillary, who was responsible for bringing Madison Guaranty as a client to the Rose Law Firm. At the time, Massey was in his first year at Rose, and he questioned Hillary's assertion before the Senate Whitewater Committee.

(62) Hillary Clinton lied when she denied having a conversation with Don Denton, concerning a possibly fraudulent option agreement she had been working on in conjunction with Castle Grande.

(63) Bill Clinton lied when he said he never discussed a $300,000 SBA loan for Susan McDougal with Judge David Hale. Susan McDougal, her husband James, and David Hale all ended up going to prison, because of fraud attached to that loan. I think Bill and Hillary should have joined them there.

(64) Bill Clinton lied when he said he never saw Kathleen Willey in the Oval Office.

(65) Bill Clinton lied when Lanny Davis claimed that Bill Clinton "had no specific knowledge of asking for help" in DNC fundraising. White House memos revealed that Bill Clinton *himself* offered to make the calls.

(66) Bill Clinton lied to his attorney Bob Bennett, who was about to discuss the Paula Jones incident on *Meet the Press and CNN Later Edition:* "You tell the American people that this did not happen."

(67) Bill Clinton lied when he called the White House's illegal possession of 900 sensitive FBI files on Republicans "a completely honest and bureaucratic snafu."

(68) Bill Clinton lied when to the people of Arkansas in 1990 when he said he would take a pledge *not* to run for President in 1992.

(69) Bill Clinton lied when he said "the Lincoln bedroom was never sold. That was one more false story we have had to endure."

(70) Hillary Clinton lied when she said she knew nothing about the official White House database being used for political purposes. A White House memo *with her signature on it* indicated the opposite to be true.

(71) Bill Clinton lied when he said that Monica Lewinsky's affidavit denying a sexual relationship was "true and accurate."

(72) Bill Clinton lied when he told Monica Lewinsky that she could claim she got her job at the Pentagon, with these words: "Well, you could always say that the people in Legislative Affairs got it for you or helped you get it."

(73) Bill Clinton lied under oath on 12-28-97, when he testified that he only remembered that Monica Lewinsky was in the White House to see Appointments Secretary Betty Currie.

(74) Bill Clinton lied when he said he never called a state official to arrange a state job for Gennifer Flowers.

(75) Bill Clinton lied when he claimed he had no prior knowledge of Roger Clinton's pending drug use, prior to his arrest in July, 1984.

(76) Bill Clinton lied when he said he had no knowledge of Roger Clinton's pending drug indictment. He eventually admitted that he knew about Roger's indictment for weeks.

(77) Bill Clinton lied when he claimed he shot a 79 in a round of golf, when he actually shot a 92!

(78) Bill Clinton lied 130 *times to the American people when he made this false claim to the American people:* "For the first time since the dawn of the nuclear age, on this beautiful night, there is not a single nuclear missile pointed at a child in the United States of America. In Lt. Col. Robert "Buzz" Patterson's blockbuster book *Dereliction of Duty,* Patterson this statement is a total lie. There *were* missiles pointed at us, all the time and every day! Patterson knew about this stuff, as the President's military aide, he carried the nuclear "football" with him at all times.

(79) Bill Clinton lied to the American people when he claimed that his administration would be "the most ethical administration in history." That is not only a lie; it's a bad joke!

The Number ONE Reason the Clintons Belong in Prison

(1) Strange, Unexplained Deaths - Never before in history have there been so many related people killed in one Presidency as during the Clinton years. People who had goods on the Clinton were dropping dead like flies. There was the mysterious death of Commerce Secretary Ron Brown, who was about to be indicted for illicit fundraising

and was in fear of his life before his very suspicious demise in a plane crash, in the mountains of Yugoslavia.[85] (see section on Ron Brown), There were the bizarre deaths of a couple of women who had been rumored to have been romantically linked to Bill Clinton- Susann Coleman and former Penthouse Pet Judi Gibbs. There was the strange death of James McDougal in prison at the age of 57. McDougal had been the partner of Bill and Hillary Clinton in Whitewater. There were the boys who somehow died on the railroad tracks in Alexander, Arkansas, Don Henry and Kevin Ives.

There was the unexplained death of former CIA Director William Colby, there was Barbara Wise, the Commerce Department employee who *was found beaten to death in her locked Commerce Dept. office on the day after Thanksgiving, 1996![86]* There was *Paul Wilcher,* the attorney who had just turned over work to Janet Reno on Arkansas drug dealing and the raid on Waco, who, *after being found dead on the toilet, his apartment was immediately "cleaned" by the FBI and CIA.* Dentist Donald Rogers was about to reveal shocking information about the Clintons and his Arkansas friends to writer Ambrose Evans-Pritchard, author of *The Secret Life of Bill Clinton. Like Ron Brown, Rogers "died in a plane crash." Ambrose Evans-Pritchard thinks Rogers was killed to keep him quiet about the Clintons and their powerful (snort) friends![87]* Then there were the 4 ATF agents shot during the raid on the Branch Davidians in Waco, TX on April 19, 1993. These 4 agents- Conway LeBleu, Steve Willis, Robert Williams, and Todd McKeehan, *all had*

---

(85) Globe, March 27, 2001, pp. 26-7.
(86) Ibid., p. 31.
(87) Ibid., p. 32

previously guarded Bill Clinton when he had been running for President. They were the only federal agents killed at Waco.*(88)* Remember, the Oklahoma City Bombing was 2 years to the day from the Clinton Government's raid on Waco. I hold Bill Clinton responsible for the deaths of the 80 innocent people at the Branch Davidian compound in Waco...Then there was the mysterious death of business man Ron Miller, who had blown the whistle on illegal fundraising connected to the Commerce Department. Miller had visited Ron Brown's associate Nora Lum "at least 13 times", according to *Chris Ruddy*. Nora Lum was very close to the Clintons. Miller died in a strange way. According to the *Globe,* "Medical experts later concluded that Miller was probably deliberately poisoned by an airborne toxin that fiercely attacked his lungs and for which there is no known cure."*(89)*

According to Ruddy, "*Miller had received death threats and had filed a complaint with local police saying that his revelations would cost him his life.*" *Miller had turned over incriminating tapes to the office of the independent counsel looking into the Commerce Dept. scandals.*(90) Let's not forget *Mary Mahoney, the White House intern who was about to blow the whistle on Bill Clinton's womanizing with female interns, when she was killed – execution style- 5 bullets- the last one to the back of the head. No money was taken in the robbery and a silencer was used by the killer- marking 2 classic signs of a "hit." Mary Mahoney was killed on July 7, 1997, just three days after Monica Lewinsky had "just*

(88) Ibid., p. 32
(89) Ibid., p. 32
(90) Ibid., p. 32

warned Bill Clinton that she was going to tell her parents about their affair unless he found here a well-paying job." Mahoney was about to describe Bill Clinton's escapades in the White House to a veteran of the Washington Press corps who frequented that Starbucks in Dupont Circle. One Carl Cooper copped a plea to the murder: was he paid by someone in the White House to take care of business?[91]

Last, but certainly not least, are the deaths of Clinton Commerce Secretary Ron Brown, (see above) Clinton Deputy White House Counsel Vince Foster, and Clinton's Arkansas security consultant Jerry Parks. See the sections on Vince Foster and Ron Brown. I am convinced that Vince Foster was murdered by someone in the White House who had to keep Vince Foster quiet. Vince Foster knew everything about the Clintons. He had been involved with Hillary for years; he had worked with her at Rose Law Firm for almost 20 years. But their relationship was now over, and Vince had the goods on Bill and Hillary. If he went public with all he knew, the Clintons could just pick out their jail cells. Vince knew all about the lying. He was an impeccably honest guy. As soon as Jerry Parks heard about the death of Vince Foster, he told his son Gary:"I'm a dead man."[92] It was Hillary Clinton who told Vince Foster to hire someone to spy on Bill Clinton. Hillary had to protect her ass, just in case she needed evidence for a divorce, or just in case she might want to be President some day! Jerry Parks started taking photos and making tapes- he started to build files documenting the infidelities of Governor Bill Clinton and the drug use of Bill Clinton at wild parties throughout Little Rock. According to a

---

(91) Ibid., p. 26-7.
(92) Ibid., p. 25

source, *"Shortly after Bill Clinton won the White House, Foster called Parks to demand that he surrender every scrap of information he had gathered. Terrified of retribution if Bill Clinton ever saw those files, Parks balked at turning them over. Foster tried again, just days before he allegedly committed suicide in a Washington area park."*[93]

"Jerry Parks didn't believe the suicide story [of Foster] and began carrying his gun everywhere- even to his mailbox", according to Limbacher-"And he was struggling to pull that gun out from under the seat in his truck Sept. 25, 1993, when two men in a White Chevy Caprice pulled alongside the truck and sprayed it with semi-automatic gunfire. One calmly stepped out and pumped a few more rounds into Parks' body before they sped off."[94]

It was just hours after Parks' death that federal agents and cops visited the house of Jerry Parks. "They swooped in and removed everything that they could find as his grieving widow, Jane, looked on helplessly," said Limbacher- "And although she's been asked to get the files and computer disks back, none has been returned and no one admits to knowing where they are."[95]

---

(93) Ibid., p. 25
(94) Ibid., p. 25
(95) Ibid., p. 25

CHAPTER NINE

The Clinton Body Count

Jerry Parks

Jerry Parks was killed on September 25, 1993, when the truck in which he was driving was sprayed with high-powered gunfire. Parks was a private investigator, hired by Vince Foster at Hillary Clinton's request, whose mission was to spy on Bill Clinton. Parks followed Bill Clinton wherever he went- taking photos, writing notes, and making audio tapes.

As soon as Jerry Parks heard about the death of Vince Foster on July 20, 1993, he told his son Gary **"I'm a dead man."** Jerry Parks was carrying his gun wherever he went. Not for a second did he think that Vince Foster's death was a suicide. After two men in a Chevy Caprice sprayed him with semi-automatic weapons, "one calmly stepped out and pumped a few more rounds into Parks' body before they sped off."

Just a few hours after his death, police and Federal agents came to his house to cart off all sorts of data. "They swooped in and removed everything they could find as his grieving widow, Jane, looked on helplessly," according to Newsmax.com's Carl Limbacher. "And although she's asked to get the files and computer disks back, none has been returned and no one admits to knowing where they are."[1]

---

(1) "Globe," March 27, 2001, p. 25

Who was Jerry Parks and what was his connection to Bill Clinton? Parks had been head of security for the Clinton-Gore campaign headquarters in Little Rock. Jerry Parks was owed a substantial amount of money by the Clinton-Gore campaign. He called the White House at least a dozen times prior to the death of Vince Foster. Four times he spoke with Vince Foster.[2] Hillary Clinton had asked Vince Foster to hire Jerry Parks to "get dirt" on her husband Bill's philandering, womanizing, cheating, and partying. Parks had done that very thing, and now that Bill Clinton had won the White House, Hillary told Vince Foster that she wanted all of Parks' files and data returned to Foster. Parks did not want to hand the files over, because he knew how damaging the information he obtained was!

Parks' son Gary felt that Ken Starr never wanted to get into the details of his father's death. Linda Tripp, who had been Vince Foster's secretary, told a grand jury that she thought "senior White House officials lied under oath about the circumstances of Vince Foster's death."[3]

To understand the web of deceit and evil surrounding the Clintons, you must understand how people like Vince Foster, Jerry Parks, Linda Tripp, Bill Clinton, and Hillary Clinton all interact with each other. Linda Tripp, who was vilified by the Clinton political hit team, to me is a wonderful person. Everyone thinks Linda Tripp taped Monica Lewinsky because she was being nosy or prying into Bill Clinton's "personal life." That, unfortunately Mr. Carville, could not

---

(2) "Bitter Legacy," Ruddy and Limbacher, p. 155
(3) Ibid., p. 155

be farther from the truth. The truth is that Linda Tripp, the former secretary of Vince Foster, was afraid for her own life after the death of Vince Foster on July 20, 1993! Furthermore, Jerry Parks, who lived for just two short months after Vince Foster died, always felt that Vince Foster was murdered!

This is what Linda Tripp told a grand jury in the summer of 1998 about the Parks murder and the Clinton body count. "There was talk that this would be another body added to the list of 40 bodies or something that were associated with the Administration. At that time, I didn't know what that meant. I have since come to see such a list."[4]

Clinton, Cocaine and Strange Deaths

There once was a woman named Sharlene Wilson. This woman had links to Bill and Roger Clinton. Though she once had a wild life, she was now trying to straighten out her life. Sharlene had been a lover of Roger Clinton, and she had unloaded bags of cocaine at Mena airport in Eastern Arkansas for several months. If anyone knew the ins and outs of drug smuggling, money laundering and who ordered hits, it was Sharlene Wilson. Another of Sharlene's lovers was Arkansas prosecutor Dan Harmon, who was about as slimy as they come. Harmon was convicted of five counts of racketeering, extortion, and drug dealing by a Little Rock jury on June 11, 1997. For years, Dan Harmon had been one of the most corrupt prosecutors in Arkansas. He worked closely under Governor Bill Clinton. When he was finally convicted, he was found guilty of using his office "as a

---

(4) Ibid., p. 153-154

criminal enterprise for six years", and "demanding money in exchange for dropping charges."[5] Years earlier, Harmon set up Charlene when a pathetic woman named Joan Potts enticed Wilson to sell her some methamphetamine. Dan Harmon himself arrested Wilson.

Harmon told Sharlene: "Bitch, I told you that if you ever breathed a word about me, I'd take you down. You're going to prison, bitch."[6]

And was he ever right! For her first conviction, Sharlene Wilson was sentenced to 31 years in prison for trafficking in methamphetamine and marijuana.

Sharlene Wilson was trouble for Bill Clinton. She knew way too much about Bill Clinton and his cocaine usage. Wilson told a grand jury of the U.S. District Court in Little Rock (on December 10, 1990) that she had given cocaine to Governor Bill Clinton at Le Bistro nightclub during his initial term as governor.[7]

On one occasion, Sharlene Wilson was at a party with Bill Clinton. According to Jean Duffey, former head of the Seventh Judicial District drug task force, "That was when she [Wilson] testified about seeing Bill Clinton get so high on cocaine he fell into a garbage can...I have no doubt she was telling the truth."[8]

---

(5) Ambrose Evans-Pritchard, "The Secret Life of Bill Clinton," p. 255
(6) Ibid., p. 260
(7) Ibid., p. 257
(8) Ibid., p. 258

Ambrose Evans-Pritchard, author of "The Secret Life of Bill Clinton" interviewed Sharlene Wilson in prison. Wilson had worked as a bartender at a Little Rock nightspot called Le Bistro. Roger Clinton, the first brother, once scored 2 grams of coke near the ladies' room. He borrowed Wilson's "tooter" and handed it to Bill Clinton.[9]

Said Wilson: "I watched Bill Clinton lean up against a brick wall. He must have had an adenoid problem because he casually stuck my tooter up his nose. He was so messed up that night, he slid down the wall into a garbage can and just sat there like a complete idiot."[10]

Wilson claimed to have been present at a series of "toga party-orgies" at the Coachman's Inn near Little Rock. According to Wilson, she was "the hostess with the mostess, the lady with the snow. I'd serve drinks and lines of cocaine on a glass mirror." At these orgies, many of the top political officials of the State of Arkansas were in attendance. There were lots of teenage girls there, and Wilson remembers at least two specific occasions when Bill Clinton was snorting cocaine "quite avidly" with Dan Harmon.[11]

Wilson gave Evans-Pritchard a detailed explanation of the type of sex Bill Clinton preferred. Additionally, she remembered a distinctive mole at the base of his stomach.[12]

---

(9) Ibid., p. 262.
(10) Ibid., p. 262
(11) Ibid., pp. 262-263.
(12) Ibid., p. 263.

Jean Duffey pointed out that Sharlene Wilson had been terrified of Dan Harmon and the Clinton administration. She was afraid her house was being watched. If you crossed Bill Clinton in Arkansas, you paid for it big time. Sometimes you paid with your life- Sharlene Wilson paid for it with a 31 year prison sentence.[13]

Said Duffey: "They couldn't silence her so they locked her up and threw away he key. That's Arkansas for you."[14]

Sharlene Wilson was actively involved in drug dealing out of Mena Airport. Twin-engine Cessnas were used to transport the cocaine. "I'd pick up the pallets and make the run down to Texas. The drop-off was at the Cowboys Stadium. I was told that nobody would ever bother me, and I was never bothered...If there was a problem I was to call Dan Harmon. According to Wilson, much of the cocaine that arrived in Mena was transported to Springdale in northern Arkansas, where it was "stuffed into chickens for reshipment to the rest of the country."[15]

I want you to remember the names **Kevin Ives and Don Henry**. We'll get to them a bit later. They were teenage boys who died mysteriously along some railroad tacks in Arkansas during the summer of 1987. **According to Sharlene Wilson, Dan Harmon was behind the murders of Ives and Henry.**[16]

---

(13) Ibid., p. 260
(14) Ibid., p. 260
(15) Ibid., p. 263
(16) Ibid., p. 265

Wilson concluded the description of her drug dealings in Arkansas:

"Every two weeks, for years, I'd go to the tracks, I'd pick up the package, and I'd deliver it to Dan Harmon, either straight to his office, or at my house...Sometimes it was flown in by air, sometimes it would be kicked out of the train. A big bundle, two feet by one and a half feet, like a bale of hay, so heavy I'd have trouble lifting it...Roger the Dodger [Clinton's brother] picked it up a few times."[17]

Jerry Parks and the Clinton Family

My research has uncovered some other interesting facts about Jerry Parks, the well-respected private investigator in Little Rock. Governor Bill Clinton had appointed Parks to the board of Arkansas Private Investigators.

In late July 1993, Parks' home was robbed in a professional burglary job. Secret files that Jerry Parks had kept on Bill Clinton, were taken, just 2 months before Parks' death. Jerry Parks' son Gary said this to British investigative reporter Ambrose Evans-Pritchard, author of "The Secret Life of Bill Clinton": **"I believe that Bill Clinton had my father killed to protect his political career. We're dealing with a secretive machine here in Arkansas that can shut anyone up in a moment."**[18]

The connection between the Parks family and the Clinton family dates back to 1984, when Jerry's wife Linda was the manager of an apartment complex known as Vantage

---

(17) Ibid., p. 263
(18) Ibid., p. 236

Point.[19] One day the real estate agents at Vantage Point told her that a "nonpaying guest would be coming to stay for a while." This guest was none other than Roger Clinton-brother of Governor Bill Clinton. At the time, Roger Clinton was a strung–out cocaine addict. According to Arkansan author Meredith Oakley ("On the Make"), "By mid 1984, Roger spent virtually every waking hour getting high or trying to get high."[20]

Roger Clinton was not some small-time drug dealer. He was a professional "who boasts of his technique for getting through airport security with bags of cocaine strapped to his body- once in the company of Big Brother. People are sent to prison for life for dealing cocaine on this scale."[21]

Roger Clinton was filmed by hidden cameras, as part of a sting by a state-federal narcotics task force. On tape, he was caught criticizing "niggers" and "cutting a rock of cocaine for sale." And Roger was an arrogant S.O.B.. He told the informant "I've got four or five guys in uniform who keep an eye on the guys who keep an eye on me." On one part of the tape, Roger orders some drugs from his Colombian buddy Maurice Rodriguez, considered by the FBI to be a key drug trafficker with links to the Colombian cartel.[22]

---

(19) Ibid., p. 238.

(20) Ibid., pp. 238-239.

(21) Ibid., pp. 238-240. This is the account of an undercover drug informant who spoke to Ambrose Evans-Pritchard.

(22) Ibid., pp. 239-240. This information Evans-Pritchard got from a confidential source from the House Banking Committee investigation into money laundering in Arkansas.

Roger Clinton became a snitch for the drug task force that had been investigating him. Although he faced six counts of drug dealing and conspiracy, he copped a plea, which, conveniently, was not announced until brother Bill was re-elected to the Governor's mansion in November, 1984! In January, 1985, Roger was sentenced to two years in federal prison. Once again, it helped knowing Bill Clinton.

Bill Clinton claimed he never knew that Roger was into drugs. That was a total lie. Bill and Roger had done lines of coke together for years. Roger told Detective Travis Bunn (former decorated Green Beret sergeant-major) on tape in 1984: "I've got to get some [coke] for my brother, he's got a nose like a Hoover vacuum cleaner."[23]

When Roger Clinton lived at Vantage Point, it was party central for Roger and brother Bill. Day and night, women showed up, and they were often brought over by the Arkansas State Troopers. Bill Clinton would show up often, usually in the mid-afternoon. According to Jane Parks, "the limousine would be parked along the side of "A" block, somewhat obscured from view...She soon learned to distinguish between the voices of the two brothers behind the thin partition."[24]

According to Jane Parks, after Roger would light up, **Bill could clearly be heard saying "This is really good shit!"**[25] Parks maintained that at least two or three times a week. Bill would do Colombian rock cocaine over at Roger's pad. Since the bed was right on the other side of the wall from

---

(23) Ibid., p. 241.
(24) Ibid., pp. 242-3.
(25) Ibid., p. 243.

Parks' desk, she could hear everything. **"Sometimes young women were invited to join, and the little party was consummated with raucous orgasms. On two occasions she heard the Governor copulating on the bed.**[26]

At that time, Linda Parks' husband Jerry was chief of the Little Rock branch of Guardsmark, a national security firm headquartered in Memphis, but he also did some detective work on the side. As his wife started filling him in on what was going on in apartment B107 (where Roger Clinton was living), Jerry started compiling data and files on the goings on. He took photos, he jotted down names, dates, and license plates. Eventually, Jerry Parks had a hefty folder of damaging information about the drug usage and carousing of Bill and Roger Clinton. Linda Parks noted that much of that material was taken in the robbery of their house, in July 1993.[27]

Jane Parks' story is 100% corroborated by her assistant. "Everything Jane Parks told you is true. That woman does not know how to tell a lie...**Bill had his girlfriends in there. You could hear them through the walls. They looked to me very young girls, probably 17, 18 years old."**[28]

Vince Foster and Jerry Parks became friends and business associates over the course of a decade, going back to the early 80's. Eventually, Foster trusted him enough to recruit Parks to launch a comprehensive reconnaissance of Bill

---

(26) Ibid., pp. 242-3.
(27) Ibid., pp. 243-4.
(28) Ibid., p. 244.

Clinton's sexual trysts. **This was done at the behest of Hillary Clinton.**

Ambrose Evans Pritchard- "By the late 1980's Vince trusted Jerry enough to ask him to perform discreet surveillance on the governor."

Jane Parks- "Jerry asked him why he needed this stuff on Clinton. He said he needed it for Hillary. It appears that Hillary wanted to gauge exactly how vulnerable her husband would be to charges of philandering if he decided to launch a bid for the presidency."[29]

And now for some more shocking information. According to Ambrose Evans-Pritchard, author of "The Secret Life of Bill Clinton", Vince Foster paid Jerry Parks $1,000 each time Parks drove out to Mena airport, located in the Ouachita Mountains of western Arkansas. Was Vince Foster involved in running drugs? Was any drug money being funneled to the Clinton campaign? Jane Parks discovered "what must have been hundreds of thousands of dollars in the trunk...It was all in $100 bills wrapped in string, layer after layer. It was so full I had to sit on the trunk to get it shut again."[30]

Linda Parks asked Jerry if he was running drugs. He told her that Vince paid him $1,000 for each trip to Mena. "He didn't know what they were doing, and he didn't want to know either, and nor should I. **He told me to forget what I'd seen.**" Linda Parks recounted that Jerry would leave his

---

(29) Ibid., p. 246
(30) Ibid., p. 246

Lincoln Continental at a hangar at the Mena airport and go off for a cold drink. By the time he would return, the money was loaded in the trunk by forklift. He never touched the money. He would then drive to Little Rock, where he'd deliver the cash to Vince Foster in the K-Mart parking lot on Rodney Parham Blvd. According to Parks, they would switch briefcases to expedite the exchange.[31]

Vince Foster started calling Jerry Parks quite often, in mid-July 1993. Hillary Clinton was all worked up about the files. She needed the files, to see if any information harmful to her or Bill was in them. Jerry Parks told Vince Foster that yes "there was plenty to hurt both of them. But you can't give her those files, that was the agreement."[32]

Foster called again, either on July 18 or 19. He decided he needed the complete set of files to give Hillary. Jerry Parks responded "You're not going to use those files."[33] Foster replied that he was going to meet Hillary at "the flat" and he was going to give her the files "You can't do that, said Parks. My name's all over this stuff. You can't give Hillary those files. You can't. Remember what she did, what you told me she did. She's capable of doing anything."[34]

I realize that this is a lot of information for you to digest, but perhaps it will help you in understanding **the circumstances behind the mysterious death of Vincent Foster on July 20, 1993.** Ambrose Evans-Pritchard raised

---

(31) Ibid., p. 247
(32) Ibid., p. 247.
(33) Ibid., p. 248.
(34) Ibid., p. 248.

the possibility that Vince Foster might have been planning a secret meeting with Hillary Clinton on the day of Foster's death, July 20, 1993.

We may never know the truth about what Vince Foster was up to. We may never know if he and Hillary were lovers, as many allege. We may never know if he was killed or took his own life. Two facts remain: on July 20, 1993 Vince Foster left this earthly existence, and his long-time pal Jerry Parks departed on September 25, 1993!

I definitely trace the deaths of Vince Foster and Jerry Parks right back to Bill and Hillary Clinton. I think they should have been tried as accessories to murder in both cases. Why did Jerry Parks die? Why did Vince Foster die?

Jane Parks spoke to a friend from church who was a top cop from the Arkansas State Police. That man told her that her husband Jerry was killed by a conspiracy of 5 men from Hot Springs who traveled in the same crowd as Buddy Young. Young was former chief of Clinton's security detail and later became a regional director for FEMA. Linda Parks was told the names of the 5 men, who flipped coins to decide which 2 would carry out the hit in her husband.

"And finally, she was told that nothing was ever going to be done about it."[35]

Mary Mahoney- White House Intern who knew too much- gunned down at Starbucks- July 7, 1997!

---

(35) Ibid., p. 237

Mary Mahoney was a White House intern who had been hearing stories of sexual harassment by Clinton from other White House interns. She was about to tell one of the White House beat reporters who frequented the Starbucks at which she worked **all about Bill Clinton's behavior in the White House.**[36]

On July 7, 1997, White House intern Mary Mahoney was killed, along with 2 of her fellow workers, in a strange "hit" at the Starbucks in Georgetown! Mary was shot 5 times; the last shot was delivered execution style to the back of her head.

Furthermore, no money was taken from the Starbucks and a silencer was used by the killer, one Carl Cooper. **These are classic signs of a professional "hit."** Furthermore, it is likely that Cooper was paid by someone at the very highest level of the White House to send a message to Monica Lewinsky!

July 7, 1997 was a very significant date. Just three days earlier, on July 4, 1997, in sworn testimony before a grand jury, Monica Lewinsky indicated that she warned Bill Clinton that she would soon tell her parents all about her relationship with Bill Clinton unless he got her a good job[37]

It is entirely possible that Mary Mahoney was killed just to send a message to Monica Lewinsky and everyone else who had stuff on the Clintons to keep quiet.

---

(36) "Globe," March 27, 2001, pp. 26-7.
(37) Ibid., pp. 26-7.

As former Clinton girlfriend **Gennifer Flowers** said, the Clintons are fully capable of committing murder!

Judi Gibbs- Penthouse Pet, Exotic Dancer and Former Lover of Bill Clinton- Burned alive in a Mysterious House Fire in Fordyce, Arkansas.

For years Hillary Clinton has maintained a divorce file, chronicling all the infidelities of her husband, William Jefferson Clinton. Within that file is contained information about **Judi Gibbs,** who was a lover of Bill Clinton back in the early days in Arkansas. An associate of Bill Clinton told the "National Enquirer" that "Bill met Judi Gibbs at a house of prostitution in Fordyce, Arkansas, which lured political and law enforcement personnel to seek their favors, and photographed them for blackmail purposes. Gibbs, who appeared in the December 1979 issue of Penthouse, was one of the key women used in the operation...After agreeing to help police in an investigation into Arkansas cocaine trafficking, she was found murdered, having been burned to death in her house."[38]

It was a well-known fact in Fordyce that Bill Clinton had been Judi Gibbs sex partner on several occasions. Gibbs met Clinton when she was working as a topless dancer in Hot Springs, Arkansas, and she had boasted to many of her friends that she and Clinton had been lovers. Gibbs had been running a high-price prostitution ring out of her mansion in Fordyce. The fire that engulfed her house killed her and her middle-aged boyfriend Billy Putterbaugh. Naturally, the Arkansas authorities ruled the fire "accidental", but many

---

(38) Globe, March 27, 2001, pp. 28-29.

people in Fordyce believed that it was a work of arson to get rid of Judi Gibbs.[39] I put the death of Judi Gibbs into the same category that I put the deaths of Vince Foster, Ron Brown, Barbara Wise, Mary Mahoney, Jerry Parks, and so many others- somehow traceable and connected to Bill and Hillary Clinton!

Judi Gibbs was being pressured by law enforcement officials to spill the beans about her illegal attempts to blackmail some of her wealthy and politically connected clients.

When Governor Bill Clinton was doing a flyover, surveying the damage in the Fordyce fire that consumed his ex-lover Judi Gibbs, Clinton told a state trooper, "it had been the home of one of the most beautiful women he'd ever met. The trooper said an eerie look came over Clinton's face."[40]

Barbara Wise- Barbara Wise was a long-time employee of the Department of Commerce whose partially nude and bruised body was discovered in her locked office on the day after Thanksgiving, 1996. An autopsy listed her death as being from natural causes, but police said they were handling it as a homicide.

Why did Barbara Wise die? What did she know about illegal fund-raising between Red China, the Clinton White House, and the Democratic National Committee? Why did Bill Clinton make an unscheduled trip to the White House from Camp David on the very day of Wise's death? He was

---

(39) Ibid., pp. 28-29.
(40) Ibid., pp 28-29.

observed with an aide carrying a big box of documents. Clinton's explanation for the unannounced trip from Camp David to the White House was to pick up a book that he had left behind. Give me a break!

Barbara Wise's boss was Ron Brown, who died under mysterious circumstances in a plane crash in Yugoslavia, in April, 1996. Brown had been linked to illicit fundraising between the Chinese Government and the Clinton Administration/DNC. What did Barbara Wise know? What was in her office that might have incriminated the Clintons?

Never in modern history has a cabinet staffer died under similar circumstances. The death of Barbara Wise was largely overlooked by the mainstream media, but it certainly should raise people's suspicions![41]

ATF Agents Conway LeBleu, Steve Willis, Robert Williams, and Todd McKeehan were the only ATF agents killed in the 1993 raid on the Branch Davidian compound in Waco, TX. All four had guarded Bill Clinton when he was a Presidential candidate. Were their deaths coincidental or did they have something to hide? **Why did these agents die?**[42]

Donald Rogers- This Arkansas dentist was about to reveal shocking information about Bill Clinton and his buddies to British investigative journalist Ambrose Evans-Pritchard, author of The Secret Life of Bill Clinton. Rogers died in a plane crash in Lawton, Oklahoma. Evans-Pritchard

---

(41) Ibid., p. 32.
(42) Ibid., p. 32

thought Rogers' plane was sabotaged to keep him quiet. **Why did Donald Rogers die?**[43]

Shelly Kelly- the sole survivor of the Dubrovnik plane crash which killed Ron Brown and dozens of others were traveling. Although she walked to a helicopter on her own, she arrived d.o.a. at a Dubrovnik hospital. Cause of death: a severed femoral artery, according to her autopsy report. Give me a break! It is impossible to walk to a waiting helicopter with a severed femoral artery! I believe someone killed Shelly Kelly. **Why did Shelly Kelly die?**[44]

Ron Miller- was a 58 year-old whistle blower who secretly taped conversations linking an Asian-American couple to illicit fundraising for the Democratic National Committee.

Nora and Eugene Lum, long-time friends and contributors to Clinton, were suspected of laundering money through Millers' company, Dynamic Energy Resources. Miller had turned over his conversations to the Independent Counsel investigating scandals within the Commerce department.

Miller died in a mysterious way. Doctors suspect he was intentionally poisoned by a toxin which attacked his pulmonary system. According to Chris Ruddy of Newsmax.com, "Miller had received death threats and had filed a complaint with the local police saying that his revelations would cost him his life." Apparently that threat was made good. **Why did Ron Miller die?**[45]

---

(43) Ibid., p. 32
(44) Ibid., . 32
(45) Ibid., p. 32

Paul Wilcher- This well-known D.C. attorney had submitted a stack of information related to Arkansas drug dealing to Attorney General Janet Reno. After he was found dead slumped on his toilet, CIA and FBI agents immediately cleaned his apartment. The data Wilcher had has never been made public. Officially, the cause of death was listed as "unknown", but **why did Paul Wilcher die?**[46]

Deaths in Marine Helicopter Unit

Two members of the special Marine Corps HMX-1 unit, the helicopter unit that transported Bill Clinton around D.C. died in a mysterious car accident. Helicopter pilot Lt. Col. Mark Cwick, who flew Clinton around, was driving home in Fredriksburg, VA, when "a car Cwick was trying to pass moved in front of him and to avoid it, he swerved off the road into an embankment and hit some trees."[47]

In March,1999, Marine corporal Eric S. Fox was killed when his van ran off the road and hit a guard rail. Fox was found dead, with a gunshot wound to the head. Authorities ruled it a suicide.[48] We will never know the truth behind the deaths of Cwick and Fox. Clearly, they knew a lot about the personal life of Bill Clinton. Were they about to go public with some information that could have damaged Bill Clinton? Was this Mary Mahoney all over again?

---

(46) Ibid., p. 32
(47) "Bitter Legacy, Ruddy and Limbacher, p. 128-129. This information came from a police report to AP.
(48) Ibid., p. 129.

The authorities want you to believe that these 2 fellows were just random victims of an automobile accident.

If I were you, I would just add Lt. Col. Mark Cwick and Marine Corporal Eric S. Fox to the Clinton body count.

Death of CIA Director William Colby

William Colby was a contributing editor to "Davidson's Strategic Investment", a periodical which ran several articles exposing the crooked deals of Whitewater and investigated the death of Vince Foster. In one issue, it was alleged that Fosters' suicide was a forgery.

Every time an issue of the newsletter came out, the Clinton White House would get upset. According to Chris Ruddy, author of "The Strange Death of Vince Foster", "Clinton and his troops suspected that Colby was supplying the information, even though he wasn't the official author of the stories."[49]

Several facts of William Colby's death don't make sense. Colby always would wear a life jacket, yet his body was found without a life jacket. He was barefoot, yet this had been a chilly day. In his house, the radio and computer were running, and a partially eaten meal of clams was on the table. But Colby was a meticulously neat, organized person who would never leave his appliances on or leave food unattended before going canoeing.

---

(49) "Globe," March 27, 2001, p. 31

Do I believe the Clinton White House ordered the murder of former CIA director William Colby on April 29, 1996 near his Maryland home on the Wicomiso River? You bet I do!

Ron Brown

The mysterious death of Clinton Secretary of Commerce **Ron Brown on April 3, 1996** is steeped in controversy, inconsistencies, and troubling, unanswered questions. The government wants you to believe that Ron Brown died in a plane crash in Yugoslavia, and that's the end of the story…

If only that *was the end. In reality, it's just the beginning.* Consider the following:

(1) Why did the White House ask the military not to conduct autopsies on Brown and the others on that plane?
(2) Why was there no in-depth investigation of the plane crash and the circumstances surrounding Brown's death?
(3) Why was an autopsy not immediately performed on Ron Brown?
(4) Why were head X-rays destroyed?
(5) Why did the chief of the air force's photography unit claim that she was told that the X-rays of Brown's skull were destroyed to remove evidence of a gunshot wound?[50]

---

(50) "Cover-Up in the Death of Ron Brown," Newsmax.com, p. 1. Most of the material on Ron Brown is from this report, which consists of several articles Christopher Ruddy wrote for "The Pittsburgh Tribune-Review" on Nov. 24, 1997, Dec. 3, 1997, Dec. 6, 1997, Dec. 9. 1997, Dec. 11, 1997, Dec. 17, 1997, Jan 11, 1998, and Jan. 13, 1998.

At the time of his death, Ron Brown was being investigated by Independent Counsel Daniel Pearson. Brown and his former business partner and mistress Nolanda Hill allegedly were dealing in several sham financial transactions allowing him to artificially inflate his net worth. Brown and Hill were facing an indictment in the spring of 1996. Brown was being investigated for possible bribery and influence peddling, along with allegations of illicit fundraising in connection with the Democratic Party and the Clinton campaign.

Before his death, Ron Brown was a defiant and cautious man. He was quoted as saying **he was not going to take the "rap" for the Clinton administration. Brown warned friends in the government 'I won't go down alone if this thing gets blown open.'[51]**

Before he died, Ron Brown feared for his life. He hired extra bodyguards and was very cautious about being seen in public. Nolanda Hill thought that Ron Brown might have been killed on the ground before the plane ever left the ground. Brown was feeling a cold coming on, and he usually would retire to his private airplane cabin in such circumstances. It is quite possible that Ron Brown could have been killed in his cabin by a hit man with a silencer **before the plane crashed!**

Larry Klayman of Judicial Watch discovered that there was a link between trading U.S. encryption technology to the Red Chinese and contributions to the Democratic Party.

---

(51) "Globe," March 27, 2001, p. 26.

According to Hill, Brown had at least one secret meeting with Wang Jun, the moneyman for China's People Liberation Army. Amazingly, the Clinton administration had transferred **the control over export of sensitive technology from the Departments of State and Defense to the Commerce Department.**

Bill Clinton needed cash for his 1996 reelection campaign. A lot of people have forgotten how Clinton's popularity nosedived after the Republicans took control of Congress in 1994. Clinton's top advisor Dick Morris told Clinton he would have to raise some **$200 million in contributions to assure his re-election in 1996.** Suddenly, the Clinton Presidency became **one big garage sale!** Everything was for sale- the Lincoln bedroom, rides on Air Force One with Bill Clinton, coffees with Bill Clinton, golf with Bill Clinton, jogging with Bill Clinton, etc. People paid big money to get access to Bill Clinton and gain favors from him. **But Ron Brown was in over his head with illicit fundraising deals with the Chinese.** And Brown used to be chairman of the Democratic Party, so he knew all about fundraising!

Remember, Ron Brown died in April 1996, two full years before Monica Lewinsky was even an issue. **The Chinagate scandal could have easily brought down the Clinton Presidency.** What is encryption? It is the key to unlocking the secrets of our nuclear codes and technology. Strict controls were in place to protect this technology, until Clinton was in desperate need for cash.

Immediately after Ron Brown's death, Pearson closed the investigation and turned the inquiry into Hill and Ron Brown's son Michael over to the Department of Justice.

After Ron Brown's death, the medical experts- military pathologists- started to question the cause of Ron Brown's death. Among those who thought that Ron Brown might have had suffered a gunshot wound to the head were **Lt. Col. Steve Cogswell, Naval Chief Petty Officer Kathleen Janoski, and Air Force Major Thomas Parsons.**
Professionals who dared to question the "official" findings were either (a) discredited and/or demoted (Lt. Steve Cogswell received his first negative job review in eleven years, and he was demoted to an assignment in oral pathology,) (b) reassigned (Army Col. David Hause was reassigned to Fort Leonard Wood, Mo. And CPO Kathleen Janowski was both relieved of her duties in her photography unit and reassigned to a different office at Walter Reed, (c) simply dismissed as wacky conspiracy theorists.

I come from a family of clinical scientists. My late father spent over half a decade working in the health care field as a clinical biochemist, an administrator, and an internationally-recognized expert in his field of clinical research. I learned from him that cover-ups in the area of autopsies, causes of death, and clashes between professional egos are as common in the field of pathology as hot dogs are at Coney Island!

Do I believe there is a cover-up in the death of Ron Brown? You bet I do. Let's consider some facts...

(1) The weather- Sources in the media (such as "Newsweek") originally reported the weather in Dubrovnik, as a factor

in the plane crash: they reported heavy rains, winds, and lightning. Yet according to the Air Force investigation, "the weather was not a substantially contributing factor to this mishap." Translation: there *was no big storm that day*. Fact: winds were 14 mph, there was a light rain falling. In the moments before Brown's plane crashed, 5 other planes landed without incident.

(2) The backup navigation beacon at the Dubrovnik airport had been stolen before the crash, and three days after the crash, the airport maintenance chief, one Niko Junic, committed suicide!

(3) Air Force Tech Sergeant Shelley Kelly survived the crash for 4 hours; she was able to get to an ambulance on her own power. Her autopsy report says she died of a severed brain stem. You try walking with a severed brain stem. I suspect that she was killed too, after the crash.

(4) No autopsy was ever carried out on the remains of Ron Brown!

(5) All of the original X-rays of Ron brown's head have mysteriously disappeared from his case file.[52]

On March 19, 1996, independent counsel Daniel Pearson obtained subpoenas requesting the records of the Asian Pacific Advisory Council (APAC), a fundraising organization associated with the Democratic National Committee. Who was named to be subpoenaed? Ron Brown, his son Michael Brown, Gene and Nora Lum (from Dynamic Energy), the

---

(52) "Second Officer: Wound appeared to be from Gunshot," Christopher Ruddy, from "Pittsburgh Tribune-Review," Nov. 24, 1997.

DNC, and "several APAC fund-raisers who were brought to the Commerce Department by Brown."[53]

Lt. Col. Steve Cogswell had amassed 12 years of experience as a forensic pathologist. His examination of the X-rays of Ron Brown led him to believe that Ron Brown might have very well died from a gunshot wound. According to Cogswell, "Essentially…Brown had a .45-inch inwardly beveling circular hole in the top of his head, which is essentially the description of a .45-caliber gunshot wound." Cogswell was quoted as saying "I talked to Col. Gormley and he told me there is a .45(-inch) inward beveling, perfectly circular hole in the top of Brown's head…Open him up. This man needs an autopsy. This whole thing stinks."

Cogswell continued: "You can't ignore who this person is. You can't ignore the controversy surrounding him. To stack up the coincidences: one of 36 people has got a hole; the hole is in their head; the hole is dead center in the top of their head; and it just happens to be the most important person on that airplane from a political point of view. That's a whole reason to investigate it."[54]

Cogswell's findings were confirmed by the opinion of U.S. Army Lt. Col. David Hause, who was a deputy medical examiner whose military service included a tour of duty in Vietnam (recipient of purple heart), duty as a surgeon during

---

(53) "Questions Linger about Ron Brown Plane Crash," Ruddy and Sprunt, "Pittsburgh Tribune-Review," Nov. 24, 1997.
(54) Christopher Ruddy, "Brown's Head Wound Raises Assassination Specter," "Pittsburgh Tribune-Review," Dec. 3, 1997.

the Gulf War of 1991, and service as the Army's regional medical examiner in Germany.

Hause was in Dover, Delaware when Ron Brown's body arrived from Yugoslavia. He recalled that a commotion erupted when the various pathologists saw Ron Brown's body. One exclaimed **"Gee, this sure looks like a gunshot wound."** When Hause looked at the body, he said **"Sure enough, it looks like a gunshot wound to me, too."**[55]

Hause felt that the Armed Forces Institute of Pathology (AFIP) had messed up in the Brown case. Soon the AFIP started reprimanding Steve Cogswell, trying to limit his discussion with the press about the Brown case. Hause said "One of the things I'm wondering is why all the attention is focused on Cogswell, who never had the original X-rays... The question you have to ask yourself is: Are (officials) upset that AFIP may have blown a case, or are they upset the American public found out that AFIP may have blown a case?"[56]

The chief medical examiner for AFIP distributed a memo to 20 AFIP staff members announcing that an investigation was underway "regarding procedures and individual actions related to the (Tribune-Review) article 'Experts disagree on Ron Brown Head Wound" authored by Christopher Ruddy and other matters."

Dr. Jerry Spencer's memo instructed AFIP staffers to (1) refer all press inquiries to the public affairs officer, (2) stay at

---

(55) Ruddy, op. cit., Dec. 9, 1997.
(56) Ibid.

the AFIP throughout the work day and to seek approval to leave the building during the lunch hour, and (3) turn over "slides, photos, X-rays and other materials" related to the case of Ron Brown.[57]

One of the nation's foremost authorities on forensic pathology Cyril Wecht (M.D. and J.D.), felt that an autopsy on Brown should definitely have been performed. Wecht, a veteran of 13,000 autopsies and reviewer of 30,000 additional cases said "Evidence of a possible gunshot wound should not be ignored. It's not even arguable in the field of medical legal investigations whether an autopsy should have been conducted on Brown...I'll wager you anything that you can't find a forensic pathologist in America who will say Brown should not have been autopsied...Forget about Brown being a cabinet member, or being under investigation. He was in a plane crash. That alone should have meant he was autopsied...There was more than enough evidence of a possible homicide to call in the FBI so that (the autopsy could have been conducted) and a gunshot could have been ruled out. The military had a duty to notify the Brown family, and if the family didn't allow an autopsy, go to another authority to have it conducted. (AFIP) had a duty to do an autopsy...I'm troubled...They did a tremendous disfavor to the families by not conducting autopsies."[58]

Speaking of the circular hole in Ron Brown's skull, Dr. Wecht stated: "Anytime you have a circular, symmetrical

---

(57) Christopher Ruddy, "Gag Order Broadens," Pittsburgh Tribune-Review," Dec. 11, 1997.
(58) Christopher Ruddy, "Top Pathologist Says Assassination Possible," Pittsburgh Tribune-Review," Dec. 17, 1997.

hole, a pathologist knows that one of the distinct mechanisms for making such a defect is a bullet."[59]

And what about the missing X-Rays? Dr. Wecht told Chris Ruddy about Wecht's Law: "The frequency of lost X-Rays, hospital records, documents, autopsy materials and other materials in a medical-legal investigation is directly in proportion to the complexity, controversy and external challenges" to a given case.[60]

Translation: Doctors lie just like everybody else!

Wecht emphasized that "you'll find it very, very rare" to have X-rays missing from a file case.

In early January 1998, a third pathologist spoke out on the Brown case. Air Force Major Thomas Parsons, who had been conducting autopsies, supported the comments of Cogswell and Hause. Parsons had told his boss Dr. Spencer that "the circular hole was both suspicious and unusual, and could not reasonably be accounted for by the plane crash. He also said the head wound was just one of many reasons an autopsy should have been performed."[61]

Chief Petty Officer Kathleen Janowski was chief of forensic photography for two and one-half years for AFIP. When she first saw the hole in Ron Brown's head, she remarked: "Wow, look at the hole in Ron Brown's head. It

---

(59) Ibid.
(60) Ibid.
(61) "Military Officers Challenge Washington Post Story," Christopher Ruddy, "Pittsburgh Tribune-Review," Jan. 11, 1998.

sure looks like a gunshot wound." Janowski felt that AFIP had botched the investigation into the death of Ron Brown. She said: "The investigation is nothing more than a witch hunt. (AFIP) should be investigating what happened to the missing head X-rays. No one at AFIP seems to care that Brown did not receive an autopsy."[62]

It is quite possible that the wound to Ron Brown's head might have come from a captive-bolt gun. Such a weapon was used in the murder of U.S. DEA agent Eugene Camarena in Mexico in 1985.

I realize this is a lot of detail, but I want you all to understand the lengths that the Clinton administration went to cover up mysterious deaths such as Ron Brown's. Vince Foster's death is similarly loaded with unanswered questions. It is quite evident that Ron Brown was a very dishonest guy, and he was over his head in illicit fundraising activities. But remember, his death in April, 1996 occurred at a time when he was on the verge of being indicted. Had Brown been indicted and told all he knew, he might very well have toppled the Clinton Administration.

It is a real crime that no autopsy was carried out on the body of Ron Brown. The FBI should have investigated the death of Ron Brown, but it never did. It is entirely possible that Ron Brown might have been the victim of terrorism (there were 2 Croatians aboard the doomed flight), a crazed gunman, or might have been killed even before the plane took off. Sadly, we will never know the truth. We will never

---

(62) "4th Expert Claims X-Ray Evidence Destroyed," Christopher Ruddy, "Pittsburgh Tribuen-Review," Jan. 13, 1998.

know if Bill Clinton had anything to do with the death of Ron Brown, or if Bill Clinton had anything to do with the lack of FBI and Dept. of Justice investigation into the real cause of the death of Ron Brown.

What we do know is what happened to the whistleblowers who questioned the "official" findings into the death of Ron Brown:

- Lt. Steve Cogswell- for the first time in his 10 year career in the Air Force, Cogswell was written up with a negative job performance evaluation. According to the evaluation, "Cogswell is disruptive to the work environment with immature behavior. He has been unresponsive to counseling, it continues, adding that he has used inappropriate language and worn inappropriate dress. Cogswell is even criticized for his manner of driving on the AFIP facility's parking lot."[63] In addition, Cogswell was demoted to work in dental pathology, a field for which he had no background.

Yet all of Cogswell's previous job evaluations had been excellent. Just one year earlier, the very pathologists that were so critical of him had cited Cogswell as "the number one forensic pathology consultant in the Department of Defense!"[64]

-Kathleen Janowski- the 22 year veteran Air Force forensic photographer – was ordered to vacate her office in

---

(63) "Pentagon Retaliates," WorldNetDaily, Feb. 20, 1998.
(64) Ibid.

Rockville. MD. She and her staff of three were relocated to Washington D.C. Janowski was stripped of her duties.

- Major Tom Parsons was transferred to Andrews Air Force Base.
- Army Colonel David Hause was transferred to Fort Leonard Wood, Missouri.
- As if to add insult to injury, the boss at AFIP canceled the planned attendance of Janowski, Parsons, Hause, and Cogswell at the American Academy of Forensic Sciences in San Francisco. All other staff members were permitted to attend this important conference, which was critical to professional development for AFIP staff.[65]

The moral of the story- don't cross Bill Clinton!

Cogswell, Hause, Parsons, and Janowski should look at the bright side. Unlike Vince Foster, Ron Brown, Jerry Parks, Ives & Henry, Susann Coleman, Judi Gibbs, Mary Mahoney, William Colby, and so many more...at least they weren't killed!

Back in 1996, Commerce Secretary **Ron Brown** was about to be indicted by special prosecutor Daniel Pearson. Brown, his lover and business partner Nolanda Hill and Brown's son Michael were all being investigated, according to Hill.

---

(65) Ibid.

According to Hill, Ron Brown went to the White House and told Bill Clinton that he (Brown) was not going "to take the fall for an administration rampant with corruption."[66]

Brown wanted Pearson to back off from his investigation. Perhaps the FBI could obstruct the Pearson investigation by withholding critical information. Brown knew that Ken Starr was being controlled by the Clintons. Brown knew that the FBI was reporting to and accountable to Janet Reno and the White House, **not to Ken Starr.**

In short, Ron Brown wanted the same treatment from Daniel Pearson that Ken Starr was giving to Bill Clinton. Again, according to Nolanda Hill, Bill Clinton told Ron Brown: "I'll take care of it."

Bill Clinton didn't have to take care of anything. He didn't have to worry about Ron Brown's imminent indictment damaging his already corrupt administration. In April, 1996, Ron Brown died in a plane crash in Dubrovnik, Yugoslavia, in a case as strange as the deaths of Vince Foster, Jerry Parks, Ives & Henry, William Colby, and so many more!

There is so much more to the death of Ron Brown than simply a plane crash in the mountains of Dubrovnik, Yugoslavia. Coincidentally, I was in Dubrovnik in the summer of 1964. I was on vacation with my parents- I was 13 and ½ years old. To this day I remember the old and new cities of Dubrovnik. It was a beautiful place to visit!

---

(66) Ruddy and Limbacher, "Bitter Legacy," p. 66. and Chris Ruddy, "The Strange Death of Vince Foster," pp. 18-19.

Yes, the death of Ron Brown is tied to the sale of encryption technology to the Chinese government. What is **encryption?** It is the key to unlocking the secrets of our nuclear codes and technology. Strict controls were in place to protect this technology, until Bill Clinton was in desperate need of cash to finance his 1996 re-election campaign.

During 1995-1996, Clinton pimped out the entire White House. He rented out the Lincoln bedroom on a daily basis to the highest bidder. Rides on Air Force One, jogging and golfing with the President, nights at the Lincoln bedroom- all of these went to the Democrats with the fattest bank accounts! Each day people paid big money for access to and favors from Bill Clinton.

Ron Brown was in over his head with illegal fundraising deals with the Chinese. Think about it. The year was 1996. Ron Brown's illicit activity could topple *the* Clinton administration, which was facing a tough re-election campaign in November. By eliminating Ron Brown, he could never "rat out" Bill Clinton and the Democratic Party. Remember, no one ever heard of Paula Jones or Monica Lewinsky at this time.

After Ron Brown's death, at least 3 military pathologists questioned the official findings as to the cause of death. Only an autopsy could conclusively answer their questions, but *incredibly, no autopsy on Ron Brown was ever performed!* Despite the fact that a cabinet member had died a very suspicious death- despite the overwhelming evidence that Ron Brown had a bullet hole in his skull- the FBI was never called in to investigate the case.

Army Col. David Hause, a pathologist who had served as a flight surgeon during the Gulf War, Lt. Col. Steve Cogswell, and Air Force Major Tom Parsons all suspected that Ron Brown had what looked like a .45 bullet would to his skull.

Naval Chief Petty Officer **Kathleen Janowski,** head of the Armed Forces Institute of Pathology's Photography Unit, believed that Ron Brown's head X-rays were intentionally destroyed to hide evidence of bullet remnants in Brown's head. To this date, *no one knows what happened to the X-rays of Ron Brown's skull!*

Vince Foster's Unexplained Death- July 20, 1993

There are many strange circumstances surrounding the death of Vince Foster. Just about the only thing I will accept as truth is that his dead body was discovered in Ft. Marcy Park (outside D.C.) on July 20, 1993.

Consider the following:

Skull X-Rays of Foster were either missing or never taken. Unusual carpet fibers were found on Fosters' clothing. Internationally-known pathologist/attorney Cyril Wecht described the U.S. Park Police's handling of the Foster case as "horribly botched" and "bungled." "Relationship" photos, usually taken by investigators to provide a lasting record of a corpse's location, with respect to its environs, were never taken.[67]

---

(67) Ruddy, op. cit., pp. 20.

Chris Ruddy raises several great questions:

(1) Why was Vince Fosters' death treated as a suicide from the outset?
(2) What happened to key evidence, like crime-scene photos?
(3) Why was the Clinton White House allowed to decide how key evidence was to be handled?[68]

"On the night of his death, senior aides to the president [Clinton] entered, searched, and allegedly removed documents from Foster's office without the approval or even knowledge of the Park Police, who had directed the room be sealed."[69]

The Park Police should never have been in charge of such an important investigation to begin with. This should have been the job of the FBI- why they weren't put in charge of the Foster death probe is as big a mystery as the case itself! Park Police made serious errors in the preservation of Fosters' physical evidence (hair, blood and fingerprints) and in the autopsy process.

There is serious doubt as to where Fosters' body was actually found in Ft. Marcy Park. It is possible that the Park Police lied about the location of the discovery of the body in their reports. No videotape was made of the murder scene, although this is standard operating procedure for the Park Police and indeed all murder cases. The first cannon in Ft. Marcy Park was removed by the Park Police in July, 1994, after Ruddy's reports questioned the true location of Fosters'

---

(68) Ibid., pp. 19-20.
(69) Ibid., p. 21

body. The FBI "refused to draw a map of the park for use during the grand jury proceedings."[70]

Two men were observed in the exact area where Vince Fosters' car had been parked at about 5p.m. on the afternoon of his death. Who were these men? Might they have been the killers? Two witnesses in the park that day- Mark and Judy- told the FBI that they observed a man standing next to Fosters' Honda who was "mid-to-late forties, approximately six feet in height, medium build, long blond hair and beard, appearing unclean and unkempt."[71] Mark and Judy felt the Park police report was not an accurate account of the facts as they seemed to them. Park Police failed to search the neighborhood for witnesses or other evidence, even though U.S. Senators, the Saudi ambassador, and many others lived in the ritzy community right around the park.

The death of Vince Foster is nothing but a lot of unanswered questions.

(1) It is quite likely that Fosters' body may have been moved to that park from someplace else. There were rumors (from the staff of one Senator's office) that Foster had been killed at a Georgetown apartment. There were rumors that Foster had died in the parking lot of the White House.

(2) Paramedics on the scene at Ft. Marcy Park said that Fosters' body appeared "coffin-like", as if it had been moved there from someplace else.

---

(70) Ibid., p. 36
(71) Ibid., p. 41

(3) There was a very small amount of blood on Vince Fosters' body. In fact, EMT worker Corey Ashford classified Fosters' death as a homicide in his official report.[72]

(4) The Park Policeman who was the first to respond to the scene, Kevin Fornshill "had never seen a suicide by gunshot before." A cardinal rule in criminology is that "All deaths should be considered homicides until the facts prove otherwise."

Mysteriously, seven key Polaroid **photos** of the crime scene **disappeared.** The Park Police concluded that Foster had killed himself in a sitting position. If this hypothesis is correct, how did the gun end up under Foster's leg? **No one has determined what happened to 2/3 of the Polaroids taken by the Park Police. They just vanished in thin air.** Kevin Fornshill claimed to have discovered Fosters' body almost **100 yards** away from where the Park Police claimed the body was found, according to the latter's official report. Similarly, Foster was found with the gun "firmly in Foster's hand after he was said to have fired it." Yet, according to the coroner, the gun's recoil and human reflexes will practically always cause the gun to be cast fifteen feet or more away from a body, in a suicide.[73]

In mid- 1994, **Ken Starr** took over for Robert Fiske as special counsel. Starr never investigated the discrepancy in the location of Starr's body, since the first cannon in Ft. Marcy Park had been moved. The FBI felt the case was closed. It was far from closed.

---

(72) Ibid., pp. 44-45.
(73) Ibid., p. 25

The Park police did not secure the rear entrance to the park with yellow crime-scene tape. By not canvassing the area, the Park Police contradicted the "Suicide Investigation" section of the Park Police homicide manual, which states that "in most cases, it is appropriate to canvass the area to locate any witnesses who may have seen or heard something related to the incident."[74]

Fairfax, VA paramedic Richard Arthur didn't believe that Foster committed suicide or that the death of Foster had occurred at Ft. Marcy Park. Arthur was never interviewed by the media. Sgt. George Gonzalez noted the small amount of blood found on Fosters' body. EMT worker Corey Ashford transported the body of Vince Foster to the morgue. After observing no blood and never finding an exit wound, Ashford considered Foster's death to be a homicide, and he stated this in his official report.

Many of the police investigating the Foster death lacked experience in suicides. Kevin Fornshill of the Park Police had "never seen a suicide by gunshot before."[75] For lead criminal investigator John Rolla of the Park Police, this was his first homicide case.[76] According to detective Cheryl Braun, it was determined that Foster had killed himself before the scene had been examined and before "her partner or any other detectives arrived at the scene."[77]

---

(74) Ibid., p. 42.
(75) Ibid., p. 45.
(76) Ibid., p. 45
(77) Ibid., p. 45

New York homicide experts policemen Vincent Scallice and Fred Santucci felt that the position of Fosters' body was "inconsistent with suicide."[78] They noted the absence of blood, brain matter, bone, and other tissue, which should have emanated from an exit wound. None of the 20 officials on the murder scene noted "any blood on the vegetation around the body."[79]

NYC police Detective Jerry Giorgio noted the small amount of blood trickling out of Foster's mouth. A .38 gunshot wound to the head would normally result in **"tremendous amounts of blood, blood all over the place, it would be a mess."[80]**

There is serious question as to whether the gun officially found in Fosters' hand was planted or exchanged for a prior gun. According to the official report, a .38 caliber revolver was found in Foster's hand, even though Fairfax County medical tech. Richard Arthur was convinced the gun he saw was a semiautomatic- either a .45 or a 9 mm. Furthermore, the only revolver Foster's wife Lisa could link to her husband was a silver revolver- *totally unlike the black one found at Ft. Marcy Park.* Mrs. Foster distinctly remembered packing the silver revolver, when the Fosters moved to Washington. Foster's children and his nephew, Lee Foster Bowman, did not recognize the old black colt revolver found at Ft. Marcy Park from their grandfathers' gun collection.

---

(78) Ibid., p. 47
(79) Ibid., p. 47
(80) Ibid., p. 48.

Larry Wilson, an expert on antique Colt weapons felt that someone placed the gun at the scene to confuse investigators, and several detectives agreed with Wilson- that it seemed like a "drop gun."[81] None of the ammunition found in the Colt revolver matched the ammunition found in the Foster home.[82]

The first witness to find Foster's body, a man identified in the reports as "CW" (confidential witness) claimed he saw no gun in Foster's hand upon the discovery of Foster's corpse. "There was no gun in the hand, His- both palms were face up- thumbs out to the side...I did not see a gun next to the body."[83]

In their report, detectives Scaldice and Santucci said that "in their combined experience of fifty years of investigating homicides, [we have] never seen a gun positioned in a suicide's hand in such an orderly position."[84]

So there are lots of questions surrounding the mysterious death of Vince Foster. Vince Foster's crime scene was filled with unanswered questions, inconsistencies, and classic mistakes in policing. Vince Foster was last seen alive at 1 p.m. on July 20, 1993. No one has been able to account for his whereabouts between 1 p.m. and 4:45 p.m. that day. No one ever saw him enter Fort Marcy Park. No investigation was ever undertaken by the Park Police, by the FBI, by the

---

(81) Ibid., p. 54.
(82) Ibid., p. 71
(83) Ibid., p. 54
(84) Ibd., p. 56

White House, or by anyone for that matter, as to Foster's whereabouts that afternoon.

The fatal bullet was never found. Several forensic experts and medical examiners had serious problems with the Park Police's version of events. Accord to Massad Ayoob, a leading forensic expert for the States of California and Michigan, the powder burns on Foster were consistent with those of a suicide that had been "faked." Furthermore, the powder burns on Foster indicate that Foster had to have held the gun in "an extremely unnatural and awkward grasp totally inconsistent with what experience and logic shows us to expect of a suicidal person."[85] Leading firearms forensics expert Dr. Vincent DiMaio agreed. "It doesn't make any sense. It is not consistent with suicide." DiMaio, a Medical Examiner from San Antonio, is an expert on gunshot trauma.[86]

The Park police closed its case on August 5, 1993. Yet the alleged death weapon was never sent for testing (to see if it even fired) until 11 days after the case was declared closed.[87]

Scalice and Santucci conducted a 4-month comprehensive investigation of the death of Vince Foster, under the auspices of the Western Journalism Center. Too many things just didn't add up. No one heard any gunshots. There was no matching ammunition. Vince Foster had not been suicidal.

---

(85) Ibid., p. 66
(86) Ibid., p. 68
(87) Ibid., p. 69

But Vince Foster had been the Clinton's personal lawyer. Vince Foster had been working on the Whitewater Partnership tax returns. Jim McDougal had been calling Vince Foster. When Vince Foster was found dead, Jerry Parks (Arkansas private eye) said "I'm a dead man." According to Parks, Hillary had asked Vince Foster to hire Jerry Parks to spy on Bill and his women. She wanted photos, tapes- evidence she might need someday in a court of law. Parks had been hired years before Bill Clinton was President. Now Bill and Hillary were in the White House. Hillary needed the files and photos Jerry Parks had taken. Vince Foster must have known that Hillary meant business. Jerry Parks couldn't give all that stuff to Vince Foster. Either way, Parks knew he was finished.

Do I think the Clintons were involved in the murder of Vince Foster? You bet I do.

The Mysterious Deaths of Don Henry and Kevin Ives

I mentioned these earlier in connection with Dan Harmon. Don Henry and Kevin Ives were run over by a freight train on an August night in 1987. They may very well have been at the scene of a drug drop, which may have led to their untimely deaths. The deaths were ruled accidental by State Medical Examiner Fahmy Malak. Malak was the same doctor who covered up for Bill Clinton's mother Virginia Kelley in the death of 17-year-old Susie Deer in 1981. Clinton's mother had been the nurse anesthetist in Deer's case- and according to subsequent accounts in "The LA Times" and "Dateline NBC" - her negligence and malpractice caused the death of Susie Deer. Deer had died from a lack of oxygen, when Clinton's mother "fumbled the breathing with

disastrous results."[88] Yet Malak ruled that Deer had died
from "blunt trauma" to the head. True, Deer had been hit by a
rock "that broke her jaw and nose," but she was not in serious
danger. Indeed, she was sitting up and chatting before
surgery at the Ouachita Memorial Hospital. In addition,
Malak had botched many other cases. He was an appointee of
Bill Clinton, who had a highly questionable background.
According to Meredith Oakley, author of the Clinton
biography "On the Make", that "Malak survived in Arkansas
is a testament to Clinton's power. He repeatedly lied about
his credentials, misconstrued his findings and misrepresented
autopsy procedures. In the lab, he misplaced bodies and
destroyed evidence. On the witness stand, he was a
prosecutor's dream."[89]

There is a lot more to the deaths of Henry and Ives.
According to Sharlene Wilson's account to Ambrose Evans-
Pritchard, one of the drops along the railroad tracks in
Alexander, Arkansas had disappeared–Wilson used to pick
up cocaine deliveries along those railroad tracks. For years,
she would pick up the dropped packages and deliver them to
prosecutor Dan Harmon. According to Wilson, Roger Clinton
picked up the packages of cocaine a few times.

On the night of August 22, Dan Harmon had brought out
a few of his goons to supervise that night's delivery. They
were awaiting of 3 to 4 pounds of cocaine and 5 pounds of
marijuana. Sharlene Wilson had been strung out on a mixture

(88) Ambrose Evans-Pritchard, "The Strange Death of Bill
Clinton," p. 266
(89) Ibid., 266.

of cocaine and crystal- so she couldn't make that night's pickup. She stayed in her car, parked off Quarry Road.

Wilson recounted the events of the evening. "It was scary. I was high, very high. I was told to sit there and they'd be back. It seemed forever...I heard two trains. Then I heard some screams, loud screams. It...It..(Wilson then stammers, unable to complete the thought)...When Harmon came back, he jumped in the car and said, 'Let's go.' He was scared. It looked like there was blood all down his legs."[90]

Wilson later learned that group of boys had been "intercepted" at the drop sight. A few of them managed to get away, but Ives and Henry were not as lucky. According to Sharlene Wilson, "Ives and Henry were captured...Harmon's men interrogated them as they were lying on the ground, face down, hands tied behind their backs. They were kicked and stabbed to death with a "survival knife." The bodies were wrapped in a tarpaulin, carried to a different spot on the line, and placed across the railway tracks so the bodies would be mangled by the next train.[91]

The next day Dan Harmon dispatched Sharlene Wilson to Rockford, Illinois, to deliver a package of cocaine. Harmon had given her $500 in cash, with which she bought an Olds Cutlass for $450 at an auto auction. From Rockford, she subsequently fled to Nebraska.

Sharlene Wilson called Ambrose Evans-Pritchard at his D.C. office. She told him, in a collect call, "Everything I told you is off the record." Evans-Pritchard, however, was more

---

(90) Ibid., p. 264.
(91) Ibid., p. 264

concerned with the facts of the case getting out than preserving the corrupt power base of the Saline County judicial authorities. Thus, he went ahead and printed Wilson's shocking account of the events surrounding the deaths of Ives and Henry.[92]

Linda Ives persisted to have another doctor examine the remains of her murdered son. "She immediately ran into a roadblock from the office of the Arkansas governor, Bill Clinton...But eventually she succeeded in having the boys' bodies exhumed and re-examined.[93]

In April 1988, Dr. Joseph Burton, chief medical examiner for Atlanta, conducted a second autopsy. After consulting with six other forensic investigators, Dr. Burton concluded that Don Henry had suffered "a stab wound consistent with it having been inflicted by something such as a large cutting knife." Burton concluded that Kevin Ives had been "smashed in the head with a large rifle butt, probably Don Henry's .22 caliber hunting rifle."

Burton concluded: "The preponderance of evidence in this case indicates that Kevin Ives and Don Henry sustained injuries prior to impact with the train, that these injuries were inflicted on them by another individual or individuals, that their bodies were placed on the track."

Remember what I have been telling you throughout this book: anyone who crossed the Clintons would get destroyed.

---

(92) Ibid., p. 264.
(93) "Globe," March 27, 2001, p. 28. Testimony of informed source.

If you crossed the Clintons, their political hit squad would discredit you, get you fired, intimidate you, scare you, and- in extreme cases- kill you!

Barbara Wise

Barbara Wise was a long-time employee of the Department of Commerce whose partially nude and bruised body was discovered in her locked office on the day after Thanksgiving, 1996. An autopsy listed her death as being from natural causes, but police said they were handling it as a homicide.

Why did Barbara Wise die? What did she know about illegal fund-raising between Red China, the Clinton White House, and the Democratic National Committee? Why did Bill Clinton make an unscheduled trip to the White House from Camp David on the very day of Wise's death? He was observed with an aide carrying a big box of documents. Clinton's explanation for the unannounced trip from Camp David to the White House was to pick up a book he had left behind. **Give me a break!**

Barbara Wise's boss was Ron Brown, who died under mysterious circumstances in a plane crash in Yugoslavia, in April, 1996. Brown had been linked to illicit fundraising between the Chinese government and the Clinton Administration/DNC. What did Barbara Wise know? What was in her office that might have incriminated the Clintons?

Never in modern history has a cabinet staffer died under similar circumstances. The death of Barbara Wise was

largely overlooked by the by the mainstream media, but it
certainly should raise people's suspicions![94]

Still More Lies told by Bill and Hillary Clinton!

(80) Hillary Clinton lied when she told Dan Rather (on "60
Minutes") that she would never run for President. She
said: "People have said that to me, but it is something
that I don't take seriously at all; it's not even in the
universe of my thinking."

(81) Hillary Clinton lied when she claimed to be a long-time
fan of the New York Yankees.

(82) Bill Clinton lied when, speaking of the possibilities of
Hillary's running for President- he said: "Oh, she'd be
great at it. But I don't think she'd ever run- not in a
hundred years!"

(83) Bill Clinton lied when he said he was never drafted.

(84) Bill Clinton lied (Jan. 21, 1998) when he told John
Podesta that he did not have a sexual relationship with
Monica Lewinsky.

(85) Bill Clinton lied when he told John Podesta that he never
asked anybody to lie.

(86) On January 21, 1998, Bill Clinton lied again to John
Podesta when he told him that he never had sex with
Monica Lewinsky.

(87) Bill Clinton lied to Podesta when he told his aide that
"he had never had sex with her in any way whatsoever-
and that *they had not had oral sex.*

(88) Bill Clinton lied to Sidney Blumenthal on Jan. 21, 1998,
when (a) he portrayed Monica Lewinsky as being the
aggressor in their relationship, (b) he portrayed

---

(94) "Globe," 3-27-01, p. 32.

Lewinsky as a "stalker", (c) Clinton presented himself as the innocent victim of Monica Lewinsky's behavior.

(89) Hillary Clinton lied when on April 19, 1999, after she attended 8 events in NYC, she made the following remark about the possibility of her running for the Senate from NY. "I'm obviously still considering, and exploring, and am very interested. But right now I'm very focused on the situation in Kosovo."

(90) Bill Clinton lied, when he said, speaking of Hillary, "She was not interested in being in elected office and she has always said that publicly."

(91) Hillary Clinton lied when she said she never called Paul Fray a "fucking Jew bastard." Why would Paul Fray lie? We have hundreds of other examples of Hillary talking this way. Hillary has every reason to be lying.

(92) Bill Clinton lied when he said that "in 29 years, my wife has never uttered an ethnic or racial slur against anybody else."

(93) Hillary Clinton lied when she said she kissed Yassir Arafat's wife only because she didn't understand the Arabic translation of Mrs. Arafat's racist comments that Israelis were "poisoning" Palestinian children.

(94) Hillary Clinton lied when she said she played no role in the firing of the White House Travel Office,

(95) Bill Clinton lied when he swore he never touched Monica Lewinsky on the breasts or genitalia for the purpose of giving her sexual gratification.

(96) Bill Clinton lied when he said he was a "non-reciprocating recipient" of Monica Lewinsky's services.

(97) Bill Clinton lied when he told Monica she could say she was coming to the White House to see Betty Currie or to bring Clinton letters.

(98) Bill Clinton lied in his deposition in the Paula Jones case when he said he didn't know if Monica told Clinton that she had been subpoenaed. Again, Clinton's own previous statements on 12-19-97 (to Vernon Jordan) and 12-28-97 (to grand jury) indicate he knew all along about her having been subpoenaed.

(99) Bill Clinton lied in his deposition in the Paula Jones case when he answered "I don't think so" to the question: **did anyone besides his attorney tell him that Monica Lewinsky had been served with a subpoena?**

So there you have it. I think the case is open and shut-the Clintons belong in prison. In fact, I don't think they should ever get *out of* prison. You may not like the things I have written in this book, but every fact *has been checked and re-checked for accuracy. Every fact has been cross-checked. I have not made up one thing in this book! My research has been done by just two people, Andrew and me. I hope George Bush wins big in November, giving him a mandate to indict the Clintons and put them in prison, where they belong. I call on Attorney General John Ashcroft to re-open the investigations in the deaths of Ron Brown and Vince Foster. I call on all of you, my readers, to call your Congressmen to get Congress to reauthorize an independent counsel to investigate and ultimately indict the Clintons.*

The pardons looked like bribery to me. Bill and Hillary Clinton have been a team since the days of Yale. They are partners in crime, *just like Bonny and Clyde. Unlike Bonny and Clyde, though, the Clintons are lawyers, and there is nothing more dangerous than a crooked lawyer. Every step of the way, Bill and Hillary had a plan. They made sure to both be on the same page every day. Hillary should be disbarred, just like Bill was. A crooked lawyer knows how to*

*avoid going to prison. A crooked lawyer "can't recall"
incriminating facts. A crooked lawyer "isn't sure" about key
facts and evidence. A crooked lawyer "has no knowledge."*

*There is only one thing worse than a crooked lawyer- that
is two crooked lawyers.*

Hillary wasn't always lying. She once made a statement
to the *Today Show on January 27,1998 I that was partly true
and partly nonsense..* Hillary said: "Bill and I have been
accused of everything, including murder, by some of the very
same people who are behind these allegations...For anybody
willing to find it, and write about it, and explain it, is this vast
right-wing conspiracy that has been conspiring against my
husband since the day he announced for president."[1]

As my father used to say, lock 'em up and throw away
the key.

---

1 The Deck of Hillary from Newsmax.com

Melrose Larry Green

Appendix

White House Guests Database (from *opensecrets.org*)

This database shows all campaign contributions made in the 1999-2000 election cycle by guests who stayed at either the White House or Camp David. The list is conservative, since the White House provided only names — not addresses, city or state of the guests. Where names were too common to positively identify, the Center did not include them in this database. Dates of the overnight stays were not provided by the White House, nor was it specified whether the guests stayed in the Lincoln Bedroom or at Camp David.

(Only contributions of $10,000 or more are listed.)

White House Guest Political Contributions

Guest	Total	To Democrats	To Republicans	To Hillary Clinton [*]	To the DSCC[**]
Abraham, S Daniel W. PALM BEACH, FL	$1,174,500	$1,174,500	$0	$76,000	$138,000
Opperman, Vance MINNEAPOLIS,	$411,462	$410,212	$1,250	$8,712	$114,500

---

*Includes donations made to Hillary Rodham Clinton for US Senate and affiliated joint fundraising committees (New York Senate 2000, New York Senate 2000 Non-Federal, New York Democratic Victory Committee and New York Democratic Victory Committee Non-Federal).

**Includes all committees affiliated with the Democratic Senatorial Campaign Committee.

MN					
Levine, Philip MIAMI, FL	$401,500	$401,000	$0	$35,000	$3,000
Pattiz, Norman LOS ANGELES, CA	$328,000	$328,000	$0	$16,000	$50,000
Saban, Haim BEVERLY HILLS, CA	$239,100	$237,600	$1,500	$18,100	$0
Spielberg, Steven LOS ANGELES, CA	$227,000	$227,000	$0	$17,000	$40,000
Gupta, Vinod LAS VEGAS, NV	$217,000	$216,000	$1,000	$101,000	$5,000
Manning, John BOSTON, MA	$188,750	$188,750	$0	$12,000	$62,500
Goldberg, Michael MIAMI, FL	$157,750	$157,750	$0	$0	$0
Gary, Willie STUART, FL	$138,500	$138,500	$0	$2,500	$0
Kessler, Howard BOSTON, MA	$99,000	$98,000	$1,000	$2,000	$10,000
Bagley, Smith WASHING-TON, DC	$94,000	$94,000	$0	$2,000	$1,000
Savage, Frank STAMFORD, CT	$85,000	$84,500	$500	$12,000	$0
Bagley, Elizabeth WASHINGTON, DC	$84,000	$84,000	$0	$2,000	$20,000
Kessler, Patricia Michelle BOSTON, MA	$81,750	$79,750	$2,000	$18,000	$0
Bowles, Erskine CHARLOTTE, NC	$80,000	$80,000	$0	$26,000	$10,000
Perry, Lisa NEW YORK, NY	$77,000	$77,000	$0	$4,500	$26,000
Iscol, Jill POUND RIDGE, NY	$68,000	$68,000	$0	$21,000	$0
Patricof, Susan NEW YORK, NY	$67,000	$67,000	$0	$8,250	$1,000
Tullman, Howard CHICAGO, IL	$66,500	$66,500	$0	$16,000	$0
Heyman, Samuel WEST-PORT, CT	$56,470	$9,000	$47,470	$1,000	$0

Perry, Richard NEW YORK, NY	$49,000	$48,000	$1,000	$2,000	$31,000
Patricof, Alan NEW YORK, NY	$47,037	$47,037	$0	$2,000	$0
Heyman, Ronnie WEST-PORT, CT	$41,500	$23,500	$18,000	$1,000	$0
Ornish, Dean SAUSA-LITO, CA	$40,200	$40,200	$0	$11,000	$0
Free, James WASHINGTON, DC	$34,993	$30,493	$4,500	$1,000	$0
Saban, Cheryl BEVERLY HILLS, CA	$33,500	$32,500	$1,000	$12,000	$0
Jones, Quincy BEVERLY HILLS, CA	$32,000	$31,000	$1,000	$10,000	$0
Cherry, Myron Mike LINCOLNWOOD, IL	$31,750	$31,750	$0	$3,000	$250
Cherry, Pat LINCOLNWOOD, IL	$31,000	$31,000	$0	$2,000	$0
Schuster, Gerald CHESTNUT HILL, MA	$26,000	$26,000	$0	$1,000	$0
Rendell, Edward Mayor PHILADELPHIA, PA	$24,000	$24,000	$0	$1,000	$0
Schuster, Elaine CHESTNUT HILL, MA	$24,000	$24,000	$0	$1,000	$0
Adler, Karen NEW YORK, NY	$21,250	$21,250	$0	$4,000	$0
Korge, Chris MIAMI, FL	$21,000	$21,000	$0	$0	$0
Tullman, Judith CHICAGO, IL	$20,250	$20,250	$0	$5,000	$0
Yorkin, Cynthia LOS ANGELES, CA	$19,750	$18,750	$1,000	$14,000	$0
Hatkoff, Craig NEW YORK, NY	$18,250	$17,250	$1,000	$1,250	$0

Iscol, Kenneth POUND RIDGE, NY	$18,000	$16,000	$2,000	$12,000	$0
Opperman, Darin MINNEAPOLIS, MN	$17,500	$17,500	$0	$5,000	$2,500
Brandt, William COCONUT GROVE, FL	$17,000	$16,000	$1,000	$2,000	$0
Robbins, Liz WASHINGTON, DC	$16,750	$15,750	$1,000	$7,000	$0
Sykes, John NEW YORK, NY	$16,600	$15,250	$1,350	$6,000	$0
McAuliffe, Terry MCLEAN, VA	$15,000	$15,000	$0	$2,000	$0
Miller, Ruby THE DALLES, OR	$14,686	$0	$14,686	$0	$0
Cohn, Betsy NEW YORK, NY	$14,550	$14,550	$0	$9,300	$0
Yorkin, Alan "Bud" LOS ANGELES, CA	$14,500	$14,500	$0	$2,000	$0
Coleman, Lynn WASHINGTON, DC	$14,250	$14,250	$0	$2,000	$0
Simon, Arnold SADDLE RIVER, NJ	$14,000	$14,000	$0	$2,000	$10,000
Cohn, Alan NEW YORK, NY	$13,000	$13,000	$0	$2,000	$0
Danson, Ted LOS ANGELES, CA	$12,500	$12,500	$0	$11,000	$0
Altshuler, Fred SAN FRANCISCO, CA	$11,000	$11,000	$0	$8,000	$0
Brooks, Robin LAKE FOREST, IL	$11,000	$11,000	$0	$0	$0
Schulman, Marc CHICAGO, IL	$11,000	$11,000	$0	$2,500	$0
Stout, Diann MCMUR-RAY, PA	$11,000	$11,000	$0	$0	$0
Pattiz, Mary LOS ANGELES, CA	$10,500	$10,500	$0	$1,000	$0
Patton, Paul Governor PIKEVILLE KY	$10,000	$10,000	$0	$1,000	$1,000

Bill Clinton's Legal Defense Fund Top Donors *(from www. opensecrets.org)*

Name	City	State	Amount	Occupation	Year
Peter Angelos	Baltimore	MD	$10,000	Lawyer	2000
William and Mary Jane Brinton	San Francisco	CA	$10,000		2000
Eli Broad	Los Angeles	CA	$10,000	Chairman and CEO, SunAmerica Inc.	2000
Charles W. Carroll	Landrum	SC	$10,000	Timber-farmer, Beckham Corporation	2000
Fred Eychaner	Chicago	IL	$10,000	President, Newsweb Corp.	2000
JB Fuqua	Atlanta	GA	$10,000		2000
Jimmy W. Janacek	El Paso	TX	$10,000		2000
Gloria Jarecki	Rye	NY	$10,000	Business Executive, Guana Hotel Corporation	2000
Henry G. Jarecki	Rye	NY	$10,000	Business Executive, Falconwood Corporation	2000
Joan S. Lane	Burlingame	CA	$10,000		2000
Norman Lear	Los Angeles	CA	$10,000	Chairman, ACT III Communications	2000
John P. Manning	Boston	MA	$10,000		2000
George Smith	San Francisco	CA	$10,000	Business, SRA	2000
Edmund A. Stanley	Oxford	MD	$10,000		2000
Chiao Jen Wang	Arlington	VA	$10,000		2000
Yuen Fung Chu Wang	Arlington	VA	$10,000		2000
Edith Wasserman	Beverly Hills	CA	$10,000		2000
Lew R. Wasserman	Beverly Hills	CA	$10,000	Chairman Emeritus, Universal Studios, Inc.	2000
Harvey Weinstein	New York	NY	$10,000	Co-chairman Miramax Film Corp.	2000
Agnes D. Williams	Potomac	MD	$10,000		2000

S. Daniel Abraham	West Palm Beach	FL	$10,000		1999
Peter G. Angelos	Baltimore	MD	$10,000	Attorney/Law offices Peter G. Angelos	1999
Janet Edwards Anti	Pittsburgh	PA	$10,000		1999
Farhad Azima	Kansas City	MO	$10,000	CEO, ALG Inc.	1999
Gilbert Bachman	Atlanta	GA	$10,000	Retired	1999
Smith Bagley	Washington	DC	$10,000	Executive/ ARCA	1999
Frederick M. Baron	Dallas	TX	$10,000	Lawyer, Baron and Budd	1999
Meyer A. Berman	Boca Raton	FL	$10,000	Stock Broker/ MA Berman Co.	1999
William A. Brandt	Coconut Grove	FL	$10,000	Consultant	1999
Susie T. Buell	San Francisco	CA	$10,000	Retired	1999
Patrice Bugelass-Brandt	Coconut Grove	FL	$10,000		1999
Janet E. Burkle	Los Angeles	CA	$10,000	Homemaker	1999
Ron Burkle	Los Angeles	CA	$10,000	Investor	1999
Ely Callaway	Carlsbad	CA	$10,000		1999
David Chang	Cresskill	NJ	$10,000	Senior Advisor/ Panacom Inc.	1999
Rashid Chaudary	Bethesda	MD	$10,000		1999
Kathleen Y. Daley	Boston	MA	$10,000		1999
James Daley	Boston	MA	$10,000		1999
A. Richard Diebold	Tucson	AZ	$10,000		1999
Michael Douglas	Los Angeles	CA	$10,000		1999
Mark J. Doyle	Chicago	IL	$10,000		1999
Stefan T. Edis	Chicago	IL	$10,000	Executive	1999
Richard Eskind	Nashville	TN	$10,000	Investment Broker, A.G. Edwards and Son	1999
Jane G. Eskind	Nashville	TN	$10,000	Investor	1999
Zachary Fisher	New York	NY	$10,000		1999
M. Anthony Fisher	New York	NY	$10,000	Partner/ R.E. Finance	1999

David Geffen	Universal City	CA	$10,000	Principal, Dreamworks SKG	1999
Paul Goldenberg	La Habra Heights	CA	$10,000	Businessman, Paul's TV	1999
Robert Green	Amarillo	TX	$10,000	Investor	1999
Sally Hembrecht	San Francisco	CA	$10,000		1999
William R. Hembrecht	San Francisco	CA	$10,000	Chairman WRH & Co. LLC	1999
Hope Harrington	Easton	MD	$10,000	Member, Board of Education	1999
Charles U. Harris	Carefree	AZ	$10,000	Retired	1999
Edwin A. Joseph	Gloucester	VA	$10,000	Real Estate, Self	1999
Gilbert S. Kahn	Coral Gables	FL	$10,000		1999
Jeffrey Katzenberg	Beverly Hills	CA	$10,000	Principal, Dreamworks SKG	1999
Walter Kaye	New York	NY	$10,000	Chairman Emeritus/ Kaye Ind.	1999
Selma Kaye	New York	NY	$10,000	Housewife	1999
Ralph Lauren	New York	NY	$10,000	Executive/ Polo Ralph Lauren Corp	1999
Peggy McCrory	Beckley	WV	$10,000	Secretarial, Non-employed	1999
Cappy R. McGarr	Dallas	TX	$10,000	Money Manager, McGarr Capital Management	1999
Robert B. Menschel	New York	NY	$10,000	Senior Director, Goldman Sachs Group	1999
Paul M. Montrone	Hampton	NH	$10,000		1999
John J, Noffo	Coral Gables	FL	$10,000		1999
William P. O'Reilly	Southfield	MI	$10,000	Business, Ectnax Systems Inc.	1999
Carole E. O'Sullivan	Old Westbury	NY	$10,000	Homemaker	1999
Kevin P. O'Sullivan	Old Westbury	NY	$10,000	Retired	1999
Cheryl Saban	Los Angeles	CA	$10,000	Philan-thropist	1999
Haim Saban	Los Angeles	CA	$10,000	Executive/ Fox Kids Worldwide	1999
Robert Shaye	Los Angeles	CA	$10,000	CEO, New Line Cinema	1999

George D. Smith	San Francisco	CA	$10,000	Business, SRA	1999
Susan Lewis Solomont	Weston	MA	$10,000	Consultant	1999
Alan D. Solomont	Weston	MA	$10,000	Entrepreneur/Solomont Bailis Ventures	1999
S. Donald Sussman	Greenwich	CT	$10,000	CEO/ Paloma Partners	1999
Edward Z. Tabash	Beverly Hills	CA	$10,000	Lawyer/Self-Employed	1999
Peg Yorkin	Los Angeles	CA	$10,000	Peg Yorkin Productions	1999
Audrey Yu	Fort Lee	NJ	$10,000	President/ Hudson Mgmt. Inc.	1999
Leonard Barrack	Philadelphia	PA	$10,000	Attorney at Law/ Barrack Rodos & Bacine	1998
Jack C. Bendheim	Fort Lee	NJ	$10,000	Executive/ Philipp Bros. Chemicals	1998
Tony Bennett	New York	NY	$10,000	Entertainer/Self	1998
Neil G. Bluhm	Chicago	IL	$10,000	President, JMB Realty Corp.	1998
Donald A. Brown	Washington	DC	$10,000	Investor	1998
Tony Coelho	Alexandria	VA	$10,000	Investor	1998
Ross M. Deutsch	Highland Park	IL	$10,000	Trader/Self	1998
Samia Farouki	McLean	VA	$10,000		1998
Arthur M. Goldberg	Las Vegas	NV	$10,000		1998
Don Henley	Los Angeles	CA	$10,000	Recording artist, Environmental Activist	1998
Robert L. Johnson	Washington	DC	$10,000	President and CEO, Black Entertain-ment Television	1998
Glenn B. Laken	Highland Park	IL	$10,000		1998
James B. Levin	Skokie	IL	$10,000	Chairman-Pres./JHL Ent.	1998
Hayden McIlroy	Dallas	TX	$10,000	Housewife	1998
David Miller	Daly City	CA	$10,000	Manufacturer/ Rollamatic Roofs Inc.	1998
Dean Ornish	Sausalito	CA	$10,000	Physician, Preventive Medicine Research Inst.	1998
Sol Price	La Jolla	CA	$10,000	Investor	1998

Steven Rattner	New York	NY	$10,000	Investment Banker/ Lazard Freres & Co.	1998
Paul Simms	Beverly Hills	CA	$10,000	Producer at NBC	1998
Herbert Simon	Indianapolis	IN	$10,000		1998
Earl B. Sloan, Jr.	Walnut Ridge	AR	$10,000	Retired	1998
Howard A. Tullman	Chicago	IL	$10,000		1998
Lorena F. Walker	Muskogee	OK	$10,000	Retired	1998
Rita Weil	Woodland Hills	CA	$10,000	Retired	1998

Top Contributors to Clinton/Gore Campaign in 1996*
(from opensecrets.com)

Ernst & Young	$135,750	Accountants
Government of Guam**	$51,800	Govt. Workers
US Dept. of Agriculture	$39,010	Govt. Workers
Goldman, Sachs and Co.	$35,884	Securities
Skadden, Arps et al	$32,250	Lawyers
AT&T	$31,225	Telephone
Bear, Stearns and Co.	$27,550	Securities
Merrill Lynch	$27,150	Securities
US Sprint	$25,500	Telephone
Jenner & Block	$24,650	Lawyers
Time Warner**	$24,000	Communications
Raytheon Co.	$23,000	Defense
US Dept of State	$22,650	Govt. Workers
Arnold and Porter	$22,300	Lawyers
Future Tech International	$22,000	Computers
Walt Disney Co.**	$21,950	Entertainment
Energy Corp.	$21,250	Electric Utilities
Smith Barney	$21,250	Securities
US Dept. of Justice	$20,600	Govt. Workers
Holland & knight	$20,550	Lawyers
IBEW **	$19,875	Industrial Union
Lazard Freres & Co.	$19, 750	Securities

Molten Metal Technology	$19,750	Misc. Defense
Patton Boggs	$19,475	Lawyers
ICE Kaiser International	$19,035	Construction Services
Reef Funds**	$19,000	Real Estate
Fulbright & Jaworski	$18,850	Lawyers
Goodwin, Procter & Hoar	$18,400	Lawyers
Fisher Scientific	$18,250	Misc. Manufacturing
ION Pharmaceuticals Inc.	$18,000	Pharmaceuticals
Milberg, Weiss et al	$18,000	Lawyers
Anheuser-Busch Co.	$17,450	Beer
Well, Gotshal & Manges	$16,750	Lawyers
Latham & Watkins	$16,625	Lawyers
Chrysler Corp.	$16,500	Automotive
US Dept. of Commerce	$16,350	Govt. Workers
US Dept. of Transportation	$15,850	Govt. Workers
Wright, Lindsey & Jennings	$15,025	Lawyers
Barrack, Rodes & Bacine	$15,000	Lawyers
MacAndrews and Forbes	$15,000	Entertainment
Newmont Gold Co.	$15,000	Mining
O'Melveny & Myers	$15,000	Lawyers
PaineWebber	$14,750	Securities
Wilikie, Farr & Gallagher	$14,500	Lawyers
Verner, Lilpfert et al	$14,150	Lawyers
Mintz, Levin, et al	$14,000	Lawyers
Sills, Cummis et al	$14,000	Lawyers
Paul, Weiss et al	$13,900	Lawyers
Montgomery, McCracken et al	$13,650	Lawyers
Lehman Brothers	$13,250	Securities

*   The list above identifies the top financial supporters of the Clinton/Gore campaign, based on donations given by company officers or employees and their families. The listing does not imply direct contributions by the companies listed, as that is prohibited by federal law.

**   Contributions came from more than one affiliate of this organization.

Top Contributors to Clinton/Gore Campaign in 1996
Analysis (from opensecrets.com)

It is interesting to see who the biggest donors were to Bill Clinton's campaign in 1996. Nineteen big law firms donated big bucks- firms such as *Skadden, Arps* ($32,250), *Patton Boggs* ($19,475), *Fulbright & Jaworski* ($18,850), *Latham & Watkins* ($16,625), *O'Melveny & Myers* ($15,000), and many more. The government of Guam gave Bill Clinton $51,800. U.S. Dept. of Agriculture donated $39,010. The U.S. Dept. of Transportation gave Bill Clinton $15,850. The U.S. Dept. of Commerce gave Bill Clinton $16,350. Disney and Time Warner kicked in $21,950 and $24,000, respectively.

So don't buy into the myth that the *Republicans* are the party of money and greed. There are plenty of greedy lawyers and accountants, who are *Democrats* and gave hundreds of thousands of dollars to the Clintons. Look at the numbers. By the way, the top donor to Bill Clinton was accounting giant Ernst & Young ($135,750).

Top Contributors
2000 Race: New York SENATE *(from www. openseccrets.org)*

Rick A. Lazio (R)

Morgan Stanley Dean Witter & Co	$136,950
Citigroup Inc.	$126,690
Bear Stearns	$111,300
Goldman Sachs	$104,050
Credit Suisse First Boston	$77,700
State of New York	$73,774

Spear, Leeds & Kellogg	$68,250
AXA Financial	$66,250
Merril Lynch	$63,550
Chase Manhattan	$63,311
JP Morgan & Co	$58,800
Verizon Communications	$56,283
PricewaterhouseCoopers	$52,836
PaineWebber	$51,100
Bristol-Myers Squibb	$46,913
Deloitte & Touche	$46,750
Sullivan & Cromwell	$46,250
Anderson Worldwide	$44,050
New York Stock Exchange	$40,300
Corning Inc.	$38,500

Hillary Rodham Clinton (D)

Kushner Companies	$82,000
Citigroup Inc.	$78,480
Goldman Sachs	$73,250
Walt Disney Co.	$62,550
Int.' Brotherhood Of Electrical Workers	$59,825
Emily's List	$52,275
Skadden, Arps et al	$47,350
Credit Suisse First Boston	$47,200
Time Warner	$44,750
PaineWebber	$39,450
Kirkland & Ellis	$38,000
Patton Boggs LLP	$37,250
Cablevision Systems Corp.	$36,950
Deloitte & Touche	$34,750
Viacom Inc.	$32,450
General Electric	$30,550

Bear Stearns	$30,150
Ernst & Young	$28,950
Wasserstein, Perella & Co.	$27,000
US Dept. of State	$26,750

Jeffrey E. Graham (3)

| Neiman Investments | $1,000 |

Mark Dunau (3)

| *This candidate received no contributions large enough to generate this list.* |

John Clifton (L)

Harbor Power Co.	$2,000
Fish & Neave	$1,000
Manchester Trading	$1,000

Louis P. Wein (3)

| *This candidate received no contributions large enough to generate this list.* |

John O. Adefope (3)

| *This candidate received no contributions large enough to generate this list.* |

Jacob J. Perasso (3)

| *This candidate received no contributions large enough to generate this list.* |

Analysis and Comparison of Political Contributions to Races involving the Clintons

2000 Race: New York Senate (from www. opensecrets.org) - Hillary Clinton (D) beat Rick Lazio (R). – It is amazing to see just how biased the media companies were with their contributions. Four of the biggest media conglomerates donated a combined $ 170,300 to Hillary Clinton. General Electric, which owns NBC, gave Hillary $30,550. Viacom, the owner of CBS, gave $32,450 to Hillary Clinton. Time Warner, which owns CNN, gave $44,750 to Hillary Clinton. Walt Disney Co., which owns ABC, gave $62,550 to Hillary Clinton.

That's a total of $170,300 donated to Hillary Clinton for her Senate run in 2000. Now what about Rick Lazio, her Republican opponent in the 2000 race for the U.S. Senate. How much do you think those 4 media giants gave him? All together, Viacom, GE, Disney, and Time Warner gave Congressman Rick Lazio, a lifelong New Yorker, a former prosecutor, and a devoted husband and father...0! That's right, the media giants gave Hillary $170,300 and Rick Lazio, they gave nothing. And you wonder why the media never has anything bad to say about Bill or Hillary Clinton. Just look at who they supported in the 2000 Senatorial race.

A closer look reveals that the law firm *Kirkland & Ellis LLP* gave Hillary $38,000. According to the firm's website, Kirkland.com, the firm's clients include Brown & Williamson (tobacco), Dow Corning (sued for breast implants), and General Motors (product liability on defective cars and trucks). How could Hillary accept money from a firm that represents such clients? By the way, one of

Kirkland & Ellis's most famous partners is none other than *Kenneth Starr!*

Chronological Clinton Timeline [*]

1993

January 20 - William J. Clinton inaugurated 42nd president of the United States. Vince Foster joins White House staff as deputy White House Counsel.

January 23- Clinton withdraws his nomination of Zoe Baird for the post of Attorney General. Shortly after, his second choice, Kimba Wood, is also withdrawn from consideration.

February 26: In New York, the World Trade Center is bombed by Islamic terrorists. Six people are killed by a bomb planted in an underground garage. Investigators suspect the mastermind, Ramzi Yousef, to be connected to Osama bin Laden.

April 12: NATO air forces begin enforcing the UN-mandated no-fly over Bosnia, involving sixty U.S., French, and Dutch antiaircraft sites.

April 9-18 In Iraq, U.S. planes bomb Iraqi antiaircraft sites that had tracked and attacked U.S. aircraft.

---

[*] This timeline is taken from three sources: *Dereliction of Duty* by Buzz Patterson; *The Strange Death of Vince Foster* by Chris Ruddy; and *Unlimited Access* by Gary Aldrich.

April 13: U.S. Forces in association with NATO enforce the ban on all unauthorized military flights over Bosnia-Herzegovina.

May 4: In Somalia, Operation Restore Hope is replaced by the United Nations Security Council operation UNOSOM II (United Nations Operation in Somalia) with enforcement powers and a mandate to disarm warring factions, in accordance with the Addis Ababa agreements of January 1993. Out of 22,700 multinational troops and logistics personnel, up to 2,000 are U.S. forces, primarily combat support personnel assigned to the UN Logistics Support Command.

May 8- Foster gives commencement address at University of Arkansas.

May 19- Clinton administration fires longtime employees of the White House Travel Office.

June 4- Lani Gunier, Clinton's choice for assistant attorney general for civil rights, is withdrawn. She was vetted by Foster.

June 17- Wall Street Journal editorial, WHO IS VINCENT FOSTER?, appears.

June 19: US aircraft fire on an Iraqi antiaircraft site displaying hostile intent.

June 24- A second wall street Journal editorial entitled VINCENT FOSTER'S VICTORY appears.

June 26: The United States attacks the Iraqi Intelligence Service Headquarters in Baghdad, launching twenty-three tomahawk cruise missiles in retaliation for an attempted assassination of the former U.S. president George Bush.

July 3- White House management review of the travel office firing released. Associate counsel William Kennedy is criticized.

July 9: UN protection forces, including 350 soldiers, are deployed to participate in the UN protection for the former Yugoslav Republic of Macedonia.

July 15- Senator Robert Dole calls for appointment of special counsel to investigate the travel office firings.

July 16- Foster and wife, Lisa, leave for weekend on Eastern shore of Maryland.
Freeh offered job as FBI director at White House meeting with Clinton.

July 17- Early morning meeting at Justice Department with FBI director William Sessions. Attorney General Janet Reno, Nussbaum, and Hubbell, tell Sessions to resign or be fired. Sessions refuses.

July 18- Foster calls Clinton attorney James Lyons. They agree to meet on Wednesday, July 21.

July 19- Hubbell meets with Chief of Staff McLarty to talk about Foster's state of mind.
Hubbell meets with Foster.

President Clinton fires FBI director William Sessions. Deputy director Floyd Clark named acting director. Clinton calls Foster at home and invites Foster to join him, Hubbell, and Bruce Lindsey for a private White House showing of the movie *In the Line of Fire.* Foster declines but agrees to meet Clinton on Wednesday.

July 20- Freeh nominated as FBI director at Rose Garden ceremony. Foster makes repeated efforts to speak with William Kennedy on phone but fails. Warrant issued for offices of David Hale's Capital Management Services in Little Rock. **Foster found dead at Fort Marcy.**

July 21- Secret Service officer Bruce Abbott observes Craig Livingstone suspiciously carrying documents from the area of Foster's office. Park Police investigators arrive at White House but are denied access to Foster's office or the right to conduct interviews. Autopsy conducted on Foster by deputy medical examiner for Northern Virginia.

July 22- White House counsel Nussbaum conducts search of Foster's office. Williams and counsel aide Thomas Castleton remove Clinton's papers from Foster's office and store them in closet located in Clinton's residential quarters.

July 23- Foster buried in Hope, Arkansas.

July 26- Associate White House counsel Stephen Neuwirth finds torn note in Foster's office briefcase.

July 27- Lisa Foster views note at 2:30 PM. Susan Thomases and the Clintons' personal attorney Robert Barnett arrive at the Clinton White House. Barnett takes possession of the Clinton's personal papers that were found in Foster's office.

6:29 PM. Webster Hubbell arrives at White House residence and meets with Hillary Clinton. Susan Thomases is already in the residence and meets with Hillary Clinton. Both Hubbell and Thomases leave together at 8:20 PM.

7:00 PM. Reno and deputy Attorney General Philip Heymann arrive at White House and are informed of note.

8:00 PM. Park Police are informed of note.

July 29- Park Police interview Lisa Foster for first time.

August 3: An Army Ranger task force of more than 1,100 soldiers is deployed to Somalia as a quick reaction force.

August 5- Park Police conclude investigation, rule Vince Foster's death a suicide.

August 9- FBI concludes investigation into the torn note.

August 10- Justice Department press conference chaired by Heymann. Park Police chief Robert Langston and FBI special agent in charge for Washington Robert Bryan announce results of inquiries. Contents of torn note revealed to press. Officials decline to release Park Police report.

August 15- Washington Post reveals that Park Police report says Nussbaum, Williams, and Thomasson conducted late-night entry into Foster's office on the night of the death.

August 16- Park Police hand-delivered the Colt revolver found in Foster's hand to the ballistics laboratory of the

Bureau of Alcohol, Tobacco, and Firearms. This is the first time the gun is tested.

August 31: The Oslo Accords are agreed to by Israel and the Palestine Liberation Organization during the secret talks in Norway. After forty-five years of conflict, the two agree to recognize each other. Within days, Yasser Arafat signs a letter recognizing Israel and renouncing violence.

September 13: The Oslo Accords are signed by Israeli and Palestinian leaders at a White House ceremony.

October 3: In Somalia, 18 American soldiers are killed in a Mogadishu firefight with irregular forces loyal to warlord Mohammed Aidid. Some 500 to 1,000 of Aidid's fighters are killed by U.S. troops.

October 7: President Clinton announces that the United States will withdraw all combat forces and most logistics units from Somalia by March 31, 1994.

December 20- Washington Times reports that Clinton aides removed Whitewater papers from Foster's office on night of death.

1994

January 6: President Clinton labels three types of satellites as civilian, thus circumventing sanctions on China in order to allow exports to proceed.

January 9- Senator Daniel Patrick Moynihan calls for appointment of special counsel to probe Whitewater.

January 12: Under media pressure, President Clinton asks that a special prosecutor be named to investigate the Whitewater scandal. A week later, Attorney General Janet Reno names Robert Fiske as special prosecutor.

January 20- Robert Fiske appointed special counsel by Janet Reno.

January 27- New York Post report by Christopher Ruddy details doubts of paramedics at the death scene about Foster's "suicide."

January 28- Wall Street Journal files lawsuit against the Justice Department for not releasing the Park police report completed on August 5, 1993.

February 2- William Sessions issues a statement to New York Post that his firing by President Clinton "compromised" the FBI's role in the Foster death case.

February 23- Special Counsel Fiske's investigators begin interviewing first paramedics at the death scene.

February 28: U.S. military aircraft under NATO shoot down four Serbian Galeb planes in the former Yugoslavia while patrolling the no-fly zone.

March 5- White House Counsel Bernard Nussbaum tenders his resignation.

March 14- A page one New York Daily News story by Mike McLary entitled CASE CLOSED reports that Fiske had concluded Foster's death a suicide at the park.

Webster Hubbell offers his resignation as associate attorney general.

April 4- The FBI begins a search and "excavation" for the missing bullet at Fort Marcy at Fort Marcy.

Wall Street Journal story by Ellen Joan Pollock reports that Fiske has concluded Foster committed suicide.

April 10-11: US combat-equipped forces are deployed to Burundi to assist with the evacuation of US embassy personnel and other citizens from Rwanda.

May 4: In Cairo, Israeli prime minister Yitzhak Rabin and Yasser Arafat sign the Agreement on the Gaza Strip and Jericho Area, setting terms for the withdrawal of Israeli military forces.

May 6: Paula Jones files a sexual harassment lawsuit against President Clinton.

May 9- Fiske's investigators interview Lisa Foster for the first time.

First significant FBI laboratory and forensic reports relating to death case completed by mid-June.

June- A team of four independent pathologists reviews Foster case for Special Counsel Fiske.

June 6: President Clinton issues Executive Order 12919, on "National Defense Industrial Resources Preparedness," which consolidates previous executive orders to give the executive branch sweeping powers for emergency control of food resources, all forms of civil transportation, water resources, construction material, and labor supply. The order gives the director of FEMA (Federal Emergency Management Agency) a key role in developing and implementing the policy. Critics claim this order is extra-constitutional in scope and could grant a president virtually dictatorial powers.

June 30- Fiske releases his report on Foster's death, concluding that Foster killed himself at Fort Marcy.

President Clinton signs re-authorized Independent Counsel law.

July 13: President Clinton issues presidential waivers under PL 101-246 to allow US satellites to be launched from Chinese rockets.

July 22: In Rwanda, US forces begin a three-month intervention to assist non-governmental and international organizations to provide relief to refugees of the civil war and to assist with the deployment of UN peacekeeping troops. By mid-August, US troops participating at the peak of the mission total 3,600 with most deployed outside of Rwanda.

July 29- Senate Banking Committee holds one day of hearings into Foster's death.

August 5: US aircraft, operating under NATO and acting upon requests of UN protective forces attack Bosnian Serb heavy weapons in Sarajevo's heavy-weapons exclusion zone.

August 5- Three-judge panel created by newly authorized independent counsel statute selects Kenneth W. Starr as independent counsel. Fiske inquiry ends.

September- Starr hires Mark H. Tuohey III as Washington deputy, as well as assistant US attorney Miguel Rodriguez to be the lead prosecutor reviewing matters relating to Foster's death.

September 19: 20,000 US forces enter Haiti under code name Operation Uphold Democracy, as the lead force in the multinational operation to restore Jean-Bertrand Aristide to power.

October 15: President Clinton lifts sanctions he had imposed on China for selling missile technology to Pakistan.

October- Prosecutor Russell G. Hardin resigns from Starr's Little Rock office over matters relating to Webster Hubbell.

November 1: President Clinton issues a waiver on sanctions on China for missile-technology exports.

November 10: Iraq accepts the UN-designated land border with Kuwait as well as Kuwaiti sovereignty as confirmed by Resolution 833.

November 19: The UN Security Council approves Resolution 958, which authorizes the use of air power to support the UN Protection Force in Croatia.

December 1994-1995
Gary Aldrich helps decorate Hillary's Blue Room Christmas Tree. Ornaments sent in by art students made of condoms and drug paraphernalia. One year later, same room-new tree. Hillary decorates room with notorious South Florida drug dealer Jorge "Gordito" Cabrera.

December 6- Hubbell pleads guilty to fraud and tax evasion charges and agrees to cooperate with Starr.

December 12: China reportedly begins to transfer ring magnets to an unsafely guarded nuclear facility in Pakistan. This violates US laws that require sanctions.

December 13- Associate White House counsel Jane Sherburne writes White House "Task List" memo identifying White House concerns over scandals, including Foster's death.

December 22: President Clinton announces that the US Army peacekeeping force in Macedonia will be replaced by 500 soldiers from the 1st Cavalry Division.

1995

January 3- Senate Banking Committee releases report agreeing with conclusion made by Fiske.

January 5- Starr's office begins grand jury proceedings into Foster's death.

January 6- A Scripps Howard wire story by Lisa Hoffman appears on the front page of *Washington Times* claiming that Starr has closed his review of Foster's death and has concluded the death a suicide.

January 9: Bernard Schwartz, chairman of Loral Space and Communications Corporation, signs a letter to the president advocating the shift of satellite export responsibility from the Department of State to the Department of Commerce.

February 27: In Somalia, some 1,800 US combat forces arrive in Mogadishu to assist with the removal of the United Nations Operations in Somalia (UNOSOM II) peacekeeping operation.

March- Rodriguez and his assistant resign.

March 3: The UNOSOM II international peacekeeping force is withdrawn from Somalia, in the midst of continuing instability.

March 8: Three unidentified gunmen kill two US diplomats and wound a third in Karachi, Pakistan.

March 31: The US- led peace operation in Haiti gives way to a United Nations peacekeeping operation, called the UN Mission in Haiti, or UNMH.

April 19: In Oklahoma City, a terrorist attack on the federal building by American extremists kills 168 and wounds hundreds more.

April 27- The Western Journalism Center releases report prepared by two former New York City police homicide experts. The report concluded that murder cannot be ruled out and Foster's body had been moved to the park.

May 3- Christopher Ruddy's story in Pittsburgh Tribune-Review reports that Rodriguez resigned over policy dispute in Foster case.

May 3: President Clinton issues residential Decision Directive 25 (PDD-25), in secretive classified form. The directive outlines US roles in UN-authorized and other international peacekeeping activities. The document, which effects the deployment of US military forces into hostile zones, is denied to the public and the US Congress, which has constitutional responsibility to approve military deployments. The directive calls for the elimination of the War Powers Act provision requiring withdrawal of US troops within sixty days, without congressional approval. That provision is not addressed by Congress.

June- Starr hires O.J. Simpson defense expert Henry Lee and the San Diego medical examiner Dr. Brian Blackbourne to review Foster's death.

June 3: NATO and other European Union countries agree to protect UN peacekeepers in Bosnia. The United States offers to provide air support, intelligence, transport, and other equipment, and rules out ground troops.

June 8: A US Marine search-and-rescue team successfully rescues Captain Scott O'Grady of the US Air Force, shot down by a Bosnian Serb Missile and stranded in Bosnia for six days.

June 25: In Haiti, first-round parliamentary and municipal elections are held. Although deadly violence does not occur, election observers state that there are numerous irregularities, including ballot burning in some locations.

June 28- Hubbell sentenced to twenty-one months, of a possible ten-year sentence, for fraud and evasion charges. Starr admits Hubbell reneged on his agreement and failed to cooperate.

July- White House publishes and distributes a 331-page file called "Communication Stream of Conspiracy Commerce." The file deals largely with issues pertaining to Foster's death.

July 6- House Speaker Newt Gingrich publicly states there will be hearings on Foster's death.

July/August- Senate Banking Committee now chaired by Senator D'Amato holds hearings into actions of White House aides involving Foster's office.

August 8: Two of Saddam Hussein's sons-in-law, both key aides, defect and are granted political asylum abroad. One of the defectors, Hussein Kamel, is the political architect of Iraq's programs of mass-destruction weapons and claims that Saddam intends to invade Kuwait and Saudi Arabia.

August 14- Senator D'Amato publicly states that questions remain on the Foster death.

August 22- Dr. Lee testifies as defense expert for O.J. Simpson.

September 1- Starr's deputy Mark Tuohey resigns and joins Washington law firm representing the Rose Law Firm before Starr's office and Congress.

August 30: NATO begins a campaign of massive air strikes against Bosnian Serb military targets around Sarajevo under Operation Deliberate Force, which lasts for around one month.

September 3- Profile of Lisa Foster appears in the New Yorker. Lisa states that she accepts official conclusions.

Mid-September- Starr begins two-month FBI search for the bullet at Fort Marcy Park.

September 28: The Israeli-Palestinian Interim Agreement on the West Bank is signed in Washington. Following the signing, President Clinton hosts a summit attended by Jordan's King Hussein, Egypt's President Hosni Mubarak, Israel's Prime Minister Yitzhak Rabin, and PLO chairman Yasser Arafat.

October 8- Mike Wallace segment on 60 Minutes reports the Foster case is closed.

October 9: After long debate in the administration, in which the Defense Department, CIA, and State Department oppose American satellites' being launched on Chinese rockets, President Clinton initials a classified order maintaining the State Department's authority over the Commerce Department on such launchings.

October 22- Ambrose Evans-Pritchard reports in the London Sunday Telegraph that Fort Marcy witness Patrick Knowlton claims the FBI falsified his testimony in their report.

October 25- Strategic Investment and James Dale Davidson hold press conference announcing the findings of three handwriting experts that the torn note is a forgery.

November 1: In Dayton, Ohio, "proximity peace talks" begin between the United States and other contact group countries to resolve the Balkan conflict.

November 4: Israeli Prime Minister Yitzhak Rabin is assassinated in Tel Aviv by an Israeli university student.

November 13: A bomb hidden in a van explodes at the US military headquarters in Riyadh, Saudi Arabia, killing seven, including five Americans.

November 21: The Dayton Peace Accords are signed to end the Balkan conflict.

December- Banking Committee threatens to hold White House in contempt for not turning over notes written by William Kennedy.

December 17: Presidential elections are held in Haiti. Although former president Aristide is not permitted to run, his protégé, Rene Preval, wins with 89 percent of the votes cast. The vote is marred by only a 28 percent voter turnout and by the boycott of the election by many parties.

1996

January 1996
Howard Schapiro leaks Aldrich typescript to White House Counsel Jack Quinn.

January 1996
Howard Schapiro sends two FBI agents to White House FBI Office to interview Dennis Sculimbrene about Aldrich's book.

January 1- Lisa Foster marries US District Court Judge James Moody, a Clinton appointee.

February 6: President Clinton issues a waiver to lift sanctions and permit four satellites, including a Loral product, to be launched on Chinese rockets despite the January reports that China continues to export nuclear technology to Pakistan. On the same day, Clinton's friend- and Chinese Triad mafia member- Charlie Trie attends a White House coffee with Wang Jun, China's top military-industrial arms dealer, who had a multibillion-dollar stake in getting access to American satellites.

February 14: On liftoff, the Chinese launch of its Long March rocket fails, killing scores of people and destroying an $85 million US satellite belonging to Loral Space and Communications Corp.

March- Starr hires Memphis federal prosecutor Steve Parker to review Foster death case.

March 1996

After Sculimbrene testifies before Senate and House investigating committees, FBI pulls Sculimbrene from White House and seizes his White House pass.

March 10-11: The United States deploys two carrier battle groups to the waters off Taiwan, calling China's live-fire exercises, intended to intimidate Taiwan, "reckless" and "risky."

May 12, 1996

Southeastern Legal Foundation provides Aldrich with legal backstopping, allowing Aldrich to pursue his first amendment rights and go ahead with his book. Further attempts to win FBI approval fail, and the typescript is eventually submitted to Regnery Publishing.

March 14: The Clinton administration announces a decision to move a commercial communications satellite from the Munitions List to the Commerce Control List of dual-use items. The export license is moved from the Department of State to the Department of Commerce.

March 25- Starr's most cooperative witness, David Hale, pleads guilty to lying to the SBA and is sentenced to twenty-eight months, of a possible fifty-seven month sentence. Hale receives stiffest sentence to date for any sentenced in the scandal.

April 1996

FBI closes its White House Liaison Office, ending a more than thirty-year presence that served seven presidents.

April 5: The *Los Angeles Times* reports that the Clinton administration tacitly approved a shipment of Iranian arms to the Bosnian government in 1994.

April 9: President Clinton orders US military forces to Liberia to evacuate "private US citizens and certain third-country nationals who had taken refuge in the US embassy compound" because of the "deterioration of the security situation and the resulting threat to American citizens."

April 21- *New York Times* reports that Starr will soon be releasing report concluding Foster committed suicide.

May 1, 1996
Gary Aldrich abandons book project after FBI refuses to approve the typescript.

May 5, 1996
Craig Livingstone hosts fundraiser for President Clinton with Yogesh Ghandi and John Huang at the Sheraton-Carlton Hotel in Washington, D.C. Three weeks later the Filegate scandal breaks, and President Clinton and Mrs. Clinton claim they do not know Craig Livingstone. A group photo of Bill Clinton, Craig Livingstone, John Huang, and Yogesh Ghandi is taken, but the DNC can't find the photo, according to news reports. It is later determined by the Senate investigating committee that the funds were given to the DNC by Ghandi were first wired to Ghandi from an Asian bank on Foreign soil.

May 30, 1996
House Oversight Committee lawyer Barbara Comstock discovers "smoking gun" Billy Dale FBI file request form,

signed by Bernard Nussbaum, in box of documents hidden from committee by White House for two years. The FBI Filegate scandal is born.

May 10: Loral completes an engineering report that instructs China on how to improve its faulty rockets and missiles, including solving fatal problems in guidance systems. This assistance enhances the ability of Chinese ICBM's to hit American cities with precision.

May 10: Loral's commission studying the failure of China's Long March missile launch completes a preliminary review that is shared with China, finding that the cause of the accident was an electrical flaw in the electronic flight-control system. This report allegedly discusses weaknesses in the Chinese rocket's guidance-and-control systems.

May 10: Sudan expels Osama bin Laden because of international pressure applied to the United States and Saudi Arabia. He returns to Afghanistan.

May 20: President Clinton reports to Congress the continual deployment of US military forces to evacuate the US embassy in Liberia and to respond to the various isolated "attacks on the American Embassy complex."

May 23: The Clinton Administration announces that China will not be sanctioned for transferring the ring magnets to Pakistan, saying that there is no evidence that the Chinese government (as opposed to a state-owned company) has "willfully aided or abetted" Pakistan's nuclear-weapons program.

May 28- Little Rock jury convicts Jim and Susan McDougal and Arkansas Governor Jim Guy Tucker of bank fraud and conspiracy charges.

June 1: In Hong Kong, Clinton donor Johnny Chung meets Chinese Aerospace Corp. executive Liu Chaoying, a lieutenant colonel in the People's Liberation Army who attended counterintelligence school. Her company builds satellites and rockets and provides equipment for China's nuclear tests. The company also owns China Great Wall Industry Guangzhou Corp., which had been sanctioned by the United States in 1991 and 1993 for selling missiles to Pakistan.

June 1996
Gary Aldrich writes commentary piece for the *Wall Street Journal*, disputing White House and FBI statements on the Filegate scandal. Media hurricane for Aldrich begins. White House "masters of disaster" start negative spin operation to discredit Aldrich.

June 17, 1996
The 24th anniversary of the Watergate break-in.

June 19, 1996
Dennis Sculimbrene appears before Senate Judiciary Committee and confirms past drug use of Clinton staffers, Hillary's recommendation of Craig Livingstone, and other key allegations made in *Unlimited Access*. White House has no comment.

June 23: President Clinton waives sanctions under P.L. 101-246 for the Asia-Pacific Mobile Telecommunications (APMT) satellite to be exported for launch from China.

June 25: Khobar Towers, a military housing facility in Dhahran, Saudi Arabia, is attacked as a fuel truck carrying a bomb explodes, killing nineteen US military personnel and wounding 515 more. Several groups claim responsibility for the attack.

June 28: Front page New York Post headline regarding *Unlimited Access*, "Bill Romped as Hill Stomped in Wild and Crazy White House."

June 30: Almost one year to the day from Aldrich's retirement from the FBI, he appears on *This Week With David Brinkley*. White House sets off firestorm of protest and counterattack.

July 2: Syndicated columnist Maureen Dowd describes *Unlimited Access* as "Civil servants vs. uncivil kids. Starched shirts vs. short skirts. Scotch vs. Bongs. Men with guns vs. men with men."

July 4: Official launch of *Unlimited Access* and of the movie *Independence Day*, which shows White House blown up by space aliens. Cartoon in the *Washington Times*: Little boy holding dad's hand, standing in line to see *Independence Day* asks, "Daddy, is Gary Aldrich an alien?"

July 9: President Clinton waives sanctions under P.L. 101-246, allowing the Globalstart satellite to be exported for launch from China.

July 12: *Unlimited Access* debuts at number five on the *New York Times* bestseller list.

July 17: Two Secret Service agents confirm in sworn testimony before the House Oversight Committee Gary Aldrich's allegations regarding drug use by the Clinton White House staff members. White House Press Secretary Michael McCurry comments, "Of course I smoked marijuana."

July 20: Speaker of the House Newt Gingrich blasts Michael McCurry for his casual attitude about using illegal drugs. Speaker Gingrich had accused the White House of illegal drug laxity in 1994, but was roundly criticized for making "false allegations." No media apologies to the speaker after McCurry's confession.

July: Treasury inspector general opens criminal investigation of two secret service agents after they testify about Filegate scandal, contradicting White House version of events.

July: Internal Revenue Service begins audit of the Western Journalism Center.

July 19-26: Liu Chaoying, a Chinese aerospace executive, arrives in the United States and at the home of the Democratic fundraiser Eli Broad, and subsequently shakes President Clinton's hand for a picture taken with him. Liu and Johnny Chung incorporate Marswell Investment, Inc., similar to a Hong Kong company that is a front for the political department of the Chinese People's Liberation Army

(PLA). Deposits to Marswell Accounts reportedly travel from the PLA to U.S. Democratic Party causes.

July 28- *60 Minutes* re-airs October 1995 segment on Foster. Wallace states that Starr will issue report closing the case by the end of the summer.

August 4: Unlimited Access is number 1 on the *New York Times* bestseller list. It remains on the list for more than one hundred days.

August 23: Osama bin Laden issues a Declaration of Jihad, or religious war, against the United States, and calls for support of Islamic revolutionary groups around the world.
August 1, 1996
Dennis Sculimbrene retires after FBI continues nonstop harassment.

September: Retiring Chairman of House Oversight Committee William Clinger praises Gary Aldrich at Republican fundraiser for Senator John Warner and Congressmen Tom Davis. He declares Aldrich book to be "highly credible."

September 3-4: US forces launch forty-four cruise missiles at military targets in Southern Iraq. President Clinton announces the widening of the no-fly zones.

September 21: 1996 House oversight committee reveals that many Clinton staff members had a history of hard drug use, vindicating Aldrich's account in *Unlimited Access*.

September 27: The Taliban movement captures Kabul, Afghanistan's capital, and gains control of 90 percent of the country. The mostly Pashtun tribal Taliban are resisted in northern Afghanistan primarily by Tajik, Uzbek, and Hazara ethnic groups. The Clinton administration hopes the Taliban will bring stability to Afghanistan.

December 20: The NATO-led Implementation Force (IFOR) peacekeeping mission ends in Bosnia, and the UN-mandated Stabilization Force (SFOR) mission begins. The 54,000 troops of IFOR- which include 16,600 SU troops in Bosnia and some 6,000 support personnel stationed in the region- are replaced by just 18,000 SFOR troops. The US contingent is reduced to 3,600 troops in Bosnia and an additional1,000 personnel stationed in neighboring countries to participate in NATO operations in the Balkans.

October 4: Former FBI special agent Dennis Sculimbrene is interviewed by a reporter for the *Wall Street Journal*, and confirms that *Unlimited Access* is a truthful account of the Clinton White House.

October 16: The *Wall Street Journal* reports Senator Paul Coverdell's discovery that seven drug dealers have received pardons or offers of pardons from President Clinton.

October 22: USA Today reports that Starr's Foster report delayed due to "several unforeseen complications."

November 5:Clinton reelected to second term.

November 5: *Human Events* newspaper publishes evidence that George Stephanopoulos annotated his own copy of *Unlimited Access*. The Marriott Hotel section is marked "National Security Breach." In contrast, other sections of the book are marked "fabrication" or "partisan." The White House and Stephanopoulos refused to comment.

November 12- Witness Patrick Knowlton files suit in federal court alleging the government violated his civil rights.

November 21- Hubbell appears before Starr's grand jury in Little Rock, which begins investigating various payments made to Hubbell shortly before he signed a plea agreement with Starr's office.

December 2- Starr appears on Newsweek cover and gives exclusive interview. Magazine reports Starr had concluded Foster killed himself at Fort Marcy.

December 4- Washington Post reports that James Carville has launched a grassroots campaign "to discredit Kenneth W. Starr."

1997

January 1: George Stephanopoulos resigns from White House and accepts job as a regular member of ABC's *This Week* Sunday morning discussion panel-joining George Will and Sam Donaldson. It is reported that ABC will pay Stephanopoulos many times his White House salary.

January 1: *USA Today* ranks *Unlimited Access* number 36 of the100 bestselling books -fiction and nonfiction, soft cover and hard cover- published in 1996. *USA Today* also ranks *Unlimited Access* in the top 25 of all nonfiction hard cover books sold in 1996. Meanwhile, *Unlimited Access* continues to sell briskly, defying all conventional wisdom. Regnery declares, "book has a life of its own."

February 13- Hubbell exits prison after seventeen months and defiantly says he will not cooperate with Starr or inquiries into campaign financing abuses.

February 17- Pepperdine University announces Starr will step down as independent counsel by August 1 to become dean of its law school.

February 21- Starr says he made a mistake by giving a resignation date of August 1 and will stay on as independent counsel.

February 23- Jack Nelson reports in Los Angeles Times that Starr had completed a "voluminous report" on Foster's death, concluding suicide.

February 23: As punishment against the "enemies of Palestine," a Palestinian sniper opens fire on the observation deck of the Empire State Building in New York City. One person is killed and many are injured before he turns the gun on himself.

March 1: *Unlimited Access* passes 500,000 copies in sales.

March 13: President Clinton utilizes US military forces to evacuate certain US government employees and private American citizens from Tirana, Albania, and to enhance security for the U.S. embassy in that city.

March 25: US military forces deploy to Congo and Gabon for a standby evacuation.

March 29: Department of Justice releases internal report on conduct of FBI lawyer Howard Schapiro, accusing him of "horrific blunders, poor judgment, and serious mistakes." The report recommends no sanctions. Schapiro tells newspaper reporters he is out looking for a job.

April 1: Gary Aldrich logs 500th radio talk-show appearance and 50th personal speaking appearance.

April 4: Congressional investigators learn of a deal struck by convicted drug felon Jorge "Gordito" Cabrera to give $20,000 to the DNC. The money swap was made in Havana, Cuba, at the Copacabana Hotel. In return for the dirty money, Cabrera meets Al Gore in Miami. Eventually Cabrera is invited to the White House for a meeting with President and Hillary Clinton, and is photographed with the first lady in front of her Christmas tree in the Blue Room. This Kodak moment takes place on December 21, 1994, one year after the Blue Room Christmas tree sported condoms and roach-clips.

April 25- Court of Appeals for the Eighth Circuit rules against White House claims of attorney-client privilege involving notes taken by government lawyers assisting Hillary Clinton.

May 7: Regarding alleged hush money payments to Webster Hubbell, the *Washington Times* asks: what did the Cluntons know, and when did they know it? Hubbell reportedly received nearly $500,000 in questionable payments from friends after Hubbell's indictment but before his "cooperation" with Kenneth Starr's prosecutors.

May 12- White House appeals circuit court ruling to Supreme Court.

May 15: President Clinton issues the Secret Presidential Decision Directive 56 (PDD-56), "The Clinton Administration Policy on Managing Complex Contingency Operations," which purportedly guides the policy for PDD-25 on the US role in international peacekeeping operations. A controversial feature of the directive is that UN-associated nongovernmental organizations (NGOs) are given a "voice in the field" through the creation of a "Civilian-Military Operation Center." The directive also urges the inclusion of the NGOs "in the planning and policymaking circles in Washington."

May 16: A classified report at the Department of Defense's Defense Technology Security Administration (DTSA) concludes that Loral and Hughes Electronics Corp. have transferred expertise to China that significantly enhances the reliability of its nuclear ballistic missiles and that "United States national security has been harmed" (cited in the April 13, 1998, *New York Times.*

May 25: Author Gary Aldrich and Publisher Al Regenry appear on NBC's Sunday morning *Meet the Press* program. Evidently, the Clinton "ban" on having Aldrich on network television, at least as far as NBC is concerned, has been lifted. Tim Russert announces that Aldrich will not be prosecuted by the FBI and Department of Justice for printing book without FBI approval.

May 29-30: President Clinton orders US military forces deployed to Freetown, Sierra Leone, to prepare for and undertake the evacuation of certain US government employees and private US citizens.

June: Congressman Robert Livingstone, Chairman of House Appropriations Committee, demands that director Freeh fire Howard Schapiro. Livingstone's demand joins chorus of Congressmen and Senators who insist, "Howard Schapiro must go!" Director Freeh tells Congressman Livingstone that Schapiro will leave soon.

June 6: Newspapers report Howard Schapiro resigns as FBI chief counsel and takes a job practicing law with former Clinton White House counsel Lloyd Cutler, where he will earn triple his former FBI salary.

June 23- Supreme Court refuses to hear Clinton administration appeal on notes made by government lawyers during their conversations with Hillary Clinton.

June 25: Hillary blames aides for missing law firm billing records discovered in her personal quarters. Records are believed to have come from the office of Vince Foster the night he died.

June 28: President Clinton claims he cannot remember calling anyone from the White House to ask them to send money for his reelection, though it appears that more than $500,000 was solicited in this fashion.

June 30: Democratic Congressman James A. Traficant, Jr., is quoted in the *Washington Times* criticizing the Department of Justice and the FBI for attempting to block publication of "Unlimited Access." Traficant states, "Something is seriously wrong in our democracy if criminal and unethical behavior at the nation's top law enforcement agency goes unpublished."

June: Veteran UPI White House reporter Helen Thomas complains that President Bill Clinton is sneaking out of the White House, "to visit friends." Thomas states that Clinton and his aides lie to the press about the president's whereabouts, and make the press believe the president is home asleep in his bed when he is actually out on the town. Thomas does not confirm the Marriott Hotel as one of the president's destinations.

July 5-7: In Cambodia, the former Khmer Rouge co-prime minister stages a coup against the freely elected royalist prime minister, Prince Ranariddh.

July 1: Congressman Gerald Solomon, chairman of the House Rules Committee, alleges that top secret documents appear to have been given to the Chinese communist government by John Huang, former DNC fundraiser, Commerce Department employee, and friend of President Clinton. Congressman Solomon stated that he is worried about "economic espionage."

July 1: Rush Limbaugh interviews Gary Aldrich for his monthly newsletter and applauds Aldrich's efforts, stating "There are too many people like you all over the country who are not going to sit idly by and watch freedoms be eroded, and watch standards be declined- on purpose."

July 2: Strengthening the "masters of disaster" team, the Clinton administration announces the hiring of Paul Begala, a Texan who had worked in the 1992 "war room" in Little Rock with George Stephanopoulos and James Carville. Joining Begala is Sidney Blumenthal, a longtime Clinton supporter and journalist for the *New Yorker*, the *New Republic*, and the *Washington Post*.

July 8: Senate Chairman Fred Thompson states that the Chinese may have tried to "buy" the 1996 presidential election, in his opening statement before the Senate committee investigating Clinton fundraising scandals. It is also reported that former "bimbo eruptions" specialist Jack Palladino, a private investigator who worked for the 1992 Clinton campaign, is now working to reelect Ron Carey as president of the Teamsters Union.

July 11: Human Events newspaper reports that John Huang was given top secret CIA reports while he was working at the Clinton administration, but lost track of the reports. The CIA admitted that the didn't keep track of the material given to Huang, now suspected of being an agent for the Chinese government.

July 20: Gary Aldrich is appointed Director of Special Events for the Virginia-based Freedom Alliance Foundation. He will also serve as Investigative Research Fellow. His mission is to ferret out and report wrongdoing in the federal government.

August 1: Kathleen E. Willey, a former White House staff member, is subpoenaed after confessing she was groped by President Clinton near the Oval Office.

September 9: The Department of Justice begins a criminal investigation into allegations that Loral and Hughes illegally passed technical assistance to China.

September 10-12: With the Middle East peace process stalled for more than a year, Secretary of State Madeleine Albright makes her first official trip to the Middle East.

September 26: Representing the administration, Secretary of State Madeleine Albright signs three agreements related to the Anti-Ballistic Missile (ABM) Treaty at the United Nations. Defense experts criticize the agreements as threatening US national security by reimposing restrictions on a national missile defense system. Although the treaty expired in 1991, with the fall of the Soviet Union, the Clinton administration continues to observe the requirements of the treaty as a policy.

September 10: Ex-DNC chief Donald Fowler testifies in front of a congressional committee that he cannot recall asking the CIA to help arrange a meeting between President Clinton and Roger Tamraz, a foreign national of highly questionable character. The meeting with President Clinton in the White House was for the purpose of fundraising.

September 11: The *Washington Times* reports that a fired White House chef was paid $37,000 "hush money" from a secret White House slush fund. The chef was in a position to give damaging testimony about how the Clintons abused White House staff.

September 12: Appearing before a congressional committee, Sandy R. Berger, head of the White House National Security Council, fully admitted that the Clinton administration dismantled security procedures, which enabled unsuitable persons to enter the White House. NSC's Berger was quoted as saying the Clinton administration had only an "informal system" to review the backgrounds of various foreign nationals, including the infamous Roger Tamraz. Others at NSC tried to keep Tamraz out but were overruled, according to sworn testimony.

September 26: White House Drug Czar Barry McCaffrey defends White House staff members who used hard drugs. McCaffrey is quoted as saying, "No American should be barred from serving their country in any position as long as they now reject all illicit drug use."

September 29: House Speaker Newt Gingrich describes President Clinton and Vice President Al Gore as "defendants in chief" and charges that conduct during the reelection campaign was "a systematic violation of the rule of the law." On the same day, the *Washington Times* reports on alleged IRS harassment of conservative groups through threatened audits.

October 12: Billy Dale's $80 million lawsuit against Harry Thomason is thrown out of court. Meanwhile, the *Washington Times* reports officials of the Paula Jones Legal Defense Fund experiencing break-ins, harassment, and IRS audits.

October: David S. Broder writes in a column in the *Washington Post*, "It is maddening to know that this kind of cynical manipulation drives our elections." He was commenting on the dishonest actions of George Stephanopoulos, Dick Morris and others in the 1996 election. Continuing, Broder says, "It is worse to know that we in the press have celebrated these consultants, who are our sources, and in some instances, even installed them in prominent positions in our own business." This was a clear reference to Morris and Stephanopoulos.

October 3: The Washington Post describes chaos and serious missteps in the Department of Justice task force investigating the Clinton fundraising scandals. Subsequent articles claim the FBI and DOJ lawyers are not working well together. FBI sources charge DOJ lawyers are preventing senior FBI agents from conducting serious investigations.

October: President Bill Clinton announces the appointment of several homosexuals to key posts in his administration, continuing to honor his quid pro quo to wealthy homosexuals and lesbians who contributed to his 1992 and 1996 elections.

October 8: New York Times columnist William Safire suggests that FBI Director Louis Freeh should do the right thing and submit his resignation, unless the White House allows him to do his job and protect national security. Safire: "That would crack the stonewall- one honorable law officer."

October 10: Attorney General Janet Reno appears on Tim Russert's Meet the Press and declares herself "mad" at the White House for withholding key videotape evidence proving that President Clinton conducted illegal fundraising at the White House.

November 5: Congressman Bob Barr and 17 co-sponsors announce House Resolution 304 calling for an "inquiry into whether grounds exist to impeach William Jefferson Clinton, the President of the United States." Speaker of the House Newt Gingrich describes Congressman Barr as "a serious man."

November 6: Former Democratic Senator Dennis De Concini meets Gary and Nina Aldrich at a Meet the Press celebration and praises Gary for "doing the right thing" by coming forward and blowing the whistle on the Clinton White House.

November 8: President Clinton becomes the "first sitting president in history to attend and address a major gay and lesbian event." He had provided a campaign videotape message to the same group in May 1992.

November 10: Congressman David M. McIntosh complains the White House hid memos that prove a massive computer database, housed in the New Executive Office Building at the White House, was going to be used by the Democratic National Committee for fundraising and other political activities. According to Congressman McIntosh, this is a clear violation of federal law.

November 12: R. Emmett Tyrrell is honored at the thirtieth anniversary celebration for the American Spectator magazine. Guests include Rush Limbaugh, former senior Resolution Trust Corporation investigator Jean Lewis, Gary

Aldrich, and hundreds of others. Rush Limbaugh declares Gary Aldrich and Jean Lewis to be "courageous," for standing up to the Clintons and their corrupted administration.

November 13: David Brock learns he's been fired from his six-figure salaried position at the American Spectator. Brock promptly declares magazine's management and staff to be "homophobic."

November 17: Craig Livingstone found alive, well, still a free man, living in Southern California, working for a firm friendly to the Clinton Administration. A $90 million civil lawsuit is pending, charging Livingstone, Anthony Marceca, and Hillary Clinton, among others, with violating the rights of more than 900 persons in the Filegate scandal. Gary Aldrich is one of the 900, according to the former chairman of the House Government Reform and Oversight Committee, Congressman Bill Clinger.

November 17: The Washington Times changes the name of the FBI to "The Federal Bureau of Incompetence" in a lead editorial, complaining that the FBI could not find key evidence of Communist attempts to influence elections, hidden in its own files and "found" only after Senator Fred Thompson anounced the suspension of Senate Hearings on the matter. Director Freeh and Attorney General Janet Reno apologized to Thompson. The same day, Pulitzer Prize winning journalist Seymour Hersh is attacked in "unusually personal terms" for reprinting "the most salacious tidbits about JFK and his frenetic sex life" in his book, *The Dark Side of Camelot*. Hersh also accused President Kennedy of campaign funding abuses and "buying" a presidential election through bribes and illegal acts. Hersh paints a picture of a president cozy with mobsters. Like *Unlimited Access,* Hersh's book links flawed presidential character with the endangerment of national security.

December 5: President Clinton issues a "presidential determination" waiving provisions of the Anti-Terrorism Act of 1987 to authorize the reopening of the Palestine Liberation Organization's office in Washington, D.C.

December 15: President Clinton issues highly classified Presidential Decision Directive 60 (PDD-60), which involves a significant change in US strategic nuclear doctrine by formally abandoning guidelines issued by the Reagan administration in 1981 that the United States must be prepared to fight and win a protracted nuclear war.

December 15: FBI lawyers assigned to review Unlimited Access notify Gary Aldrich that his manuscript for a new paperback edition has been approved. The new manuscript was submitted to the FBI in the very same manner as the first manuscript. But this time approval is granted a mere ten calendar days after submission to the FBI director. The letter, in part, reads as follows: Based upon our review, it has been determined that the chapters contain no information of a classified or sensitive nature. As a consequence, Mr. Aldrich is free to seek publication of these materials."

December 18: A New York Times editorial praises FBI Director Louis Freeh for arguing in favor of an Independent Counsel to investigate President Clinton and Vice President Gore, despite Attorney General Reno's opposition. Headlines announce: "The Federal Bureau of Independence."

December 19: Gary Aldrich begins his next book, investigating William Jefferson Clinton.

December 19: Monica Lewinsky is issued a subpoena to appear at a deposition in the Paula Jones suit.

1998

January 1: Gary Aldrich announces creation of non-profit foundation dedicated to the support of Constitutional government and Bill of Rights, particularly the first amendment. The Patrick Henry Center for Individual Liberty, based in Virginia, will support witnesses who wish to come forward to expose wrongdoing and corruption in the federal government.

January 26: President Clinton declares publicly, regarding Lewinsky, "I did not have sexual relations with that woman."

February 15: Bin Laden issues a joint declaration with the Islamic group Al Jihad, the Jihad Movement in Bangladesh, and the Jamiat-ul-Ulema-e-Pakistan under the banner of the 'World Islamic Front" which states that Muslims should kill Americans, including civilians-anywhere in the world.

April 18: The US ambassador to the United Nations, Bill Richardson, visits Afghanistan and Pakistan. In Afghanistan, he asks the Northern Alliance resistance to stop its successful offensive against the Taliban and their al-Qaeda allies. He is rebuffed by the Taliban when he asks them to hand over

Osama bin Laden. Richardson calls for an end of military supplies to all warring factions, and voices support for a religious clergy conference, or ulama, called for by Pakistan to discuss peace. The arms embargo is largely honored by the Northern Alliance resistance, Pakistan, however, steps up arms supplies to the Taliban and sends in military reinforcements from the army and religious schools. Within a few months, the Taliban and the al-Qaeda regain a military advantage and, with support from Pakistani air power, capture most of the Northern Alliance areas of resistance.

June 8: A US grand jury investigation of bin Laden, initiated in 1996, issues a sealed indictment, charging bin Laden with "conspiracy to attack defense utilities of the United States." Prosecutors charge that bin Laden heads a terrorist organization called al-Qaeda, "The Base," and is a major financier of Islamic terrorists around the world.

August 6: Monica Lewinsky testifies under immunity to a grand jury.

August 7: US embassies in Nairobi, Kenya, and Dar es Salaam, Tanzania, are bombed simultaneously, killing 224, inlcuding 12 Americans, and injuring more than 5,000. It is determined that Osama bin Laden is responsible for the attacks.

August 17: President Clinton undergoes four hours of questioning before a grand jury. Afterward, he says in a televised speech, "I did have a relationship with Ms. Lewinsky that was not appropriate."

August 20: President Clinton orders the bombing of a pharmaceutical factory, in Sudan, suspected of being a chemical weapons factory.

August 20: President Clinton authorizes cruise missile and air strikes in Afghanistan and Sudan camps used by the Osama bin Laden organization after convincing information is found linking the bin Laden organization to the bombings of the US embassies in Kenya and Tanzania on August 7, 1998.

September 9: Kenneth Starr tells House leaders that he has found "substantial and credible information...that may constitute grounds for an impeachment."

September 15: Following the Taliban and al-Qaeda capture of Bamiyan, the Hazara tribal stronghold in central Afghanistan, massive atrocities are committed against the civilian population. On Afghanistan's western border, Iran masses 200,000 troops in response to the Taliban's northern offensive, which is backed by Pakistan.

September 23: The *New York Times* reports that, in August, a small group of presidential advisors met with Clinton, reportedly with evidence that bin Laden wished to obtain weapons of mass destruction and chemical weapons to use against US installations.

October 15-23: At the Wye River Conference in Maryland, President Clinton and Secretary Albright broker an intensive conference-ending all-night session between Israeli and Palestinian leaders. The meeting results in the Wye River

Memorandum, which is signed at the White House on October 23.

November 23: The UN Security Council adopts Resolution 1199, demanding a cessation of hostilities in Kosovo and warning that "additional measures" to restore peace will be considered.

November 30: President Clinton hosts a Middle East Donors Conference in Washington, at which some forty nations pledge over $3 billion to the Palestinian Authority.

1999

January 13: The *Washington Times* reports that President Clinton backed away from an announcement on funding the first part of a deployed national missile defense after US attacks on Iraq prompted Russia to halt its ratification of the START II arms treaty.

March 24: NATO air strikes begin in Kosovo, initiating a war against Serb forces.

March 24: US military forces in coalition with NATO allies commence a seventy-eight-day bombing campaign against Serbia and Serb forces in Kosovo in response to the Yugoslav government's campaign of violence and repression against the ethnic Albanian population in Kosovo.

May 7: NATO airplanes mistakenly bomb the Chinese embassy in Belgrade, killing seven. China accuses the United States of conducting a deliberate attack.

May 25: The US House of Representatives Select Committee on US National Security and Military/ Commercial Concerns with the People's Republic of China (the Cox Commission) releases a three-volume report detailing the transfer of sensitive "dual-use" US military-related technologies to China. The report includes the satellite/rocket related cases pertaining to the Loral and Hughes companies. "The seriousness of these findings and their enormous significance to our national security," the commission states, includes theft of some of America's most sensitive technologies, including nuclear weapons design.

May 27: The Russian Duma adopts a resolution condemning the NATO actions and postpones ratification of the START II treaty.

June 10: NATO suspends bombing in Kosovo after Serb forces begin to withdraw.

June 11-12: Kosovo forces (KFOR) troops begin entering Kosovo. Russian troops arrive in Pristina three hours before NATO troops arrive in Kosovo.

July 14-20: Israeli Prime Minister Ehud Barak visits the United States for the first time since taking office on July 6. He and President Clinton pledge to make peace a top priority.

June 20: Serb forces completely withdraw from Kosovo, which signals NATO to end its bombing campaign in the former Republic of Yugoslavia.

July 15: A congressionally mandated Commission to Assess the Ballistic Missile threat to the United States, led by former secretary of defense Donald Rumsfeld, concludes that "Ballistic missiles armed with weapons of mass destruction pose an immediate strategic threat to the United States." The commission's findings are in stark contrast to the Clinton administration's definitive 1995 National Intelligence Estimate that there would be "no threat from long-range ballistic missiles for at least 15 years." The report adds, "The threat to the US posed by these emerging capabilities is broader, more mature and evolving more rapidly than has been reported in estimates and reports by the [Clinton Administration] Intelligence community."

July 19: President Clinton reports to Congress that, "consistent with the War Powers Resolution," about 6,200 US military personnel continue to participate in the NATO-led SFOR operation in Bosnia, and another 2,200 troops will support SFOR from other parts of the region. In addition, US military personnel will remain in Macedonia in support of the international security presence in Kosovo.

November 2: At a ceremony in Oslo commemorating the anniversary of Yitzhak Rabin's assassination, President Clinton meets with Barak and Arafat, who agree to designate a framework agreement on the permanent status of peace issues.

November 13: President Clinton agrees to pay Paula Jones $850,000 to drop her sexual harassment lawsuit.

December 11-12: The House Judiciary Committee approves impeachment articles 1, 3, and 4 against President Clinton, which involve perjury and obstruction of justice in the Jones case.

December 15: President Clinton reports to Congress, "consistent with the War Powers Resolution," that 8,000 U.S. combat-equipped military personnel will continue to serve as part of the NATO-led KFOR security force in Kosovo. Another 5,000 US troops are deployed in other parts of the region in support roles.

December 19: President Clinton is impeached in the House of Representatives.

December 20: Polls show that President Clinton's approval ratings continue to rise.

2000

February 12: The US Senate votes to acquit President Clinton of two impeachment articles.

February 25: President Clinton announces that a small number of U.S. military personnel will be assigned as part of the United Nations Transitional Administration in East Timor. The contingent includes three military observers and one judge advocate. The president also assigns a thirty-troop military support group to facilitate and coordinate US military activities on the island.

October 12: In Aden, Yemen, a small boat laden with explosives blows up alongside the USS *Cole*, killing seventeen American sailors. Al-Qaeda operatives and bin Laden are suspected.

November 26: In Haiti, Jean-Bertrand Aristide is elected President again, although the election is boycotted by most of the opposition.

December 18: President Clinton reports to Congress, "consistent with the War Powers Resolution," that 5,600 US troops remain as part of the NATO-led KFOR security force in Kosovo. Another 500 US-support troops are deployed in neighboring Macedonia.

Vince Foster's Last Day - April 20, 1993

8:00 AM- Foster leaves home for work. Drives daughter to work and son to Metro Station.

9:00 AM- Foster attends counsel's office daily staff meeting.

9:27 AM- Foster atends Rose Garden ceremony. President Clinton introduces Louis J. Freeh, his nominee for the directorship of the FBI.

9:40 AM- Rose Garden Ceremony ends.

9:50 AM- Deborah Gorham states Foster arrived at counsel suite.

10:30 AM- Foster leaves his office for unknown location.

Approx. 11:30 AM- Foster returns to the office and stops in at Nussbaum's office. Nussbaum offers congratulations for the apparent success of the nominations of Louis J. Freeh and Ruth Bader Ginsburg to the Supreme Court.

12:00 PM- Linda Tripp, Nussbaum's assistant, says that Foster asked her to get his lunch from the White House cafeteria.

Approx. 12:30- White House claims Foster eats lunch in office.

1:00 PM- Foster leaves White House counsel's office.

Approx. 1:00 PM- Secret Service officer John Skyles sees Foster exit West Wing. Last sighting of Foster alive.

Approx. 4:30 PM- Motorist Patrick Knowlton drives into Fort Marcy's parking lot. The couple observes two men in and around the Honda.

5:30 PM- Confidential Witness claims he entered the parking lot driving a white utility van. Witness said he found Foster's body in front of the second cannon. Witness then drove to nearby parkway headquarters to notify authorities.

Approx. 5:45 PM- Confidential Witness claims he discovered Foster's body in park.

5:59 PM- Park service employee Francis Swann calls Fairfax County911 notifying them of a possible dead body in Fort Marcy.

Approx. 6:00 PM- Arkansas Trooper Larry Patterson arrives in his little Rock Apartment and receives a phone call from Trooper Roger Perry informing him of Foster's death. Patterson said the call came no later than 6:00 PM E.S.T.

6:03 PM- Swann makes second call to Park Police.

6:03 PM- Swann, after calling 911, hangs up and notifies Park Police.
Arthur claims he saw Park Police entering Foster's car in search of identification.

6:10 PM- Fairfax Fire and Rescue personnel and Park Police officer Kevin Fornshill arrive at Fort Marcy.

Approx. 6:15 PM- Body of unknown male found in Fort Marcy Park. Park Police officer transmits radio call of "suicide" in park.

Approx. 6:15 PM- Dead body located in park. Fornshill radios Park Police headquarters and notifies them of a "suicide" in the park.

Approx. 6:30 PM- Park Police investigators and supervisors begin to arrive at park.

Approx. 6:35 PM- Paramedics return from death scene to parking lot.

6:37 PM- Fairfax personnel leave park to return to firehouse.

6:40 PM- Fairfax Fire and rescue workers exit park to return to station house.

Approx. 6:45 PM- Fairfax Fire and Rescue workers arrive at station house. Rescuers report to station supervisor

Lieutenant William Bianchi that a White House official was found dead in park.

7:00 PM- Latest possible time former state police commander Lynn Davis claims he was notified of Foster's death by Trooper Perry.

Approx. 7:00 PM- Park Police senior investigator Cheryl Braun claims she first entered Foster's Honda in search of identification. She claims she was still unaware of deceased's name. After finding Foster's White House identification, Braun asks Lieutenant Watson to call shift commander Lieutenant Gavin to notify him of death.

Approx. 7:15 PM- According to a New York Post report, White House administrative chief David Watkins is paged at Georgetown theater and notified of death.

Approx.7:30 PM- Braun discovers that Lieutenant Gavin was not called by Watson. She calls Gavin herself to notify him of Foster's death.

Approx. 7:40 PM- Gavin calls White House and notifies Secret Service of Foster's death.

7:40 PM- Fiske reported that Dr. Donald Haut, the medical examiner, arrived at Fort Marcy Park to view the death scene.

Approx. 7:50 PM- Deputy Chief of Staff Bill Burton calls Gavin to confirm death.

8:00 PM- Latest possible time trooper Roger Perry claims he was notified of Foster's death by Helen Dickey at the White House. Perry says call likely came earlier.

Approx. 8:00 PM- According to grand jury testimony, Gayle Kennedy put her two children to bed when call came notifying her husband William Kennedy of Foster's death.

8:02 PM- Fairfax ambulance arrives at park to pick up body and bring it to morgue.

Approx. 8:15 PM- According to his FBI statement, William Kennedy first was called by Craig Livingstone and notified of Foster's death.

8:17 PM- Ambulance leaves Fort Marcy.

Approx. 8:30 PM- Lead Park Police investigator testified under oath that for the first time he enters Foster's Honda in search of of Foster's identification and only then was White House notified.

8:30 PM- According to a Secret Service memo to the White House, this is the exact time when the Park Police in the person of Liuetenant Gavin first notified the White House of Foster's death. According to the Secret Service, the first official notified by the Secret Service was David Watkins sometime after 8:30.

8:30 PM- White House claims that Secret Service is first notified of Foster's death. Ambulance arrives at Fairfax Hospital. Hillary Clinton's plane makes unscheduled stop in Little Rock returning to Washington from West Coast trip.

Approx. 8:45 PM- Park Police investigators Cheryl Braun and John Rolla clear scene at Fort Marcy and exit park.

Approx. 8:45 PM- CNN makeup artist preparing president for Larry King Live overhears the president being informed about the finding of a document in Foster's office.

8:45 PM- Park Police "Evidence/Property Control Receipt" shows police investigator Braun retrieved two rings of keys from Foster's front pocket. (Braun states she was at morgue at the time.)

9:00 PM- President Clinton appears on CNN's Larry King Live program from White House Library.

Approx. 9:00 PM- Senior White House aides claim to be first notified of the death.

9:00 PM- Larry King Live begins.

Approx. 9:05-9:15 PM- Senior White House aides, including McLarty, Lindsey, Livingstone, and Gearan, first claim they learned of Foster's death.

Between 9:00 PM and 10:00 PM- Craig Livingstone and William Kennedy identify Foster's body at morgue. Park Police investigators Rolla and Braun drive to morgue to retrieve Foster's car keys.

9:25 PM- Foster's Honda towed from Fort Marcy Park.

9:45 PM- White House claims Hillary Clinton first notified of death.

9:55 PM- White House claims that Livingstone and Kennedy made positive identification of Foster at morgue.

9:55 PM- White House claims it confirmed Foster was dead.

10:00 PM- Clinton leaves King program, takes elevator to White House residential quarters. Mack McLarty informs Clinton of Foster's death. Park Police arrive at Foster's Georgetown home and notify family of death.

10:00 PM- Clinton departs King program and takes elevator to residential quarters. Once there McLarty informs him of Foster's death.

10:06 PM- Dickey claims she made call to her father, after which she called Arkansas governor's mansion and spoke to Perry informing him of death.

10:13 PM- Hillary Clinton calls Maggie Williams and informs her of death.

10:45 PM- Nussbaum arrives at White House counsel's suite.

10:48 PM- Patsy Thomason arrives at White House. Thomasson, Nussbaum, and Williams enter Foster's office. Williams observed by Secret Service officer Henry O'Neill exiting Foster's office with documents.

11:00 PM- Clinton arrives at Foster home.

11:41 PM- Officer Henry P. O'Neill sets security alarms in the White House counsel's suite after Thomasson, Nussbaum, and Williams have left.

11:45 PM- Clinton leaves Foster home.

Melrose Larry Green

Recommended Reading for Further Knowledge:

I recommend the following books and magazines, if you want more information than I have provided for you in this book. I have read all of these books, in the course of my research on this book.

(1) Laura Ingraham, *Shut Up & Sing,* Regnery, 2003- This book provides great information about the phonies of the Hollywood community, and it gives great insight into just how stupid and ignorant some of our biggest Hollywood stars are, when it comes to the truth.

(2) Laura Ingraham, *The Hillary Trap,* Hyperion, 2000- Gives wonderful data about how Hillary Clinton amassed her power base in politics. This book tells you how Hillary operates. Ingraham is a brilliant attorney who graduated from *Dartmouth College and the University of Virginia School of Law.*

(3) Howard Kurtz, *Spin Cycle,* Touchstone, 1998. Kurtz describes how the Clinton team spun the news their way for eight years, and how the press by-and-large gave Bill and Hillary Clinton a free ticket out of prison, through a calculated program of spin control, deception, lying, and good old press relations, and p.r.

(4) Gary Aldrich, *Unlimited Access,* Regnery, 1998- The Clintons tried to stop the publication of this *N.Y. Times bestseller.* Gary Aldrich takes you inside the Clinton White House- it is not a pretty picture. Aldrich was a decorated veteran of more than 25 years with the FBI!

This book is a fascinating read. You won't be able to put it down!

(5) Christopher Ruddy and Carl Limbacher, Jr., *Bitter Legacy,* Newsmax.com, 2001. *This book is required reading!* Newsmax never disappoints, and this book is chock full o' the stories you'll *never see on CBS, ABC, NBC, and CNN.* There are articles on Chinagate, Clinton, the Strange Deaths, and lots more. I keep my copy (personally autographed by Chris Ruddy) right on my desk.

(6) Qiao Liang and Wang Xiangsui, *Unrestricted Warfare,* Pan American Publishing Company, 2002- This is a frightening book. It describes "China's Master Plan to Destroy America." The authors are from Communist China. This is not fun, but every American has to read it. Get it from Newsmax.com!

(7) Christopher Ruddy and Carl Limbacher Jr., *Catastrophe,* Newsmax.com, 2002- Another great Newsmax book. This covers how Clinton blew several opportunities to capture Bin Laden, the bias of the media, intelligence failures of the FBI and CIA, threats from Russia, China, and Iraq- and a whole lot more.

(8) Christopher Ruddy, *The Strange Death of Vince Foster,* The Free Press, 1997. This classic could be titled *Everything You Wanted to Know about Vince Foster but were afraid to ask!* Ruddy's meticulous research is matched only by his captivating writing style. The appendices and chronologies at the back of the book are

shocking. If you have any doubts that Vince Foster didn't kill himself, this book will remove them.

(9)   Rikki Klieman, *Fairy Tales Can Come True,* Reagan Books, 2003. This is the autobiography of the Court TV Anchor who is a buddy of Bill and Hillary Clinton. She and her husband, LAPD Chief William Bratton, both slept in the Lincoln Bedroom. I would skip this book, *except* for the part where she describes meeting Hillary Clinton. I almost vomited when I read her gushing. Then again, Rikki Klieman gladly defended cop-killer Katherine Power. I'm sure Hillary also admires Katherine Power.

(10) David Brock, *The Seduction of Hillary Rodham,* Free Press, 1996. This is a detailed look into the diabolical mind of Hillary Rodham Clinton. Brock has done exhaustive research, but I am warning you: this is not an easy read. Check out the photo of Webb Hubbell in the middle of the book. Young Webb Hubbell looks like the spitting image of Chelsea Clinton. That picture of Webb Hubbell alone is worth the price of the book.

(11) David Horowitz. *Left Illusions- An Intellectual Odyssey,* Spence Publishing, 2003. This is a collection of the essays and articles of one of the brightest guys on the political scene. David Horowitz is brilliant, and I recommend his book to all. It's 500 pages long, so you definitely get your money's worth. The stuff on Bill Clinton is gold. At $29.95, this book is a bargain! I had the pleasure of meeting David Horowitz at a Newsmax.com luncheon that Chris Ruddy hosted earlier this year in Los Angeles.

(12) Rich Lowry, *Legacy,* Regnery, 2003. This great book is a scholarly study of the Clinton years. It is painstakingly documented- *there are over 100 pages of long, detailed footnotes.* This is not an easy read, but you will learn a lot from Lowry's epic. Lowry, the editor of the *National Review,* put a lot of work into this. I recommend it to all.

(13) David Maraniss, *First in His Class,* Touchstone, 1995. This is a detailed biography of Bill Clinton. But it is dated- from 1995. Most of the scandals hadn't broken yet. Still, this 500-page book is worth the $15 I paid for the paperback.

(14) Susan McDougal, *The Woman Who Wouldn't Talk,* Carrol & Graf, 2003. Skip this book. It is a piece of fluff, by a woman who has lots of problems. This convicted felon is about as credible as Bill and Hillary, her partners in Whitewater.

(15) David Gergen, *Eyewitness to Power,* Touchstone, 2000. Scholarly examination of Presidential leadership. This is not must reading, but it is very interesting. I enjoyed the book.

(16) Bob Kohn, *Journalistic Fraud- How the New York Times Distorts the News and Why It Can No Longer be Trusted,* WND Books, 2003. This unique book examines the *N.Y. Times* in great detail. Kohn points out just how biased the *Times is to the left.* Since I have read the N.Y. Times for years, I especially enjoyed this book.

(17) Zell Miller, *A National Party No More,* Stroud & Hall, 2003. Miller is one of the few Democrats in Congress who has exposed the Party for what it has become. Zell Miller reveals a lot about the human side of people such as Jimmy Carter. Miller has been a Governor and Senator from Georgia. He will be leaving the Senate soon, and he is not holding back anything in this book.

(18) Sean Hannity, *Let Freedom Ring,* Reganbooks, 2002. Sean Hannity blasts Bill Clinton in this book. He tells it like it is, and I am certain that he *wrote every word of this book.* When you read it, you can hear Sean Hannity speaking!

(19) Larry Elder, *The Ten Things you Can't Say in America,* St. Martin's Griffin, 2000. Very informative read- Elder is an African-American conservative Republican-Libertarian, who does a daily syndicated radio show.

(20) David P. Schippers, *Sellout,* - Regnery,2000. This *is the best book written about the true story of the behind-the-scenes activity with the Senators and Congressmen.* Schippers, a Democrat and an attorney with 40 years of trial experience, writes a brilliant expose of the phonies in Congress. Schippers was the Chief Investigative Counsel for the Clinton impeachment.

(21) Lt. Col. Robert "Buzz" Patterson, *Dereliction of Duty,* Regnery, 2003. An expose of how Bill Clinton weakened the U.S. military and pulled off a surplus by closing military bases, axing our armed forces, and putting our soldiers on food stamps. Patterson carried

the "nuclear football" for Clinton, and *this book will scare the hell out of you!*

(22) Dick Morris, *Off With Their Heads,* Reganbooks, 2003. *I really dig Dick Morris! Although I have never met him, whenever I see him on the Fox News Channel, I feel as if I really know him.* Morris was a consultant for Bill Clinton for years, and his book is must reading. Pay special attention to chapters 3 and 4. Chapter 3 talks about how Bill Clinton dropped the ball in fighting Osama Bin Laden and terrorism. Chapter 4 takes on the frauds who make up much of the Hollywood community- it's called "The Hollywood Apologists."

(23) L.D. Brown, *Crossfire,* Black Forest Press, 1999. L.D. Brown was an Arkansas State Trooper who worked with the Clintons for years. His book is a *tell-all book, which has plenty of juicy details about Bill Clinton's sex life.* Learn all about how Bill and Hillary Clinton behaved when the TV cameras are off. This was one of my favorite books.

(24) Jason D. Fodeman, *How to Destroy a Village,* PublishAmerica, 2003. What's unique about this book is the author's age. He was 17 *years old when he wrote this book.* Fodeman outlines how the Clintons destroyed the concept of honesty and made lying a national pastime. The ethical lapse that has permeated this country is exemplified in the lives and conduct of Bill and Hillary Clinton. All teenagers, college students, and young adults who think Bill Clinton was "cool" should read *How to Destroy a Village.*

(25) Gennifer Flowers, *Passion and Betrayal,* Emery Dalton Books, 1995. This is the autobiography and also tell-all book of the girlfriend of Bill Clinton for 11 years. Gennifer's book is definitely written by her alone, Like L.D. Brown's book, *Passion and Betrayal has lots of juicy stories about sex. Best of all, the book is compact, so you can carry it on the plane and enjoy it. You will read this book in one sitting. It's that good!*

(26) Barbara Olson, *Hell to Pay,* Regnery, 1999. This classic gives the reader a chilling peek into the dark side of Hillary Clinton. Olson, who died on the plane that hit the Pentagon on Sept. 11, was an attorney who did extensive research in this book. Everything is documented and explained in easy language. You must read *Hell to Pay!*

(27) Barbara Olson, *The Final Days, Regnery, 2001. This is the best account* of the last-minute pardons of Bill Clinton. Olson describes the drug dealers, international fugitives, and terrorists pardoned by the most corrupt President in U.S. history.

(28) Jerry Oppenheimer, *State of a Union,* Harper Collins, 2000. A good account of the story of the Bill and Hillary 'arrangement.' The book concentrates on the family background of both Clintons. It is a fascinating read. It has some great stories you won't find in many of the other books.

(29) Andrew Morton, *Monica's Story,* St. Martin's Press, 1999. This account of Monica Lewinsky's life and her

affair with Bill Clinton is fascinating. I recommend it to you.

(30) Ann Coulter, *Treason,* Crown Forum, New York, 2003. Ann Coulter is highly opinionated. I have a lot of respect for her- she is a brilliant attorney, with an encyclopedic mind. Her work is thoroughly researched and documented. I really enjoyed this book.

(31) Joyce Milton, *The First Partner,* William Morrow, 1999- This is an excellent biography of Hillary Clinton. In fact, I think it will someday be a classic!

(32) Gail Sheehy, *Hillary's Choice,* Random House, 1999- Also a great book about Hillary. This is one of the most famous books on Hillary. Gail Sheehy is a wonderful writer. Read it!

(33) Carl Limbacher, *Hillary's Scheme,* Crown Forum, 2003. This is one of the best books about Hillary Clinton ever written. In a lot of ways, this is my favorite book of all.

(34) Bernard Goldberg, *Bias,* Perennial, 2002- a fascinating look into the liberal bias so prevalent in the media. Goldberg knows about the media- *he spent 28 years with CBS as a national correspondent.*

This book is wonderful, and it demonstrates just how pro-Clinton the media is.

(35) Bernard Goldberg, *Arrogance,* Warner Books, 2003,- this sequel to *Bias* is so refreshing. I just *love Bernie Goldberg!*

(36) Ambrose Evans-Pritchard, *The Secret Life of Bill Clinton,* Regnery 1997, I found this book to be a real thriller. It is through, well-footnoted, and *downright scary. The chapters on the Dixie Mafia (ch. 18), Mena Twins (Ch. 21), Jerry Parks (Ch. 16), the Death Squad (ch. 17), and Dan Lasater Drug Trafficking Organization are scary, but accurate. There are three Appendices, chock full of documents that will leave you shaking!*

(37) Wall Street Journal, *Whitewater,* Dow Jones, 1994- This 575-page work is the last word on Whitewater. It is not pleasure reading, but it is a great reference book. Very complicated stuff is broken down here.

(38) The Starr Report- this is the report that you must read. It details the lies of Bill Clinton like you've never seen before.

(39) Ronald Kessler, *Inside the White House,* Pocket Books, 1995- A fascinating peek into the White House very few of us will ever see. The section on the Clinton White House is gold! I love this book.

(40) Gary Aldrich, *Thunder on the Left,* Patrick Henry Center,. 2003- This sequel to *Unlimited Access* explains what's wrong with the Left today. Read it.

(41) Ann Coulter, *High Crimes and Misdemeanors,* Regnery, 1998- Ann Coulter gives a strong case for why Bill Clinton committed a bevy of impeachable offenses.

(42) R. Emmett Tyrrell, Jr., *Madame Hillary,* Regnery, 2004- The most recent book on Hillary. Tyrrell (American Spectator) does his homework. Get it.

(43) Webb Hubbell, *Friends in High Places,* William Morrow, 1997- this is the autobiography of Webb Hubbell, who worked with Hillary Clinton at Rose Law Firm, who worked for Bill Clinton in the White House, and who went to jail to save the Clinton's hide. Check out the photos of a young Webb Hubbell- he looks *exactly like Chelsea Clinton!* This book was a bargain- Andrew found it on the internet for 20 cents! Such a deal!

Recommended Publications: I recommend the *Washington Times, Human Events, and Newsmax Magazine.*

Recommended Websites: *Newsmax.com, Drudgereport.com*

Recommended TV Programs- First, I will tell you a secret: I keep my TV on *Fox News Channel all day and night long! I recommend The O'Reilly Factor, Hannity & Colmes, and all the other programs on Fox News Channel.*

Recommended Radio Programs:

I recommend *Larry Elder, Sean Hannity, Michael Savage, Bill O'Reilly, and Howard Stern. They are all syndicated. As they say, check your local listings.*